ecpr PRESS

Series Editors:
Dario Castiglione (University of Exeter) and
Vincent Hoffmann-Martinot (Sciences Po Bordeaux)

the state tradition in western europe

a study of an idea and institution

Kenneth H. F. Dyson

ecpr PRESS

First published by the ECPR Press in 2009

Originally published in 1980 by Martin Robertson, Oxford

The ECPR Press is the publishing imprint of the European Consortium for Political Research (ECPR), a scholarly association, which supports and encourages the training, research and cross-national cooperation of political scientists in institutions throughout Europe and beyond. The ECPR's Central Services are located at the University of Essex, Wivenhoe Park, Colchester, CO4 3SQ, UK

Typeset by Newgen Imaging
Printed and bound by Lightning Source

British Library Cataloguing in Publication Data
A catalogue record for this book is available from the British Library

Paperback ISBN: 978-0-9558203-5-9

Hardback ISBN: 978-1-907311-2-4

www.ecprnet.eu/ecprpress

Publications from the ECPR Press

ECPR Classics:

Identity, Competition and Electoral Availability: The Stabilisation of European Electorates 1885–1985 (ISBN: 978-0-9552488-3-2)
Stefano Bartolini and Peter Mair

People, States and Fear: An Agenda for International Security Studies in the Post-Cold War Era (ISBN: 978-0-9552488-1-8)
Barry Buzan

Elite and Specialized Interviewing (ISBN: 978-0-9547966-7-9)
Lewis A. Dexter

System and Process in International Politics (ISBN: 978-0-9547966-2-4)
Morton A. Kaplan

Democracy (ISBN: 978-0-9552488-0-1)
Jack Lively

Individualism (ISBN: 978-0-9547966-6-2)
Steven Lukes

Political Elites (ISBN: 978-0-9547966-0-0)
Geraint Parry

Parties and Party Systems: A Framework for Analysis (ISBN: 978-0-9547966-1-7)
Giovanni Sartori

ECPR Monographs:

The Return of the State of War: A Theoretical Analysis of Operation Iraqi Freedom (ISBN: 978-0-9552488-5-6)
Dario Battistella

Gender and the Vote in Britain: Beyond the Gender Gap? (ISBN: 978-0-9547966-9-3)
Rosie Campbell

Paying for Democracy: Political Finance and State Funding for Parties (ISBN: 978-0-9547966-3-1)
Kevin Casas-Zamora

The Politics of Income Taxation: A Comparative Analysis (ISBN: 978-0-9547966-8-6)
Steffen Ganghof

Joining Political Organisations: Institutions, Mobilisation and Participation in Western Democracies (ISBN: 978-0-9552488-9-4)
Laura Morales

Citizenship: The History of an Idea (ISBN: 978-0-9547966-5-5)
Paul Magnette

Representing Women? Female Legislators in West European Parliaments (ISBN: 978-0-9547966-4-8)
Mercedes Mateo Diaz

Deliberation Behind the Closed Doors: Transparency and lobbying in the European Union (ISBN: 978-0-9552488-4-9)
Daniel Naurin

Globalisation: An overview (ISBN: 978-0-9552488-2-5)
Danilo Zolo

General Interest Books

Parties and Elections in New European Democracies (ISBN: 978-0-9558203-2-8)
Richard Rose and Neil Munro

Masters of Political Science (ISBN: 978-0-9558203-3-5)
Campus and Pasquino

| contents

the state | new introduction to the
tradition in | ECPR Press edition by
western europe | Kenneth Dyson

WHY THE BOOK WAS WRITTEN

The State Tradition in Western Europe is an attempt to capture, through the cross-cultural study of ideas, a particular European way of thinking about public power. The tradition to which it alludes emphasises the autonomy, distinctiveness and normative character of public power. It attributes action in the service of this power to a fictional person and deliberative agent – the state – in ways that recall Thomas Hobbes, Samuel Pufendorf, and Christian Wolff. The classic state tradition serves to depersonalise public power in a dual sense, seeing it as distinct from both ruler and ruled. In the words of John Dunn (1996: 32), the state is '… constituted for the express purpose of denying the claims of any populace to be itself the continuing locus of political authority.' Such claims are denied as much to governments as to public opinion, from both of which the state is viewed as distinct. Simultaneously, and in a way paradoxically, it privileges those actors who are understood to represent the state and whose institutional milieus and actions give it material as well as symbolic expression.

In consequence of this paradox, the book pictures state as a problem-solving and a problem-creating concept (see Chapter 9 of *The State Tradition*). State is an abstract, holistic concept that is a source of certain virtues but also of enduring difficulties (on which I reflect later in this introduction). In particular, it exists in tension with concepts of democracy, with managerial models of efficiency, with instrumental conceptions of government, with accounts that reduce 'the state' to its parts (notably the government and discrete governmental institutions), and with notions of the welfare state that see it as just a set of activities. Also, in different settings elites contest each other's claim to embody the state. Hence state remains contested.

The State Tradition was conceived in the process of writing a much more modest book – *Party, State and Bureaucracy in Western Germany* (1977). This last book argued that analysts of post-war German political parties, who used conventional Anglo-American party system theory to focus on party system 'concentration' and on narrowed 'ideological space', missed capturing a key dimension of the party system – the *character* of these parties. Valuable insights into party system behaviour were to be gained by counting the number of competing parties and by analysing the ideological distance between them (Sartori 1976). However, this two-dimensional approach neglected how the parties were affected by prevailing concepts about the nature of the state in which they were embedded, concepts that reflected the de-legitimation of traditional elites, like the army and the bureaucracy, and the subsequent power vacuum. These effects were apparent in the identities and role conceptions of party elites: in the German case in the primacy of political parties in the constitution of 1949, the distinctive emphasis on 'militant' democracy (after the horrors associated with the collapse of the Weimar Republic), and the opinion-shaping role of party leaders. *Party, State, and Bureaucracy in Western Germany* traced how the different character of the political parties of the Bonn Republic as compared to those of the Weimar Republic – and to those in the UK – had to do with the historically transformed and distinctive relationship of political parties to the idea of the state. This relationship remained a source of reference and controversy for the German political parties. It begged questions about the German idea of the state, specifically the 'party state'.

I sought to contextualise this single-country observation within my wider comparative interest in French and West European government and politics. This search led me, first, to recognise that theorists of public administration had for some time argued that the *character* of public bureaucracies could not be understood apart from prevailing conceptions of public power (notably Chapman 1959; Armstrong 1973; Suleiman 1974). Two processes seemed to be at work here and are central to establishing and understanding the significance of state as an integrating and legitimating concept. Certain special properties were attributed to the state; and particular elites succeeded in identifying themselves, and their self-interests, with this concept and, in consequence, gained a privileged status and power. Their identities and self-interests became bound up with the concept of the state. In this respect the state is best conceived as a fictional entity to which an extraordinary power of action is attributed, along with the capacity to act through those who are identified with it (Runciman 2003). It also became bound up with the self-interests of the academic elites who educated and trained these elites (see Chapter 3 of *The State Tradition*; later Bourdieu 1989).

In addition, I sought to place the idea of the state in the context of the debate about 'strong' states and 'weak' states. It was clear that the claim to autonomy and distinctiveness of public power was not the same as the possession of financial, institutional and professional capacity to act as a 'strong' state and to provide 'heroic' leadership. Indeed, though Britain and the United States might be 'stateless' in lacking this idea of the state, they could act as 'strong' states in discharging particular functions and could generate heroic leaders (and not just in wartime). This capacity drew on close links with society and convergence of public and private power, for instance the role of private litigation in strengthening the state, rather than on claims to autonomy and distinctiveness of public power (on the United States as 'not stateless' in this respect, see King and Lieberman 2009 and Novak 2008). In not making such claims the United States remained 'stateless'; at the level of the concept of state, it remained an historical enigma (Skowronek 1982). States that shared in the classic state tradition were not to be equated with 'strong' states; 'stateless' societies were not necessarily 'weak' states.

Finally, I noted the strong emphasis in the literature on the historical state- and nation-building differences between France and Germany. They had contrasting institutional configurations (France's centralised state and Germany's federal state) and different state/economy configurations (French *dirigisme* and German Ordo-liberalism). The French state was classically pictured as centralised and *dirigiste*, the German state as federal and pledged to the 'social market economy'. These differences bore some relationship to a more complex and changing reality. However, they seemed to mask a commonality. In their historical and legal frames of reference, especially discourses about the autonomous and distinctive character of public power, they were 'state societies' (see *The State Tradition* pp. 243–50).

The next question was whether the notion of 'state societies' was more than just a way of summarising Franco-German commonalities. Was I just writing about 'The State Tradition in France and Germany'? My reading into Belgian, Dutch, Italian, Swedish, and Swiss literature on the state had to rely to a greater extent on secondary sources. It suggested that France and Germany had served as the 'core', from which ideas of the autonomous and distinctive power of the state had evolved. It had been elaborated in, and disseminated from, this 'core' through the nineteenth and into the twentieth centuries, notably through the French Revolution and Napoleonic Europe and then through Prussian unification of Germany and the process of legitimating the new German state. Hence the book was largely about France and Germany. Nevertheless, concepts of public power that shared the properties of French and German thinking about the state were emulated across continental Europe in the search for legitimacy and above all order, not least in the troubled Habsburg Empire of the late nineteenth and early twentieth centuries and in post-1918, truncated Austria. In some instances, these concepts gained strong footholds in domestic institutional structures, for instance in Belgium and the Netherlands. In others, like Italy, state played an important role in discourse. However, its institutional imprint was much weaker so that reference to the state functioned more at the level of political and administrative symbolism. Nevertheless, the book has something to say about the independent contributions that Austrian and Italian thinkers made to the elaboration of the classic state tradition.

Hence what began as a single-country study was soon transformed into a cross-cultural history of ideas. As *The State Tradition* emphasises, the concept of the state was variously interpreted in France and Germany, and contextualised as part of different political traditions. However, there appeared to be a shared nucleus of meaning, particularly a shared preference for attributing certain qualities and certain actions to the state. The question was whether it was possible to elucidate a shared set of properties attributed to the state that accounted for this commonality. Both France and Germany seemed attached to the idea of 'unitary', rationally-ordered power, to the state's role in constituting markets as 'market maker' and 'market modifier', and to the notion of socially-embedded markets (cf. Polanyi 2001: Dyson and Quaglia 2010). These ideas distinguished German federalism from US federalism and German thinking about the 'constitution' of the market from Anglo-American economic thinking, which preferred to see the market as an autonomous, spontaneous and evolutionary phenomenon (Dyson and Quaglia 2010).

My hesitation about taking on this task in the cross-cultural study of ideas at such an early stage in my academic career was compounded by recognition that the state remains an extraordinarily elusive and contested concept. In the words of Runciman (2003: 37), 'it is a fictional entity, a canvas onto which various kinds of ideas and elite interests are pinned, and thus condemned to remain puzzling and contested'. Hence I was wading into intellectually murky waters. I also faced enormous complexity. The research that underpinned the book involved a huge amount of reading across a range of scholarly texts covering different time periods, languages and disciplines, as well as exposure to a variety of ontological and epistemological positions. Not least, I had to stretch beyond political science into history and law. Only later, in various articles and books, did I begin to fully explore how the state concept was manifested in economics, beginning with the volume *Industrial Crisis* (Dyson and Wilks (eds) 1982) and most recently in the first volume of *European Economic Governance and Policies* (Dyson and Quaglia 2010). My later work in comparative European economic policies retained this fascination with the role of state in discourse about, and within, institutions and policies.

I faced the enormous challenge of weaving individually complex literatures together, across linguistic and cultural barriers, and over long time periods, into a coherent narrative. Looking back, I very much doubt that, had I encountered the Research Assessment Exercise (RAE) in those early years of my career, I would have attempted to write such a book. It would have focused on one or maybe two countries and a discrete time period and issue area (see Laborde 2000b; Meadowcroft 1995).

Now, after many years of not reading the book, and trying to look back without undue pride in having been selected for the ECPR 'Classics' Series, my reaction is mixed. On the one hand, I am genuinely surprised at the amount of ground that I covered at such an age and so quickly. It is less 'immature' than I at first feared. On the other hand, I now have the advantage of many more years of scholarly experience, which has made me more able to be self-critical. In particular, the loss of the central position of this particular concept of the state in political and legal discourse during the intervening period underlines more forcefully the historical contingency and specificity of the phenomenon about which I wrote in the late 1970s. And, not least, I have read critiques of the book, which have led me to look at it afresh with a more sceptical eye. In writing this introduction, and re-reading these critiques, however, my sceptical eye fell as much on the critics as my own work.

In particular, *The State Tradition* is marked by the historical conditions in which it was written – at the tail end of the 'golden age' of this tradition. I must therefore ask whether the book is dated in the sense that the classic state tradition itself has declined, lost its dynamism and its hold on minds. This decline might be attributed in substantial part to the steady consolidation of the hegemony of Anglo-American approaches to the study of government and politics and of law, with their much more utilitarian view of the public realm and reductionist view of the state (Birnbaum 1982; Loughlin 2005). However, to the extent that this is true of law and of political science, it reflects much deeper historical changes on which I reflect below. We might ask whether, in consequence, debate about the nature of public power has been impoverished.

On the other hand, as I argue below, conditions are emerging in which the idea of public power as autonomous and distinctive may gain greater credence. Reworking the state tradition means going beyond a static picture of public power to a dynamic analysis of change in its internal interactions and in its interactions with business and civil society (Elias 2007; Migdal and Schlichte 2005: 19–20). A static picture of the classic state tradition will not suffice for this purpose.

THE STATE TRADITION

The shared properties of the classic concept of the state with which *The State Tradition* was concerned were manifested in a discourse that focused on the intimate connections between legal authority, political power and community in creating the conditions for an 'ordered' society (see p. 206). Hence state was a generalising, integrating and legitimating concept that was irreducibly normative. It commended certain forms of behaviour and condemned other forms. Its core values focused around the role of hierarchy, integration and identity (including conflation with 'nation') in securing the overriding public good of order in society. They included public interest, legality, impersonality, predictability, continuity, probity and precision in exercising public power. Above all, the classic state tradition rested on the core distinction between public and private and the importance attached to solidarity.

Through these values the concept of the state was seen as giving purpose and meaning to what would otherwise be a chaos of fragmented and competing individuals and interests (p. 84). It fashioned unity out of diversity by affirming shared identity (Nora 1986). In the French case the core values of the 'one and indivisible republic' stood in contrast to an Anglo-American counter-identity, in terms of which a persisting anti-economic liberalism was fashioned (Hayward 2007, 2008). Equally, this identity was very much shared at elite level and could be contested, for instance in the French republican and revolutionary tradition. In Wilhelmenian Germany and conservative circles in the Weimar Republic state became conflated with *Volk* and *Nation*.

State was conceived as depersonalised power; it was attributed to certain institutions that embodied public power, and it became a focus for identity formation (Chapter 9). It was, in short, a legal, political and sociocultural construct that addressed the core problem of order in society. In particular, the notion of the state permeated, and in turn was permeated by, the discourse of public law (pp. 107–15).

I defined a 'state society' as one in which political and legal discourse centres on:

'the abstract, impersonal state as an entity or personality above and distinct from both government and governed; as an institution which is autonomous, formally coordinated and differentiated from other organisations which operate in a defined territory; as an object of universal service and respect; and as the source of a distinct public morality... State societies exemplify strongly non-economic, non-utilitarian attitudes towards political relations, which attitudes deny that the public interest is simply the sum of private interests; a rationalist spirit of inquiry; a stress on the distinctiveness of state and society;... an emphasis on impersonal political symbols of community; a stress on the unitary character of the 'public power'...; a moralistic view of politics which involves strongly collectivist and regulatory attitudes... These features find their coherence in a rationalist conception of the technical requirements of an 'ordered' society' (pp. 51–52).

'The concept of the state... is articulated as a body of values, powers, procedures and offices and represents a concern for logic and order in collective arrangements' (p. 270).

This definition of shared properties suggests historical contingency is at work in the rise and fall of discourse about the state. In geo-strategic, cultural and socio-economic conditions in which the problem of order is acutely experienced, this type of thinking about the state can flourish. One thinks of Thomas Hobbes in seventeenth-century Civil War England, of the earlier French wars of religion, of the French Revolutionary period, and of the vortex of challenges that beset Europe in the latter part of the nineteenth and first part of the twentieth centuries. The theme of historical contingency of the tradition is developed later in the new introduction. In particular, geo-strategic ambition and war emerge as powerful conditioning factors in stimulating conceptions of the state as an autonomous, distinctive public power (cf. *The State Tradition*; also Tilly 1973). Hence in the French context, its primacy is especially associated with the figures of Cardinal Richelieu, the Emperor Napoleon Bonaparte, and General Charles de Gaulle (Hayward 2007).

In addition, the definition highlights the intimate connection with public law. The state was the judicial form in which public power was exercised (Troper 1994). Law was not just the articulation of the state in its role as the impartial and impersonal regulator of society. Also, through law, the state constituted society and, not least, the market, as French *dirigistes* and German Ordo-liberals argued. This property contrasted these societies from the English-speaking countries. In the United States law held a central position, but discourse centred on very different values and commended different forms of behaviour. The classic state tradition reflected a shared set of normative commitments.

The classic state tradition was impossible to understand apart from the edifice of public law with which it came to be intimately associated, especially from the second part of the nineteenth century, from when we can date its 'golden age' (Jones 1993; Möllers 2008). It became permeated by Roman law notions of *potestas* and *imperium*, which were much less influential in Anglo-American political thinking. Firstly, the state was seen as a corporation that possessed an inherent power to act through its representatives. Secondly, in acting, the state embodied a distinctive public interest which was set apart from the voice of particular electoral majorities or what could be agreed with or amongst powerful lobby groups. The public institutions identified with the state had attributed to them autonomy of action (a life of their own), a specificity of moral purpose, and a unique ethos of public service in the general interest. They were there to protect the values of the public sphere from the self-interested behaviour of special economic, social and cultural groups whose behaviour threatened to 'fracture' society. Hence the state was identified with 'services of general economic interest' (*Daseinsvorsorge* in the work of Forsthoff 1968, and first used by him in 1938; also Bull 2008) or with safeguarding principles like economic stability, a sound currency and competitive markets (in the work of a founding father of Ordo-liberalism, Eucken 1952), or more generally the integrity of the nation, the unification of the territory and the direction of the economy (see Kuisel 1984; Nora 1986; Rosanvallon 1993; Hayward 2007).

LONG-TERM TENSIONS IN THE STATE TRADITION

The irreducibly normative character of discourse about the autonomous and distinctive power of the state meant that it served as both a 'problem-solving' and a 'problem-creating' concept (see Chapter 9). The identification of certain values with the state, and the emphasis on the state as distinct from both its rulers and from the ruled, was a source of social, economic and political tensions. Firstly, the classic state tradition existed in various conditions of political tension with democracy, ranging from authoritarian alternative to liberal corrective to democratisation (*Machtstaat* versus *Rechtsstaat*). It provided a focal point of reference in legal, economic, historical and political debates. State served as a pervasive and polarising source of identification (as a source of order and identity) and of disaffection (as authoritarian and oppressive). On the one hand, the idea of the state was seen as a counterweight to the threat of political instability, government irresponsibility and ineffectiveness associated with party and parliamentary government. It claimed to stand outside and above partisan politicking. In its extreme form, expressed by state theorists who followed

Carl Schmitt in Germany, the 'authoritative' state was contrasted with 'totalitarian' society *(The State Tradition*: 126). It was to be measured by its decisiveness in dealing with exceptional circumstances.

On the other hand, the classic state tradition helped spawn specific forms of *anti-étatisme*, for instance in continental European syndicalism and in the ideological form that the 1960s student movement took there (p. 16). Here the claims of the state were seen as hypocritical, as camouflage for the self-interests of established elites (e.g. Bourdieu 1989). More balanced positions – and more influential in the maturing Federal Republic of Germany – were those of Konrad Hesse and Ulrich Scheuner. They followed Rudolf Smend, Carl Schmitt's Weimar-period rival, in seeking to determine the appropriate relationship between the 'state ruled by law' (*Rechtsstaat*), understood as having a material (as opposed to formal) character, and political structures and processes (*The State Tradition*: 125–7).

In addition, the classic state tradition existed in economic tension with the emerging model of commercial society, which emphasised individual choice, the market as arbiter of values, and managerial models of efficiency and performance management. In particular, the state and the market offered rival claims to embody 'modernisation' and 'modernity'. The emergence of a new 'managerial' class, alongside the new social prestige of the entrepreneur, offered the basis for a critique of the classic state tradition as a source of inflexibility, inefficiency and waste. The state was a burden on society. A change took place in the dominant image of the individual. The individual was seen less as a citizen (possessed of certain rights and obligations) and more as a consumer (enjoying a market status). In the words of Bauman (Bauman and Barth 2009): 'I shop, therefore I am...' In consequence the notion of the distinctiveness of public power began to lose its centrality.

A further source of cultural tension stemmed from deeper social changes associated with greater social mobility (through increased real incomes and access to education) and with exposure to more and varied sources of information (notably the media and later digital revolutions). Those who claimed to represent the state had to contend with a much more questioning and critical public, one less trusting in public authority. Values of accountability and transparency began to count for more. In addition, the media revolution contributed to a process of personalisation of government, in which political leaders were continuously soliciting the support of often fickle public opinion through the media. In this changing environment neither politicians nor the media, both locked in an incestuous relationship, had much time for the values represented by the classic state tradition.

Finally, the classic state tradition had to contend with more pronounced and intrusive internationalisation in economic and cultural terms. It existed in tension with the new models and pressures associated with 'globalisation', 'Europeanisation', and the emergence of English as the world language in whose terms politics, administration, law and the economy were increasingly debated and scholarly benchmarks of excellence established. The 'logic' of globalisation and of the single European market assumed a central legitimating role in domestic discourse. This 'logic' went along with a renewed belief in the disembedded nature of the global economy as an autonomous phenomenon (Polanyi 2001; Caporaso and Tarrow 2008). The academic agenda shifted to the opportunities for non-state actors to engage in collective action at different levels (Tarrow 2005: 25) and to emerging counter-movements on behalf of global justice (della Porta 2007). Together, the various social, economic and cultural challenges associated with globalisation and Europeanisation served to undermine the distinctive claims of the classic state tradition. These challenges, and the historical contingency of the state concept, are examined later.

THE IMPACT OF THE BOOK: MISUNDERSTANDINGS AND CLARIFICATIONS

The State Tradition has been received in three ways, varying from warm welcome, through indifference, to criticism. Many comparative scholars, working on continental European governments, politics and policy making, have made positive reference to the work (e.g. Birnbaum 1988; Hancher and Moran 1989; Page 1985; Pierson 1996; Schmidt 2002 and 2006). Some have used the state/stateless distinction as an independent variable in cross-national empirical studies (e.g. Atkinson and Coleman 1989; Knill 1998). Above all, it has been most warmly welcomed by European country and area specialists who tend to be very 'context-aware': on Britain (e.g. Barker 1990; Bevir and Rhodes 2003; Harden and Lewis 1988; Marquand 1988), on France (e.g. Hayward 1983 and 1986; Schmidt 1996; Stevens 2003; Wright 1989), and on Germany (e.g. Johnson 1983; Kvistad 1999, Smith 1986). For them the study of politics was about 'getting inside politics' to 'politics as it is experienced and lived'. Ideas and the discourse surrounding them were central in this process of understanding 'politics from within'. Many empirically-minded political scientists who work on France, and who have embraced multi-level governance and the 'disaggregated' state, continue to argue that France still retains a state-centred tradition (cf. Cole 2008: 27–9, 51). In their work on the French central state bureaucracy, on public-sector reforms, on regionalisation of power and on privatisation, they stress the way in which discourse continues to conceptualise a coherent centre over and above conflicting economic, societal and territorial interests (Cohen 1996; Jobert and Muller 1987; Le Galès 2003; Muller and Surel 2002; Schmidt 1996 and 2002; Cole 2008: 27). Similarly, the classic state tradition finds its way into German political studies (e.g. Benz 2001) but more especially legal studies (e.g. Bockenförde 1991, 1999; Möllers 2008, Schuppert forthcoming). In addition, various political theorists and historians of ideas have taken up the challenge to explore further the historical and normative underpinnings of the state understood as autonomous and distinctive public power (e.g. Bartelson 2001; Jordan 1985; Morris 1998; Runciman 1997; Skinner 2008; Vincent 1987). British public lawyers have also responded (e.g. Harden and Lewis 1988; Loughlin 1999, 2003, 2009; McLean 2003, 2005; Prosser 1996).

Unsurprisingly, indifference has been notable on the part of the most entrenched practitioners of Anglo-American approaches to political science and law, especially rational choice models that attribute utility-maximising preferences to actors, public choice theories, and the so-called 'positive political theory' of the Yale Law School. The advocates of these approaches tend to remain focused on the functions and the structure of the state and on theories of the state that help to explain its functions and structure – pluralist, corporatist, realist and neo-Marxist (Dunleavy and O'Leary 1987) and pluralist, elitist, Marxist and market liberal (Dryzek and Dunleavy 2009). This emphasis on the functions of the state and preference for disaggregating the state, rather than exploring underlying ideas about the character of public power, has grown since *The State Tradition* was published (cf. Dunleavy 1995; Coen and Thatcher 2008; Héritier and Lehmkuhl 2008). Continental European thought about the nature of the state as a collectivity, above all in its public law aspects, remains foreign to these essentially instrumental and reductionist approaches to structures and functions of the state. This indifference also affected country studies, like Katzenstein's (1987) study of the 'semi-sovereign' German state. To the extent that *The State Tradition* reflected this continental thinking, it was too elusive for their tastes and too 'foreign' to their models. In particular, the conflation of state with government impoverished thinking about public power (cf. McLean 2003; Skinner 2008). At the same time this indifference to the classic state tradition was by no means universal. Of Anglo-American approaches, 'historical' institutionalism has been perhaps the most open to thinking about ideas of public power. Its stress on path dependency has helped to highlight continuities, for instance in the centrality of state in European administrative systems (e.g. Page 2003) and in economic policy (Schmidt 2002).

Similarly, some influential attempts to construct conceptual maps of the history of European state-building have ignored the concept of the state with which this book is concerned. Barrington Moore (1993) and Immanuel Wallerstein (1979) examined processes of state formation using socio-economic variables and focusing on the distribution of state power rather than the nature of state power. In contrast, Stein Rokkan concentrated on political variables, especially relating to the state-economy and state-culture dimensions of centre-periphery relations (see Flora, Kuhnle and Urwin 1999). However, his broad historical narratives about 'centre formation', 'system building' and 'political structuring' were not used to elucidate similarities and variations in conceptions of public power.

Historians have also cited the book (e.g. Shennan 1986). However, indifference has been notable amongst those historians and lawyers who have been wedded to Anglophone legal and political thought. The primacy of the notion of the Crown in their work has not proved hospitable to evolving the idea of the state as a fictional person and has not spawned a clear distinction between government and state. Furthermore, many of them have also been hostile to the high level of abstraction required to examine long-term and fundamental political changes in political ideas. Thus Skinner (2002) has argued that the genealogy of state is bound up with the history of its use in individual linguistic communities rather than in longer-term and broader structural developments (cf. Richter 1995). Paradoxically, this position did not prevent him from transcending his 'context-dependent' view of ideas to subscribe to the republican model of civic duty as a prescriptive basis for political argument. At the same time Skinner (2008) is by no means indifferent to the classic state tradition, suggesting that the disappearance of Thomas Hobbes' notion of the state as a fictional person has impoverished English political thought. However, his discussion of state remains very Hobbes-centric.

On reflection (spurred by the invitation to write this introduction) I regret not having earlier addressed some of the key criticisms of the book (notably Meadowcroft 1994, 1995; Laborde 2000b). Two considerations prevailed in my lack of response. Firstly, I had moved on in personal research agenda into comparative European and European Union (EU)-level economic policies, if still focusing on the intimate nexus between conceptions of the state and economic policy ideas and markets. This shift led me to see that, behind the apparent highly visible differences between French *dirigiste* and German so-called Ordo-liberal economic ideas, there lurked a fundamental commonality. They shared the notion that the state constitutes the market economy, as 'market maker' and 'market modifier' (Dyson 2002). The market was not perceived, in the Anglo-American manner, as a spontaneous order on which governments imposed intrusive restrictions. It was created by the operation of the public sphere (cf. on the French stability paradigm of 1870–1914 Jobert and Muller 1987; on French *dirigisme* from 1945 to the 1980s see Kuisel 1984; on Ordo-liberalism Eucken 1952; from a German non-Ordo-liberal perspective Bofinger 2009; more generally Polanyi 2001). Both *dirigiste* thought and German Ordo-liberal ideas were concerned with the problem of private economic power and with establishing the political legitimacy of the market economy. These concerns with the institutional requirements of the economy, and the importance of strong and independent public authorities, demarcated French and German economic thinking from Anglo-American ideas about the liberal market economy (even if French and German thinkers differed about the underlying principles that should guide policy). So, after my shift of direction, the central argument of the classic state tradition remained intact, and I remained relaxed about its value.

Secondly, my reading of the critics led me to conclude that they actually seemed to agree with the central thrust of my argument. This was not always at first apparent. My central claim was that Britain was a 'stateless society' *in a juridical sense*, reflecting the absence of a vigorous public law tradition. As Frederic Maitland (1901) claimed, 'English lawyers... liked their persons to be real'. Having criticised my dichotomous analysis of 'state' and stateless' societies with respect to Britain, Laborde (2000a: 552) refers almost as an afterthought to the absence of public law in the form of endowment of the state with a corporate existence. In her words about Britain: '... law never became intimately bound up with the concept of the state.'

The difference seems to be one of emphasis. In *The State Tradition* the central argument is that law matters and has been central to whether and how the concept of the state manifests itself in discourse. Given this difference in legal tradition, Laborde (ibid: 553) writes of: 'the absence of an integrated state tradition... the absence of a single discursive idiom about the "state"... the absence of a strong distinction between state and society'. Laborde (ibid: 550–51) goes on to concede: '... the British state was rarely theorized as the upholder of an integrated, self-contained normative order, and was more likely to be perceived as an unproblematic technical requirement or a 'lesser evil'... there was not in Britain one encompassing idea (one might say "ideal-type") of the state, incorporating moral, legal and institutional elements.' I cannot disagree, at least not without abandoning my central argument.

So what the critique amounts to in this case is the detail of whether my interpretation of the British Pluralists (like Frederic Maitland, J.N. Figgis, Harold Laski and G.D.H. Cole) and of the French Pluralists (notably Leon Duguit) was right or wrong. Even here, on closer examination, I can find little to separate our narratives. If anything, Duguit's role as a foremost critic of the ascendant French sovereignty-based conception of the state helped his ready reception in British political and legal thinking. The connection with Duguit was a shared functionalist 'style' of thinking about public law and political commitment to promoting the role of government in social solidarity (Loughlin 2005). A further factor was political: the attempt by writers like Ernest Barker, J.A. Hobson and Leonard Hobhouse to discredit influential pre-1914 British Idealist philosophers as heirs to the German state and its militarism. Their Hegelian-inspired idea of the state having a moral will above that of the people it represented was intensely contested for reasons that were political as well as rooted in ascendant intellectual style.

Three more serious criticisms deserve attention in that they are more central to the work. Here clarifications are needed in the interests of dispelling some misunderstandings. Firstly, Meadowcroft (1994) suggests that the book 'conflates' the *institutions* of the state and the *idea* of the state into a single object. More precisely and accurately, *The State Tradition* deals with the idea of the state as it evolved in continental Europe. It also examines both how it has been used by different elites to legitimate their special position and how it has come to endow particular institutions with special authority. In this respect state takes a material form. The idea of the state becomes significant because it enters into action as tools in political and legal debates and because it permeates institutions, their functioning, their socialisation processes and thus the role definitions of certain actors. As Skinner (2008) points out, we want to know whose actions properly count as actions of the state and to understand the processes through which certain actions are *attributed* to the state as an artificial person. However, as *The State Tradition* emphasises, we need first to understand the idea of the state – and how and why this idea took on a distinctive form in continental Europe.

Secondly, contrary to Meadowcroft (1994) and Laborde (2000b), essentialist definitions of the state are not necessarily 'misguided'. They may be misguided in particular cases, perhaps in very many, and even in this case. However, some form of distinction between the 'essential' and the 'accidental' properties of concepts is implicit in the practice of political science. Certain historians of political thought, such as Skinner (2008), make a case for 'context is all' in the examination of concepts, focusing on their use. However, he too ends up making broader 'non-context-bound' conceptual commitments, in his case to the republican model of civic engagement. Political scientists are not just interested in collecting an undifferentiated list of features of the state or plotting its use as a concept.

The State Tradition is interested in asking whether thinking about the state shares certain properties in some contexts that make it distinctive from ideas about the state in other contexts (of time as well as space). If special and distinctive properties are attributed to the state in certain contexts, these properties are of significance for political science. The book argues that there is a shared continental European concept of the state that has precisely such properties, that they were shared across contexts, and that political science is the poorer for not recognising them. It should, however, be emphasised that this exercise is not based on any assumption about eternal or universal properties of the state. The classic state tradition that is identified here is historically contingent as well as spatially context-bound.

Thirdly, *The State Tradition* did not argue that 'British thinkers, while occasionally using the word, *never* comprehended the concept of the state', or that it was 'something that *only* continental minds can grasp', or that 'the state concept was a *mere* continental import to Britain' (Laborde 2000a: 542) (my italics). However, it did contend that modern and dominant Anglo-American-centric approaches to political science and law have made it difficult to grasp the continental European concept and its significance – which Laborde (ibid: 554) endorses. These approaches have been more concerned with what states do (their functions), with their interaction within international relations (their external sovereignty), with how they are organised (institutions, governance and networks), and with who holds power (socio-economic analysis). They are much less concerned with the nature of the state, what the state is in itself. In terms of debates about functions, sovereignty, structures and 'who governs' there is of course a clear, strong and continuing sense of the state in Anglo-American thought. Moreover, this sense of the state is shared right across Europe and the wider world. 'Bringing the state back in' and discussion about the state is very meaningful in all these respects (cf. Skocpol, Evans and Rueschemeyer 1985; Dunleavy and O'Leary 1987). Seen in these terms, Britain and the United States are not 'stateless societies' and never have been; and it can be claimed (Stråth and Skinner 2003: 4) that '... the state has become the master noun of our political discourse.' However, this is not the sense of state with which *The State Tradition* is concerned.

If there is a main weakness in the book's discussion of 'stateless societies', it is perhaps the failure to underline sufficiently the point that I was not claiming that state was a foreign concept in *all* its dimensions. The claim was that in continental Europe a concept of the state emerged that was distinctive in its views about public power. This claim is made in the book but needs reinforcement. In the sense of state with which this book is concerned, the English-speaking societies are 'stateless'. This claim is far from saying that in the past, when Anglophone political science approaches were less dominant, or even now, American and British minds have been unable to comprehend the different ways in which the concept has been understood and used in continental Europe. The British Idealists such as T. H. Green and Bernard Bosanquet; the Pluralists such as Harold Laski, Frederic Maitland, and Ernest Barker; cultural theorists such as Matthew Arnold; and American Progressives such as Woodrow Wilson – all understood very well continental European thinking about the state as central to moral self-development and about rights as socially constructed. In the late-Victorian, Edwardian and inter-war period they engaged actively with these ideas. For instance, William Robson (1928) sought to carry Idealism into his advocacy of a distinct system of public law in the UK. My main points were that Idealist thinking did not displace or deflect the predominant British currents of pragmatic and utilitarian thinking about public law and government; that Pluralist thought pursued a functionalist style of thinking about public law; and that modern political science and law had lost the active engagement with the autonomy and distinctiveness of public power displayed by Laski, Maitland and Robson.

The stress on the specific character and the pervasiveness of the concept of the state in continental European thought does not mean that there was an absence of discourse about the state in Britain; that it was a mere continental import to Britain; or that there were not counter, anti-*étatiste* discourses in continental Europe (cf. Hayward 2007). It suggests that British discourse about the state took different forms from that ascendant in continental Europe. This discourse shifted its centre of gravity over time. However, the prevailing tendency over the last two centuries has been to embrace a utilitarian conception of the state and to equate the state with the power of an established government (Skinner 2008). Discourse focused much more on the *functions* of the state, what it does and should do, and how it was *organised* for this purpose. To the extent that there were normative formulations of the *nature* of the state, it was seen as of secondary importance to the vibrancy of civil society or as an historical emanation from this society and thus fused with society (cf. Laborde 2000a: 551–2). According to T.D. Weldon (1953: 50), no hard and fast line can be drawn between state and society; there is nothing special about the state. The key point is that, when the nature of the state was debated, and continental thinking about the state drawn on for this purpose, these debates were not inspired by Roman law conceptions of public law. In the words of Loughlin (2003: 2): 'Modern British history is based on rejection of the idea of public law.'

In a strongly Anglophone account of the state, Quentin Skinner (2002, 2008) has usefully reminded us that the English political philosopher

Thomas Hobbes made an important contribution to emerging continental European debates about the nature of the state as distinct from both ruler and ruled and as having the attributes of a fictional person (also Jaume 1986; Runciman 1997; but see also *The State Tradition*: 188–89). Indeed, he attributes its origins to Renaissance England and France (Skinner 1989). However, Skinner also points out that the reception of Hobbes was much more sympathetic in continental Europe than in England and that this type of notion of the state made no substantial progress in English legal thinking after William Blackstone in the eighteenth century (Skinner 2003: 320–3). More tellingly, Hobbes influenced debates in international law, for two reasons: first, with his conception of the state as an artificial person, which was modified considerably; and, secondly, for making the conceptual move that eventually led to distinct concepts of the law of nature and the law of nations, to which the state was subject.

A HISTORICALLY CONTINGENT CONCEPT: THE *LONGUE DURÉE* AND THE UNRAVELLING OF THE 'GOLDEN AGE'

From a later vantage point of nearly thirty years, we can ask what long-term changes have occurred in and to the continental European state tradition (cf. Koselleck 2000; Richter 1995). Are there features of contemporary experience that suggest that its core values might be returned to as a source of inspiration in moral arguments about politics, economy and society? Or, alternatively, have its core claims to autonomy and distinctiveness of public power lost relevance and credibility?

The overall impression has been that its 'heroic age', culminating in the debates about state theory between Carl Schmitt, Rudolf Smend, and their disciples, has passed (Möllers 2008). Indeed, as early as the 1920s Otto Hintze (1964) was claiming that the state had been reduced to just another type of business operation (*Betrieb*). The classical state tradition has unquestionably withered, though it seems premature to speak of its demise (Reinhard 2007; Schuppert forthcoming; Wahl 2006). Caney (2005) argues for a new global political theory, focusing on institutions beyond the state; Caporaso (1989) refers to the elusive state; Benz (2008) argues that the search for a general theory of the state must give way to a dynamic political analysis of how state and societal actors build and transform states in very differing ways; with specific reference to Germany, Benz and Goetz (1996) and Goetz (2005) point to the narrowing of the domain of the 'classic' bureaucratic state as a new public sector takes root; Héritier and Lehmkuhl (2008) see new modes of network governance operating in 'the shadow of hierarchy'; MacCormick (1999) writes of 'post-sovereign' states; and Schuppert (2003) refers to a new 'post-national' model of public law. More fundamentally, Loughlin (2003) and Möllers (2008) claim that the idea of public law has waned even in continental Europe and that there is a resulting sense of loss and disorientation amongst scholars and teachers of *Staatsrecht* and *Staatslehre*.

On closer examination it is evident these judgements need qualification both with respect to what we mean when we talk about the 'decline of the state' and with respect to different societies. First, in forming judgements we must distinguish between the many and ongoing changes that affect the form of the state, especially its claims to sovereignty and how collectively binding decisions are made and implemented, and state as a set of beliefs about the distinctive character and ordering of public power (Genschel, Leibfried and Zangl 2008; Genschel and Zangl 2008; Schuppert forthcoming). It can be plausibly argued that the underlying form has fundamentally changed: from the state as the *monopolist* of public power to the state as the *manager* of public power (ibid). It is no longer the exclusive or necessarily even the main provider of public goods. The cooperative creation of law in conjunction with the private sector and with civil society is manifested in new modes of 'co-regulation' and 'self-regulation', including increasing use of voluntary agreements in target setting, benchmarking and monitoring mechanisms like 'naming and shaming' (Héritier 2002; Héritier, Knill and Mingers 1996). In consequence, new debates have opened about whether the appropriate form of state is best characterised as 'lean', 'enabling', or 'preventative'. However, these changes at the level of the form of state do not amount to displacement of the centrality of state as a set of beliefs about the distinctive character and exercise of public power. Moreover, they do not mean that a state necessarily becomes 'weaker' because it ceases to be a monopolist of public power. Erosion of sovereignty, internal and external, and new modes of governance do not equate with the demise of state as a set of beliefs about the distinctiveness and legitimation of public power as the prerequisite of order. Indeed, these beliefs can be strengthened by public agencies acting in association with other non-state actors, like international institutions, non-governmental organisations (NGOs) and businesses as governments 'outsource' provision of public goods (Zürcher 2007: 14–15).

Secondly, though generally in continental European and EU thinking about law there is a continuing sense of the central role of public law in maintaining order by clarifying the foundations of authority, state has been reconstituted differently across societies, notably in the core cases of France and Germany. State as representing autonomous and distinctive public power continues to occupy a more central role in French discourse than elsewhere. This centrality is evident in work on the sociology of particular academic and bureaucratic elites, the *grands corps*, as 'custodians of the state' (Bourdieu 1989; Eymeri-Douzans 2001, 2009; Suleiman and Courty 1997) and as guarantors of the 'strong' state as opposed to the supposedly 'weak' American and British states (Birnbaum 1982); in political economy (Cohen 1996; Kuisel 1984); in political history (Guéry 1985; Nora 1986); and in public law (Troper 1994). The contrast is characteristically with 'Anglo-Saxon neo-liberalism' as a counter model and identity.

In contrast in post-war Germany, state is a much more problematic concept. Its negative historical associations with the Wilhelmenian, Weimar and Nazi periods implicate its use with the conferral of legitimacy on politically dubious memories about public power (cf. Assmann 1993; Möllers 2008)). In consequence, historians, political scientists and many lawyers tend to exhibit little of the national nostalgia for the old 'certainties' of the classical state tradition that are manifested in France (cf. Nora 1986). If Anglo-American economic liberalism serves as a counter identity in prompting reflection on the legitimacy of the French state, state thinking – as exemplified in Wilhelminian, Weimar and Nazi Germany – provides a more inward-looking source of 'counter identities' in the Federal Republic. Historical interest focuses above all on the 'Nazi state', on the juristic and political controversies surrounding the role and influence of Carl Schmitt and Ernst Forsthoff, and on the pernicious legacy for Weimar and potentially post-1949 liberal democracy from traditional thinking in terms of the 'authoritative state' (*Obrigkeitsstaat*). In its early post-war form, German political science broke with this type of thinking in favour of the 'party state' (and 'militant' democracy) and the 'social state' as core conceptual references. Later, from the 1960s, under the influence of the new social movements, and an agenda of democratisation (Willy Brandt's pledge in 1969 to 'dare more democracy'), political science developed critiques of the 'party state' (see Kvistad 1999).

It was mostly amongst lawyers in the tradition of *Staatslehre* and *Staatsrechtswissenschaft*, and amongst economists associated with 'Ordo-liberalism', that the sense of anxiety about the weakness of the post-war state and about threats to its legitimacy and integrity was most strong. In the case of 'Ordo-liberal' economists, economic crises (as in the mid-1960s, 1970s and early 2000s) were classically the catalysts for calling for a stronger state to push through fundamental reforms. They reflected Alexander Rüstow's (1963: 258) famous speech to the *Verein für Sozialpolitik* in 1932: 'the new liberalism... demands a strong state, a state standing where it belongs, above the economy and above interest groups.' Post-war Germany economic policy was seen as captured by special interests.

Amongst lawyers, a similar sense of anxiety and threat was caused by the new political movements of the 1960s and 1970s as tests to the authority of the state. Later the Maastricht Treaty debate and the Lisbon Treaty debate, and above all the two related rulings of the Federal Constitutional Court in 1993 and 2009, opened up a cleavage between defensive traditional *Staatsrechtler* and European lawyers who criticised the anachronism of traditional conservative ideas of the state. The two rulings indicated a new defence of the 'statehood' (*Staatlichkeit)* of the Federal Republic against deepening European integration (Mőllers 2008: 72–3).

German discourse about the state as the model for ordering political authority was kept intellectually alive in the law faculties as *Staatsrechtswissenschaft* and in the scholarly networks around two particular academic periodicals. The journal *Der Staat* serves as an interdisciplinary forum for reworking *Staatslehre* and *Staatsrecht*, which still figure prominently in public law and 'state examinations' (*Staatsexamen*). It is closely associated with the work of Ernst-Wolfgang Bockenfőrde (1991, 1999) and, more recently, with Christoph Mőllers (2008). Similarly, the yearbook *Ordo* retains state as a concept of reference in continuing Ordo-liberal discussions about the principles of economics and their application (see Bőnker, Labrousse and Weisz 2001). More recently, Bremen University and the Free University Berlin have become sites of large-scale projects studying new modes of governance and change in 'statehood'. These projects seek to reconnect modern political science analysis of the dynamics of public-private and domestic-international interactions ('governance') with traditional concerns of public law.

Despite this continuing intellectual engagement and new efforts to radically rework the classic state tradition, it is difficult to escape the impression that much of the post-war juristic reworking of the classic state tradition in Germany has been defensive, distancing it from its federal origins and practices. This defensiveness is most apparent amongst certain lawyers who retain a national conservative orientation (e.g. the former Federal Constitutional Court judge Paul Kirchhof 2008). It surfaced in the much-disputed ruling of the German Federal Constitutional Court on the Lisbon Treaty in 2009, in which a traditional conception of the state, uniting nation with state, left little room for supra-national institution building and deepening of European integration. The result was sharp critiques of anachronistic German *Staatsrechtslehre* (e.g. Becker and Maurer 2009; Rüttgers 2009). Ordo-liberalism too has been defensive. German economics has lost its old embeddedness in *Staatswissenschaft*, weakening the idea that the state is essential to deliver order to the market economy and that institutions are central to economic life (Bofinger 2009). Here the global, financial and economic crisis of 2008 acted as a catalyst for economists on both centre-Left and centre-Right to argue that Germany needs a return to the values of the state (ibid; Sinn 2009).

Overall then, Germany has witnessed the unravelling of the 'golden age' of the classic juristic state tradition (Möllers 2008). At the same time there is evidence of new attempts to rethink, rejuvenate and modernise the state tradition in the context of multi-level and multi-actor governance (e.g. Genschel, Leibfried and Zangl 2008; Genschel and Zangl 2008; Schuppert forthcoming). These contributions share the view that, though the forms of the state has changed, in ways that are contested, state remains the central model for ordering and legitimating public power. State needs to be reconstructed in the context of radical changes across a number of dimensions, from internationalisation and Europeanisation, through new forms of social and political organisation, to changes in cultural values. More recently, German debates about forms of state have focused on the 'lean state' (Jann 2006), the 'enabling state' (Bogumil and Jann 2009), and the 'preventative state' (Denninger 1988). However, the new consensus seems to be a fundamental shift from state as monopolist to state as manager of public power, cross-nationally and domestically (Genschel and Zangl 2008). In particular, Hoffmann-Riem (2000), Schuppert (forthcoming) and Zürcher (2007) focus on the 'co-production' of 'statehood', based on the interplay of the 'enabling' state with business and civil society, including NGOs and international organisations. New reliance is placed on 'guidelines', 'framework rules' and forms of 'self-regulation' that induce public responsibility and the 'cooperative provision of public goods'. There are, in short, various providers of 'statehood'.

Looking back, there seems a strong argument that the mode of thinking about public power with which *The State Tradition* was concerned may be historically contingent in more than the sense that it has been specific to some states rather than others. The explanations for this first sense of historical contingency are discussed at length in the book. They are to be found in long-term differences in trajectories of political development between England and most continental European states. England did not pass through a similar stage of absolutism. It evolved a tradition of common law as a law of the people, understood as a cultural rather than a political entity. There was either a failure to recognise public law or a narrow functionalist style of thinking about public law that distrusted abstract conceptual debates about fictional persons in favour of what governments actually do. Law was seen as a function of society and as evolving with it (cf. Loughlin 2005). In either case the judiciary was reluctant to develop a body of public law, and the Crown remained a 'poor substitute for the idea of the State' and 'has never been systematically cultivated as a juristic concept' that distinguishes government and state (Loughlin 1999: 33 and 75; Maitland 1901; Mitchell 1965). A telling comparison is between two British and German textbooks on constitutional and administrative law. Compared to Kirchhof (2009) on German *Staatrecht*, Allen and Thompson (2005) on the UK provide a mere five pages out of 786 on the state (within which the concept of the state as a juristic person is absent).

However, in a second sense, even in those states which had a strong '*sens de l'Etat*', state seems to be in retreat as a central organising concept of analysis and in debate. It is plausible to argue that this distinctive vocabulary of the state enjoyed an ascendancy within continental Europe that lasted from the latter third of the nineteenth century to the mid-twentieth century. This argument does not amount to saying that the '*sens de l'Etat*' was absent before this period. In French and German public law the conception of the state as a fictional and moral person, distinct from both ruler and ruled, was firmly established from the 1830s onwards, though it had earlier roots in the Enlightenment (Bartelson 2001; Runciman 1997). Clearly, for instance, the French Revolution and the Napoleonic period were preoccupied with the saliency and distinctiveness of state power, whilst in the eighteenth century Prussia and the Hapsburg Empire built up attributes of the 'police state' (*Polizeistaat*) dedicated to intervention on behalf of public welfare (classically Maier 1966). Nevertheless, an examination of the key thinkers, to whom reference is made in *The State Tradition,* suggests the centrality of the period *circa* 1870s to *circa* 1960s. It is neatly framed by the process of German unification, with the geo-strategic and political challenges it provoked, and the rise of the so-called 'new social movements' that challenged traditional hierarchical conceptions of state power.

What were the specific features of this period that gave rise to this particular and distinctive preoccupation with the state? Above all, the centrality of the state in legal and political discourse was rooted in the defensive reactions of traditional elites to a set of challenges: geo-strategic rebalancing, military competition, and the threat of intra-European war; the rise of parliamentary democracy, extension of the suffrage, and new mass political parties; the industrial revolution, the scale of technological and economic modernisation, and new class-based political organisation; alternative social and cultural models; and consequent fears of cultural decline, social breakdown and chronic political instability. It was the age of the rise of modern political parties and the power of legislatures, of large corporations and of trade unions, of mass-circulation print media, and of 'modernist' artistic movements, each challenging traditional elites as new elites sought to share power. It was the age of demands for state intervention on a new scale and the emergence of modern bureaucracy, requiring clarification of what they meant for public and private power. Not least, it was the age of emerging big power rivalry and military competition, consequent on German unification around Prussian power and the crushing, onerous and humiliating military defeat of France in 1870–71. Preoccupation with public power was kept alive in the interwar period by the equally humiliating context in which the Weimar Republic was born and by the collapse of the Hapsburg Empire.

The state offered an organising concept, albeit used in different ways, to legitimate the coherence and unity of public power in the face of these multiple challenges by defining its autonomy and specificity. Its different uses – like 'public-service' state, 'state ruled by law', 'cultural state', and 'power state' – reflected the self-interests of those who sought to identify themselves and their interests with the state. Not only was distinctive public power attributed to the state; also, the right to exercise this state power was attributed to certain elites. They incarnated the state. One might say that out of this context the 'age of the classic continental European state tradition' reached its full maturity. The state was conceived as a *sui generis* collective person who represented the permanent common interests of a body of people and thus had an existence – even if fictional – independent of the democratic process and of 'public opinion'. Its central values were those of public service such as professional autonomy and integrity, impersonality, impartiality, legality and predictability.

If one analyses the period since the 1960s, the evidence overwhelmingly suggests that this particular sense of the state has withered with deeper transformations in economic, social and political life. It has lost its role as a central reference point in normative debates about European government and politics, either as a source of commendation or as a source of condemnation. Not least, with the progressive broadening of policy scope, the institutional deepening and the territorial widening of European integration, the threat of intra-European war and dynamic of military competition has ceased to impact on conceptions of the state. In providing a new 'security community', further reinforced by the NATO umbrella for collective defence, European integration seemed to erode the classic state tradition. These 'top-down' processes appeared to testify to profound changes in elite attitudes and behaviour consequent on the traumas of the period 1914–1945.

However, there were also 'bottom-up' changes at work. The condemnation of statist thought and its authoritarian assumptions of hierarchy and integration was a common theme uniting French and German radical student-based movements in the late 1960s; whilst the German Green Party attacked the 'party state' in the name of 'grass-roots' democracy and 'hori-zontal' forms of democratic membership (Kvistad 1999). They attested to deep generational and cultural changes, which affected both policy agen-das and political processes. However, by the end of the century this type of critique had subsided. This change reflects the fact that the patterns of con-duct traditionally associated with classic state discourse are seen to have lost their social and political significance. As its vocabulary has withered, so anti-*étatiste* political thinking has subsided.

More importantly, new concepts have arisen as sources of commenda-tion and condemnation. They reflect new forms of social behaviour and the prestige of new social models. Debates have come to focus around glo-balisation, Europeanisation, 'post-Westphalian' state systems, New Public Management, 'multi-level governance', 'new modes of governance' such as 'network governance', and 'post-modern' polities. Strategic debates have shifted to common security, collective defence, and joint NATO and EU crisis management capabilities. In domestic politics the new values de-emphasise hierarchy and community in favour of accountability, transpar-ency and efficiency, based around market models of individual consumer choice. The values of the classic state tradition were premised on social and political trust in the professionalism and integrity of public servants who pursued the overarching public interest. This trust waned with gener-alised critiques of social hierarchy, the prestige of the market model, the in-trusiveness of media investigation, and the general loss of social deference. The operation of government and politics became more dependent on the volatile quality of public trust in the personal qualities of political leaders as mediated through the proliferating media of communications.

Of course, the centrality of debates about the 'Europeanisation' and 'globalisation' of European states, about 'New Public Management', 'multi-level governance' and 'network governance', which emerged later, played no role in *The State Tradition*. The book was the product of histori-cal reflection from the perspective of the 1970s. Whilst seeking to tran-scend particular spatial and temporal contexts, it inevitably bears some of their imprints. It was not an exercise in thinking about the future. European integration was still a new and uncertain process, with a much more lim-ited agenda . It was much less intrusive as a process and in outcomes than today. European government and politics were analysed and debated with-out much reference to the 'Europeanisation' of states, except as a marginal reference. Similarly, debates about 'globalisation' and about 'hollowing out' versus 'redefinition' of the state were for the future (e.g. Cassese and Wright 1996; Müller and Wright 1994; Rhodes 1994) – and at that time were cast very much in terms of functions and structures. Certainly there was a sense of change in the 1970s. States were seen as 'over-extended' in commitments, especially to the welfare state, and subject to 'excessive' demands. In consequence, there was a problem of the 'overloaded' state. The central manifestation of this problem was in the state's inability to master a growing inflation problem and the phenomenon of 'stagflation'. In consequence, the politics of the 1980s were to be preoccupied with radical redefinition of the functions of the state and remodelling of the structures through which these (more limited) functions were delivered. Similarly, there was an emerging recognition of the power of the international financial markets and the external vulnerability of European states to destabilising capital flows and speculation. Credibility and reputation with international markets – as opposed to 'controls' – became the core reference points in discourse about economic policies (Dyson and Quaglia 2010). By the 1990s it seemed to some that the 'hollowing out' of the state was being witnessed (Rhodes 1994).

In addition, since the 1970s the private sector has achieved much greater prestige as the source of a managerial model of efficiency, economy and accountability and also of individual values of entrepreneurship. The New Public Management represents a new agenda of competition in public services, based on market models of choice and managerial models of performance measurement (Pollitt 1993). These models de-emphasise hierarchy and formality of procedures in public services, displacing traditional values of legality, probity and predictability. Ideas of the autonomy and distinctiveness of public power seemed to vanish in a vapour of performance management, multi-level 'governance' and policy 'networks'.

More generally, one might conclude that European integration (at least since the 1980s), globalisation (especially in its economic and cultural manifestations), and New Public Management have been underpinned by the intellectual triumph of Anglo-American ideas and models of analysis and forms of discourse. French and German social scientists have looked increasingly to participate in international debates framed in these terms rather than in terms of domestic state traditions. Even in continental Europe, academic self-interests have become defined in terms of international benchmarks set around Anglo-American models (and journals and book publishers). In this way careers are to be made.

In this context it is hardly surprising that the classic state tradition that this book examined in the 1970s has withered in the interim. As early as 1992 and 1994 respectively, Beaud and Troper were bemoaning the lack of an adequate legal theory of the state in France. In particular, the EU's rise to a new salience in debates about power and policies in Europe has not been associated with a renewal of 'the sense of the state'. The EU is not a state, at least not in the sense of having the values of the classic state tradition attributed to it (least of all by the German Federal Constitutional Court in its wide-ranging Maastricht and Lisbon treaty rulings). Its expanded functions and 'deepening' structures have initiated a debate amongst lawyers about the nature of EU powers and whether it is 'a state in the making'. However, amongst political scientists attention has focused on the connections between boundary redefinition and 'internal restructuring' of states (Bartolini 2007). The EU's characterisation as an 'association of states' in the ruling on the Lisbon Treaty by the German Constitutional Court in July 2009 underlines that it is a 'reversible self-commitment' by states, which remain the 'masters of the Treaty' on which the EU claims to authority rest. Instead, academic and political debates have focused on the EU's functions, structures and processes. According to Majone (1996), in the absence of independent resources, it is a 'regulatory state', focused on efficiency gains; in the view of Hooghe and Marks (2001) it is a structure and process of 'multi-level governance'; whilst for Coen and Thatcher (2008) it represents European regulatory network governance. However, neither Majone nor Hooghe and Marks are talking about the nature of the EU's authority so much as about what it distinctively does and how. Similarly, lawyers ask whether the EU possesses *Kompetenz-Kompetenz* (where does ultimate authority reside in interpreting the treaties?) and about the relationship between the superiority of EU over domestic law and the legal pluralism of the EU. These debates fall short of asking whether the EU's powers as an association are distinctive. They do not appear to be autonomous, at least according to the German ruling on the Lisbon Treaty, according to which the Member States remain 'masters of the Treaty'. In fact, theories of European integration, notably functionalist theories, intergovernmental theories and governance theories, take an essentially utilitarian view of the EU. This utilitarian approach fits well with the dominant conception that the EU's legitimacy rests on the fragile basis of its outputs ('output' legitimacy). In this institutional context there is little room for the EU to be attributed with the features of the classic state tradition.

The inability of the EU to catalyse a debate about its 'stateness' is complemented by the argument that its extension of powers over policies has undermined any residual claims to autonomy and distinctiveness of its Member States. They are subject to the pressures of conditionality with EU law and of convergence. This argument might apply with even more force to the newer Member States, who must take on the accumulated and very extensive and detailed *acquis communautaire* (the entire body of legislation of the European Communities and Union), remoulding their domestic institutional frameworks and policies to 'fit' the EU. Even so, such pressures for transformation and accommodation, whether originating from the EU or from other international bodies, do not mean that claims to the autonomy and distinctiveness of public power have lost credibility or meaning.

ARE EUROPEAN INTEGRATION AND GLOBAL GOVERNANCE REVITALISING, RESCUING AND DISSEMINATING THE STATE TRADITION?

Despite this formidable evidence of the retreat of the classic state tradition, one should beware of writing it off as dead or redundant. Firstly, as Craig and De Burca (2003: 279) argue, the bold rulings of the European Court of Justice (ECJ) demonstrate a teleological as opposed to textual approach in which the aims and spirit of the Treaties are invoked to establish the special and original nature of Community law. Thus the ECJ has interpreted the social objectives of the Treaties broadly and used the jurisprudence of the European Court of Human Rights to fill the principle of freedom of movement with social policy content in areas like family solidarity, gender equality and state liability in order to protect Community citizens (Höpner and Schäfer 2007). In the process it has evolved the potential to act 'as an agency for the construction of a European civil society as well as a unified market' (Caporaso and Tarrow 2008: 17).

The idea of the EU as 'market making and shaping' has played a role in the accumulating jurisprudence of the Court in other ways. Thus in various rulings, the ECJ has clarified the scope for 'services of general economic interest' under Article 86(2), thereby setting certain limits on the market model. This principle has been taken up in Article 16 of the Amsterdam Treaty, in Article 36 of the Charter of Fundamental Rights, and in Protocol 26 of the Lisbon Treaty. The ECJ has also established the principle of state liability for breaches of EC law (Craig and De Burca 2003: 257). These developments are important with respect to placing requirements on domestic courts, not least in the UK, to exercise powers that they would not have under national law (ibid: 282). In fostering juridification in this 'top-down' manner, the ECJ has provided the conditions for the reinvigoration of public law and more widely for *Staatslehre*.

At the same time, in a 'bottom-up' fashion, many ideas from continental administrative law, especially French, and continental constitutional law, especially German, found their way into the ECJ's jurisprudence. Thus the ECJ 'uploaded' into its rulings the three-step procedure for examining basic rights in German constitutional law, alongside basic German constitutional principles of protection of confidence and of proportionality (Schuppert 2003). The result of this uploading into ECJ jurisprudence has been a further source of stimulus to the evolution of new thinking about public law in the UK.

Secondly, numerous empirical studies of the processes of European integration and of Europeanisation of member states have attested to important elements of continuity in elite attitudes and behaviour. Milward (1992) pointed to the function of European integration in 'rescuing' European states by making them more effective in delivering security, prosperity and welfare to their citizens. In the French case the humiliating defeat of 1940 served to reinforce the classic state tradition, especially under President Charles de Gaulle (Hayward 2007), and to create the conditions for the emergence of the idea of the state as 'moderniser of capitalism' (Kuisel 1984). Europeanisation studies too have highlighted the continuities in domestic legal and political traditions (e.g. Dyson and Goetz 2003; Goetz 2003; Page 2003; Müller and Wright 1994; Cole 2008). Historical path dependencies remain strong and refract the pressures for convergence from European integration in different directions. Europeanisation is not synonymous with convergence.

Thirdly, EU law and emerging global governance have been conduits through which a body of jurisprudence relating to the state (e.g. on liability) has developed and the conditions for a reinvigoration of public law strengthened (Loughlin 1999: 75). In particular, through EU law and World Trade Organisation (WTO) agreements, governments are able to bind their successors to commitments on which the reputation of the state – and through that the credibility of the government of the day – comes to depend. More widely, international law can be seen as promoting a legal concept of the state as a unified legal person entering into enduring commitments. This development of international, and above all European obligations, can be seen as introducing the idea of the state as a legal person into the domestic law of Anglo-American societies and, in the process, creating new tensions between state and government, and between EU/international law and democracy (McLean 2003). EU and international law do not function on the basis of the Anglo-American common law tradition, according to which the law relates to disaggregated government bodies. As we see below, scepticism about the claims to sovereignty and to control over territorial borders (van Creveld 1999; Strange 1996) does not mean that state is without virtue as a concept (Morris 1998). Equally, the erosion of the distinction between the domestic and the international does not mean that state has lost value as a foundational and constitutive concept (Bartelson 2001; Schuppert forthcoming). It seems to be reinforced and disseminated.

Hence, despite much talk of its retreat or its demise in favour of multi-actor and multi-level 'governance', the classic state tradition still offers a valuable source of values and modes of thinking about public power, its distinctive nature and exercise, and how it is legitimised. In particular, the distinction between the state and the government of the day supports normative arguments about the continuing importance of correctives to democracy and of the maintenance of disincentives to short-term political expediency. It stresses the importance of procedures that are designed to act, in the words of a German public lawyer and later President of the Federal Republic of Germany, as 'the better conscience of society' (Herzog 1971). Such procedures are needed to frustrate constitutionally subversive actions by governments that seek to wrap their actions in the flag of the state and in the process threaten political legitimacy. Barker (1990: 183–4) refers to the Clive Ponting case in which the judge directed the jury that 'in the interests of the State' meant 'in the interests of the Government of the day'.

Equally serious questions arise about how territorially and temporally delimited democracies, whose decisions profoundly affect current non-voters, are to deal with long-term global challenges like managing climate change, correcting economic and financial imbalances, securing financial and monetary stability, tackling poverty, famine and disease, and dealing with large-scale demographic changes like population ageing. It has proved enormously difficult to design and operate democratic political arrangements that offer strong incentives to move beyond short-term, parochial thinking and action. The combination of tight domestic electoral timescales with territorially delimited democratic political space tends to trivialise and narrow horizons of debate and frustrate approximation to the ideal of 'justice as impartiality' (Barry 1995). Within this confined temporal and territorial space political parties are prone to compete by 'over-promising' and then failing to deliver; media and elections become focused on personality rather than issues; and electorates are disposed to lose trust in politics as a self-referential game played out amongst party elites (cf. Crouch 2004). In this context it proves difficult to reconcile what public opinion will 'accept' with what is 'acceptable' for long-term sustainability. Enriching the quality of public deliberation has proved a formidable challenge.

Concern about the quality of consent in democratic societies and about long-term sustainability opens up a new opportunity to reflect on the values of the continental European state tradition. It may be premature to write off the classic state tradition as an historical curiosity, of interest mainly to antiquarian political scientists and lawyers. As challenges to the sustainability of existing institutions and policies mount, it becomes important for political scientists and lawyers to ask whether the idea of the autonomous and distinctive nature of public power has renewed relevance. Its value resides in legitimating government actions around the notion of the security and welfare of the people as a whole (defined across generations and across borders) and in enabling governments through appropriately designed procedures to bind their successors to commitments that are essential for long-term sustainability (cf. Barker 1990; Loughlin 2003, 2009; McLean 2003; Skinner 2008). These ideas have assumed a new relevance in the context of the post-2008 global financial and economic crisis and of challenges like climate change.

The broad direction in which debate needs to move is away from narrowly conceived and contested debates about the functions of the state ('welfare', 'intervention', 'lean', 'enabling', 'preventative' etc.) and from the elusive search for the location of sovereignty ('hollowing out' of the state?). It requires fresh thinking about the nature of the political compact between European governments, the EU, and emerging global institutions and between public, business and civil society bodies. Fresh thinking suggests returning to the idea of the distinction between public and private power, whilst recognising that the concept of the state must be reworked in the profoundly transformed context of multi-level and multi-actor governance, especially at European and global levels , new modes of governance and the cooperative creation of law (cf. Genschel and Zangl 2008; Hoffmann-Riem 2000; Loughlin 2009; Schuppert forthcoming; Zürcher 2007)

In reflecting on this distinction, debate needs to refocus on the concepts of public service, solidarity and 'justice as impartiality' (Barry 1995) as foundations for thinking about political authority. Political science and law need to replenish and consolidate their thinking about the importance, distinctiveness and normative character of public power as the state's role transforms from monopoly provider to manager of public power in association with business and civil society. At the same time, as emphasised above, they will have to live with, and make their individual accommodations to, the continuing tensions in which this concept of the state is embroiled. As *The State Tradition* emphasised, state remains a problem-solving and a problem-creating concept.

GHOSTLY SHADOW OR REJUVENATION?

Over the last thirty years we have witnessed the decline of the classic state tradition. However, it is less appropriate to speak of its demise than of a period of uncertainty and confusion in beliefs about public power, out of which emerges opportunity for reworking of the state tradition in transformed circumstances. This period of uncertainty and confusion was associated with traditional advocates of the classic state tradition becoming much more defensive as they sought to respond to the impacts of new social movements since the 1960s, accelerating European integration since the 1980s, and deep-seated changes to the two core pillars of the state tradition – the civil service and the law (notably from the New Public Management, privatisation, and signs of convergence in Roman and common law thinking). One might speak of state in its classic continental European sense as having become a ghostly presence in public debate about European and domestic politics, law and society.

Nevertheless, there are some indications that debate about the distinctiveness of public power is being reinvogorated, above all in German public law. The traditional conservative German *Staatslehre* that found its way into the unexpectedly restrictive ruling on the Lisbon Treaty by the German Constitutional Court in 2009 was a wake-up call to rethink more profoundly the state in an EU context. In this sense the EU serves as a major catalyst to rework the state tradition. The reassertion of national conservative interpretations of the state tradition produced new cleavage about public power in the context of European integration, especially in Germany (e.g. Kirchhof 2008). A further catalyst is global and Europe-wide financial and economic crisis, as it throws the nature of public power and the issue of the constitutive role of the state in the market economy into clearer relief.

The idea of the autonomy and distinctiveness of public power in relation to ruler (government) and ruled (public opinion) remains a cornerstone in the edifice of fully-informed debate about political legitimacy. Given the scope and depth of the changes that have ended the golden age of the classic state tradition, it is necessary to rework notions about how this autonomy and distinctiveness works in relation to markets and civil society. In the process the state tradition has to be disengaged from a preoccupation with monopoly provision of public goods and with sovereignty as its leading signs (already questioned in *The State Tradition*).

State opens up debates about how public power constitutes markets; about the social construction of rights; and about rights and obligations in international, and not least European, law that attach to states as artificial persons who can be held to account for honouring their commitments. As I argued earlier, statements about the institutional capacity and strength of a state to deliver on commitments, to act decisively to secure rights, and to organise markets are another matter. After all, claims made on behalf of state autonomy may not translate into 'strong' states in action. Equally, close symbiotic links with society may emerge as a source of state strength and capacity (in relation to the United States see King and Lieberman 2009 and Novak 2008; more generally Zürcher 2007). The state tradition has to be disentangled from confusion with debates about 'strong' and 'weak' states.

At the same time reworking the state tradition reveals an unresolved tension between state as a fictional person – reinforced by EU and international legal obligations – and state as no longer a monopoly provider but a manager of public power. The process of 'binding Leviathan' is associated with compliance problems, whether in meeting EU and global environmental targets or fiscal policy commitments under the Stability and Growth Pact. The attempt to 'name and shame' states may only reveal just how 'shameless' governments can be with respect to their obligations. Moreover, the shift to managing public power involves some abridgement of the traditional core notion of the autonomy of public power. The debate has shifted much more to the distinctiveness of public power in taking and implementing collectively binding decisions (binding governments as well).

We should beware of assuming that any (partial) convergence of 'state' and 'stateless' societies is based simply on the withering of the classic state tradition. Unquestionably, one element is the erosion of traditional notions about the autonomy of public power in 'state' societies. However, we are also witnessing the gradual, piecemeal dissemination of a reworked state tradition, in part through the development of European and international law, and in part through a reworking of state in public law, informed by political science concepts like 'governance'. Public law remains central in the retention of the idea of the state and in its reworking in the context of internationalisation, Europeanisation, new modes of governance and the co-creation of law by public and private actors. It serves as the intellectual anchor and sociological basis of this debate. What public law needs from political science is a more fruitful debate about the nature of public power as opposed to a preoccupation with the structures and functions of government and with the processes of governance.

REFERENCES

Allen, M. and Thompson, B. (2005) *Cases and Materials on Constitutional and Administrative Law*, 8th edition. Oxford: Oxford University Press.
Armstrong, J. (1973) *The European Administrative Elite*. Princeton: Princeton University Press.
Assmann, A. (1993) *Arbeit am nationalen Gedächtnis: Eine kurze Geschichte der deutschen Bildungsidee*. Frankfurt am Main: Campus.
Atkinson, M. and Coleman, W. (1989) 'Strong State and Weak State: Sectoral Policy Networks in Advanced Capitalist Economies', *British Journal of Political Science*, 19: 47–67.
Barker, R. (1990) *Political Legitimacy and the State*. Oxford: Oxford University Press.
Barry, B. (1995) *Justice as Impartiality*. Oxford: Oxford University Press.
Bartelson, J. (2001) *The Critique of the State*. Cambridge: Cambridge University Press.
Bartolini, S. (2007) *Restructuring Europe: Centre Formation, System Building and Political Structuring between the Nation State and the European Union*. Oxford: Oxford University Press.
Bauman, Z. and Barth, R. (2009) *Leben als Konsum*. Hamburger Edition.

Beaud, O. (1992) 'L'honneur perdu de l'État?', *Droits*, 15: 10–21.

Becker, P. and Maurer, A. (2009) 'Deutsche Integrationsbremsen: Folgen und Gefahren des Karlsruher Urteils für Deutschland und die EU', *SWP-Aktuell*, 41, July.

Benz, A. (2001) *Der moderne Staat: Grundlagen der politologischen Analyse*. Munich: Oldenbourg.

Benz, A. (2008) 'Der Staat als politisches Projekt – eine theoretische Skizze', in S. Bröchler and H. -J. Lauth (eds) *Politikwissenschaftliche Perspektiven*. Wiesbaden: VS Verlag, pp. 71–92.

Benz, A. and Goetz, K. (eds) (1996) *A New German Public Sector*. Aldershot: Dartmouth/ ASGP.

Bevir, M. and Rhodes, R. (2003) *Interpreting British Governance*. London: Routledge.

Birnbaum, P. (1982) *La logique de l'Etat*. Paris: Fayard.

Birnbaum, P. (1988) *States and Collective Action: The European Experience*. Cambridge: Cambridge University Press.

Bockenförde, E. -W. (1991) *Recht, Staat, Freiheit. Studien zu Rechtsphilosophie, Staatstheorie und Verfassungsgeschichte*. Frankfurt am Main: Suhrkamp.

Bockenförde, E. -W. (1999) *Staat, Nation, Europa: Studien zur Staatslehre, Verfassungstheorie und Rechtsphilosophie*. Frankfurt am Main: Suhrkamp.

Bofinger, P. (2009) *Ist der Markt zu retten? Warum wir jetzt einen starken Staat brauchen*. Berlin: Econ Verlag.

Bogumil, J. and Jann, W. (eds) (2009) *Verwaltung und Verwaltungswissenschaft in Deutschland*, 2nd edn. Wiesbaden: VS Verlag.

Bönker, F., Labrousse, A. and Weisz, J. -D. (2001) 'The Evolution of Ordoliberalism in the Light of the *Ordo* Yearbook: A Bibliometric Analysis', in A. Labrousse and J. -D. Weisz (eds) *Institutional Economics in France and Germany*. Berlin/Heidelberg: Springer, pp. 159–82.

Bourdieu, P. (1989) *La noblesse d'État: grandes écoles et esprits de corps*. Paris: Editions de Minuit.

Bull, H. -P. (2008) 'Daseinsvorsorge im Wandel der Staatsformen', *Der Staat*, 47, 1: 1–19.

Caney, S. (2005) *Justice Beyond Borders: A Global Political Theory*. Oxford: Oxford University Press.

Caporaso, J. (ed.) (1989) *The Elusive State: International and Comparative Perspectives*. New York: Sage.

Caporaso, J. and Tarrow, S. (2008) *Polanyi in Brussels: European Institutions and the Embedding of Markets in Society*, RECON Online Working Paper 2008/01, January.

Cassese, S. and Wright, V. (eds) (1996) *La recomposition de l'Etat en Europe*. Paris: La Découverte.

Chapman, B. (1959) *The Profession of Government: The Public Service in Europe*. London: Allen & Unwin.

Coen, D. and Thatcher, M. (2008) 'Network Governance and Multi-level Delegation: European Networks of Regulatory Agencies', *Journal of Public Policy*, 28, 1: 49–71.

Cohen, E. (1996) *La Tentation Hexagonale. La Souveraineté à l'épreuve de la mondialisation*. Paris: Fayard.

Cole, A. (2008) *Governing and Governance in France*. Cambridge: Cambridge University Press.

Craig, P. and De Burca, G. (2003) *EU Law: Text, Cases and Materials*, 3rd edition. Oxford: Oxford University Press.

Creveld, M. van (1999) *The Rise and Decline of the State*. Cambridge: Cambridge University Press.

Crouch, C. (2004) *Post-Democracy*. Cambridge: Polity.

Della Porta, D. (ed.) (2007) *The Global Justice Movement*. Boulder: Paradigm Press.

Denninger, E. (1988) 'Der Präventionsstaat', *Kritische Justiz*: 1–15.

Dryzek, J. and Dunleavy, P. (2009) *Theories of the Democratic State*. Basingstoke; Palgrave.

Dunleavy, P. (1995) 'The State', in R. Goodin and P. Pettit (eds) *A Companion to Contemporary Political Philosophy*. Blackwell Companions to Philosophy. Oxford: WileyBlackwell.

Dunleavy, P. and O'Leary, B. (1987) *Theories of the State: the Politics of Liberal Democracy*. Basingstoke: Macmillan.

Dunn, J. (1996) *The History of Political Theory and Other Essays*. Cambridge: Cambridge University Press.

Dyson, K. (1977) *Party, State, and Bureaucracy in West Germany*. Beverly Hills, Calif: Sage.
Dyson, K. (2002) 'The German Model Revisited: From Schmidt to Schröder', in S. Padgett and T. Poguntke (eds) *Continuity and Change in German Politics. Beyond the Politics of Centrality?* London: Frank Cass, pp. 135–54.
Dyson, K. and Goetz, K. (eds) (2003) *Germany, Europe and the Politics of Constraint*. Proceedings of the British Academy 119. Oxford: Oxford University Press.
Dyson, K. and Quaglia, L. (2010) *European Economic Governance and Policies: Commentary on Key Documents, Volume I: History*. Oxford: Oxford University Press.
Dyson, K. and Wilks, S. (eds) (1982) *Industrial Crisis*. Oxford; Blackwell.
Elias, N. (2007) *Über den Prozess der Zivilisation. Soziogenetische und psychogenetische Untersuchungen, Band II: Wandlungen der Gesellschaft. Entwurf zu einer Theorie der Zivilisation*. Frankfurt am Main: Suhrkamp.
Eucken, W. (1952) *Grundsätze der Witschaftspolitik*. Tübingen: Mohr.
Eymeri-Douzans, J. -M. (2001) *La fabrique des énarques*. Paris: Economica.
Eymeri-Douzans, J. -M. (2009) *Les gardiens de l'Etat. Sociologie de la haute administration française*. Paris: Economica.
Flora, P., Kuhnle, S. and Urwin, D. (1999) *State Formation, Nation-building, and Mass Politics in Europe: The Theory of Stein Rokkan*. Oxford: Oxford University Press.
Forsthoff, E. (ed.) (1968) *Rechtsstaatlichkeit und Socialstaatlichkeit*. Darmstadt: Wissenschaftliche Buchgesellschaft.
Genschel, P., Leibfried, S. and Zangl, B. (2008) 'Der zerfaserte Staat', *Vorgänge. Zeitschrift für Bürgerrechte und Gesellschaftspolitik*, 182: 4–13.
Genschel, P. and Zangl, B. (2008) 'Metamorphosen des Staates – Vom Herrschaftsmonopolisten zum Herrschaftsmanager, *Leviathan*: 430–54.
Goetz, K. (2003) 'Executives in Comparative Context', in J. Hayward and A. Menon (eds) *Governing Europe*. Oxford: Oxford University Press, pp. 74–91.
Goetz, K. (2005) 'Administrative Reform: Is Public Bureaucracy Still an Obstacle?' in S. Green and W. Paterson (eds) *Governance in Contemporary Germany*. Cambridge: Cambridge University Press, pp. 239–60.
Guéry, A. (1985) 'L'État, l'outil du bien commun' in P. Nora (ed.) *Les lieux de mémoire*, Vol. 1. Paris: Gallimard, pp. 4545–84.
Hancher, L. and Moran, M. (eds) (1989) *Capitalism, Culture and Economic Regulation*. Oxford: Oxford University Press.
Harden, I. and Lewis, N. (1988) *The Noble Lie: British Constitution and the Rule of Law*. London: Hutchinson
Hayward, J. (1983) *Governing France: The One and Indivisible Republic*, 2nd edition. London: Weidenfeld and Nicolson.
Hayward, J. (1986) *The State and the Market Economy*. Brighton; Harvester.
Hayward, J. (2007) *Fragmented France: Two Centuries of Disputed Identity*. Oxford: Oxford University Press.
Hayward, J. (2008) 'La Persistance de L'Antilibéralisme: Rhétorique et Réalité' *Pouvoirs*, 126, September: 115–32.
Héritier, A. (2002) 'New Modes of Governance in Europe: Policy-Making without Legislating', in A. Héritier (ed.) *Common Goods: Reinventing European and International Governance*. Lanham, MD: Rowman and Littlefield.
Héritier, A., Knill, C. and Mingers, C. (1996) *Ringing in the Changes in Europe: Regulatory Competition and the Transformation of the State. Britain, France and Germany*. Berlin: W. de Gruyte.
Héritier, A. and Lehmkuhl, D. (2008) 'The Shadow of Hierarchy and New Modes of Governance', *Journal of Public Policy*, 28, 1: 1–17.
Herzog, R. (1971) *Allgemeine Staatslehre*. Frankfurt am Main: Athenäum Verlag.
Hintze, O. (1964) 'Der Staat als Betrieb', in G. Oestreich (ed.) *Hintze: Gesammelte Abhandlungen, Band II: Soziologie und Geschichte*. Göttingen: Vandenhoeck und Ruprecht.
Hoffmann-Riem, W. (2000) 'Verantwortungsteilung als Schlüsselbegriff moderner Staatlichkeit', in P. Kirchhof et al. (eds) *Staaten und Steurn. Fetschrift für Klaus Vogel zum 70. Geburtstag*. Heidelberg: Müller, pp. 47–64.
Hooghe, L. and Marks, G. (2001) *Multilevel Governance and European Integration*. Lanham, MD: Rowman and Littlefield.
Höpner and Schäfer, A. (2007) *A New Phase of European Integration Organized Capitalisms in*

Post-Ricardian Europe, MPIfG Discussion Paper 07/4. Cologne: Max Planck Institute for the Study of Societies.

Jann, W. (2006) 'Wandlungen von Verwaltungsmanagement und Verwaltungspolitik in Deutschland', in W. Jann, M. Röber and H. Wollmann (eds) *Public Management. Grundlagen, Wirkungen, Kritik. Festschrift für Christoph Reinhard.* Berlin: Sigma, pp. 35–48.

Jaume, L. (1986) *Hobbes et l'État representatif moderne.* Paris: PUF.

Jobert, B. and Muller, P. (1987) *L'État en Action: politiques publiques et corporatisme.* Paris: PUF.

Johnson, N. (1983) *State and Government in the Federal Republic of Germany.* Oxford: Pergamon Press.

Jones, H. (1993) *The French State in Question. Public Law and Political Argument in the Third Republic.* Cambridge: Cambridge University Press.

Jordan, W. (1985) *The State: Authority and Autonomy.* Oxford: Oxford University Press.

Katzenstein, P. (1987) *Policy and Politics in West Germany: the Growth of the Semisovereign State.* Philadelphia: Temple University Press.

King, D. and Lieberman, R. (2009) 'Review Article: Ironies of State Building. A Comparative Perspective on the American State', *World Politics*, 61, 3: 547–88.

Kirchhof, P. (2008) *Das Gesetz der Hydra: Gebt den Bürgern ihren Staat zurück!* Droemer.

Kirchhof, P. (2009) *Staats- und Verwaltungsrecht Bundesrepublik Deutschland: Mit Europarecht.* Heidelberg: Müller.

Knill, C. (1998) 'European Policies: The Impact of National Administrative Traditions', *Journal of Public Policy*, 18: 1–28.

Koselleck, R. (2000) *Zeitschichten. Studien zur Historik mit einem Beitrag von Hans-Georg Gadamer.* Frankfurt am Main: Suhrkamp.

Kuisel, R. (1984) *Le capitalisme et l'Etat en France.* Paris: Gallimard.

Kvistad, G. (1999) *The Rise and Demise of German Statism: Loyalty and Political Membership.* Oxford: Berghahn.

Laborde, C. (2000a) 'The Concept of the State in British and French Political thought', *Political Studies*, 48, 3: 540–57.

Laborde, C. (2000b) *Pluralist Thought and the State in Britain and France, 1900–25.* London: Macmillan.

Le Galès, P. (2003) 'The Changing European State: Pressures from Within', in J. Hayward and A. Menon (eds) *Governing Europe.* Oxford: Oxford University Press, pp. 380–94.

Loughlin, M. (1999) 'The State, the Crown and the Law', in M. Sunkin and S. Payne (eds) *The Nature of the Crown: A Legal and Political Analysis.* Oxford: Oxford University Press, pp. 33–76.

Loughlin, M. (2003) *The Idea of Public Law.* Oxford: Oxford University Press.

Loughlin, M. (2005) 'The Functionalist Style in Public Law', *University of Toronto Law Journal*, 55: 361–403.

Loughlin, M. (2009) 'In Defence of *Staatslehre*', *Der Staat*, 48, 1: 1–27.

MacCormick, N. (1999) *Questioning Sovereignty: Law, State and Nation in the European Commonwealth.* Oxford: Oxford University Press.

Maier, H. (1966) *Die Ältere Deutsche Staats- und Verwaltungslehre (Polizeiwissenschaft).* Neuwied-Berlin: Luchterhand.

Maitland, F. W. (1901) 'The Crown as Corporation', *Law Quarterly Review*, 17: 131–46.

Marquand, D. (1988) *The Unprincipled Society: New Demands and Old Politics.* London: Fontana.

McLean, J. (2003) 'Government to State: Globalization, Regulation, and Governments as Legal Persons', *Indiana Journal of Global Legal Studies*, 10: 173–97.

McLean, J. (2005) 'Divergent Legal Conceptions of the State: Implications for Global Administrative Law', *Law and Contemporary Problems*, 68: 167–87.

Meadowcroft, J. (1995) *Conceptualizing the State. Innovation and Dispute in British Political Thought 1880–1914.* Oxford: Oxford University Press.

Migdal, J. and Schlichte, K. (2005) 'Rethinking the State', in K. Schlichte (ed.) *The Dynamics of State. The Formation and Crises of State Domination.* Farnham: Ashgate, pp. 1–40.

Milward, A. (1992) *The European Rescue of the Nation-State.* London: Routledge.

Mitchell, J. D. B. (1965) 'The Causes and Effects of the Absence of a System of Public Law in the United Kingdom', *Public Law*, 95.

Möllers, C. (2008) *Der vermisste Leviathan: Staatstheorie in der Bundesrepublik*. Frankfurt am Main: Suhrkamp.

Moore, B. (1993) *Social Origins of Dictatorship and Democracy: Lord and Peasant in the Making of the Modern World*. Boston, MA: Beacon Press.

Morris, C. (1998) *An Essay on the Modern State*. Cambridge: Cambridge University Press.

Muller, P. and Surel, Y. (2002) *L'Analyse des politiques publiques*. Paris: Montchrestien.

Müller, W. (2003) 'The Changing European State', in J. Hayward and A. Menon (eds), *Governing Europe*. Oxford: Oxford University Press, pp. 369–79.

Müller, W. and Wright, V. (eds) (1994) 'The State in Western Europe: Retreat or Redefinition?', *West European Politics*, 17, 3.

Nora, P. (1986) 'Les mémoires d'Etat: De Commynes à de Gaulle', in P. Nora (ed.) *Les lieux de mémoire, II, La nation*. Paris: Gallimard.

Novak, A. (2008) 'The Myth of the 'Weak' American State', *American Historical Review*, 113, 3: 752–72.

Page, E. (1985) *Political Authority and Bureaucratic Power*. Brighton: Harvester.

Page, E. (2003) 'Europeanization and the Persistence of Administrative Systems', in J. Hayward and A. Menon (eds) *Governing Europe*. Oxford: Oxford University Press, pp. 162–76.

Pierson, C. (1996) *The Modern State*. London: Routledge.

Polanyi, K. (2001) *The Great Transformation: The Political and Economic Origins of Our Time*. Boston: Beacon Press. First published 1944.

Pollitt, C. (1993) *Managerialism and the Public Services: Cuts or Cultural Change in the 1990s*, 2nd edn. Oxford: Blackwell.

Prosser, T. (1996) 'Understanding the British Constitution', *Political Studies*, XLIV, pp. 473–87.

Reinhard, W. (2007) *Geschichte des modernen Staates. Von den Anfängen bis zur Gegenwart*. Munich: Beck.

Rhodes, R. A. W. (1994) 'The Hollowing Out of the State: The Changing Nature of the Public Service in Britain', *The Political Quarterly*, 65: 138–51.

Richter, M. (1995) *The History of Social and Political Concepts: A Critical Introduction*. Oxford: Oxford University Press.

Robson, W. A. (1928) *Justice and Administrative Law*. London: Stevens.

Rosanvallon, P. (1993) *L'Etat en France de 1789 à nos jours*. Paris: Le Seuil.

Runciman, D. (1997) *Pluralism and the Personality of the State*. Cambridge: Cambridge University Press.

Runciman, S. (2003) 'The Concept of the State: The Sovereignty of a Fiction' in Q.
–   Skinner and B. Strâth (eds), *States and Citizens. History, Theory, Prospects*. Cambridge: Cambridge University Press, pp. 28–38.

Rüstow, A. (1963) 'Die staatspolitischen Voraussetzungen des wirtschaftlichen Liberalismus', in W. Hoch (ed.), *Alexander Rüstow, Rede und Antwort*. Ludwigsberg: Hoch.

Rüttgers, J. (2009) 'Speech on the EU Amending Law to the Lisbon Treaty', Bundesrat, Berlin, 18 September.

Sartori, G. (1976) *Parties and Party Systems: A Framework for Analysis*. Cambridge: Cambridge University Press.

Schmidt, V. (1996) *From State to Market? The Transformation of French Business and Government*. Cambridge: Cambridge University Press.

Schmidt, V. (2002) *The Futures of European Capitalism*. Oxford: Oxford University Press.

Schmidt, V. (2006) *Democracy in Europe: The EU and National Polities*. Oxford: Oxford University Press.

Schuppert, G. (2003a) 'Public Law: Towards a Post-National Model', in K. Dyson and K. Goetz (eds) *Germany, Europe and the Politics of Constraint*. Proceedings of the British Academy 119. Oxford: Oxford University Press, pp. 109–25.

Schuppert, G. (2003b) *Staatswissenschaft*. Baden-Baden: Nomos.

Schuppert, G. (forthcoming) *Staat als Prozess: Eine Staatstheoretische Skizze in sieben Aufzügen*.

Shennan, J. H. (1986) *Liberty and Order in Early Modern Europe: The Subject and the State, 1650–1800*. London: Longman.

Sinn, H. -W. (2009) *Kasino Kapitalismus*. Berlin: Econ.

Skinner, Q. (1989) 'The State', in T. Ball, J. Farr and R. Hanson (eds) *Political Innovation and*

Conceptual Change. Cambridge: Cambridge University Press, pp. 90–131.

Skinner, Q. (2002) *Visions of Politics: Volume III Hobbes and Civil Society*. Cambridge: Cambridge University Press.

Skinner, Q. (2008) 'What Is the State?', 12th Annual British Academy Lecture, 13 May. London. British Academy.

Skocpol, T., Evans, P. and Rueschemeyer, D. (eds) (1985) *Bringing the State Back In*. Cambridge: Cambridge University Press.

Skowronek, S. (1982) *Building a New American State: The Expansion of National Administrative Capacities, 1877–1920*. Cambridge: Cambridge University Press.

Smith, G. (1986) *Democracy in Western Germany: Parties and Politics in the Federal Republic*. Aldershot: Gower.

Stevens, A. (2003) *The Government and Politics of France*. Basingstoke: Palgrave.

Strange, S. (1996) *The Retreat of the State: The Diffusion of Power in the World Economy*. Cambridge: Cambridge University Press.

Stråth, B. and Skinner, Q. (2003) 'Introduction' in Q. Skinner and B. Stråth (eds), *ibid*, pp. 1–27.

Suleiman, E. (1974) *Politics, Power and Bureaucracy in France*. Princeton: Princeton University Press.

Suleiman, E. and Courty, G. (1997) *L'Âge d'or de l'État: Une métamorphose annoncée*. Paris: Éditions du Seuil.

Tarrow, S. (2005) *The New Transnational Activism*. Cambridge: Cambridge University Press.

Tilly, C. (1973) 'Reflections on the History of European State-Making', in C. Tilly (ed.) *The Formation of National States in Western Europe*. Princeton, N.J.: Princeton University Press.

Troper, M. (1994) *Pour une théorie juridique de l'Etat*. Paris: Presses Universitaires de France.

Vincent, A. (1991) *Theories of the State*. Oxford: Blackwell.

Wahl, R. (2006) *Herausforderungen und Antworten. Das öffentliche Recht der letzten fünf Jahrzehnte*. Berlin: Gruyter.

Wallerstein, I. (1979) *The Capitalist World-Economy: Essays*. Cambridge: Cambridge University Press.

Weldon, T. D. (1953) *The Vocabulary of Politics*. Harmondsworth: Penguin.

Wright, V. (1989) *The Government and Politics of France*, 3rd edition. London: Unwin, Hyman.

Zürcher, C. (2007) 'When Governance Meets Troubled States', in M. Beisheim and G. Schuppert (eds) *Staatsverfall und Governance*. Baden-Baden: Nomos, pp. 11–27.

The author is indebted to the following for their helpful comments on the first drafts of this introduction: Professor David Boucher (Cardiff University), Professor Alistair Cole (Cardiff University), Professor Andrew Gamble (Cambridge University), Professor Bruce Haddock (Cardiff University), Professor Jack Hayward (Hull University), Professor George Jones (the LSE), Professor Desmond King (Oxford University), Professor Martin Loughlin (the LSE), Professor Janet McLean (Dundee University), Professor Christoph Möllers (Humboldt University Berlin), Professor Michael Moran (Manchester University), Professor Ed Page (the LSE), Professor Jiri Priban (Cardiff University), Professor Gunnar Schuppert (Humboldt University Berlin), Professor Daniel Wincott (Cardiff University), and Dr. Richard Wyn-Jones (Cardiff University).

| preface

This book has not proved easy to write. Indeed, colleagues have frequently revealed by their facial expressions (rather than by unkind words of discouragement) a feeling that I was embarking on a hazardous enterprise. It was, however, an exciting task to undertake and full of immediate rewards. Nevertheless, on occasion, I could not help experiencing a sense of vulnerability in the face of so vast a topic. The book is aimed at the sophisticated student of politics who is prepared to work hard at an important concept of authority that is likely to be outside his range of immediate political, legal and cultural experience and even perhaps of his intellectual experience. Such an endeavour is recommended because the idea of the state as the institution of political rule lies right at the heart of the continental European tradition of political thought about authority, whether 'taken-for-granted' in the form of a deep-rooted subconscious conception, and its meaning and significance scarcely reflected upon at all, or consciously elevated to a leading place in the interpretation of public affairs.

On reflection I am aware of the extent to which I may have become entrapped within the mannerisms of that tradition of authority, its combination of complex allusion and density of meanings. Moreover, the deliberate attempt to be comprehensive and at the same time to compress the richness of this historical and intellectual tradition of the state may reinforce an impression of linguistic strangeness in the text, a strangeness that is likely to be more keenly experienced by an English reader used to an economical and common-sense style than by an American who may be accustomed to the abstractness of the German tradition of scholarship. All of the weaknesses of this text, formal and substantive, are of course attributable to the author. Nevertheless, some of them illustrate problems of the tradition of thought with which it is concerned.

In order to prepare for what follows, it is necessary to clear up some misunderstandings that might arise from the attempt to compare 'state' societies with 'stateless' societies (for definitions, see pp. 51–2 and notes 2 and 4 of the Introduction). The term 'stateless society' is applied to a society that lacks a historical and legal tradition of the state as an institution that 'acts' in the name of public authority (or rather to which certain acts are attributed), as well as a tradition of continuous intellectual preoccupation with this idea of the state right across the political spectrum. It does not refer, in a more familiar sense, to a primitive society, which lacks the political structure of parliament, political executive, public administration, law courts and local authorities associated with the modern state. Members of this type of 'stateless' society can also recognize themselves to be part of a 'state system', to be a territorial association that interacts with other such associations on the level of international relations. The book is not concerned with the latter dimension of the state. It deals with the notion of the state as the institution of political rule, as the embodiment of the 'public power', and with the idea that this institution materializes and by which it is supposed to be directed; in other words, with the state as idea and institution. Second, a focus on 'state' societies does not suggest the absence of wide variation within and between such societies. It does, however, offer an alternative to approaches that stress internal continental European contrasts and ignore the common, often inarticulate, environment that is provided by the historical and intellectual tradition of the state as an institution. Similarly, identification of an Anglo-American, English-speaking political tradition that is characterized by its 'statelessness' (i.e. by the absence of this historical and legal heritage of the state) does not imply the absence of interesting contrasts within that tradition.

I have benefited greatly from the helpful advice and criticism of Professors Malcolm Anderson (Edinburgh), Brian Chapman (Manchester), Jack Hayward (Hull), George Jones (LSE), Geraint Parry (Manchester) and Fred Ridley (Liverpool), as well as that of Rodney Barker (LSE), Joe Femia (Liverpool), David Miller (Oxford) and Gordon Smith (LSE). I am also grateful to Ray Thomas for his scrutiny of an untidy manuscript, and to Mrs Gillian Haspell for her careful and efficient work on the typescript. Finally, I acknowledge with gratitude the sympathetic encouragement and support of my wife Ann, whose efficient management of two small boys gave me the freedom to write this book.

Liverpool   KENNETH DYSON
July 1979

introduction | the state as idea and institution

When we study national variations in political theory, we are led to semantic considerations of a delicate kind. ...

Louis Hartz (1955, p. 59)

... To know that the balance does not quite rest,
That the mask is strange, however like.

Wallace Stevens

The term state, when used to refer to a political association, evokes, perhaps even within the same person, a complex variety of responses, among which are hope, fear and puzzlement. It is a central term of political discourse in some societies and one with whose meaning this book is concerned. Why study the idea of the state? In the case of France, where state is a central term of political discourse, the disjointed and untidy character of political activity seems to possess no clearly observable relationship to the unity of action that is promised by the idea of the state (Machin, 1977). State is not, however, a concept whose relevance depends solely on its offering an accurate picture of the observable political arrangements of all or some societies. Words are a part of human behaviour. They are mental categories which both represent, and are part of, the world and which impose intentionality and coherence on that world. Language is not just an intellectual activity distinct from the reality of the material world. Concepts and contexts are inseparable. Language is part of the social and political structure; it reveals the politics of a society. Hence analysis of political discourse will indicate how the political world is perceived, and a diachronic analysis of concepts can be helpful in uncovering long-term structural changes by showing how words acquire new meanings in the context of such changes. With a word like state one would expect to find a multiplicity of usages. Words are not, therefore, reliable and unchanging labels firmly attached to the things one wants to study and describe. Indeed, the usefulness of state as a political term derives from its 'open-textured' quality (Waismann, 1945), from the fact that it can be taken to mean so many different, even contradictory, things in various linguistic and social contexts. Its virtue is its uncertainty, for it leaves room for something unexpected to be said. Its intellectual problem—and this is a problem that this book reflects rather than resolves—is that it is a general idea which is terribly amorphous. Attitudes towards the state in Western Europe vary across an enormous spectrum. State is not therefore a concept with the sort of definite boundaries that would enable a complete description; the evasiveness and ambiguity surrounding state would suggest the impossibility of finding an agreed specific meaning of the term.

The view that an interest in the idea of the state distracts attention from the reality of political conduct poses the question of what counts as reality. Reality is a function not just of sense data but also of the conceptual apparatus that men have developed, for concepts shape experience by providing categories in terms of which men see and understand the world. Experience of the world, as well as processes of reasoning and imaginative reflection about it, find their expression in words. A study of the concept of the state is not therefore simply concerned with an autonomous, self-perpetuating field of vague and abstract thought unrelated to political practice. Nor is the idea of the state to be lightly dismissed as a decorative facade, a smokescreen of elevated language, by which men seek to provide cynically expedient *ex post facto* rationalizations for their manipulative politicking. Ideas are, of course, used as tools or weapons in politics, and they do reflect political activity. They are not, however, merely expedients or reflexes of political practice. Men are as much prisoners as manipulators of the ideas by which they seek to explain and legitimate their actions in terms acceptable to others. This latter requirement helps to make ideas an important aspect of political reality. An idea can be linked to a visible set of events, being formulated in the context of specific problems and deliberately used to legitimate and even implement policy (Church, 1972; Skinner, 1979). It can then develop a momentum of its own as an implicit working assumption or requirement of action. The notion of the state is neither a passive reflection, nor a determinant, of political conduct. Being in part constitutive of political activity and of the state itself, the idea of the state is connected in an intimate, complex and internal way with that conduct, shaped by and shaping it, manipulated by and imprisoning the political actor whose political world is defined in its terms. As political actors must legitimate their conduct by describing and evaluating it with reference to the notion of the state, it seems likely that at least some men are sometimes motivated by it. The concept of the state *per se* may not be explanatory of political action, but it does help to make sense of that action.

Conversely, a concern with the state tradition must avoid the category mistake of conflating the state with the idea of the state (in this study the former is referred to by the term 'the state apparatus' or 'the state itself'). Although they are inseparable in so far as the state is partly constituted by the beliefs that people hold about it, they are obviously different. For example, if anarchy broke out tomorrow, there would be no state apparatus, but the idea of the state would still be present. The danger of failing to make this distinction is a 'super-idealism', through which changes in the idea of the state are equated with changes in the state itself, nullifying questions about the causal effectiveness of ideas. However, because this category mistake pervades the literature on the state and individual theorists are so ambiguous in their use of the word, it is difficult to avoid its reproduction in a comprehensive survey.

We are not dealing with a conceptual monolith created in the minds of a few great thinkers and capable of being shifted about over space and time at will, enjoying a perfectly autonomous explanatory power. State is a theoretical term, one associated with the great themes of political discourse and interwoven with political activity, simultaneously a part both of eloquently formulated intellectual constructions and of the working assumptions of political action. It is a category of mind, which is an important aspect of experience of political reality in certain societies, both representing and shaping experience of them. For example, values, beliefs and expectations characteristic of the state tradition of authority in which they operate affect groups' perceptions of their interests and foster in them a disposition to explain their positions in abstract terms, to fit their particular concerns into a larger framework. The idea of the state forms part of the considerations which groups have in mind when determining where their interests lie and what types of conduct will appeal to decision-makers and the public.

As Nettl (1968) has emphasized, the idea of the state has been neglected in the English-speaking world. From the traditional British empiricist and the American pragmatist viewpoints a useful concept must be grounded in experience. However, the concept of the state was not firmly grounded in American or British experience. The absence of the notion of the state as a 'lived' historical and socio-cultural phenomenon did not, in the context of such a philosophical outlook, encourage its emergence as a central concept within the intellectual tradition. In other words, a complex mutually reinforcing interaction between, on the one hand, historical experience in which the state was not recognized as a legal institution and as a living entity and, on the other, an empiricist or pragmatist intellectual outlook was hostile to the development of a sense of 'stateness'. It was to prove as difficult to explore the distinctiveness and unity of the state as a rational entity by an empirical method that sees the world as a mass of discrete, directly observable facts or events as by a Marxist method that begins by dismissing this unity as a delusion. In particular, the understanding of West European politics has suffered recently from a tendency of so many scholars of comparative politics to confine themselves unreflectively within the framework of thought of the Anglo-American cultural and intellectual tradition.[1*] Numerous scholars who have sought to explain the similarities and differences between West European political systems have been blinkered by an empirical outlook that emphasized contingency and advocated a 'method of detail', a method that consists in treating wholes by resolving them into their parts and breaking every question into pieces before attempting to resolve it; and by a fascination with the methodology of natural science. Both perspectives promised to deal economically with experience, and both contributed to the 'realistic' and 'demystifying' orientation of much comparative politics. Consequently, comparative politics has had little patience with abstract political ideas or legal concepts, particularly those which are unfamiliar in the sense of outside immediate 'felt' experience. And yet in the continental European political context, where consciousness of institutions is developed and closely associated with the notion of the state, it seems sensible to explore the relevance of ideas and the institutions that embody them to an understanding of political conduct. A 'feel' for the peculiar character and diversity contained within continental European politics, for politics as it is 'lived', is only

---

* Notes are to be found at the end of each chapter.

possible if the historical, legal and intellectual tradition of the state is taken into account. Moreover, comparison with that tradition of authority rather than with the United States (with which Britain shares a 'stateless' quality) helps reveal some of the distinctive features of political arrangements and conduct in Britain.[2] As Sir Ernest Barker (1930, p. 173) noted:

> the State as such does not act in England; a multitude of individual officials each separately and severally act.... There is a bundle of individual officials, each exercising a measure of authority under the cognizance of the Courts, but none of them, not even the Prime Minister, wielding the authority of the State.

This book is an exploratory venture whose objective is to offer a 'map-and-compass' guide to the rich complexity of a tradition of thought and practice which for historical and linguistic reasons has proved partly inaccessible to the English-speaking world.[3] Consequently, it does not provide a rigorous, technical analysis of particular legal, political and philosophical theories of the state in their linguistic and social context. Nor does the book develop an elaborate theoretical argument. Because it contains a great deal of specific information about a tradition that appears somewhat amorphous and that incorporates a broad spectrum of attitudes and because many detailed references are made about an unfamiliar terrain, it resembles (to vary the metaphor) a mosaic whose pieces are widely dispersed. There are many ways of organizing such complex material and many connections which others (encouraged, I hope, by this book) will make. The book is concerned with the character of a tradition of authority, supplying neither apologetics for, nor denunciation of, that tradition but rather an appreciation of its strengths and weaknesses. Like any tradition, it tolerates and unites an internal variety and displays an ability to change without losing its identity. Thus the politics of the Bonn Republic has been shaped by the process of exploring the intimations of this tradition of ideas about political rule in the context of the experience of the Weimar Republic and the Third Reich as well as of international, economic and social developments (Dyson, 1979). Like any tradition, its legacy is ambivalent, notably in its relationship to democracy. State is a complex concept which has been associated with some formidable problems. For example, as Wilhelmenian Germany revealed, its emphasis on the importance of the 'public power'[4] can lead to the seductions of power, relapses into political irresponsibility and inhumanity. A state tradition harnessed to fear and pessimism, and to aggression and the desire for conflict, is likely to produce reckless policy (Craig, 1978). The same period in German history illustrates the dangers of treating the concept of the state divorced from, or as a substitute for, consideration of the political character of the regime. Gustav Radbruch (1930, p. 289), a *Staatsrechtler* and Social Democratic Justice Minister in the Weimar Republic, referred to impartiality as the 'living lie' of the conception of the *Obrigkeitsstaat,* a view of an authoritarian state above politics and one which had been influential during the Second Empire. Some French commentators (Crozier, 1970; Peyrefitte, 1976), and Max Weber with reference to the German Second Empire, have emphasized the bureaucratic inefficiencies that have been associated with the historical tradition of the state. And yet at its best this tradition has been characterized by an ennobling sense of purpose, an idealism transcending egoistic self-interest and a concern to reflect critically on the relationship between idea and conduct, form and practice, in public life. 'State' societies display a particular sensitivity to the requirements of institutions and to the importance of the internalization of their standards for cultural survival. This consciousness of institutions informs both the outlook of their members and the academic approach to the study of public power. Institutions pose problems of rule and are not to be understood exhaustively by describing their formal structures or the patterns of interaction within them. A high-minded moralistic concern with the requirements of rule may also be associated with a contemptuous attitude towards 'material'-interest politicking and a failure of insight into the complex problems involved in the accommodation of competitive interests. A didactic style of leadership, preoccupied with the moral integration promised by the idea of the state, has difficulties in accepting the diversity implicit in a vigorously politicking society. Political leaders can become ensnared in the authoritarian implications of the search for a single theory of political rule, one that produces a rigid view of the requirements of citizenship. The anti-Semitism of the German Second Empire was in part an instance of this phenomenon (Pulzer, 1964).

Recognition of the complexity of the state tradition does not imply that it is impossible to achieve a clearer conceptualization of the term, to identify that distinctive ethic which gives it cultural significance. The attempt to arrive at a definition which might form a basis for a constructive comparison of West European political systems must, however, be combined with insight into how the idea of the state is grounded in more general metaphysical assumptions and historical traditions and is sensitive to social and economic changes. By placing the notion of the state in its historical and intellectual context in Parts I and II of the book it is possible to identify the forces and interests, material and ideal, from whose interaction it emerged and the important changes that have taken place in its ideological, sociological and organizational character over time. It is helpful to illustrate the developments in political theory that accompanied its emergence, and to show how its meaning has been contested between different groups and how it has served an ideological function, springing out of particular social conditions and helping to transform those conditions. This focus on history and political theory, on the social function rather than inherent logic of theories of the state, highlights the background against which state became an interesting and important concept as well as the wide range of contested meanings and consequent imprecision it has acquired. Attention to usage helps in the process of 'unpacking' the concept, of identifying, through a process of discrimination, the interrelated 'unit ideas' or simpler elements which comprise it. It is, then, possible to offer in Chapter 8 an ideal-type definition of its formal characteristics, for what gives coherence to these elements is the rationalist pursuit of order (in its broadest sense) in a society subject to ceaseless change. The fullest flowering of the historical and intellectual tradition of the state as an institution of rule is to be found in those societies in which at particular periods the problem of order was most vividly experienced and where the perception gained ground that an adequate response to this problem required a rationalist reflection on the nature of public authority. Political authority could not be taken for granted; its defence depended on an explicit institutional focus.

This book will have succeeded if it reverses the tendency in English-language studies of West European politics to ignore the idea of the state, to write it off as an historical burden on the development of a democratic political consciousness (Bracher, 1968, quoting C. J. Friedrich: 'in a strict sense the state does not exist in democracy') or of some specialists on a particular country to handle it selectively with reference to the experience of their political system. Nevertheless, there are linguistic and cultural problems in dealing with a theme that is not present in the political tradition of one's own society. For example, the disposition within the Anglo-American intellectual tradition to analyse wholes into specific, discrete parts is alien to the emphasis upon the interrelationships amongst parts contained in the concept of the state. The latter promotes a sense of the whole and a concern for the terms of its operation. As a philosophical and culturally rich concept, state is not amenable to the elaboration of 'operational indicators' involved in the sort of rigorous definition desired by advocates of the natural science paradigm and systems builders. Its importance lies in its holism, its normative concern with the nature of public authority and the terms on which it is to be exercised, its rationalist preoccupation with the creative role of institutions and with giving its constituent ideas institutional expression as a way of 'fixing' certain meanings within public life. The state tradition reflects a series of intellectual preoccupations which have not been as strongly represented in the Anglo-American tradition.

The affective and open-ended nature of the concept of the state needs to be stressed. It is a complex concept, capable of being interpreted in various ways with reference to very general beliefs about human conduct and relationships in society. While state communicates distinctive meanings and purposes, it is characterized by an ambiguity and an imprecision that make it impossible to find an agreed specific meaning for the term. This ambiguity stems in part from the amorphous idea of an 'ordered' society upon which it rests. It is also the product of its incorporation with other concepts in a complex variety of theoretical frameworks, of different degrees of institutional commitment to its purposes and of attempts to redefine it to meet changing circumstances. State is an ideological concept; it provides individuals with certain categories of awareness and knowledge and certain standards of evaluation with reference to which expectations and objectives are to be formulated and purposive action taken. It has been a central reference point for political discourse within 'state' societies. In political debate the term state is used approvingly (although it is not, *ipso facto,* a term of approval or condemnation). Particular policy stances are derived from or rationalized with reference to the idea of the state: witness the concern for the 'unity of the state' in French debates on regionalism and on direct elections to the European Parliament in the 1970s. The term state is also used pejoratively. For example, in continental European anarchist and radical libertarian thought (more than in its Anglo-American equivalents) the whole ethos of the 'repressive' state is denounced. Conversely, others vilify those forces and interests that appear to be eroding its autonomy and professional public-service values. If the Weimar Republic could be seen as an example of the 'crisis of the party state', the *Verbändestaat* or *Gewerkschaftsstaat* (interest-group or trade-union state) was, in the view of some critics, a threat to the governability of the Bonn Republic.

Serving as both a highly generalizing philosophical–ethical concept and a weapon in political argument, the idea of the state has been viewed as a source of confusing vagueness, tantalizing mystery and exploitation. Thus an early nineteenth century German Romantic like Adam Müller glorified in an expansive, poetical conception of the state as 'a great individual encompassing the individuality of lesser men.... Man cannot be imagined outside of the state...the state is the totality of all human concerns' (Aris, 1929). If an Idealist like Hegel was concerned to penetrate to its innermost secret core, a historical materialist (for example, Marx), a positivist (for example, Duguit) or a legal positivist (for example, Kelsen) sought to unmask its mystification. Thus Hans Kelsen produced a highly restrictive view of the state as the expression of the logical completeness and inner consistency of the system of legal norms. Thereby he hoped to avoid the political abuses that could follow from personification of the state as an entity different from the legal order. It would, nevertheless, be more accurate to speak of these three influential critics as correcting rather than breaking with the state tradition.

The rich variety of theorizing about the nature and functions of the state suggests the danger of assuming or seeking a single accepted or monolithic theory of the state in any particular society. For example, Franco's Spain rested on a fluid combination of conceptions of a personalized state, a corporatist state and an administrative state, whose common concerns were unity and public order. Even more theoretical competition is to be expected in less authoritarian societies. Differences exist over the priority of the ideals that the state embodies, over the interpretation of shared principles, and over the institutions that best give expression to the idea of the state. One thinks of the clashes within the French public bureaucracy between those corps pledged to the conception of the technocratic state and the rest; of disagreements between traditional conservative welfare state and radical participatory interpretations of the West German conception of the *Sozialstaat* (social state);[5] and of opposed views about whether the law, the bureaucracy or the parties embody the distinctive ethos of the notion of the state. An example of the conflict between idealistic and realistic theories of the state is provided by the differences between the jurisprudence of the Council of State (*Conseil d'État*) relating to theories of *l'État de Droit* (the state of law) and the critiques levelled by the French union of magistrates which often rest on a view of the repressive character of the state. Realistic theories of the state gravitate between those which contrast ideal and real in order to show the hollowness of the ideal (leading to denunciation of the liberal bourgeois state) and others which use this observation to stress the urgency of a more determined effort to secure the ideal. This ambivalence, characteristic of left-wing realistic theories, has made for some difficult problems in handling dissent in 'state' societies. The question of how to distinguish a constructive critic from an enemy of the state bedevilled the application after 1972 of the so-called 'Radicals' Decree', which sought to exclude enemies of the 'free democratic basic order' from the West German public service (Dyson, 1975). Although the idea of the state promises unity of action and community of sentiment, it is associated with considerable theoretical and practical conflicts. It has functioned simultaneously as a source of affect and disaffection.

Continental European reflection about the idea of the state has been beset by some fundamental difficulties. First, there was the issue of just how important it was as a factor in understanding political conduct. For many writers it was not the concept of the state *per se* that was central. In his Addresses to the German Nation (1807–8) the philosopher Johann Gottlieb Fichte outlined the *Volkstaat* in which the nation was 'the bearer and pledge of earthly eternity' and 'went far beyond the state in the ordinary sense of the word—beyond the social order'. Marxists and some on the right during the French Third Republic stressed the existence of the 'bourgeois' state, one that was simply the instrument of a dominant class. By contrast, French 'structuralist' Marxists like Poulantzas (1973) concentrated on the 'capitalist' state.[6] This state was seen to possess a 'relative autonomy' of the economic structure and to maintain the unity of the 'social formation' as a whole by balancing and reconciling the different social forces within it. Post-war German conservative theorists such as the sociologist Helmut Schelsky (1965) have emphasized the development of the 'technical' state whose concern for performance or functional effectiveness was reflected in the dominance of scientific method in decision-making.

The idea of the state has attracted most those, like the disciples of Maurice Hauriou in France, with an Idealist perspective which conceives of man, acting through the state, as a subject in history. In addition to the rationalistic and Idealist neo-Thomism of Hauriou's account of the state as an institution which offsets the fallibility of the individual, German Hegelianism in its concern for the spiritual life has been particularly conscious of the significance of the state as a basis of community and altruistic commitment. Swiss theories of the state took much of their inspiration, and drew a great deal of their character, from Jacob Burckhardt's philosophical and cultural conception of history, one that was indebted to German liberalism of the 1840s. According to Burckhardt, the state was constantly being made by men and was to be understood in terms of the general 'conception of the world' through which men in a particular context made their discoveries (Schindler, 1932; Kägi, 1945). Burckhardt's contemplative historical vision was inspired by a view of civilization as a delicate and precious thing, an awareness of the human costs of history and a recognition of the creative importance of invisible historical forces. An aristocratic pessimist and, like his own country, a somewhat isolated and independent figure, he offered a broad and ascetic conception of the state as a protective shield for the moral life of society, as an institution of anchorites. It was a part of the history of civilization, indeed the custodian of civilization. An Idealist and neo-Hegelian conception of the state and one sensitive, like Burckhardt's, to cultural change was also the legacy of Benedetto Croce's philosophical history in Italy (Chabod, 1958; d'Entrèves, 1967). The abstract rationalism of neo-Kantianism has had an especially powerful influence on continental European philosophy, legal theory and social science. Its search for a pure notion of rational truth was also conducive to the idea of the state; either to the *Kulturstaat* or the material conception of the *Rechtsstaat* as the embodiments of certain absolute, transcendental ethical values (Radbruch, 1950) or to the formal conception of the *Rechtsstaat* as the embodiment of a logical objectivism because it rested on a formal epistemology that guaranteed objectively valid knowledge, removed from the transitory world of experience (Kelsen, 1925).

Some theorists have attempted to bring Idealism and economic materialism into an intellectual system. For example, the German sociologist Lorenz von Stein's (1850) solution to this problem conceived of a society of class struggle and competition for personal development being 'overcome' by a state which expressed the idea of the unity of the *Volk*. Society was a non-personal and natural community and the object of the state's activity. By contrast, the state was viewed as the community of the wills of every individual, a community that expressed itself as a personality through will and action and found its highest expression in a constitutional or social monarchy. As Stein recognized that each had a logic of its own, he emphasized the struggle between state and society. The logic of a society that expressed the particularity of individual and class interest, an interest that was centred on property, would reassert itself as soon as state activity was withdrawn.

A second difficulty arose over whether the concept of the state had an objective meaning, whether it represented a real phenomenon that was external to the consciousness or the conceptual apparatus of the observer. In Max Weber's view, the concept of the state was merely a representation of certain meanings understood by social actors, and it changed as these meanings altered. 'For sociological purposes there is no such thing as a collective personality which 'acts'... what is meant [by the state] is ... *only* a certain kind of development of actual or possible social actions of individual persons' (Weber, 1964, p. 102). Weber, an eminent German sociologist, was concerned about the tendency to reify state as a *deus ex machina,* even to deify state by attributing to it mysterious powers and qualities. This tendency was reinforced by the metaphorical, figurative language that was often used in Germany to characterize the state, in particular by the organic analogy and an associated language of 'collective forces'. The concept of the state had an intoxicating effect on the mind, an effect that hindered rigorous analysis. According to a Scandinavian legal 'realist' like the Danish jurist Alf Ross (1969) state was a mental tool, the name for a legal subject to which certain acts (acts-in-law and factual acts) by individuals could be attributed. It was possible to identify a common core in the varied usage of the term: acts-in-law are attributed to the state when they are expressions of the qualified power referred to as 'public authority' as opposed to 'private autonomy'; while factual acts are attributed to the state when they are manifestations of a privilege to perform acts of physical force. However, the question of what the term state stood for as an acting subject was not, in Ross's view, a meaningful one.

The influential French jurist Maurice Hauriou sought to avoid the sort of relativism that Weber displayed. He conceived of two worlds— the subjective world embodied within each conscience and the objective world of social reality—worlds that opposed and balanced each other. In his view, the concept of the state belonged to the subjective world; it was a representation of the organic unity or individuality of a political body. Similarly, Jacques Donnedieu de Vabres (1954, p. 14), like Georges Renard, saw the state as a legal subject and a moral personality that was constructed by reason. It had a fictional character and, consequently, most of the problems that were associated with it were psychological. According to another eminent member of the French school of institutional theory, Georges Burdeau (1949–57, vol. 2, p. 230), 'the state exists because it is thought'. However, institutions like the state itself gave an objective expression to certain ideas through their structures and procedures

(Hauriou, 1923; Renard, 1930). The concept of the state was therefore viewed as both external to and internal to (that is, internalized by) any given individual. The attempt of Weber and later legal 'realists' to avoid the fallacy of the reification of the concept of the state (a fallacy that involves regarding an abstraction as a real phenomenon) led conversely to their unwillingness to emphasize the role of institutions as both idea and object in generating and sustaining authoritative meanings defined in terms of purpose. Hauriou was particularly concerned to emphasize that the subjective world of the state was capable of achieving a greater degree of coherence and consistency than was the objective world of 'social movement'. By contrast, Weber was fascinated by the way in which the same institution meant different things to different people and, moreover, could change in meaning over time. He attributed great importance to the distinction between legal norms and human conduct orientated to such norms and emphasized that the former in no way determined the latter. Institutions were seen as the vehicles of human action. While Weber recognized that they enabled man to orientate his action towards certain expectations and that their structures provided a coherence and permanence, he did not fit this observation into a general theory of institutions (Lachmann, 1970).

The German sociologist Ferdinand Tönnies (1887), who was a contemporary of Weber but, like Hauriou, closer to the sociological ideas of the Frenchman Gabriel Tarde, was prepared to accept that the concept of the state was in part to be conceived of as an empirical reality. However, he rejected the German view, associated even with a liberal like Otto von Gierke, that the state 'is' an organism as well as the view of the concept of the state as simply an empirical fact. According to Tönnies, the state was an artificial cultural unit, a fictitious moral person in whose name certain individuals acted. It possessed an ideally conceived character, being created or made by men, but could achieve an external objective power over the individual. As we shall see later, Tönnies argued that all institutions, social relationships and values, in so far as they existed for their subjects, were created and affirmed by the will of those subjects. This psychological condition constituted their essence; in this manner they were seen 'from within'.

Some theorists argued even more forcefully that the concept of the state had an objective meaning. For French neo-positivists like Émile Durkheim and Léon Duguit, who diverged sharply from Weber, the concept of the state was simply a social fact, an objective social reality or force, one that was both external and constraining to the individual. Its meaning stemmed from the organization of society. In the view of such eminent jurists as Georg Jellinek (1900) and Raymond Carré de Malberg (1920) state was not just an abstract legal subject but was represented by an object which confronted the mind, whose organs were held to 'act' (because authorized to do so by the legal order) and which could be described and defined. By contrast, to the German philosopher Georg Hegel[7] and, more recently, to Jürgen Habermas, the concept of the state was not a reality *sui generis*. It was part of a more comprehensive 'totality' and partook of the quality of a larger developing historical whole from which it derived its meaning. If Weber suggested a relativistic view of the state as involving an irreducible conflict of values, these theorists were attached to the notion of enlightened human beings who could agree on a determinate set of needs and values (even if the preconditions for such emancipation were different: for Karl Marx, for example, the 'withering away' of the state). Their ambition to achieve comprehensiveness in their account of the state promised a normative critique of political practice. It also contained dangers. Extraordinary claims for sociology or philosophy were accompanied by ambiguity on important questions of political details, while enthusiasm for particular exciting ideas could lead to a loss of a sense for balance in political argument. Above all, it was tempting to 'force' connections that might not be written into political reality.

One awkward problem which plagued juristic conceptions of the state was the idea of corporate personality. Jurists who sought to offer a sociological account of the state either rejected this idea on the ground that there was no observable fact corresponding to it or argued that the state was a real corporate person, a social reality. Duguit (1911) represented the former view, von Gierke (1915) the latter view. By contrast, Jellinek drew a clear distinction between sociological and juristic accounts of the state and insisted on the reality of corporate personality only as a juristic phenomenon. He proposed two conceptions of the state: as an empirical reality, a social fact or object of observation; and as a legal phenomenon, a subject of rights whose corporate personality was a purely abstract, but not fictitious, juristic conception. This juristic conception was an ideal synthesis of its empirical elements, necessary to explain society as a unified legal organization. At the same time, corporate personality was part of the reality of law. However, Jellinek's rigorous distinction between social and juristic conceptions of the state, and his particular skills as a jurist, led him to neglect consideration of the social elements of the state. He favoured a formal rationalistic view of the state as the source (through its inherent superiority of will) of standards and norms. Jellinek neglected to show how the abstraction is bound up with reality, how the formal character of the state as a juristic person is bound up with the character of the social fact, which is its real content (Hallis, 1930). Hauriou offered a more sociological approach, one which suggested that the personality of the state as an institution had a 'substratum of reality' and hence was a social force rather than just a legal form. We have seen that he sought to synthesize the objective element of continuity and the subjective element of action or creation in his account of society. Correspondingly, the institution was composed of both elements. As the institution was founded on the subjective element of action, it was not simply an objective reality distinct from the individual human being. The institution comprised an idea, organized power, directive organs and rules of procedure. It involved both intellectual agreement, communion in an idea, and the will to act, communion in action. Corporate personality became in this sociological analysis something real, a natural and spontaneous phenomenon of social life. Personification of the state was the product of a real subjectivization of the common interest which was the bond uniting the members of the corporate body. The eminent French jurist Raymond Saleilles (1922) followed Hauriou's analysis of the institution. However, he construed the juristic person of the state as a subject of right, as an ideal synthesis that was a juristic interpretation of social facts, rather than as itself a social fact. Legal personality avoided becoming just an abstract form by its attribution to a living being, an entity in itself, which acquired thereby juristic capacity. In other words, legal personality depended on organized power, on a motive force.

The juristic conception of the state was much influenced by the extent to which particular theorists were prepared to recognize it as a social reality (Hallis, 1930). Jellinek insisted upon the distinction between the state and law and gave priority to the state as a social organization, as the historical product of an act of will that was extrinsic to the law. The state was the essential presupposition of the law, for it alone supplied the power necessary to guarantee the binding force of the law. However, the idea of the state as a juristic person implied the subordination of the state to the law which it created. In this process of auto-limitation the state retained its inherent power of will; in submitting to the rule of law it limited itself. Hans Kelsen attempted to overcome or avoid the subsequent problem of why the state must obey its own law by refusing to treat the state as a social organization outside the law. 'The state as a social fact exists for the jurist as little as the symphony exists for the physiologist' (Kelsen, 1922, p. 116). He offered a purely juristic and formal conception of the state as an organization of legal norms. Law and the state were one and the same. The distinction between juristic and sociological conceptions of the state remains important: the one is concerned with the imperative and formative character of the state, the other with its factual nature and the forces that create deviations from its rules. However, Kelsen was not prepared to recognize that they were complementary, that they threw light on each other.

It is clear that there is a great variety of incompatible or ill-fitting views about the concept of the state in continental Europe. Moreover, ideologies exist which are not deeply concerned with state as a theoretical term.[8] In 'state' societies it is not the sole idea motivating conduct. Nevertheless, even for anti-*étatistes,* it is a central point of intellectual reference. The concept of the state permeates continental European thought. On the one hand, theories of the state appear to present a disorderly and, in historical terms, very provisional picture reflecting the contested character of the assumptions on which they rest. On the other, they are united by a concern to go beyond 'common-sense' empiricism and its fascination with detailed questions about discrete relationships and with the factual record of the contingent complexities of life. Theorists of the state have sought to connect the particular with the general, with philosophical questions concerning the properties and possibilities of human nature and man's relationship to the external world. Answers to these larger questions were to provide the framework within which settled solutions could be found for more detailed questions. Assumptions, however contestable, were more readily articulated, and their implications tested, in terms of a theoretical framework. The result was often a greater readiness to challenge the *status quo* by offering a rational defence of particular premises (rather than by making implicit appeals to social conventions) and by providing a rational and comprehensive account of patterns of change (Hawthorn, 1976). In contrast to the 'atomistic' approach of English analytic philosophy, an attempt was made to understand particular concepts in time, in the context of social structure and historical background as well as of an examination of wider systems of ideas in terms of which they have at least in part acquired their meaning (Kägi, 1945). Moral concepts were seen to be embodied in, and partly constitutive of, forms of social and political life.

The importance of the idea of the state within the continental European historical and intellectual traditions was reinforced by the way in which it provided a rationale for the very institutions and activities in which most academics, administrators and leading politicians were profession-ally engaged. Not surprisingly, their theories of the state tended to reflect their respective professional interests: the *Kulturstaat* (cultural state) of the philosophers, the *Rechtsstaat* (state ruled by law) of the jurists, the *Beamtenstaat* of the public officials, and the *Parteienstaat* of party mem-bers. By and large, British and American political thought and practice have shown a marked inwardness, a preference for taking institutions for granted rather than for exploring them in a theoretical manner. It has been during periods of doubt about Britain's institutional arrangements that certain thinkers have turned to the continental European intellectual tradition and have rediscovered the term state. For example, the exten-sion of the functions and powers of government from the 1870s prompted reflection on fundamental principles and a concern about the limits of proper 'state' activity. A liberal like Herbert Spencer (1884) saw the state as just 'a joint-stock protection-company for mutual assurance', 'a hin-drance of hindrances', whereas an advocate of the New Liberalism like John Hobson (1909) could speak of the 'central organizing intelligence' of the state. The shift toward Edwardian welfare policies under Asquith, Lloyd George and Churchill found its legitimation in the stress of moral reformers like Leonard Hobhouse and Hobson on the function of the state in the moral improvement of the community (Freeden, 1978). Similarly, in the 1960s the New Left, disenchanted with gradualism and the appar-ent impotence of governments, turned to continental discussions about the state (for example, the works of Althusser and Gramsci). While these 'European-minded' thinkers may have influenced the climate of politi-cal argument, their intellectual impact was restricted. The state was not a legal institution that could be universally recognized to exist or could command attention as a relevant object of political reflection. Moreover, elite training had not been formalized and systematized as in continental Europe, where it served to implant the idea of state interests and require-ments. Consequently, the notion of the state had little cultural resonance. Britain maintained an intellectual tradition that was distinctive without being insular (Barker, 1978).

The intellectual 'strangeness' of the continental European state tradition is compounded by its association with the idea of law as the articulation of the state, and the dominant role of lawyers in theorizing about the state and in its administration. Hence the student of this tradition must be prepared to deal in juristic categories and to see behind the emphasis on the legal dimension of public life the expression of a distinct culture involving attitudes about the nature of law, about the role of law in society (both as a normative commitment to certain political values and as a regulator of institutions), and about how law should be made, applied and studied. An understanding of law is fundamental to an understanding of continental European government.[9]

Emphasis on the importance of state as an intellectual and legal tool of analysis must not distract attention from the concept's role in political debate, for its norms enter into man's practical reasoning and guide conduct. It represents not only a particular manner of arranging political and administrative affairs and regulating relationships of authority but also a cultural phenomenon which binds people together in terms of a common mode of interpreting the world. As we shall see, its effects are to be traced in the character of institutional arrangements, attitudes of elites and political opposition, and in modes of interest accommodation that range from France's absolutist exercise of public authority to Austria and West Germany's 'social partnership'. The notion of the state is associated with the affective appeals and sense of duty which accompany a moral idea, the endowment of material purposes and interests with a moral significance and an unwillingness to distinguish moral and material life; with a rejection of the neutral language of political 'machinery'; with the normative character of the legal order (*Staat als Rechtsordung*); and with the non-rational character of human community (*Staat als Lebens-gemeinschaft*) (Kuhn, 1967). There have been considerable changes in social and political life, brought about by alterations in social structure and attitude, historical experience and the evolution of party systems and organized groups. These changes have nevertheless been channelled through an institutional framework whose motivating ideas reach back into the past and embody inherited procedural norms shaping political conduct and constraining choice in a manner with which 'stateless' societies are unfamiliar. The state tradition of authority has been concerned to provide man with direction in his behaviour, and to avoid 'aimless' conduct, through the idea of order in values. It has stressed the importance of a hierarchical and normative element in society, of a common set of public principles rather than 'private' standards of taste and opinion as the basis of order, and of an intellectual contribution to the clarification of the normative order. And yet it appears an internally complex and variegated tradition. At one level the idea of the state emerges in specific policy debates, at another in attempts to gain coherence through reflection on general principles. The relationship between these two levels of discourse is far from straightforward or one-way. Arguments about the state reflect the changing practice of politics, and shape, however diffusely and indirectly, ways of thinking and acting in politics.

NOTES

1   As will be argued in the book, this framework of thought owes much to the fact that historical experience has not generated the state as an institution (whether perceived as an object or a personality) that cannot be avoided in political, sociological, historical and juridical reflection.

2   The term 'state society' refers to societies which have a historical and intellectual tradition of the state as an institution that embodies the 'public power' (see n. 4). They recognize state organs which establish legal norms and/or apply them to particular cases. A 'stateless society' lacks a historical experience of this institution. Within such a society there may be some intellectual interest in the state which takes the form of rationalist reflection on the interconnected principles that characterize the political order or on the proper limits of 'state' activity. However, this reflection is not intense and falls short of seeing the state as an institution which acts. There may also be a general sense of being members of a state. In other words, a 'stateless' society can possess the idea of the state as a territorial association which interacts, on the plane of international relations, with other such associations. 'State' and 'stateless' societies share also the notion of sovereignty, but they interpret that notion differently. The composite character of the English idea of parliamentary sovereignty, an idea that comprises king, Lords and Commons and represented an appeasement or settlement between these traditional powers, contrasts with the integrated 'public power' of continental Europe, a rationalist conception which was the product of the attempt to achieve peace by offering an explicit defence of public authority in abstract and impersonal terms.

The striking similarity between Britain and the United States lies in their view of the nature of public authority, of its composite and pluralistic character if liberty is to be safeguarded. Their major differences are the product of different geographical situations, in particular the American experience of the frontier; America's economic abundance which reduced perceptions of scarcity; a more complete break with the hierarchical social order of the feudal past in the American case, outside the South (Hartz, 1955); and successive waves of non-British immigrants to the United States. Above all, both countries hold somewhat different conceptions of democracy, with implications for the constitutional shape of public authority. America is more completely wedded to a Lockean individualism; its liberalism takes on a natural, 'matter-of-fact' quality as a common moral code or way of life which itself provides a peculiar sense of community that Europe, with its theocratic, feudal and clerical past, has not known (Hartz, 1955). Nevertheless, the United States appears to be very traditional in institutional terms. Huntington (1968, pp. 125–6) emphasizes that early English immigrants sought to perpetuate what they perceived to be the characteristics of Tudor society, in particular its localism and balance of powers. He quotes (pp. 97–8) Charles McIlwain for support: 'The breach between colonies and mother country was largely a mutual misunderstanding based in part on colonists arguing the case of the old English constitution against the new British constitution.' The American Revolution, like the English revolutions of the previous century, was 'past-minded' and practical (in the tradition of English pre-industrial, rural and small-town, anti-Tory radicalism) rather than speculative. According to Huntington, American politics unites Tudor institutions with the 'modern' late eighteenth century notion of popular sovereignty.

One does not have to accept the thesis of Huntington in full in order to see the historical connections between English and American political institutions (despite their different context) and their distinctiveness from continental European conceptions of the 'public power' and its constituent institutions. Consequently, one can exaggerate the similarities between the American and French revolutions of the eighteenth century: the first was in the tradition of English dissent, sought to appeal to historic rights and political practices, but was required by the circumstances of independence to give an abstract formulation to these rights and practices; the latter was a reaction against, and only comprehensible in terms of, the *ancien régime,* a quite different political heritage.

3   Also unfamiliar to an English-speaking audience is the textbook-manual nature of much writing on the state, highly eclectic in content (drawing on law, history, politics, sociology, etc.) and schematized in form in order to be useful to mass student audiences. As an example, see Ermacora (1970).

4   The 'public power' is an unfamiliar term in the English language. The German term is *öffentliche Gewalt* or *Staatsgewalt.* It denotes the totality of the legal power of decision and administration of a state and refers to the organs of power (*Staatsorgane*) through which the state functions or to the power of rule exercised by an officer appointed to such organs. Distinctions are made between 'constitutional' organs and 'subordinate' organs (which are instructed by constitutional organs), and between creative organs (which can create other organs), organs of will (which form the political will of the state), and executive organs (which apply the will of the state). *Staatsgewalt, Staatsvolk* (those who are 'nationals' of the state, *Staatsangehörigen*) and *Staatsgebiet* (territory) are the three elements of the German idea of the state.

The equivalent French term is *puissance publique* or *puissance étatique* which refers to the totality of 'powers' (*pouvoirs*) of the state. While jurists are sometimes concerned to distinguish power (*potestas*) from force *potentia*), usage is not clearcut, and the term 'public power' often carries the implications of superior force as well as of legal competence. For example, *puissance* is closer to the idea of *potentia, pouvoir* to *potestas.* The Dutch refer to *staatsmacht,* the Norwegians to *statsmakt* and the Danes to *statsmagten.*

5   *Sozialstaat* was a term popularized by the German legal theorist Hermann Heller towards the end of the Weimar Republic, but it can be traced back to Lorenz von Stein (1850). It refers to a state whose legal, economic and social system is founded on the principles of social security (avoidance of material distress for the citizen), social justice and social equality (of opportunity). In contrast to the collectivism and centralization of the 'welfare state' (*Wohlfahrtsstaat*) the state is limited to the function of compensatory assistance for those unable to help themselves (the *Subsidaritätsprinzip*). These principles of 'integration' were also endorsed by Roman Catholic social teaching and had as their purpose 'social peace'. While Heller (1963) saw the principles of the *Sozialstaat* as a necessary corollary to the formal legal rights of the *Rechtsstaat,* a tension remained between the interventionist bias of the former concept and the insistence of the latter on strict depersonalization and delimitation of power. Nevertheless, the *Sozialstaat* helped broaden the concept of the rights of the citizen to incorporate social and economic rights and found its expression in Article 20 of the West German Basic Law according to which the Federal Republic is a 'democratic and social federal state'. This firm anchoring of the idea of social and economic rights in political and legal language did not of course preclude disagreement about the interpretation of shared principles particularly as these rights were not listed in the constitution.

6   On the differences between the ideas of the bourgeois state and the capitalist state, see Lichtheim (1971, pp. 150–2).

7   In fact, Hegel uses 'state' in both a wider and a narrower sense: in the first to refer to the whole social existence of a people, in the second to refer to political arrangements in particular.

8   Thus for a democratic socialist like Fritz Vilmar (1973) democratization is the key concept of politics, creating freedom and equality throughout society and requiring a 'multi-fronted' strategy based on the student movement, economic democracy, citizen action groups, etc. By contrast, Hennis (1970) insists on an analytical distinction between state and society, seeing democracy as possible in the political sphere of the state (where the preconditions of freedom and equality exist) but not in society where inequality is a natural condition.

9   In his survey of political ideas in modern Britain Barker (1978, p. 95) concludes:

> Judicial theory has not constituted a major part of the body of political ideas...the general character of the judicial system and the general assumptions of law have been little considered in debates about the political character and goals of the nation...in general, legal ideas were invisible in the elaboration of political argument.

part i
the historical tradition of the state

chapter one | the origins of the state

The gradual awareness, from the late fifteenth century onwards, that a new kind of political association was emerging in Western Europe led to the search for an appropriate word with which to characterize this new phenomenon. *Lo stato, l'État, der Staat, el estado* or 'the state' came slowly into usage but with little precision or consistency. This lack of clarity reflected in part the complexity of the new experience and of the factors which gave rise to it, in part the very different senses of the Latin word *status* and the generality with which such words as *status* and *stato* were used. By 360 BC the Romans were speaking of the *status Romanus,* but its clearest political meaning was evident in the term *status reipublicae,* which was employed, for example, by Cicero. In the medieval period *status* was primarily non-political in its references and was not used as a word, standing alone, to refer to a political association. It meant the 'condition' of an object or order (by the fifteenth century, also of a person). Later *status* was used to describe a sound, prosperous community or a system of ranks or estates, each with its particular rights and duties. For example, as late as the eighteenth century the English jurist William Blackstone was still referring to the 'civil state' of nobility and commoners as opposed to the military and maritime states. In medieval usage *status* and its derivatives denoted positions of rank and power, whether legally recognized or not; offices and positions of eminence; and the properties and insignia of rank or office, especially the territorial rights which related to the estate of a prince (Dowdall, 1923).

By the fifteenth century, and particularly in the following century after the Dutch Independence, *status* began to acquire a more clearly political sense as a specific form of polity (for example, in the sense of contrasting a 'popular' with a 'monarchical' state). Indeed, as early as the fourteenth century Giovanni Villani was using *stato,* in the manner of Cicero, to mean a body politic of a republican type. *Status* was frequently adopted with a republican tone and was sometimes used to contrast a republic like 'the States' of the United Provinces with a kingdom.[1] Nevertheless, *status* or *stato* was also employed in a proprietary sense. Government was typically seen as a form of property and its problems as akin to those of estate management. During the medieval period emerged the concept of the *status regalis, lo stato del Principe* (Mager, 1968). There was a new emphasis on the authority and prestige of the prince. Hence the term derived in part from medieval recognition of the *status* or estate of a prince, together with the distinct duties and privileges of princes and the expression of those duties and privileges in legal terms (Hexter, 1973). The word *status* or *stato* was subsequently applied to the authority, privileges and property of government, however constituted. German legal historians like Quaritsch (1970) tend to go back before the modern idea of sovereignty to the emergence of the post-feudal *Ständestaat* (polity of estates) at the turn of the thirteenth and fourteenth centuries for the birth of the concept of the state. At that time discussions of Roman law were also making familiar the concept of the public good.

It is easy to exaggerate the speed with which the term state entered into 'official' and 'common' use. For instance, while the great French legists of the sixteenth and seventeenth centuries were much concerned with the term, many continued to use other words: Jean Bodin, *république;* Charles Loyseau, *seigneurerie*. Eventually in the eighteenth century it became a common political term in continental Europe and acquired a rich variety of new meanings. This development was in part related to the extraordinary growth in the production and consumption of printed matter and the exposure of an enlarged literate public to a greater variety of ideas. Printing accelerated the emergence of national language cultures and consequent attempts to unify the peripheral territories culturally around a standard medium of internal communication (Innes, 1950).

The Italian contribution is stressed in the claim that Niccolò Machiavelli provided the 'true and proper foundation of a philosophy of politics . . . which are beyond good and evil . . . which cannot be exorcised and driven from this world with holy water' (Croce, 1925, p. 60). *Stato* was a key word in his work, and he was important in both moving away from medieval use and popularizing the term, particularly in the context of discussions about the 'reason of state' (the idea that politics is characterized by an exceptional morality and rationale).[2] Although Machiavelli contributed a naturalistic view of the state as an autonomous realm, the achievement of man's will, he employed the term in an unsystematic and uncertain way: in *The Prince* narrowly as an inert instrument to be manipulated to preserve or enhance the power of the ruler; and in the *Discourses* rarely as a body politic. *Stato* was hardly ever the subject of an active verb in Machiavelli's writings and, moreover, was used alternatively to refer to 'position' and 'state'. The idea of the state did not acquire the 'inherent nobility' which it was to possess later (Ercole, quoted in Chabod, 1958, p. 117).

The word *Staat* was taken from the Dutch *staat* into High German in the fifteenth century, and its political use during the seventeenth century developed under French and Dutch influence.[3] However, till the late eighteenth century it seems to have been regarded as a cold and exacting abstraction (Weinacht, 1968). In France *estat,* later *état,* was derived from the Latin in the thirteenth century and used by Nicolas Oresme in its political sense in the following century. By 1595 Pierre Charron could offer a modern definition of *l'état* as 'a domination, an ordering involving command and obedience, and . . . the foundation, the internal link, and the guiding spirit of human affairs; it is the bond within society which cannot exist without it, the vital essence which brings life to human and natural associations' (Church, 1969, p. 306). During the seventeenth century Cardinal Richelieu, Bishop Bossuet and Louis XIV made frequent reference to *l'État,* their use of it with a capital letter reflecting its distinctiveness in the French vocabulary.[4] Its entry into the 'official mind' and the meaning which it came to possess was conditioned by the very practical concerns of legists like Charles du Moulin who were employed in the royal administration, the courts and the schools of law. Thus the major contribution of Bodin to the rise of the modern state, his theory of sovereignty, was not simply the product of a speculative mind. He brought his encyclopaedic knowledge to bear on the problem of disorder generated by social changes, religious divisions and the crisis in the relationship of monarchy to the estates. The immediate appeal of his solution lay in its combination of a voluntarism in rule to enable 'controlled change' with an emphasis on the ethical importance of natural law which avoided the notoriety of Machiavelli's 'reason of state'. Machiavelli's writings had, to an even greater degree, been those of the intuitive, imaginative man of affairs concerned about the contemporary problems of disorder in Italy, especially as they affected his native Florence.

It was the practical relevance of the work of the legists that helps explain how by the early seventeenth century state was established as a fundamental legal concept in France. The idea of the state connoted a

territorial unit ruled by a single sovereign; the continuity of royal government and its vast apparatus of offices apart from the mortal life of the king;
and a community enjoying a unity of sentiment as a consequence of living under a common sovereign (Church, 1972). It was a permanent entity
endowed with certain superior purposes. Nevertheless, there remained an
ambiguity in the term which made it difficult to rid it of patrimonial implications. State was closely associated with the idea of estate, whether in the
form of a man's status in society or in the form of property (the two being
closely linked). *L'État* was used ambiguously with reference both to state
and to the king's estate; in English state was a contraction from the word
estate. In addition it was unclear whether there existed in the community
itself principles limiting the princely office, to which appeal could be made
against the ruler, or whether justice inhered in the office of the prince so
that the right of resistance was a logical impossibility. The problem ac-
companying the emergence of the new absolutist state was that though an
impersonal body politic was recognized, the idea of sovereignty remained
distinct and personalized.

THE BIRTH OF THE MODERN STATE

The historical development of the modern state presents a puzzling picture.
It was slow to emerge in theory and practice, and there remain disagreements about when it reached maturity. Prussia is often seen as the paradigm
of the modern state for it seemed to express most vividly the ideal emer-
gent character of a novel association (Hintze, 1967). Bluntschli (1875) saw
the notion of the abstract impersonal state as coming to maturity in 1740
with the accession of Frederick the Great in Prussia and his idea of himself
as 'the first servant of the state' and its chief bureaucrat (Hubatsch, 1975).
In particular, the concept of office (*Amt*) served to objectify the state so
that Kant (1797) could express his sympathy for the republican style of
government in his native Prussia. Other German historians accept Georg
Hegel's view that the 'statelessness' of Germany expressed itself in the
Peace of Westphalia (1648) ending the Thirty Years' War. They see the
end of the Holy Roman Empire in 1806, and the response especially of
Prussian reformers to this dramatic crisis, as the beginning of the modern
abstract state. French scholars like Lucien Febvre and Maurice Hauriou
have tended to see the idea and practice of the state as a peculiar historical and spatial phenomenon which arose at a particular stage of civilization: in France with the 1789 revolution and its radical elimination of the

feudal and patrimonial legacy.[5] Pre-revolutionary France was a 'transitional' case. Eighteenth-century Germany and Spain were even more characterized by medieval particularism, while Prussia and Sweden were in the vanguard of development. Some continental European historians, including the legal historian Otto von Gierke, continued to apply the term state to the medieval period. Thus Heinrich Mitteis (1940) viewed the state as 'any order of the people for the realization of its political purposes' and distinguished the medieval state as an association of persons (*Personenverbandsstaat*) from the modern institutionalized state (*Anstaltsstaat*) and territorial state (*Flächenstaat*). However, Otto Brunner (1954) and Skalweit (1975) expressed the dominant view when they argued that such use of the term and especially of 'the modern state' produced an intolerable confusion of ideas. For reasons which we shall explore later, students of British history have been much less preoccupied with the question of dating the emergence of the concept of the modern state.

The emergence of the idea of the impersonal, abstract state, which controls a consolidated territory and possesses a system of offices that is differentiated from that of other organizations operating in the same territory, was a ramshackle affair, and neither identical nor simultaneous in different countries. 'State-building' was accompanied by immense conflict, uncertainty and failure. The strength and durability of each individual state were dependent on its relationship to the whole system of states and were affected by the different coalitions of classes, past and present, which supported its government. Most efforts to build states failed; a few units survived from a ruthless competition in which most contenders lost (Tilly, 1975, p. 38). The characteristics of the modern state were acquired in a complex flux of disintegration of old political units as forces of particularism or provincialism engendered revolts against the Empire and the Papacy, and of efforts at territorial integration. In addition the period from the mid-fifteenth century to the early eighteenth century witnessed a general crisis in the relation of rulers and ruled (Shennan, 1974). There was (in sixteenth-century France, for instance) a gradual establishment of the notion of individuals as 'subjects', alike in their subordination to the rule of the sovereign, as against the opposition of the special privileges enjoyed by particular localities, provinces and social groups (estates). The idea and practice of the modern state emerged in various ways from diverse local conditions: from calculations springing from personal, especially dynastic, ambitions and fears; from contests between groups whose status was threatened (for example, the nobility) or insufficiently recognized (the rising bourgeoisie, for instance); and from the search for an enduring order in the midst of the appalling consequences of the dynastic, religious, economic and social squabbles which formed the six-teenth- and seventeenth-century crises. By the eighteenth century it was clear, even in Germany, that the legal position of the estates (*Stände*) was becoming increasingly precarious with increasing territorial ownership by the princes, the formation of public services of Roman-law and Cameralist-trained officials and the new importance of princely courts in resolving dis-putes about what constituted the rights and freedoms of estates. It was a period when intellectuals were roused to reflect on a new political problem: the emergence of an unfamiliar form of political association which lacked precision of meaning in terms of what had gone before.

These new uncertainties about political identification and loyalties were related to two fundamental developments. There was, first, the general in-fluence of Italian humanism as it passed northward in the fifteenth and succeeding centuries. On the one hand, it added to the majesty, splendour and reputation of the new Renaissance courts; the prince emerged as the cultivated patron of the arts. On the other, there was a new interest in the secular role of the prince and in temporal problems of conflict and change. The new Renaissance State (Chabod, 1964, p. 26) was seen, notably by Burckhardt, as a 'work of art', the creation of the 'virtuous' prince, rather than as the product of a slow historical process. Machiavelli's concept of *virtu* in opposition to *fortuna* represented a concern for public political purposes and for creating, through the power of will, something differ-ent from, and independent of, necessity. The growth of a new rationalism and scepticism was also apparent within Catholicism (especially among jurists) which experienced a revival of Roman Stoicism. While unprepared to abandon the religious nature and purpose of the state and attacking Machiavelli, the concept of political prudence and an attempt to formulate a Catholic reason of state preoccupied political writers in Italy, Spain, the Low Countries and, later, France. The powerful *politique* party in sixteenth-century France prepared the way not only for divine-right sovereignty but also for the important *raison d'état* discusssion during Richelieu's period as First Minister. However, Richelieu's official propagandists strove con-stantly to fit *raison d'état* into a traditional theological view: it was to be 'the Reason of the Catholic and Monarchical State' in which the monarch, as the embodiment of justice, was the arbiter of a body politic composed of estates, orders and corps (Church, 1972).[6]

The process of secularization was exhibited in a number of ways. Philosophically, it was apparent in the development of natural philosophy and the rationalism of Descartes, Leibniz and Wolff. Above all, there was the rediscovery of Aristotle's *Politics,* whose concept of a self-contained, self-sufficient community, the *polis,* shifted emphasis away from the unity of the Christian community and encouraged, notably at the University of Paris in the thirteenth and fourteenth centuries, a naturalism in political writing (Ullmann, 1975). In the legal realm jurists shifted their attention from customary law to universal principles of natural law (Samuel Pufendorf's systematization and secularization of natural law is an example of this) and to Roman law concepts of public power. Socially and economically, there was the rise of modern capitalism and a growing resentment at the static pattern of rights and duties imposed by feudal society.

In addition to the influence of Italian humanism there was the more complex influence of the Reformation which both ruptured the religious unity of the Christian community and created domestic schisms. On the one hand, Martin Luther's teaching helped to fragment the Holy Roman Empire and to establish the idea of the charitable role of the secular authorities in place of monastic charity: on the other, the revived Augustinianism of the so-called Catholic Renaissance which gripped early seventeenth-century France underpinned the missionary role of Catholic monarchs in purging sin through promoting faith. These religious upheavals assisted a consolidation of princely power as agents of religious revolution or as defenders of Christian tradition. The influence of the Reformation was felt even in those countries where it failed to establish itself. It was only after the bitterness and slaughter of the religious wars of the sixteenth and seventeenth centuries that the notion of a neutral public power began to emerge: one which, like Ludwig von Seckendorff's *Christen-stat* (1685), held to Christian principles but gave priority to the secular purposes of protecting life and providing order and peace rather than to the imposition of one particular religious truth (Quaritsch, 1970, p. 293; Schnur, 1962). Hence the emergence of the idea of the neutrality of the state is not simply to be understood as the product of a rising bourgeoisie identifying its economic interests with the universal interests of the state. A dramatic instance of the process of secularization came in 1721, when Peter the Great undercut the secular political power of the Roman Orthodox Church and replaced a theocratic concept of the tsar's role with the idea of the impersonal state of which the tsar was both servant and guide. Subjects were required to take two oaths of loyalty: to the monarch and to the state (Shennan, 1974, p. 65).

There was a new element of force in politics and, in the context of the abridgement of political rights and the resistance of ordinary people which accompanied the expansion of state power, a sense of the break-down of traditional authority and of a need to redefine the basis of the authority of the ruler. In a situation of flux and tension it was clear that a static conception of the ruler as the arbiter of the traditional rights and priv-ileges of various groups was inadequate. It was Bodin who provided the solution to this problem by incorporating the element of 'will' as well as those of administration and adjudication in his crucially important theory of royal sovereignty. The ruler was a legislator, supreme or 'absolute' with respect to civil law, albeit limited by divine, natural and fundamental law. This consolidation of the authority of the ruler went along with a growth of governmental activities and of new, more rational, forms of administra-tion. Two intellectual groups which supported this development were the jurists (most prominently the French) and the German Cameralists of the eighteenth century. In Germany, however, the tensions between these two groups grew: the Cameralists were concerned with an efficient interven-tionist administration, while the jurists became anxious about control of the public power.

The new claims of the prince were buttressed by threats to the state of external aggression as rival dynasties made their territorial claims. Moreover, international commercial rivalries, inspired by the Dutch, sug-gested the need for government regulation of economic affairs, of the kind exemplified by Colbert's mercantilism in France. This dramatic change in the climate of international relations and the imminence and extent of warfare produced not only a new permanent diplomatic organization but also a sharper awareness of the problem of ends and means in politics, and of whether politics possessed a special ethic. The intensity of external threat helps to explain the appearance of an influential literature on *ragion di stato* in sixteenth-century Italy as well as the internal character of the new state itself: for example, Frederick William's campaign against the estates in Prussia and the emergence there of a bureaucratic/military state, in which the bureaucracy arose to complement the army by supervising the quartering and supply of troops and, moreover, was linked to it by per-sonal ties through common recruitment from the landed nobility. Hintze (1962a) has emphasized the importance of the model of the *Commissarius,* an office of military origin, to the civil administration of the new absolutist Prussian state.

The idea and practice of the modern state were forged out of con-flict involving medieval parliaments which centralizing rulers sought to extinguish or make subservient; the Church, as rulers attempted to acquire its authority and thereby extend their moral function in relation to their subjects; and the nobility who were either drawn into the service of the prince as members of the royal administration (as in Italy and Sweden) or ceded influence to a bourgeoisie rising as powerful officers (as in France). There was a close historical connection between the increase in 'stateness', the expansion of armed forces, rises in taxation and popular rebellion. The costs of state-building were high, and early states were characterized by immense corruption and waste. In particular, offices served, in Richelieu's phrase, 'to keep the people to their duty' and so to create a new 'fourth' estate whose interests were allied to those of the prince. Pursuit of office emerged as a new social and political phenomenon: office generated new policy initiatives (Chabod, 1964). At the same time the expense of this new Renaissance State, and the threat the new hierarchy of offices posed to the status of traditionally powerful families, were major factors in the seventeenth-century crisis between state and society across Europe. This crisis led in France to reform and in Britain to revolution (Trevor-Roper, 1967). Nevertheless, the sale of offices in France encouraged an exploitation of office for personal gain, in terms of both clientelism and profit, and underlines the difference between this new phenomenon of office and Max Weber's characterization of modern bureaucracy. It was only during the eighteenth century that the idea of a personal, private relationship to the prince was replaced by the concept of a professional relationship to a permanent impersonal state. A professional commitment to social improvement, rational action and the general welfare was impressed upon the official mind by the Cameralists and Christian Wolff and his disciples in Germany and by the physiocrats and *philosophes* in France. Particularly after 1763 the Prussian administration acquired a growing independence and began to play a more innovatory role in domestic policy (Johnson, 1975).

THE CHARACTERISTICS OF THE MODERN STATE: THE CONTINENTAL EUROPEAN PERSPECTIVE

Despite the diversity of experience, and the way in which the ideas of self-containment (from the *polis*) and of law (from the *civitas*) have influenced how theorists have interpreted this experience, it is possible to identify certain common characteristics which, in the continental European view, distinguish the state as a historical experience from the Greek and Roman forms of political association. German theorists have traditionally identified three elements: a *Staatsgebiet* (which term suggests its distinct territorial character compared with other political formations), whose 'nationals' (*Staatsvolk*) acquired a certain sentiment of community like, for example, that of nationhood and were ruled by a common centralized authority (*Staatsgewalt*) able to make as well as to apply and guarantee law.

In the first place, the state was seen as a new element of society: a structure of authority and a mechanical organization of constraint (Prélot, 1957). The special quality of its authority was expressed by the new concept of sovereignty: that 'absolute and perpetual power', in Bodin's (1962, p. 84) classic formulation, 'over citizens and subjects in a commonwealth'. By the nineteenth century, however, it had become apparent to some jurists that the use of 'power' in the definition of sovereignty had proved a source of confusion implying, for example, the possibility of its 'unconditional' or 'limitless' character. In Bodin's theory the logic of order in a dynamic situation was an ultimate decision-maker, whose authority was absolute and unique in the sense of final and binding equally on all its subjects (Stankiewicz, 1969). So abstract a formulation left, of course, a whole variety of questions to be answered, particularly about the manner in which such authority was to be distributed and exercised and the conditions by which it was to be acquired. These constitutional questions involved the clash of claims to rule on the basis of divine right, hereditary succession, virtue or democratic consent and provided some of the most dramatic political issues for the new association.

Besides its novel legal character, the state was also recognized as a distinct apparatus of power that was able to use an increasingly sophisticated mechanical and social technology to control human conduct. This aspect of the state has appealed to political 'realists' like Machiavelli and nineteenth- and early twentieth-century German theorists of the *Machtstaat*, who were obsessed by external physical threats to the survival of the state in an unstable international environment.[7] They insisted, moreover, that the authority of the ruler at home was inadequate alone to ensure loyalty and survival if resources of power were meagre. In the view of Carl Schmitt (1932), for example, what was necessary if a state were to maintain a claim to loyalty was an effective sovereign, a source of authority with a monopoly and unity of power to enforce its decisions and uphold order. His scepticism about the Weimar Republic and his willingness to accept the conception of the *Führerstaat* during the Third Reich resulted from the argument that the liberal legal norms of the conception of the *Rechtsstaat* were an empty façade, premised on shared understanding, when effective politics required a capacity to recognize and deal with one's enemies (Schwab, 1970). The issue of effectiveness also attracted twentieth-century exponents of a scientific view of politics, which saw the state in the mechanical terms of 'inputs' and 'outputs', 'pressures' and 'communication', and envisaged its central problem to be its 'steering capacity'.

Second, there was a recognition that the state was a society, with a peculiar form of collective life whose nature and purpose needed to be clarified. Its character as an association has been a topic of various disputes (Oakeshott, 1975). For some it was a divine institution to be understood theologically as a gift of God to prevent anarchy (Luther) or as the product of a God-given sociability (von Seckendorff). By contrast, to Johannes Althusius and Gottfried Leibniz, both of whom were influenced by Aristotle, it was a natural community to be understood in anthropological terms as a necessary consequence of man's needs. Immanuel Kant viewed the state in formalistic, sociological terms. It was an *a priori* requirement of the rule of pure reason. To the French jurist Léon Duguit the state was essentially an artefact, to be understood in utilitarian terms as a mechanism arising out of the division of labour by which the performance of certain functions on behalf of society was ensured. For Adhémar Esmein the state was conventional, the product of an 'anti-social contract' by which men agreed to prefer the discipline of rules to the 'brutish' world of a society of men exercising their individual free wills. Hauriou viewed it as historically acquired. The state was a phenomenon of consciousness. Hegel linked it to the development of particular powers of the mind, to the emergence of self-consciousness with the development of labour and property relations. The *Volkstaat* of Johannes Gottfried von Herder represented a natural process of organic growth in history: the concept of organism, suggesting a natural and indissoluble community, was allied to a philosophy of history.

Another fundamental dispute concerned the proper activities of this association. There were those like the younger Fichte, Wilhelm von Humboldt (1947), Kant and Klein who hesitated to acknowledge that the state had any common substantive purpose (other than security or the assurance of legal freedom) and preferred to see it in terms of certain moral rules of conduct within which subjects could pursue their own ends. It proved impossible, however, to obtain agreement about the proper purposes of the state. If Bodin was content with security and tranquillity, Leibniz saw the state as concerned with 'the whole life and the common good' and providing 'institutionalized charity'. Cameralists like J. H. G. von Justi emphasized the welfare purpose of the state, whereas the later Fichte and Herder attributed a more impressive cultural mission to the state. Underlying these two disputes—about the character of the bonds and of the purpose of this new association—was the problem posed by the state's origins in diversity: just how much uniformity should be imposed on so heterogeneous an association?

ENGLAND: AN ABERRANT CASE

The earliest political use of the word state in England was in 1538 by Thomas Starkey, who was strongly influenced by Italian sources. It entered into greater use during the sixteenth century and even into official language in, for example, the Act of Supremacy of 1558 and the new office of Secretary of State. Raleigh's 'Maxims of State' (1618) referred to the state as 'the frame or set order of a commonwealth, or of the governors that rule the same'. There was, however, a preference for such terms as 'realm', 'body politic' and 'commonwealth'. Indeed, at the level of political ideas, the sixteenth century witnessed a fresh expression, rather than dislodgement of, medieval conceptions of the meaning and purpose of the social and political order (Allen, 1928; Eccleshall, 1978). One inheritance from the Middle Ages was the notion of the Christian commonwealth, an idea of a people as common members of one body co-operating for the general welfare. The terms 'commonwealth' and 'common weal' (the latter referring to the welfare of all members of society) were the hallmark of Thomas Cromwell and the intellectuals like Starkey with whom he associated. If the paternalistic concept of the 'common weal' underpinned the major social and economic policies of the Cromwell period (Elton, 1973), it embodied an attempt to strengthen rather than overthrow the existing order. Nevertheless, what Beer (1965) has called the Old Toryism of the sixteenth and early seventeenth centuries intimated the idea of the state, in its emphasis on paternalism, the organic unity of society under the Crown and the independent authority of monarchical government as the diviner of the public interest. Indeed, into the twentieth century Toryism was to retain a loose sense of the state in its political vocabulary. England was, moreover, not notably slow in adopting an imprecise term like the Crown. Use of the Crown as a symbol above and beyond the king and indicating the residuum of rights and privileges that he enjoyed temporarily can be traced back in both England and France to the middle of the twelfth century.

At the level of political practice England appeared to share more obviously in general European development during the sixteenth century. The Tudors, aware of their 'majesty', were pioneers of the new Renaissance State, and the central figures of their period were great administrators like Cardinal Wolsey, Thomas Cromwell and the two Cecils. Even so, a society which had by the late medieval period acquired a unitary character could rely on collaborators at the local level. By contrast, a particularistic society like France was held together by a vast apparatus of *local* servants of the king, a phenomenon unknown in England. The 'mosaic' character of France reflected the successive absorption of areas with distinct traditions and institutions and depended on formalized controls for its unity (Strayer, 1970). The Tudor 'revolution in government' was only revolutionary in English terms.[8] In the absence of continuous threats of invasion, and in the context of the veto powers of the Commons, the English monarchy did not develop the sort of administrative, financial and military base which might have enabled it to withstand the seventeenth-century crisis (Stone, 1965).

The pattern of sharing in European development was apparent even in the Puritan Revolution of 1640–60 which was part of a general crisis of the Renaissance State. However, a combination of rigid, unimaginative statesmanship and a crisis in the relationship of the court with a powerful group like the gentry (rather than with the peasantry, as in the French Frondes) produced the greatest revolution in England. From the seventeenth century onwards England departed from general European development. The political and legal concept of the state was not developed and the term little used, while after the experience of the Protectorate even the concept of the commonwealth fell into disrepute.[9] Reference was made to kingdom, country, people, nation and government. The term state was occasionally used as a synonym for the nation or community as a whole, for example by Blackstone and Edmund Burke, but not as an expression for the legal personality of the executive or as a collective term for the whole or part of the machinery of government.

At the level of international relations the English, like the Americans, were able to recognize themselves as a state. Their polities represented independent political communities, 'sovereign' units in international affairs and absolved from the requirement to recognize any external authority as superior. In Britain the exercise of prerogative powers by the Crown in the realm of foreign affairs is generally referred to as an Act of State, while the Foreign Office has maintained a special, aloof status within the governmental system. The terms 'State Department' and 'Secretary of State' reflect the distinctive quality of the foreign affairs function within American government. In France or Western Germany, where the idea of the state as an institution embraces domestic policy, this kind of distinction within government is less obvious; government as a whole shares in the notion of the uniqueness of the state. Britain does, therefore, share with other West European societies an idea of the state as a territorial phenomenon referring to an entity which intereacts with other such entities (as well as, see Chapter 7, an occasional functional concern about the proper activities of the 'state' and the conditions for the effective discharge of these activities). For example, after 1945 political observers (like Smith, 1978) began to query—with reference to Britain and other West European societies—whether the idea of the state as a territorial association was any longer adequate for the discharge of the proper functions of the 'state', particularly for the effective provision of physical security and the management of economic and industrial affairs. A utilitarian argument for integration of states into a wider and more flexible political community appeared to be complemented by evidence—provided, for example, by new pressures from below in favour of a territorial diffusion of power— that popular sentiments were no longer as attached to the idea of the state as a territorial association.

From the seventeenth century onwards England's political development displayed a remarkable continuity from its medieval roots. One reason for this divergence from the European norm was the character of the medieval heritage from which it sprang. The English medieval community was, comparatively speaking, highly integrated and effective (Strayer, 1970). Unity under one monarch had been achieved as early as the tenth century, and a sense of national identity had emerged by the fifteenth century. The political system rested on a complex process of bargaining between the Crown and the great landed magnates which had, by the early seventeenth century, given way to a pattern of co-operation and conflict between 'Country', which was represented in the Commons, and 'Court'. Monarchical authority was viewed as conditional. The monarch was not above or outside the community but was a member of the 'community of the realm'. While his authority might be in an ultimate sense derived from

God, he had an immediate responsibility to his fellow lords. Out of the medieval idea of 'the king's two bodies', a mortal body natural and a body politic, derived the Puritan view that it might be necessary to 'fight the king to defend the king'. In France, by contrast, a more theocratic conception of kingship and its close relation to the notion of 'lordship' made it more difficult for ideas of constitutionalism and parliamentarianism to develop. By the reign of Edward I the English Parliament had already established itself as a major aspect of medieval society. Soon the notion was being proclaimed that Parliament embodied the whole community of the realm. At the same time monarchs (like Henry VIII, in his severing of England's ties with Rome) found it useful to use the statutory method of 'king-in-parliament' to establish the supreme law of the land (Dicey, 1895). In the process the Commons established a taste for statutory power. Moreover, unlike its continental European equivalents, Parliament had acquired a basis of territorial representation; it became the principal location for the articulation and aggregation of territorial interests. It was no longer just an assembly of estates of the realm. From a European perspective the Glorious Revolution of 1688 appeared radical, establishing consent as the principle of authority. From an English perspective, however, it was a conservative settlement which appealed to the importance of safeguarding the traditional rights and privileges of Parliament, the courts and local communities against the claims of centralizing monarchy. Public action was made relatively unobtrusive and amenable to parliamentary and local control. The subsequent gradual extension of public activity, legitimated by Parliament and local government, was not justified by reference to the notion of an autonomous state acting to realize certain inherent purposes. It took the form of a maze of statutes, the complex product of contending political groups seeking to realize their versions of the general interest through representative institutions.

The notion that sovereignty resided in Crown-in-Parliament represented a continuity with medieval institutions. An aloof monarchical executive, with a private, personalized and secretive conception of government, was made to coexist with (though maintaining some separation from) the increasingly public politics of Parliament. Nevertheless, the key feature of post-seventeenth-century political thought was that it focused on Parliament and the representative system rather than the Crown. As a notion of political rule representation was theoretically more highly developed than the concept of the Crown and was, in addition, more sympathetic to a vigorously politicking society of parties and groups. (The devolution debate of the 1970s was, for example, concerned with the character of the representative system; the Crown yielded little in the way of prescriptions about the nature of the political order.) As a general idea Crown-in-Parliament was capable of supporting different theories of representation (Beer, 1965) and was compatible with different interpretations of institutional relationships: eighteenth-century Whig ideas of a 'balanced' constitution; nineteenth-century Liberal ideas of the supremacy of Commons over Lords and of the collective and individual responsibility of ministers to Parliament (rather than to the monarch); and twentieth-century collectivist views on the role of party in integrating Parliament and government. While the monarchical tradition remained, there was a gradual shift to the idea that the executive power was an emanation of, or an agency of, Parliament.

Although the constitutional formula of Crown-in-Parliament was flexible, it precluded two options: the notion that the executive power was an emanation of the state was too reminiscent of past claims of absolute monarchy, while the idea of the nation as the state, with the associated constitutional concept of the people as citizens with rights rather than as subjects, was too radical. There was no attempt to systematize the relationship of the individual to the state. The seventeenth-century constitutional settlement was one between the distinct constituent powers of king, Lords and Commons and did not involve the people acting as a constituent power. Consequently, there was no formal distinction between the constituent power (the people as a unity) and constituted powers, and no notion of a distinct 'public power' which had been established by the people and which required its own public law. As Burke observed, the events of 1688–9 were 'a revolution, not made, but prevented', a revolution against both absolutism and the radicalism of the commonwealth (Forsyth, forthcoming). Maitland (1901) brought out the legacy of the monarchical tradition when he argued: 'Just because the King is no part of the people, the People cannot be the State or Commonwealth.' The English constitutional formula linked the public to the executive power through Parliament, which became the arena for the complex processes of co-operation and conflict between Court and Country. However, it encouraged neither an active role for the people nor an activist conception of an executive power predisposed to educate and mobilize—not just react to—public opinion. A further consequence was an anthropomorphic conception of government. The hitching of monarchical prerogatives on to parliamentarianism, combined with ministerial responsibility, meant that governments became personified in the 'over-life-size' role of ministers. Powers were conferred by statute on a named person, not on the impersonal state as a corporation, and were exercised in his, not the ministry's, name.

The continuity of the forms and essence of medieval government, which helps to explain the absence of state as a political concept, is to be understood partly in terms of the absence of powerful neighbours with adjacent land frontiers. In continental Europe a practical concern with state-building and an intellectual interest in *raison d'état* stemmed from a perceived need for a vigorous response to the combination of enemies abroad with factionalism and the threat of disorder at home (on sixteenth-century Sweden and Russia, Shennan, 1974; on France, Church, 1972). There was an attempt, in the context of protracted challenges and vulnerabilities, to construct an elaborate ideology that would justify existing or new institutions and the dependence of subjects on these institutions. An emphasis on formal controls reflected a declining ability to rely on informal collaborative arrangements in territorial politics. By contrast, the English settlement of 1688 left a fragile structure of politics which gradually constructed, or rather reconstructed, a set of political understandings. British politics was, and is still, to be understood in terms of an informal and subtle 'operational code', which comprises certain working assumptions but has no 'superstructure' of theoretical elaboration (Bulpitt, 1978). Its ideal was the practice of civility. In place of developing the Crown as an impersonal concept, an attempt was made to distinguish between 'high' and 'low' politics. 'High' politics was to be settled in Whitehall, as far as possible independently of external pressure; 'low' politics was a matter of politicking. As regards territorial politics within the United Kingdom, the informal collaborative arrangements of indirect rule were preferred to the formal controls associated with the idea of the unitary state.

A further reason for the absence of the idea of the state is to be found in the medieval character of law and of a legal profession that did not evolve the idea of the state as a formally recognized legal institution, subject to its own distinct norms and procedures and integrating diverse institutions. Both the legal profession, organized around the medieval Inns of Court rather than as a public service, and the language of law itself are noticeably remote from politics. On the one hand, the judiciary has a fierce independence; on the other, law is not regarded as the great interpreter of the pattern of politics. In comparison with continental Europe there remains a sceptical attitude towards the role of formalized and elaborate procedures in social life, a 'wholesome English contempt for legal technique' and an aversion to 'the petrifying action of juristic theory' (Maitland, 1901); a less imperative, more discretionary attitude towards the application of law (evident in the field of public prosecution); a more relaxed attitude towards using the law to regulate the power of organized groups, leading to a proliferation of autonomous private associations which remain 'unincorporated' and take advantage of the flexible English private-law concept of the 'trust'; and a political process which can be better understood in terms of a network of informal relations between roles and personalities than in terms of the formalization of office, with its rational allocation of authority and responsibilities and the possibility of authoritative legal interpretations. The elitist character of a 'clublike' world of 'high politics' dependent on mutual recognition rather than office in the sphere of public affairs is complemented by a wider unwillingness to develop public-law regulation of private relationships and a preference to allow forms of voluntary self-organization.

In England an evolutionary judge-made common law served as an instrument of unification. As the common law ceded pride of place to statute law, which expressed parliamentary supremacy, it was quite unable to provide a body of public-law principles in terms of which legislation could be framed. Hence the Rule of Law became a narrow, formal concept expressing a procedural philosophy and losing the substantive concerns that were apparent even in Dicey's later classic formulation (1895). By contrast, legal unification in continental Europe was the product of Roman law, which imported, as we shall see, distinctive ideas about the character of the 'public power' and involved the academic profession, to a much greater degree, in the systematic arrangement of its concepts. It is difficult for the Englishman to appreciate fully the political importance attached by continental Europeans to the reception of Roman law. The law was conceived of and developed as the articulation of the state, as a distinctive, binding and enforceable system. Its principles were identified as the principles of the public power, the elaborators of these principles as the fulcrum of the state. England did, of course, experience the Renaissance and the Reformation and gained from these two movements a sense of 'stateness', of the secular character of political affairs and of being an independent and sovereign political community (Skinner, 1979). However, England was not deeply affected by the other important movement—'the Reception'—that severed modern from medieval history and facilitated the emergence of the idea of the state as the public institution acting in the name of public authority and the general interest.

Britain exemplifies one extreme in the range of, and variation in, ideas about the character of collective arrangements in Western Europe. It represents in particular a disinclination to explore ideas about the distinctive character of public authority. Little or no attention is paid to state as a political concept which identifies the nation in its corporate and collectivist capacity; as a legal institution with an inherent responsibility for regulating matters of public concern; and as a socio-cultural phenomenon which expresses a new, unique form of associative bond. Whereas the continental European concept of the state referred to a living entity and inspired that entity, the Crown remained a theoretically undeveloped and lifeless abstraction. On the executive side, there was just a bundle of officials, united only by 'a mysterious Crown which serves chiefly as a bracket to unite an indefinite series of integers' (Barker, 1915, p. 101). On the legislative side, Britain lacked an idea of emancipation from civil society. Although Parliament was at the centre of the political system, it was composed of members of civil society and hence, according to Hegel (1894, p. 272), 'objective freedom or rational right is rather sacrificed to formal freedom and particular private interests'. The temptation to label Crown-in-Parliament the state institution is avoided once it is recognized that this institution does not embody, or represent a part of, the more extensive idea of the state outlined in Chapter 8.

It is instructive (see also p. 72) to compare British experience with the fate of the word state in another monarchical society, Sweden.[10] Sweden is also interesting because it exemplifies that it is possible for the idea of the state to exist without the word. *Rike* (cf. German *Reich*) was a traditional term used to refer to the 'realm' or kingdom and incorporating, like the later word *stat*, a reference both to governmental machinery and the population. As a result, the distinction between *rike* and *stat* (as between *rijk* and *staat* in Dutch) was by no means clearcut. The word *stat* was not used in the original composition of the 1809 constitution. It was not until the nineteenth century that liberal influence (the Swedish liberals were under the French spell) led to a growing use of the term in both political language and legal debate. Constitutional law (*statsrätt*) and political science (*statskunskap* or *statsvetenskap*) became concerned with the constitutional state (*konstitutionellstat*) or 'state based on law' (*rättsstaten*). Ministers were called *statsråd* (counsellors of state). The term Crown, unlike in Britain, fell slowly out of use until it referred primarily to the fiscal or economic aspects of the state (for example, to the state as landowner). During the twentieth century *stat* began to be used in all contexts relating to central government and its activities (as opposed to local government). Before the 1974 constitution the notion of king, government, administration, courts, Parliament and associated authorities as components of the more important and central concept of the state had taken firm root. It was a highly generalizing, comprehensive concept of key importance in describing public organization. The new constitution confirmed it as the basic political and legal term. *Regering* (government) is now used in the narrow sense to refer to the cabinet, but designations of prime minister (*staatsminister*) and other ministers (*statsråd*) indicate its prevalence even in this context. Official language is pervaded by the term: the state administration, the civil servant (*statstjänsteman*), state police, state railways, state planning authority, etc. In Britain, by contrast, terms like 'public' (as in public corporations, public inquiries), 'national' (as in National Economic Development Council, National Enterprise Board) and 'British' (as in British Railways, British Airways) are used variously but without any clear organizing principle. One reason for the infrequent use of the term state in Britain (as in state papers or state secrets) is that it is rarely resorted to in law—with the exception of Acts of State and the possibility of being imprisoned for acts contrary to the interests of the state under the Official Secrets Act of 1911. Although the concept of the state was not deeply explored by Swedish jurists, constitutional law was seen to be dealing with the legal relations and functions of the organs of the state (Ross, 1959–60). The actions of these organs were attributed to the state because they were its instruments.[11]

NOTES

1   In a paper on 'The Birth of the Dutch Republic' Professor G. N. Clark quotes an anonymous English author writing about 1626 as alleging that 'the word "State" was learned by our neighbourhood and commerce with the Low Countrys, as if we were, or affected to be governed by States. This the Queen saw and hated' (quoted in Marshall, 1971, p. 15).

2   Whilst Machiavelli may have had the idea of *ragion di stato,* he did not use the phrase. It appeared first in Della Casa and Guicciarcini and became current later in the sixteenth century. The French usage, *raison d'état,* began in the late sixteenth century.

3   In Dutch the word *staat* was employed for the political organization as a whole and *Staaten* (capitalized and plural) for the representative assemblies (the States of the provinces and the States General). By contrast, the French word *état* (usually capitalized) was used for both.

4   These individuals did, however, see the state differently. 'For Richelieu, of comparatively modest origin . . . the State . . . was a sort of formidable idol, to be served by methods of terror. For Henry IV, and for lesser men like Francis I and Louis XIV, the State was no Leviathan but something accessible and personal—their own domain, their family, themselves' (Guérard, 1965).

5   C. J. Friedrich (1952, pp. 215–16) offers a different, and even more precise, dating of the birth of the idea of the state. 'I am more obligated to the state,' Louis XIII declared on the famous 'Day of Dupes', 11 November 1630, when he rejected the Queen Mother and her claims for family in favour of Cardinal Richelieu and his claims for the state. According to Friedrich: 'More than any other single day, it may be called the birthday of the modern state.'

6   It would be wrong to conclude that divine right and reason of state got along easily with one another. The revocation of the Edict of Nantes of 1685 and the subsequent expulsion of Huguenots showed that these two royalist doctrines were as much enemies as friends.

7   'Between state and power in themselves there is perhaps no difference for the idea of a state originates in the idea of a certain independence which cannot be maintained without the corresponding power' (Leopold Ranke, quoted in Meinecke, 1957). Heinrich Treitschke, his successor in the chair of history at Berlin, was even more 'realistic': 'In the first place, the second place, and in the third place, the essence of the state is power' (quoted in Meinecke, 1957, p. 399). However, not all theorists who were influenced by the realistic perspective on the origin of the state found that it provided a satisfactory account of the development of the state (see Oppenheimer, 1926). While the Austrian sociologist and national liberal Gustav Ratzenhofer (1893) argued that 'absolute enmity is the essential characteristic of all politics' and that 'the essence of politics is so repulsive', he believed that the conquest state (*Frobererstaat*) would eventually evolve into a cultural state (*Kulturstaat*) of relative social equality and peace. On Ratzenhofer's influence on early American sociology, see Aho (1975).

8   Keir (1967) emphasizes that the Tudors gained absolute supremacy over the Church and not over Parliament, the common law or local administration. The Tudors relied in particular on the local gentry who had acquired important administrative as well as judicial functions as Justices of the Peace. Francis Bacon noted that the Justices of the Peace were an institution that made England unique.

    The interesting aspect of English development is that its kings had such success as nation-builders without creating a 'state-service' elite. It is notoriously difficult to find a distinction between medieval and modern times in England. When can separate government departments be clearly distinguished from the king's household: before or during the 'Tudor revolution in government' (Elton's term)? When have 'public servants' acquired a status different from that of the king's 'private' servants? The source of this problem of demarcation lies in the unitary character and sense of identity of English late medieval society and in the flexibility and adaptability of its institutions. Consequently, even the most turbulent periods of English history (the Norman Conquest, the Reformation, the Civil War and 1688) did not interrupt traditions or suppress old institutions in favour of revolutionary new devices. King and Parliament, the common law, local self-government and even a professional civil service were apparent in medieval England and persist in twentieth-century Britain (Fischer and Lundgreen, 1975).

9   The 'backwoods' gentry, which supported the revolutionary situation of the 1640s and 1650s and provided the majority of members of Parliament, were indignant at the extravagance and parasitism of the Court. However, they possessed no clear new political ideas about the form of government. The gentry and Oliver Cromwell, who was one of their ranks, looked *back* to an Elizabethan age of decentralization, concern for the 'common weal' and harmony of Court and Parliament. They destroyed persons, not institutions: parliamentarians and the king, not Parliament and the throne. These institutions were cleaned out and left temporarily vacant (Trevor-Roper, 1967, pp. 348–50).

10   The example of Sweden is also instructive because it shared less obviously and directly in continental European development than the monarchical societies of Denmark, Norway and the Netherlands. For examples of the role of the state as an organizing concept in Denmark, see Andersen (1954), Ross (1959–60), Kauffeldt (1958), Hoffmeyer (1962) and Philip (1947). On Norway, see Castberg (1947).

Unlike Sweden or the Netherlands, Ireland uses the term state as a substitute for Crown: the attributes of the Crown as a legal concept are simply shifted to the term state. However, state does not carry the range of meanings involved in continental European usage, largely because its meaning is established within a framework of common law. A similar substitution would be possible for Britain but would not involve participation in the state tradition with which this study is concerned.

11   Of central importance is the fact that the legal ties of Scandinavia, like its geography, are much closer to continental Europe than to England or America. Scandinavia represents one of the several families of the civil-law group of countries, a group which is united more by its formal technique than by its content or even by its roots in Roman law (Sundberg, 1969). The Scandinavian countries share two central characteristics with continental Europe (see Chapter 4): the drive towards legal simplicity and consistency through codification, and the bureaucratic, public-service character of judicial office whose occupants are recruited from and trained in the universities (where law courses are tailored to meet the needs of state service) and form a career service. Administrative and judicial functions are regarded as closely akin; in both cases the primary duty is the application of the law (Strömberg, 1962). Although Scandinavian codes are more fragmentary than is typical of continental

codes and there is moreover no 'general part', German *Rechtswissenschaft* (legal science) played an important role in making and developing law. Thus, Norwegian legal scholars tended to pursue studies at continental universities and to avoid the common-law world in which the law was seen as above all a courtroom game, and the major legal problem was held to be the procedural one of 'due process'. In Scandinavia it is normal to appoint to judicial office men who have helped to draft statutes in the service of the central ministries and consequently possess a strong spirit of officialdom. English and American law may have had some influence on Scandinavian law and even on continental law in general: for example, the Uppsala school showed an interest in Anglo-American jurisprudence. However, this interest in the world of common law reflected the glamour of the big and successful and coincided with the outcome of two world wars. It did not influence the essentials of legal life and actual legislation (Sundberg, 1969). Scandinavia has remained firmly within a legal tradition that is different from that of the common law.

chapter | the state as a socio-cultural
two | phenomenon*

While appreciating the complexity of dynamic historical forces that have encouraged or retarded the development of the state as idea and institution, it is helpful to try to establish an element of order in this development. In particular, the idea of the state and its expression in institutional arrangements have generated very different kinds of response in society. This chapter seeks to identify the various types of 'political world pictures' that have accompanied the emergence of the state as idea and institution.

The empirical and nominalistic temper of Anglo-American historiography and political science inclines scholars to reject the idea of the state as a myth that masks reality and to see it as a suitable case for demystification through the study of real events and that which can be directly observed. They have made little attempt to analyse its role both as part of the more or less coherent, more or less elaborate 'meaning structures' or 'political world pictures' used by Europeans to interpret and respond to their political experience and as an essential abstract idea which informs their institutional arrangements. The assumptions that underlie these European institutional arrangements, 'political world pictures' and attitudes towards the political accommodation of interests are as much a product of the degree of elaboration and articulation of 'stateness' as of the nature of social development. A twofold axis of variation based on these variables (see figure on p. 49) is one way of devising a model that will both distinguish different forms of political experience and facilitate identification of the predominant type of political organization in a concrete political situation.[1]

---

* This chapter appears, in a somewhat modified form, in the journal *West European Politics,* May 1980.

Conceptions of Public Authority

	'Stateless'		State	
	Feudal	Ständestaat/Personalized/Patrimonial	Clientelist/Patronage	State
Type of Society				
Gemeinschaft	Balanced Parliamentary	'Crisis-of-modernity' (i) bureaucratic dominance (ii) parliamentary/party dominance (iii) balanced	Dual	Crisis zone*
Gesellschaft	Adversary/Competitive	Authoritarian corporatist — Crisis zone*	Accommodative/Liberal Corporatist	

* The two crisis zones incorporate respectively: *Ständestaat*, personalized, authoritarian corporatist, and parliamentary and dual. They intersect in the 'modernity–crisis' polity.

It is a model which focuses upon the character of the authority relations contained within the 'associative' bonds that hold men together in state and society. The central premise is that 'political world pictures', in terms of which political conduct is defined, and attitudes towards the accommodation of interests typical of different polities are closely related to an experience of authority (both its organizational/procedural form and the manner or style of its exercise) exercised through both public institutions and a particular set of social relations. It is the character of this experience and the degree of congruence between experience of authority in state and society that yield the categories of polity employed in this model. These categories of polity are, of course, ideal types: in other words, a given political system at a particular point in time may display a variety of relationships to the structure of authority. 'Political world pictures' and attitudes to accommodation can be complex, contradictory and confused.

In attempting to analyse the intricate historical processes of political change in Western Europe in the context of an explicit frame of inquiry it is essential to be aware of the uses and requirements of conceptual frameworks. A central concern of such a deliberately simplifying exercise is to make some sense of the otherwise haphazard pictures that are conventionally portrayed by political history and are set against a background of broader developments like industrialization and urbanization. The historian's emphasis on the complexity of individual experiences involved in the establishment of the modern European state can easily lead to the view that the world is confused and defies generalization. By contrast, political scientists are concerned to identify basic patterns within this development and to explain (or at least make comprehensible) the character of political conduct in terms of these patterns. If the historian's stress on contingency and variety may involve a failure to identify underlying patterns or regularities, the failures of the political scientist can result from the attempt to construct an 'exhaustive' catalogue of variables relevant to his enterprise, catalogues which in turn become too complex and unwieldy to be helpful in generalization and in making political conduct intelligible. The task of those political scientists and historians who are interested in comparative analysis is assisted if an attempt is made to construct a map of the terrain, however provisional, by establishing the analytical concepts and frame of reference within which to work. Such general models are exploratory and tentative but suggest that patterns can be discerned. They do not necessarily involve the positivist assumption that the objective attributes of the variables selected determine political conduct. Above all, a model needs to provide both a rational and coherent typology which makes political conduct comprehensible and a system of categories sufficiently flexible to be comprehensive and to allow for very diverse circumstances.

THE CONCEPTS OF STATE AND SOCIETY

The utility of this model derives from the attempt to base it on the two major regularities in the development of 'modern' West European politics. First, there has been the evolution of the notion of the abstract, impersonal state as an entity or personality above and distinct from both government and governed; as an institution which is autonomous, formally co-ordinated and differentiated from other organisations which operate in a defined territory; as an object of universal service and respect; and as the source of a distinct public morality. A shift towards a 'state' society involves a preference for bureaucratic and legalistic methods of conflict resolution and for technical criteria in decision-making. Both the presence of bureaucrats in politics and the form of institutions and procedures of policy-making illustrate this phenomenon — for example, in Sweden, the administrative co-operation of groups, the 'remiss' device for circulating draft legislation and the meticulous documentation provided by commissions of inquiry. 'State' societies exemplify strongly non-economic, non-utilitarian attitudes towards political relations, which attitudes deny that the public interest is simply the sum of private interests; a rationalist spirit of inquiry; a stress on the distinctiveness of state and society, whether in terms of the special function of the state or in terms of the peculiar character of its authority; a consciousness of institutions which reflects the strength of legalism and codification within the political culture and reveals itself in the ubiquity of formal organizations and their detailed constitutions; a concern for formalization and depersonalization which lend a 'republican' character to the political system (even in the 'democratic' monarchies of the Netherlands and Sweden); an emphasis on impersonal political symbols of community; a stress on the unitary character of the 'public power', whether the state itself is centralized or federal (state is a generalizing and integrating concept); a moralistic view of politics which involves strongly collectivist and regulatory attitudes, a notion of the inherent responsibilities of the executive power and an active conception of the administrator's role; and, even when parliamentary and party government is accepted, the idea that the executive power is a public institution that is detached from, and has a basis of authority outside, Parliament. These features find their coherence in a rationalist conception of the technical requirements of an 'ordered' society. By contrast, 'stateless' societies are characterized by the strength of pluralism, representation and the debating tradition in the political culture; an instrumental view of government and a pragmatic conception of politics, both of which are associated with a passive notion of a neutral, anonymous, detached and private administrative role; a pervasive informality in politics and a sense of 'gamesmanship' which informs legal and political attitudes; a preference for 'social' models of the constitution or economic analyses of politics which emphasize the role of elites rather than institutions and the notion of 'a world of high politics'; an anthropomorphic conception of politics and the personalized and private character of the executive in which, for example, all attention is on the minister (Johnson, 1977, p. 84 quotes Lord Chancellor Hardwicke as saying, 'Ministers are Kings in this country'); and the emphasis on shared rituals and ceremony at all levels of society and/or on personalized, non-political symbols of community which focus notably on monarchy. 'Stateless' societies display, above all, a pronounced continuity of medieval feudal ideas and institutions, including a diffusion of power, and find their coherence in a conception of the customary requirements of an ordered society, in an appeal to heritage and social practice rather than to rationally ordered principles and technique. Political morality is the practice of civility; its standards are those of a civilized social conduct that involves mutual respect for individuality and, therefore, tolerance of diversity (Oakeshott, 1975).

The shift from 'stateless' to 'state' societies has been complex. Medieval society was 'stateless' in the sense that political ideas focused on the Church. Kingdom (*regnum*) and priesthood (*sacerdotium*) were parts of that body, and their relationship within that body was a major source of dispute. A turning-point in the medieval period was the emergence of feudalism as an idea of rule and the subsequent corrective which the king's function as feudal overlord offered to traditional theocratic ideas. According to the theocratic theory, all power was located in God and delegated from above to His earthly officers. This theory derived from Latin Christendom and was justified ecclesiastically by reference to the Latin (or Romanized) Bible. Theocratic kingship had appealed to an abstract principle, rested on a deductive method of reasoning and allowed only for the passive obedience of the king's subjects. The king stood outside and above the people who were under his protection; he was surrounded by a royal mystique and exercised the 'royal plenitude of power'. By contrast, feudalism rested on the notion of a contract which created a legal bond between lord and vassal (as Magna Carta of 1215 reminded King John). This bond made it possible to conceive of the king as a member of the feudal community and of the 'law of the land' (that is, what was later to be called the 'common law' in England) as the product of counsel and consent and as common to kings and barons. While the feudal idea spread across Western Europe, its importance as a system of rule varied. The medieval king embodied the functions of theocratic ruler and of feudal overlord, and the predominant among these functions in a particular society shaped the future character of its political development. In France the theocratic theory dominated, and later political ideas either were direct descendants of, or grew up in opposition to, this theory; in England the feudal theory was pre-eminent and sufficiently flexible to accommodate ideas which accorded a greater role to the people. According to Ullmann (1965, p. 154): 'The debt which the English constitution owed to feudal principles of government is very great indeed'.[2] Feudalism was an empirical growth but was not in origin an English theory. It developed in the Frankish empire in the eighth and ninth centuries and was characterized by a fragmentation of authority and reliance on the mutual loyalties and affections engendered by a network of interpersonal relations. A central problem of feudalism was that increasingly independent centres of local power engaged in costly feuds and private wars.

The first step towards the idea of the modern state was the *Ständestaat*, which emerged in the late twelfth century. Moreover, it was to prove a more important and durable system of rule than British or French historians have usually been prepared to recognize (see Myers, 1975). British history did not witness the consolidation of distinct legal privileges for the estates seen in most of continental Europe; while the dramatic decline of the French *Ständestaat* (the Estates-General was not called between 1614 and 1789) was an aberration from general European experience, which saw the continuing vitality of the estates up till 1789 (notably in German principalities like Wurtemberg and Mecklenburg, the Netherlands and Aragon) and even into the nineteenth century (till 1866 in Sweden). As Myers (1975) has emphasized, the *Ständestaat* was a phenomenon of Latin (rather than Celtic or Byzantine) Christendom, which was characterized by the

strength of Roman notions of justice and legal definition and the development of canon law. It differed from the feudal order in being more legalistic, institutionalized (it included a new administrative component) and
territorial in its reference (the estates represented the territory to the ruler),
and in being based on a partnership of prince and estates in the rule of
the territory. This partnership of two independent centres of rule implied
a dualism that was not present in the later notion of the 'unitary' modern
state (Poggi, 1978). The *Ständestaat* was associated with the thirteenth-
and fourteenth-century birth of parliaments which were held to represent
the whole realm to the ruler; the rise of towns as new, politically independent centres, which claimed new corporate rights to self-government
in order better to conduct their commercial affairs; and the growth of
canon law and the recovery of Roman law. Its history was one of tension
between its elements: the territorial ruler who stood outside and above
the estates and acquired a new public, non-feudal role; the towns, which
usually allied themselves with the territorial ruler (often to their ultimate
disadvantage); the nobility which emerged as a new corporate entity; and
the clergy (in Sweden the peasants formed an extra estate).[3] Out of the
dynastic ambitions and hunger for power of rulers and the new instability
of international affairs emerged territorial consolidation and centralizing pressures which favoured, in many cases, the emergence of the
patrimonial polity: the *Fürstenstaat* or Princes' State of the Renaissance,
then the *Hausstaat* or Dynastic State. This new polity held the 'good
old law' of the *Ständestaat* in less reverence and subordinated the idea
of law increasingly to the will of the ruler. Law became an instrument
of rule that applied uniformly to the whole population rather than the
framework of rules which embodied the customary differentiated rights
and privileges of the *Ständestaat*. The modern notion of the abstract and
impersonal constitutional state was, of course, associated with the rise
of civil society. The conception of the *Rechtsstaat* galvanized both bourgeois entrepreneurs, and their ideologues interested in the autonomy of
the market, and the bourgeois intelligentsia committed to the idea of a
'reasoning' public that was capable of developing a 'public opinion on
public affairs' (Habermas, 1965; Poggi, 1978).

The other major development has been in the character of society:
what Tönnies (1887) described as the movement from the characteristics of *Gemeinschaft* (community) to those of *Gesellschaft* (association). These two ideal types of society were, in his view, distinguished
by the quality of the will which created and sustained them. This will,

and the inner relationship of associated individuals, could vary from one situation to another. Community was united in and through the 'natural' or 'integral' will (*Wesenswille*) of its members: their thought was closely related to the whole personality, embedded in a way of life and inextricably entangled with inherited myths. Social bonds were, correspondingly, based on the close personal ties of friendship and kinship typical of rural and agricultural life. Relationships took on an intimate, broadly defined, deeply personal and emotional nature and emphasized tradition, informality and kinship. Association was, by contrast, integrated by 'rational' or 'arbitrary' will (*Kürwille*): thought took the independent form of a more impersonal, secular, emotionally and morally neutral analysis by the 'detached' individual who differentiated sharply between ends and means. Social bonds were formal, contractual, expedient, impersonal and specialized. Viewed in the light of both ideal-type concepts and their psychic correlates, actual societies were mixed. Western Europe had, nevertheless, witnessed a shift from personal forms of domination (which found their expression in medieval, patrimonial and clientelist polities) to organizational forms of domination—from personal ties to formal procedures of rule; from a politics that centred on the personal relations of notables and estates to one that was based on bargaining between mass parties and organized groups and reflected a consciousness of class; from ascription to achievement in assessment of status; from intrinsic to extrinsic valuations of relationships; and from deferential to utilitarian attitudes.

Anglo-American analyses of West European politics have tended to concentrate on the character of society or, more accurately, on specific aspects like social class and class relationships. In order to be able to identify the basic types of European polity it is also necessary to take into account variations in conceptions of public authority. The relationship between the development of the state as idea and institution and changes in the nature of society is complex. Both have raised new questions about the character of social and political bonds and have had a hot-house effect on ideas. They have involved an intellectual shift in the character of the analogies used to picture such bonds (from organic analogies, which use the language of 'nature' and 'growth', to mechanical); in legal theory (from customary law to systematic codes, which are derived from abstract principles); and in modes of social analysis (from a 'poetic' experience of the world, in which practical affairs were entangled with myths, to 'objective' rationality and conceptualism by a formal logic that is concerned with the relations of abstract entities; from culture integrated with nature to culture divorced from nature; from 'timeless' societies to societies that sense that they are 'in history'). Nevertheless, different factors were involved in the two developments. Whereas the economic transition to capitalism, itself a moral as well as a material phenomenon, was crucial in shaping the character of changes in the nature of society, a whole variety of political, religious and economic factors as well as factors of status interwove to shape the evolution of the idea of the abstract, impersonal state. Furthermore, neither axis was characterized by a smooth, regular development. Although both are represented in the model in terms of polar generalized types, with a general historical trend from one to the other, each development was a multi-dimensional process in which movements on different dimensions did not occur at uniform rates.

There was an interlocking between the two developments. For example, the state has been perceived as a countervailing model to traditional society, as an instrument of modernization that could transform social and economic relationships. From another perspective the notion of the state has been seen as a threat to the values of *Gemeinschaft*. The absence of these two perceptions in Britain facilitated a relatively smooth and slow transition from the vertical ties of deference to the horizontal relations, class tensions and more materialistic politics of 'modernity'. The link was also apparent in the peculiar amalgam of traditional and modern features which characterizes a contemporary 'stateless' society like Britain (Marx's 'old England'). *Gemeinschaft* characteristics were carried over into, and conserved within, a *Gesellschaft* type of society as public institutions perpetuated 'pre-modern' aristocratic 'value patterns' which emphasized qualities of character and gentlemanly style and gave them prestige within society: in other words, there was a spill-over of the values and norms of public institutions into wider society. One problem for such a political system was the possibility of a crisis of authority if traditional patterns of governing, which had been based on an informal fluid network of acquaintances and premised on heirarchy and deference, were subjected to criticism from more secularized, rationalist elements in society that were attached to a complex of entrepreneurial, technological and egalitarian ideas.

What is important is the independent variation possible on both dimensions. It is fallacious to assume that the idea of the state is nothing more than an expression of a *Gesellschaft* form of society. After all, the latter type of society has been associated with both the development of, and the failure to develop, a state consciousness. The notion of the state has been based on the legal and cultural distinctiveness of this political formation from the form of society (at the most extreme, on its autonomy from the class character of society)—indeed, on the significance for the wider society of the specialized peculiar values of the state as an association or enterprise with a distinct mission. In other words, in contrast to the assumptions of group theorists and of Marxists, there is the possibility of a dissemination from the state itself to society (whether through collaboration in corporatist forms, as well as informally, with organized groups or through 'pressuring' groups who come into conflict with it). While reality is observed to be distinct from the ideal of the state and attention can be drawn to the representation of predominant class interests of society in the 'real' state, the ideal—as 'internalized' norms—may still be relevant, in the sense that the ideal is rationally linked to conduct. The ideal is, moreover, expressed in intellectual forms like the *Kulturstaat* and *Rechtsstaat* by a social group (intellectuals) that may not possess particularistic economic allegiances. Even in those instances in which the 'real' state appears to serve particular interests, the idea of the state may remain important for society precisely because it represents an amalgam of dominant class representation with a distinctive collectivist ethos which gives it the potential to transcend narrowly self-interested motives. Neither class analysis nor the variation induced by clientele relations, local influences and career patterns should disguise the way in which the notion of the state imparts a set of general tendencies both to the institutions that formally comprise it and to others.

Another example of the importance of independent variation on the two axes is provided by the different forms of interest-group politics that are apparent in a *Gesellschaft* type of society. The mode of interest-group politics is shaped in relative independence of the conditions in civil society and of changes in the structure of the economy. Different views on how the power of organized groups should be constituted and exercised depend on frameworks of ideas and historical experiences of authority. The open, competitive and pluralist model of interest-group politics incorporates a view of politics as an 'arena' or process of brokerage in which contending interests determine policy: while the two corporatist models (see the figure on p. 49) involve the idea of the state as a relatively autonomous actor and the elaboration of specific criteria of public purpose, which flow from a monistic concept of the public interest and in terms of which orderly

co-operative relationships can be established. Indeed, the reason for rejecting Schmitter's (1974) distinction between 'state corporatism' and 'societal corporatism' in favour of 'authoritarian' and 'liberal' corporatism
(Lehmbruch, 1977) is that both types are dependent on a notion of the
state. The difference between them and the pluralist model rests on the distinction between 'state' and 'stateless' societies.

THE 'CRISIS-OF-MODERNITY' POLITY

Tensions that generate conflict are apparent at all points in the development
of 'stateness' and changes in the character of society, but in the 'transitional' stages they can become acute and cumulative. On the axis of 'stateness'
problems are generated by the twin processes of state-building—an attempt to design a centralized administrative system in order to 'penetrate'
society to effect policies—and the search to acquire legitimacy by, for example, appealing to dynastic loyalties or 'nation-building' (Almond and
Powell, 1966). The transitional stage may be productive of *Obrigkeitsstaat*
ideas and 'police-state' characteristics and/or of resistance by cultural pe-
ripheries and religious organizations. On the axis of types of society are
two sources of problems, both of which focus more on interests and are in
principle negotiable. First, there is the challenge of participation as new
groups press for a share in making decisions and old groups feel politically and economically threatened. The patrimonial polity was particularly
vulnerable to this challenge as it opposed a share of power both for the old
estates and for new groups that were pressing for the impersonal constitutional state. There is also the problem of distribution which is unleashed by
the effects of industrialization and of the agricultural revolution in redis-
tributing resources in society. The product is political demand for welfare
policies. In the case of changes in the character of society, the transitional
stage can be productive of riot and the beginnings of more institutionalized
dissent (for example, the early trade unions). The most vulnerable polities
are the estate, patrimonial, parliamentary, dual (especially the *tutelle* variant) and the authoritarian corporatist.

Political systems which accumulate problems on both dimensions are in danger of ending up in a 'crisis-of-modernity', of slipping
into the 'black hole' at the centre of the model.[4] The 'crisis-of-modernity' polity is likely to draw on the characteristics of the personalized and

authoritarian corporatist polities but, besides adding new features, will interpret these characteristics in a novel framework. That framework involves an ambiguous, comprehensive and expansive ideology as a means of resolving the disagreements generated by the problems of modernity. The 'black hole' character of this polity indicates that there is a radical attempt to escape from the constraints of 'stateness' to the extremes of heroic personalized leadership with Fascism or the totalitarian party of Marxism/Leninism. As a consequence 'corporate state' features of Italian Fascism amounted to little more than a facade. Fascism was a movement arising outside the existing institutional framework, which was to be captured and manipulated.[5] Above all it made profoundly ambiguous ideological appeals that combined certain 'modern' tendencies with an anti-rationalism which rested on aesthetic motifs. In the struggle for power both a 'modernist' political mobilization and the themes of 'anti-modernity' were employed. The equivocal commitment to them was manifested once in power; then the emphasis was upon control of mass society by disarming or breaking down existing institutions and upon the need for an industrial base for nationalist ambitions. Rhetoric and ritual, a combination of demagoguery with paramilitary force, were the novel features of Fascism (Tannenbaum, 1973). The term movement was more central than state. Fascism represented a phenomenon of a transitional-stage society in which there was an attempt to escape from the disciplines of 'stateness', from not only the emphasis on depersonalization which follows from the state's bureaucratic and legal character but also the idea of state and society as distinct realms.

A stress on 'crisis zones' of development should not distract attention from the difficulties that beset other polities: the clientelist polity, with its disjunction of state and social norms, is likely to experience corruption; the adversary polity, with its low problem-solving capacity, is prone to policy failure; while the accommodative polity, with its failure to live up to the model of the 'active' citizen, is likely to be concerned about political passivity and the need for participation in the face of the bureaucratization of mass organizations. It would, moreover, be erroneous to see the problems of 'penetration', legitimacy, distribution and participation as exclusive to the crisis zones; they may persist and recur. In the crisis zones, which incidentally incorporate the majority of polities in the model, these problems are characterized by their novelty and their tendency to accumulate.

FROM FEUDAL TO CLIENTELIST POLITY

In the three polities associated with *Gemeinschaft* 'political world pictures' are highly personalized; monarchy provides a symbol of the way
of life. Respect and deference combine with indifference and resignation;
politics is for 'them', the upper class and professional men in general.
The personalized, decentralized feudal order, with its static view of
reciprocal personal rights and obligations, was, of course, highly con-
gruent with this type of society. While the estate and patrimonial polities were born out of conflict with elements that supported the feudal
order, and the new-found ambitions of the ruler were financially exacting on subjects, monarchy continued to provide for personalized loyalties. In the feudal order, 'an association of persons' (Brunner, 1954), the
norm governing political accommodation was reciprocity and the right
of resistance where reciprocity was not respected. The monarch, as a
'passive' adjudicator, recognized and maintained patterns of customary rights and duties. In the patrimonial polity the monarch took on a
dynastic responsibility: as a private individual to the Christian ethic, as
a public personality to 'reason of state'. Its paternalist character derived
from the notion that the ruler inherited the state as a landowner inherited
his father's property (hence the close association of the notions of 'state'
and 'estate'), except that his authority lay in a legislative power rather
than in the ownership of land itself.

With a shift to the idea of the impersonal, abstract state as an 'institu-
tional-territorial association' (Brunner, 1954) fully completed, respect and
indifference turn to a profound estrangement from an 'imposed' institutional structure about which the public knows little and wishes to know
less (Allum, 1973). As a legal institution the idea of the state provides an
ideal-type representation of *Gesellschaft* norms and values. Its assumptions about social relationships are diametrically opposed to *Gemeinschaft*:
generalized standards of behaviour rather than the 'special' character
of mutual relationships; a narrow, clearly defined range of expectations
rather than a broad, undefined range of mutual rights and responsibilities;
collective obligations rather than private permissiveness; the primacy not
of impulse but of restraint and discipline in the service of more distant
goals; performance rather than status. The state becomes a façade. Political
accommodation is achieved by the establishment of the view that the state
itself is the major provider of a source of living. An integration between
the idea of the state and type of society is realized through patronage and

corruption. The state apparatus offers an avenue for social mobility, a pole of attraction in career terms, but society does not support the ideas to which it appeals. In particular, the state apparatus becomes a source of security against 'intellectual unemployment', both the channel for advancement of personal careers and a source of resources to distribute to one's clients. An image of the 'coercive' state is counteracted by a notion of the politician as an 'intermediary' using personal influence to protect the public from state demands. One result of this 'deputy-centred' politics is the mutual resentment of parliamentarians and civil servants at the centre. The parliamentary battle is between factions of a restricted oligarchy of local notables, who see themselves as mediators on behalf of local clienteles and help their friends and neighbours to a slice of the state's largesse. These notables do not oppose 'big' government, for the bigger it is, the more they can do for their clients. In turn such services create a personal bond between individual and party: a classic case was provided by the Republican Party of the French Third Republic. The reciprocal importance of ministerial office and a powerful local base is also recognized. Consequently, parochial issues and very particularistic interests receive inordinate attention, and 'a chain of intermediaries of diminishing honesty links the politician—often without his knowledge—with the crook' (Williams, 1970). The minister's personal staff of political friends (situated, for example, in the Third Republic's ministerial 'cabinets') provide an entrée to a *demimonde*. There is, not surprisingly, an intolerance on the part of higher civil servants towards politics.

In the clientelist polity political bosses emerge; 'place men' supercede landowners. Favours are traded down a hierarchical chain of personal acquaintances. These vertical political ties are associated with a low propensity for forming or joining voluntary interest groups. Above all, the network of patronage provides a link between national and local politics. In the French Third Republic the prefects played a key role in assisting Republican deputies by giving them special access to the administration. Similarly, the provincial governors of Restoration Spain (1874–1923) played a major political role at the centre of the patronage network, along with the *caciques* or party bosses. During this period of *caciquismo* (rule through patronage and intimidation by party bosses) Spain was plagued by *empleomania* (rage for office), by a personalized politics in which the 'right' contact (*enchufe*) came before loyalty to the idea of the impersonal state (Kern, 1966). As in that other classic period of the clientelist polity, Italy from 1860 to 1925, the result was an extraordinary administrative inefficiency which confirmed public estrangement from the state. The Second Republic tried to put an end to *caciquismo,* and it became much less evident under the Franco regime, largely because those who had practised it now found a new confidence in political arrangements. Clientelist polities are characterized by a flamboyant political life at the local level, with strong personalities and a politics of sensational scandals. Mayors act as political entrepreneurs who bypass the administration and thereby deprive it of legitimacy (Tarrow, 1977). The state itself is the object of both fear and fascination. This intense suspicion of centralized state power can be exploited particularly by the extreme right, by using scandel-mongering as an instrument to generate a crisis of confidence in the regime. It is a polity of both parasitism and riot, predisposed to elaborate a mystique of popular resistance. There is a ready resort to *jacqueries,* to extra-legal violent action. Carlism in Spain, for long the biggest anti-democratic movement in Western Europe, provides an example of Catholic peasant society resisting the demands of a centralized and secular liberal state that was introduced prematurely in terms of the stage of civic development that the country had reached. Even Germany has a history of peasant revolts.

BALANCED PARLIAMENTARY AND DUAL POLITIES

The balanced parliamentary polity was an ideal representation of the emerging characteristics of the English political system. As a type of polity it excited much admiration elsewhere, not least in continental Europe, but approximation to its features in Western Europe remained a uniquely English achievement. The balanced parliamentary polity was associated with a recognition by certain elements, old and new, of a dissolving feudal society that the new dynamic of economic, social and religious change made a static conception of government impracticable. In the context of a shift in the character of society, mainly caused by the commercialization of agriculture, and the prestige conferred on Parliament by Henry VIII's Reformation, self-confident men of property, landowning gentry amd merchants, dominant in the Commons, sought to affirm a positive constitutional position for themselves against the patrimonial and theocratic claims of the Stuarts. Compared, for example, with the *standenstaat* of the Dutch Republic, vestiges of which were to persist until 1848, England offered a different response to the problem of where the new sovereignty should lie. Parliament determined to share in it through the formula of Crown-in-Parliament rather than suffer from its application in a centralizing, bureaucratic polity. The English civil war revolved around the constitutional issue of the nature of the king's prerogative: was that prerogative tantamount to sovereignty or did it make the king co-equal with Lords and Commons in the supreme body of Parliament? Eventually, after 1688, the contestants were able to agree on a form of government that was justified both by reference to the 'ancient' constitution of the realm and inherited rights and in terms of the contractual language of a feudal past. Parliament embodied the idea of balance. It was the joint representative of the kingdom, a union of concurrent parts, at first of king, Lords and Commons, later of government and opposition. Indeed Vile (1967, p. 335) has claimed that the idea of balance remains central in the interpretation of Anglo-Saxon constitutions.

One difference between the English seventeenth-century revolutions and the French Revolution of 1789 was that the former represented a 'pre-emptive' strike against, the latter an overthrow of, the patrimonial polity. As a consequence, the post-revolutionary inheritances were very different; representative and decentralized in the one case, bureaucratic and centralized in the other. Political accommodation occurred in the fluid parliamentary arena through the mechanism of debate and the growing accountability of government and individual ministers. Debate provided both enlightment and collective entertainment and encouraged the emergence of political personalities and dramatic clashes between these personalities. Theatrical analogies pervaded 'political world views'. Linguistic performance was the currency of politics. The problems of this polity were those of transition: from a *Gemeinschaft* legacy of paternalist attitudes, which reacted to parliamentary indifference to social plight by riot, to the emergence of *Gesellschaft* institutionalized forms of dissent, notably organized labour, which appeared to challenge parliamentary supremacy; from 'old corruption' and the patronage of oligarchic politics to a broadening of representation and a shift in its character from property to universal suffrage.

The dual polity was, by contrast, a more complex phenomenon which represented different responses on the part of new bourgeois groups to a central question: how should the 'democratic' principle enshrined in the institution of Parliament and the parties be related to the 'authoritarian', hierarchical principle of the executive power? It was the product of a reaction by these groups to one of three

experiences: to the personalized and often theocratic character of the patrimonial polity (as in France in 1789), to the patronage and corruption of
the clientelist polity (a persistent concern in post-revolutionary France)
and to the 'crisis-of-modernity' polity (as in post-war Italy and Western
Germany). There was the attempt, in the first instance, to give institutional
expression to the idea of the impersonal, abstract state based on democratic principles; in the second, where democratic principles were already
formally recognized, to make the state itself more autonomous of society in order to safeguard its distinctive ethos; and, in the third, to integrate the idea of the state and democracy in terms of party dominance.
The 'bureaucratic dominance' form of dual polity was often a response to
the excesses of the clientelist polity. One variant has been the autocratic
mode of Bonapartism, a bureaucratic Caesarism that combined 'democratic' legitimacy through plebiscitary devices (rather than parliamentary
elections) with police-state features. Another has been Gaullism, which
established in the Fifth Republic of 1958 an increased insulation of the executive power from the Assembly by, for example, bestowing greater rule-
making power on the executive, direct election of the President (after 1962)
and greater recruitment of bureaucrats to ministerial office and 'cabinet'
positions. Both variants represented a shift towards bureaucratic power,
an emphasis on the *tutelle* powers of the executive, a view of politics as a
game, distinct in character from the executive's business-like nature, and
a combination of a 'limited authoritarianism' with 'potential insurrection
against authority'. Local–national brokerage takes on a different character
from that in the clientelist polity. Mayors emerge as administrative activists who legitimate the bureaucracy by working with it (Tarrow, 1977). The
official's political role could, of course, become a source of division, the
attack on the bureaucratic state a political phenomenon. Another example
of the 'bureaucratic dominance' type was provided by the 'regime of officials' in Norway from 1814 to 1884 and the cultural and territorial opposition which it generated (notably from the peasantry).

There were two other types of dual polity model. One involved
the establishment of the idea of a balance between the two powers or poles of the state, as in post-1809 Sweden and the post-1848
Netherlands. The mode of political accommodation was not the
tutelle with its notion of the executive as a moral arbiter: it was a
'business-like' co-operation of the two powers. 'Political world views'
exhibited a recognition of the significance of legal and technical values.
Parliamentarians and civil servants displayed a greater mutual respect than

in the *tutelle* type of dual polity, and in particular officials showed a political awareness and tolerance not apparent in the latter. There was not, however, that fusion of executive and legislative powers which was to be found in Britain.

A very different example was provided by the 'parliamentary/party dominance' type of dual polity, apparent in new nineteenth-century states like Belgium from 1831 and the new Confederation in Switzerland from 1848, as well as in post-'crisis-of-modernity' polities. In these cases the effective establishment and maintenance of the idea of the abstract, impersonal and autonomous state depended above all on the character of party domination. Before 1848 Switzerland had been a loose confederation that combined Liberal, predominantly Protestant and 'statist' cantons with smaller, traditionalist, Catholic cantons. The new confederation was dominated by the Liberal Radicals, who kept a majority in the federal executive, the Federal Council, until 1943. This party, which was strongly urban, Protestant and middle-class, was committed to a 'state ideology' that emphasized *Beamtenstaat* and *Rechtsstaat* elements. Besides dominating university teaching and the law, it pursued a radical patronage policy which led to the creation of a Liberal–Radical federal civil service. No Conservative/Catholic before 1919 and no Socialist before 1945 entered the federal higher civil service. Liberal–Radical dominance succeeded in establishing in politics the *Sachlichkeit* ideal, which produced an 'executive frame of mind' committed to the idea of objectivity. As this dominance gave way to a progressive proportionalization of the federal civil service by religious and linguistic groupings, the style of politics which it had established remained remarkably intact. Proportionality had quite the opposite effect in Belgium. Belgium was a contrived entity at its beginning, with few national symbols. While there was much emphasis on the idea of the state as a reaction to its deep divisions, that idea remained a formality. The particularism of Belgium had been swept aside earlier by French revolutionary forces, and it was founded in 1830–1 in the context of a revolt against the patrimonial rule of William I, king of the Dutch–Belgian union created in 1815. However, the Liberals, the 'state-bearing' party which was influenced by French ideas of the state, failed to maintain the overall (but by no means complete) dominance that they had secured from the end of the period of 'unionism' (1831–47) until 1884. At that date the Catholics began an unparalleled thirty years of control of central government. Society was dichotomized into two camps, Catholic and non-Catholic, and in addition was characterized by linguistic/regional opposition between Flanders and Wallonia. Consequently, political socialization tended to emphasize the particularistic, not the national. The bureaucracy witnessed an extreme of party penetration on a proportional basis but had already failed to establish a credible notion of its own autonomy and distinct ethos.

Despite internal variation within the 'dual polity' type, it is possible to identify a distinctive 'political world view' and mode of accommodation. 'Political world views' are ambivalent: the state is perceived as both a protector and a threat to individuality. On the one hand, its depersonalization is embraced as a method of defusing issues; on the other, there is resentment at its imposition of regulations. Accommodation is achieved through reliance on the initiatives and arbitrative role of an impartial bureaucracy dedicated to the public interest and a hierarchical style in the exercise of authority. The major concern is the autonomy of the executive power in order to safeguard its ability to determine impartially the public interest.

ADVERSARY, AUTHORITARIAN CORPORATIST AND ACCOMMODATIVE POLITIES

A *Gesellschaft* type of society is characterized by more general abstract orientations which support modern mass parties and organized groups. The adversary/competitive polity is confined to a few countries of British provenance and has come closest to realization in post-1945 Britain. Indeed, its features are an ideal representation of that country's changing politics after the 1860s. This polity has two major features: an adversary or accusatory style of party politics that stresses the role of public debate and is hostile to the requirements of inter-party coalition and the idea of power-sharing as an aspect of normal competitive party activity as well as to the effective functioning of investigative machinery in the formulation of policy (for example, within parliament); and, among the producer groups, a fluid, competitive pluralistic politics of bargaining in which a complex of groups emerge in a self-determining fashion on the model of market-place relations and the establishment of stable tripartite arrangements between government and both sides of industry proves an elusive quest. On the one hand, in contrast to the balanced polity, majority party government, government's control of the parliamentary agenda and party discipline have ensured that the exercise of political authority is more concentrated in institutional terms. On the other hand, power is diffused; there is an untidy proliferation of independent centres of decision. The executive is perceived as a broker between contending interests, the polity as adaptive and reactive, depending on society both for the dynamism for change and for standards of civilized political conduct. As Lijphart (1975) has suggested, the result is likely to be 'centripetal' politics in a homogeneous political culture and 'centrifugal' politics in a fragmented political culture.

'Political world views' are not informed by a deep institutional consciousness or constitutional awareness but rather by the notion of politics as a game in which the rules, which are often vague and subject to various interpretations, are mainly the result of mutual understandings between contestants who compete for the favour of the spectators. The game evokes ambivalent responses: on the one hand, as in the elections of 1945, 1950 and 1951, it can produce the drama that is associated with passionate commitments to particular ideologies or issues; on the other, as in the 1970s, it may generate disillusion with the outcomes of an oversimplifying and rigid pattern of partisanship between two rival teams of politicians, 'ins' and 'outs'. There is a critical support for politics. Political style rests on the premise that divergent interests are resolvable only through continuous, open, partisan conflict, public debate and majority decision rather than, as in the accommodative polity, by reference to an idea of the public interest, in the sense of an agreement that there are values which transcend particular interests. The character of this conflict and debate is moulded in turn by the assumption that political questions can best be resolved if expressed in terms of just two contrasting alternatives (Johnson, 1977). As in the balanced polity, politics reflects the 'sporting' theory of justice that is embedded in, and nourished by, the common-law tradition and parliamentary procedure, both of which are more deeply rooted in the feudal heritage. Much of the complexity and fluidity of contemporary British political arrangements stems from the legacy of a pluralistic political order and of faith in the efficacy of the spoken word, bequeathed by the balanced polity, to a public adversary polity in which the pursuit of power within the political order by the parties becomes a 'zero-sum' game (winner takes all) and is combined with a complex, changing pluralistic process of bargaining and consultation with organized groups. Assumptions that derive from both polities coexist, often with difficulty, and are united by a shared view about the character of public authority, including its private, personalized nature, and about the mode of its exercise, in particular by consent and by offering an opportunity to 'contest' government's policy.

In the polity of authoritarian corporatism accommodation is through hierarchy. Labour and capital are expected, or rather required, to collaborate under the supervision and control of the state apparatus in order to achieve common ends. The emphasis is on leadership (but without an elaborate ideology), on a restricted 'managed' accommodation of interest groups and on the importance of professional bureaucrats and jurists. A formalistic conception of the *Rechtsstaat* is accompanied by features of the *Polizeistaat*. There is little political mobilization, and 'political world views' exemplify estrangement and indifference. A tentative expression of this polity was provided by Primo de Rivera's regime in Spain after 1923 and found a later echo in the views of *Renovación Española*.

The accommodative/liberal corporatist polity has come closest to realization in the Netherlands since 1917 (Lijphart, 1975), modern Sweden (Elder, 1970), Austria's Second Republic (Steiner, 1972), the Bonn Republic (Dyson, 1977) and modern Switzerland (Steiner, 1974). Compared with the dual polity there is a heightened awareness of the political dimension of the relationship between the state apparatus and society, of their mutual dependence and of the need for more information, clarification and analysis among interests in order to broaden their perspectives. Accommodation is a political style that stresses 'coalescent' elite behaviour, based on an inquisitorial rather than an adversary approach to policy, collegiality in the making of decisions and an egalitarian style in the exercise of authority. A didactic and moralistic style of leadership, which emphasizes mutual interdependence and forebearance in the name of social responsibility, is accompanied by a 'business-like' approach of cool objectivity in the service of the public interest, and by political attitudes orientated towards results. An example of the pervasiveness of this style of policy is the spirit of 'summit diplomacy' between the powerful 'peak' associations (which represent the major producer groups) in the context of explicit criteria of public purpose: for example, Austria's Joint Commission on Prices and Wages and West Germany's 'concerted action' for a decade after 1967 and, more generally, the spirit of social partnership (*Sozialpartnershaft*) in both countries. This type of polity is not dependent on particular institutional arrangements like, for example, the devices suggested by theories of consociational democracy as necessary to 'coalescent' elite behaviour in a fragmented political culture (grand coalitions, coalition pacts and committees, *Proporz*). As will be clear from the model, such elite behaviour is not assumed to be dependent on this type of political culture. However, proportionality in appointments and depoliticization of issues (for example, by resort to law for resolution of conflicts and by reliance on economic experts) are two typical features of this polity. Emphasis is upon the role of committees of experts (which include parliamentarians, organized groups, officials and independent experts in Sweden and Switzerland) in the preparation of legislation. 'Political world views' perceive politics in terms of a rational, objective framework of institutional values which focus upon duty, public service, proper procedure and efficiency. Although the state is objectified, it remains a plausible source of affective identification.

The administration as an institution is not formally dominant over others, but its values are prevalent. Individual members are visible, active and very mobile in career terms compared with the practice in the adversary/competitive polity. The varied experience made possible by this pattern of inter-organizational mobility of the elite lends an added attraction to public-service careers. In Norway, for example, the civil service acts as a 'state elite' which integrates diverse institutions (Higley, Brofoss and Groholt, 1975). Moreover, officials are able to act as middlemen at the interfaces of various groups; they possess transcendable group commitments and have access to information, ideas and positions outside the normal run of organizational actors (Heclo, 1974). As in the dual polity, there is a strong technical orientation in policy-making, but the key difference resides in the displacement of lawyers by economists in elite positions, typically trained in the 'state' perspectives of continental European faculties of law and economics, and providing integrative macro-perspectives. The executive power is the linchpin of elite integration. However, the emphasis is not so much on the autonomy of the executive power as on its integration with the democratic framework. The result is an openness towards politics, a pragmatic style, a more consensual view of social relationships, and a recognition of the co-equal, distinctive character of bureaucracy rather than an emphasis on its superiority. Political parties seek to establish their authority over the bureaucracy and other institutions by a process of party 'penetration' or 'grip'. Appointments and promotions are influenced by party-political criteria. This phenomenon is variable—at its height in the *Parteienstaat* of Austria and the Bonn Republic, and low in Sweden, where it is largely confined to the category of 'posts of confidence' in the administration. The function of bureaucratic placement has an important influence on the character of the parties, particularly through the incentives that it offers to membership. As a result of the strong presence of officials in the parties, the ethos of the parties becomes characterized by public-service values and attitudes (Dyson, 1977).

At the centre of this polity is, however, a tension between the two elements of the policy-making system: party government, which is orientated periodically to competitive electoral stimuli, and a corporatist form of producer-group politics (Lehmbruch, 1977). While the relationship between the two is symbiotic and mediated by accumulation of offices, and while a monistic conception of the public interest may predispose both elements towards forms of collaboration, they are different in character, and the scope of their respective concerns for policy varies considerably over space and time. Corporatism characterizes major aspects or sectors of policy, particularly in the economic/industrial policy field.[6] It involves power-sharing and stresses interdependence and interpenetration of 'public' and 'private' decision-making: an incorporation of organized groups into the exercise of public power in the form of a high degree of collaboration of powerful groups (mainly capital and labour) in shaping and implementing policy. The process emerges pragmatically: in the Netherlands corporatism achieves considerable institutionalization but in Sweden it remains relatively informal. Institutionalization is given most scope perhaps in the Austrian 'chamber state', where the Joint Commission on Prices and Wages is involved even in the preparation of economic legislation. However, changes in the ideological climate underline the precarious stability and shifts in range of policy of liberal corporatism. The party system becomes a more important arena when the corporate sector proves unable to contain (or avoid) conflicts. At or near election time it is also likely to introduce an ideological competition which disrupts corporatist efforts. Despite (or because of) the congruence of 'stateness' and type of society there is a danger of exaggerating the stability of this polity by comparison with that of the competitive polity. There are various possible contradictions: between party and corporatist forms (witness the breakdown in Sweden of the so-called 'Haga' decisions of 1974–6, which involved the major parties, 'peak' associations and the central bank in economic-policy decisions); between elite agreement and 'mass' reactions (notably disruptions over the issue of the distribution of resources from within organized labour or through tax protests); between some people's 'responsible' and enlightened amicable agreements and other people's 'self-interested' collusion or conspiracy of oligarchical leaders who have an interest in the maintenance of popular passivity. The viability of particular corporatist arrangements depends on an evaluation of the success of agreements by all parties to them and on the nature of ideological divisions. While these comments underline the provisional character of these arrangements, corporatism remains a distinctive response to problems of interest-group accommodation in this polity.

CONCLUSIONS

The purpose of this model is essentially heuristic. It does not seek to explain how or why particular countries pass through, or combine, different categories of polity, and it does not identify a standard sequence or path of development. Model-building is not concerned to underestimate the complexity of political phenomena, the individual subtleties of political life or the importance of historical understanding (or, indeed, the impact of chronological events like revolution, defeat in war or civil war itself). Its purpose in this instance is to identify certain general tendencies in West European political development in the form of an ideal-type representation of the political forms that have been produced by independent variations in 'stateness' and type of society. Particular political systems do not fit neatly into the boxes. It would be to mistake the nature of model-building if an attempt were made to force each system into a specific box. Their politics display too many ambiguities and are too deeply engaged in subtle processes of political change; in practice they combine elements from different ideal-type polities.

One feature of the model is that it indicates that progression in political development is step-by-step rather than by random shifts. Although different possibilities are available in political development, some are more likely than others. In Britain development was on a 'stateless' continuum from feudal to the modern parliamentary/adversary form of politics. By contrast, France's political development was characterized by the leading role of the state as idea and institution: from a medieval, strongly theocratic polity, through the sixteenth- and seventeenth-century 'crisis zone' of estate/ patrimonial conflicts which led to the ascendancy of the patrimonial polity, and to the clientelist/dual polity character of post-revolutionary regimes. Constitutional instability after 1789 reflected at first the tensions between nostalgists for the personalized polity and the advocates of the modern idea of the constitutional state, and then the conflicts between clientelist and dual polities and subsequent disagreements about the appropriate form of dual polity. The Fourth (1946–58) and Fifth Republics have made very tentative efforts towards the accommodative polity of partnership or 'concertation' between organized groups and the state itself, notably in the national economic planning exercise: indeed, the Economic and Social Council represents a longer-standing attempt which was based on 'solidarist' political ideas. Prussia's patrimonial/*tutelle* form of political system was transferred to Imperial Germany in 1871, where it made an ambivalent appeal: personalized for traditional groups and impersonal for 'modernist' elements. Wehler (1973) has emphasized the elements of Bonapartism or Caesarism in Bismarckian Germany, which is seen as a 'plebiscitary dictatorship' on the lines of Napoleon III's Second Empire in France. The Weimar Republic was a combination of personalized polity (focusing on Hindenburg's presidency which could, and eventually did, invoke Article 48 of the constitution to rule by decree) and dual polity (party domination); while the Bonn Republic, which emerged out of the 'crisis-of-modernity' experience of the Third Reich with a reshaped social structure, rested upon dual polity (party domination) elements with a rapid ascendency of accommodative polity elements.

Before its 1809 constitution Sweden displayed a particularly interesting oscillation: within the context of a *Ständestaat* represented in the *Riksdag* there was a competition for dominance between groups which pressed for the idea of the impersonal, abstract and legal state and other groups which supported patrimonial ideas (the latter were especially powerful under Gustav Vasa and later Charles XI, with his reduction of the aristocracy's estates in 1680). At an early stage, and later encouraged by monarchical reduction (that is, the large-scale nationalization of the aristocracy's landed possessions), the aristocracy's power base became administrative office. This transformation of a large part of the aristocracy into an administrative group which served the 'realm' combines with a long tradition of independence of administrative office from direct government control to help explain why the concept of the state was to become more important and more central in Swedish than in English constitutional theory and why the transition to the welfare state went so smoothly. Whereas elsewhere it was largely the bourgeoisie that formulated political demands for the idea of the abstract impersonal state, in Sweden it was the nobility, through figures like Erik Sparre and Axel Oxenstierna, that put forward against the king the case for constitutionalism, administrative order and efficiency in the service of the realm (*rike*). Through the Council of the Realm (note, *not* the King's Council) the great families were a force pressing, however unconsciously, towards the idea of the abstract legal state. During periods of 'council constitutionalism' or 'aristocratic constitutionalism' their political ideal came close to realization. The cause of the aristocracy was, however, less popular than, and contrasted with, a demagogic style of kingship which sought to ally with the other estates against them. Indeed, their political ideas were held to be clientelist, a foil for their material interests. Popular resentment of their share of office was considerable, particularly among the politically significant independent peasantry. The 'Era of Liberty' (1718–72) appeared to be a shift towards a purer form of estate polity, and was followed by the most dramatic period of personalized rule. While the Council of State which was established as a check on the monarch's action by the 1809 constitution seemed to mark a further shift towards the idea of the abstract state, the retention of the estates till 1866 and *de facto* dominance of the political scene by the monarch, aided by bureaucracy and conservative nobility, meant considerable continuity. After 1866 a dual polity based on the notion of the separation of powers which had informed the constitution took root; after 1917 there was a gradual shift towards the accommodative polity.

A second feature of the model is that it emphasizes the imprint left on political systems by their particular path of development, including the nature of the medieval order from which they emerged. As the model offers only a set of abstract representations, one has to remember that concrete political systems which are embedded in political traditions will carry over into, and conserve within themselves, characteristics like those of *Gemeinschaft* or of 'stateless' society. The model draws attention also to the character of the 'crisis zones' through which they have passed. It suggests, for example, that the pattern of politics is likely to be rather different in political systems like those of Italy and Western Germany which have experienced crises of modernity. Such crises generate a heightened self-consciousness about legalism as well as a sensitivity towards radical dissent. Perhaps even more important, the model indicates the kind of complexity in the character of society and in conceptions of the state which shape the survival power of particular political arrangements. The longevity of Franco's authoritarian regime depended in large part on its recognition and reflection of the extraordinary complexity of conceptions of society and the coexistence of different views of the state. Franco's regime incorporated competing formulae to maximize its legitimacy: personalized elements which appealed to those, like the Carlists, attached to *Gemeinschaft* values and helped to reduce perceptions of it as a clientelist polity; *tutelle* elements for technocratic modernists; and authoritarian corporatist elements as a way of incorporating and controlling interest-group politics (Linz, 1964).

The model serves also to illustrate how the state takes on radically different meanings which depend on the character of society and, in particular, on whether social experience predisposes individuals to develop an institutional consciousness in which political conduct is expected to be governed by a larger, rational and objective framework. The inability to establish an effectively functioning state apparatus in Italy is to be understood in terms of two interrelated factors: the widespread estrangement in the south from the norms of a rational legal society because of the dominance of *Gemeinschaft* relations, and loss of respect in the north, where crass inefficiency and corruption within the bureaucracy clashes with a 'political world view' established in the context of *Gesellschaft* (Allum, 1973). From 1860 to 1925 Italian politics fused clientelist polity elements (southern land) with dual polity elements (northern capital). The patronage forces were represented politically by *sinistra storica*. Cavour's party, *destra storica*, combined a fascination with the French conception of the centralized administrative state (supporting the adoption of the prefectoral system in 1861) with Hegelian ideas. It advocated a 'Piedmontization' of the new state and was prepared to sanction state intervention on a vast scale. However, the alliance with southern land made difficult the emergence of any meaningful notion of the autonomous state. Indeed, the prefects became one of the main reference points of clientelist politics, since a large majority of them were recruited from the southern intelligentsia. Post-1945 Italian bureaucracy remained an odd mixture of the Napoleonic centralized administration inherited from Piedmont and a Bourbon paternalism which packed the civil service with a large number of southerners through political preferment: there existed also the aloof and contemptuous attitudes towards politics of surviving Fascist 'place men'. On the one hand, a system of 'underground' government through favours and jobs gave a certain flexibility to politics; on the other, the absence of an effective institutional framework produced a deterioration in human relations outside the protective function of the family.

As an explanatory device the model, like any other, has limitations which stem from its focus on regularities rather than particularities. It is necessary, for example, to remember that the simplicity of the axis of types of society hides significant detail. There are important differences in the structure of the social formation and in relationships between classes. Thus in the period of transition of society the relationship between lord and peasant takes on a variety of forms (Moore, 1969). In England the peasantry was transformed early on into a landless proletariat, while important sections of the aristocracy and gentry took on commercial characteristics and sought to protect their economic self-interest through representative and local institutions against the monarchy; in Prussia monarch and nobility allied against the peasantry who became serfs; in France the Revolution which brought down the monarchy and destroyed the feudal powers of the nobility confirmed the power of a pre-capitalist peasantry; while Sweden, which had missed the feudal stage, possessed an independent capitalist peasantry which achieved early institutionalization as the fourth estate of the *Riksdag*. The importance of different patterns of land tenure within the *Gemeinschaft* is suggested by the failure of the independent peasantry of Catalonia, secure in land tenure, to share in the 'rage for office' that gripped the rest of Restoration Spain. It is also necessary to bear in mind the detailed differences in the terms upon which particular groups were admitted to participation in the political system and the consequences for the form of political opposition (Rokkan, 1970); for example, did the rise of organized labour predate or follow universal suffrage?

There are important variations in the character of the religious framework within which state-building takes place and hence in the nature of Church/state conflicts. For Roman Catholic societies the emergence of the idea of the abstract, impersonal state posed an extremely divisive issue of secularization (especially in education) that was less apparent in Protestant societies like Lutheran Sweden or Prussia and produced very different forms of accommodation between state and Church. In post-war Italy the Church's formidable grass-roots organization which paralleled the state itself, the post-war dominance of the Christian Democratic Party, and the Church's role in the educational system safeguarded a position of initiative for the Church hierarchy and underpinned its centuries-long influence on 'political world views'. By contrast, in the French Third Republic the separation of Church and state after much bitter controversy and the aggressive role of the anti-clerical *instituteurs* in winning the support of the peasantry were conceived to be essential to the establishment of the legitimacy of the republican state.

The different character of politics in individual countries is, furthermore, influenced by the way in which they have experienced different rates of change on each axis. For example, Britain not only avoided the cultural traumas that could follow from state-building but also enjoyed a relatively gradual rate of change in society compared with the late and rapid industrialization of Germany or Sweden. On the other hand, the presence of paternalist attitudes and a strong administrative capability in pre-democratic Sweden and Germany (the product of state-building) encouraged 'defensive modernization', the anticipatory development of social policies, which had not existed in Britain during the rise of an industrial working class. While their industrialization may have been more dramatic, it probably entailed less protracted human suffering than that of Britain, with important consequences for forms of working-class political conduct.

It is clear from the model that in any one political system at a particular time the whole complex range of types of society may be present. The model underlines rather than glosses over the very untidy reality that constitutes, for example, post-war French and Italian politics. In both (and especially in Italy) different groups exhibit contrasting views of the state, which include estrangement from, ambivalence towards, and support for its abstract institutional values. These views reflect their position on the *Gemeinschaft–Gesellschaft* continuum. Correspondingly, their attitudes to political accommodation range from a parasitism, which seeks to exploit the state's resources, through qualified faith in the impartial hierarchical and arbitrative role of the state, to the 'accommodationist' views of the central planners. This fracturing of 'political world views' is reflected in the extraordinary complexity of group politics and in the fragmentation and factionalism within the interest-group structure. Even the Gaullist party has not been able to avoid ambivalence; the rhetoric of the 'strong' state is tempered by an emphasis among Gaullist deputies on their ability to use their 'privileged' relationship with the administration to provide services for clients. The collusive relationship of local notables (generally hostile to the Fifth Republic) and departmental prefects has been little permeated by the Gaullists, so that it becomes possible to identify two forms of politics; one centred on the presidency, stressing general interests; the other centred on deputies, including Gaullists as well as local notables, which has changed much less radically.

A model is a way of tying together some of the vast number of loose ends that seem to characterize the development of West European political systems, and of making the intricate process of historical change more intelligible by presenting a set of highly abstract representations. The distinctive feature of this model is that it seeks to establish not only that the past illuminates the present but also that conceptual rigour and the purposive use of analysis provided by a framework of general ideas is as relevant to the task of making sense of the past as it is to clarifying the present. The model draws attention to the dynamic of changing conceptions of the character of the public power and its link with the changing character of social relations. It underlines the political significance of the divergent views on the proper character of the state that may exist within a political system. For example, opposition between the Carlists and the Liberals of Restoration Spain, and between the National People's Party and the Democratic Party of the Weimar Republic, represented a fundamental difference between nostalgists for the patrimonial state and 'modernist' advocates of the impersonal, abstract state. Similarly, the Swedish Liberal Party's advocacy of the parliamentary polity in the early 1900s was an important element of the era of confrontation which lasted up to 1920. The latter example serves to remind us that attempts to import foreign models (in this case, the British), which suggest adopting quite different views about the character of the public power, prove not only politically disruptive but also incomprehensible in terms of historically acquired ideas about the nature of politics.

NOTES

1   A model or paradigm is a convenient shorthand, a device for presenting a succinct codification of an area of analysis. Models are tentative and limited, yet they are the building blocks of theory and interpretation. They are less vague than a perspective, for they provide a systematic, specific, and often logically exhaustive set of categories for research and speculation. At the same time they are less than a theory. A model provides a 'language', a set of interrelated questions, but no account of validated propositions.

   Much of the controversy about model-building results from confusion about their purpose. This model does not seek to deny the dynamic character of historical development (which has been emphasized in the last chapter) or the importance of events and perceptions in shaping the diverse development of political systems. It reflects only a limited aspect of the world of politics. The model does not deny that factors other than the two variables which have been selected for attention introduce further differences between political systems (for example, religion, class relations, diffusion of ideas across frontiers). By offering a set of abstract categories the model takes one type of overall view and identifies an element of order in political development. However, unlike theories of political development that emphasize the process of 'modernization', it focuses on the diversity of paths that have been followed, and it does not seek to explain how particular political systems have arrived at certain points.

2   Ullmann (1965, p. 153) stresses that the abstract concept of the Crown was intimately connected with the feudal conception of society. The Crown embraced the king and the feudal tenants-in-chief and provided both a formula to unite king and kingdom and a useful shield or buffer against papal demands. The Crown did not consist of the king alone or of the community alone, but of both.

3   The tensions within the *Ständestaat* were generated by the issue of where initiation should lie rather than by contention over the form of society. For example, the tension between the aristocracy of the towns and the house of Orange was a permanent feature of the republic of the United Provinces (with the passions of the 'common' people behind the house of Orange).

4   The term 'crisis of modernity' has its roots in the idea of 'modernization'. Modernization is a complex concept that comprises various elements which may arise separately or concurrently: industrialization, the rise of urban 'mass' society, greater social mobility, secularism and rationalization and, in particular, differentiation and specialization within society. At a general level the 'crisis of modernity' is the product of a combination of a desire to escape from political and economic underdevelopment, in order to meet aspirations for social opportunity, and the fears of the 'machine' and the 'masses' that are engendered by development. It is a summating term and refers to an accumulation and simultaneity of crises (such as those of 'penetration', legitimacy, participation and distribution).

5   The model offers no explanation for the successful rise to power of Italian Fascism or German National Socialism, only an indication of the sort of conditions in which such movements originate and which they can manipulate.

6   In 'state' societies the corporatist sector refers primarily to the producer groups, in particular the trade unions, employers' organizations and industrial associations. Outside this sector there is a pluralistic politics of interest groups.

part ii
the intellectual tradition of the
state

chapter three | the state and the intellectuals: some general considerations

Clarification of the idea of the state is not to be achieved simply by exploring in the manner of linguistic analysis the logical grammar that is associated with its vocabulary. A clear grasp of the idea of the state is dependent on establishing a historical perspective of its use by jurists, political theorists and philosophers as well as by 'men of action', for the term state has been employed in very different contexts and manners. Its use may vary from fragmentary thoughts (*pensées*) about the state to attempts to formulate a coherent theory (*philosophie*) about it. Changes in its use are grounded in the intentions of those who reflect upon the state and the background theoretical understanding that they bring to bear upon it. These intentions and understandings are in turn related to, and in part reflect, a historical experience of 'stateness' and of the social and cultural attitudes associated with 'stateness' that is not evident in English-speaking societies. Experience of living within a particular kind of inherited institutional and cultural framework shapes the manner in which the character of political, legal and societal arrangements is considered. Equally, intellectual characterizations of these arrangements provide an orientation for elites towards the framework within which they operate and a distinct vocabulary in terms of which public affairs can be considered. Around 1800, for example, the extraordinary development in Germany of a concern with the idea of the state lent a unique character to German political vocabulary and established the parameters of political discussion for a century and more. There is, in other words, a complex interaction between theory and practice and between the state as an institution that rests on an ideology, the articulate ideas that politicians, administrators and lawyers have about it and theories of the state that are held by intellectuals.

Theories of the state represent neither disembodied abstractions nor the epiphenomenal products of social conditions. As we have seen, they contain a strongly pragmatic element, in the sense that much of their meaning is established with reference to the realities of practical politics and the policies which inspire contemporary debate. Variations in German theories of the state bear witness to changing definitions of the problems that face the political community. In the seventeenth and eighteenth centuries such theories were shaped by the dramatic impact of the Thirty Years' War. Some, like Ludwig von Seckendorff and Hermann Coming, responded to the subsequent problem of physical reconstruction by devoting their theoretical attention to the practical administrative requirements of the *Fürstenstaat*. Other scholars sought to respond to the widespread sense of political and spiritual insecurity, as well as to the legacy of bitterness, either by returning to scholastic tradition or, as in the case of Samuel Pufendorf, by attempting to offer a new secular legitimation of authority (Stolleis, 1977). The problem to which Pufendorf addressed his systematization of natural law was that Germany had degenerated from a *Reich* to a *Monstrum*. An antidote to the fragmentation and mutual suspicion that characterized Germany was to be found in a firmer foundation of shared principles. In the early nineteenth century theories of the state, like the theory of Hegel, were moulded, as we shall see, by the impact of the French Revolution, the emergence of the market economy and the deficit of state organization in a Germany that was no longer even formally a *Reich*.

At the same time theories of the state are in part constituted by their authors' intentions, which may or may not be representative of the wider society, and by strictly intellectual processes which give them life of their own. On occasion they may, of course, represent little more than a justification of prevailing policy. Richelieu's attempt to exert a strong influence on political theorizing in seventeenth-century France was probably the first instance of modern political propaganda. Authors were 'inspired' to produce books and pamphlets that extolled the virtues of the new patrimonial state and of a Christian *raison d'état*. The most 'outstanding' of these authors were then appointed to the newly founded *Académie Française* (1635), which was designed as another instrument of propaganda for statebuilding (Church, 1972). Even so, theories of the state have a capacity to shift political perceptions by a creative and illuminating synthesis of concepts and by providing solutions that come to form an intrinsic part of succeeding changes. For example, Bodin, Grotius, Hobbes and Spinoza made coherent ideas that were perceived only dimly, if at all, by the participants in the sixteenth- and seventeenth-century crises; they turned to sovereignty as the precondition of order in society. While intellectuals may in this way contribute to a renewal of moral self-confidence, changing theories of the state can also reflect a collapse of intellectual confidence in the contemporary political order, as during the Weimar Republic or the Third and Fourth French Republics, and thereby contribute to a growing disillusion with the regime (Sonth-eimer, 1962; Halbecq, 1965).

ACADEMIC PATRONS AND COTERIES

The character of intellectual preoccupation with the state in continental Europe has been shaped by two factors: the typically ambitious intentions behind theories of the state; and the proximity of important sections of the intelligentsia to those in public office (the state itself). The sense of urgency and even passion, the abhorrence of inconsistency and the moral confidence that were typical of scholarship reflected both a rationalist heritage and a deep sense of the fragile condition of the political order as well as of the very premises upon which that order rested. It was difficult, in a society that was characterized by pervasive fear of 'disintegration', for the intellectual to remain satisfied with an empirical and pragmatic outlook that was concerned with limited practical matters and the patient acquisition of partial knowledge. For example, historiography took on a didactic quality, related to an urge to unravel the complexity of the world by careful conceptualization, a self-reflective concern for making explicit underlying value judgements and assumptions, and above all a theoretical character which sprang from the attempt to arrive at coherent interpretations by fitting arguments into a 'world view'. In France the impetus to institutionalize history within the educational system and the early character of the historical profession were conditioned by the context of intense ideological pressure after the Franco-Prussian war to restore national pride (Keylor, 1975). Longstanding and virulent divisions within society and the vulnerability of frontiers proved potent factors in generating a perception of the importance of the state as an institution that guaranteed order. Thus President Pompidou drew on a deep-rooted French intellectual tradition when he said to his ex-colleagues of the Council of State in 1970:

For more than a thousand years...there has been a France only because there was the State, a State to bring it together, to organize it, to make it grow, to defend it not only against external threats, but also against group egotisms and rivalries. Today, more than ever, the State's force is indispensable not only to assure the nation's future and its security, but also to assure the individual his liberty.

These theoretical ambitions, in response to great practical political problems, were further strengthened by the adaptation of religious images to the field of politics (Hawthorn, 1976). Although epistemological concerns had been secularized with the new priority accorded to reason and experience, theological outlooks continued to influence the character of intellectual models and particularly the *a priori* notions about man that these models contained. Reference has often been made to the effect of the Catholic Church as a model of intellectual authority in France (Peyrefitte, 1976). Auguste Comte has been seen as a 'Catholic atheist', his positivist sociology as an example of a 'secularized' Catholicism that sought to provide a force for unity and order, a source of authoritative knowledge and guidance. By contrast, and emerging out of the even more fragmented and confused society of eighteenth-century Germany, Idealism has been interpreted as a 'secularized' Protestantism in the Pietist tradition. On the one hand, order was to be maintained by 'external' submission to the authority of the state; on the other, the moral autonomy and integral growth of the unique, individual personality was to be safeguarded by the freedom of 'inwardness', of the 'thinking subject'. German theories of the state tended to combine a stress on duty and the supreme right of the state against the individual, who could not resist, with a recognition of the right to subjectivity and self-direction. Except in the area of scholarship, where the requirement of self-direction was stressed, the result was ambiguity about the rights of the individual.

Traditionally, the importance of theorizing on the state has been increased by the close connection between scholars and the state administration and the importance of the latter as both a decision-making centre and a source of recruitment for the political system. The role of faculties of law and economics as centres of elite socialization and recruitment, equivalent in function to the English public schools, has further aided the dissemination of theories of the state (Armstrong, 1973; Dahrendorf, 1967). For example, in the southern German states of Bavaria and Baden-Würtemberg, the three subjects of public law, administrative law and *allgemeine Staatslehre,* each of which focuses on the notion of the state, can account for the greater part of undergraduate work in law. The idea of the state is even more apparent in preparation for the French *licence* in law, in which there are compulsory courses in the history of institutions, political economy, constitutional law and administrative law. In France the notion of the state also forms the basis of teaching at *'Sciences Po'*, where many serving administrators provide or participate in courses: before 1940, as a private institution (the *École Libre des Sciences Politiques*), it provided most of the successful candidates for entry into the *grands corps;* after the war (renamed *l'Institut d'Études Politiques*) as part of the University of Paris, but with a separate legal status, it dominated recruitment into the new and eminent *École Nationale d'Administration* (ENA), to the extent of 94 per cent in 1962–3. From its very beginnings in the 1870s *'Sciences Po'* had been closely linked in terms of staff and students to the Paris Faculty of Law and Economics, although the former attempts to provide a broader training. Together both institutions have had a great influence on the assumptions that underlie the content of training at ENA. ENA has been the recruiting ground for the *grands corps,* notably the Finance Inspectorate, which is based on the Ministry of Finance, and the lawyer–administrators of the Council of State. The Council of State has itself been important as the 'conscience' of the state; its views on draft laws and decrees and its judgements in cases relating to the individual and the state have been influenced by juristic conceptions of the state. During the Third Republic the Council of State played a key role as the exponent of 'republican synthesis', a process of converting the exercise of public power into republican principles of individualism, liberty, justice and solidarity. Particularly important was the innovative role of the *commissaires du gouvernement* (notably, in the period up to the 1920s, Blum, Romieu, Pichet and Tardieu), whose reports on individual cases were often models of judicial analysis and indicated the way in which doctrine (for example, ideas of public domain, public service, public utility and public power) influenced as well as emerged from practice.[1] The two founders of French administrative law, Léon Aucoc and Laferrière, were brilliant *commissaires,* and Laferrière, the author of the first major treatise on the subject, went on to become vice-president of the Council of State. According to Aucoc, the task of the Council of State was to ensure the principle that 'the State must conduct itself like an honest man in its relation with particulars'. Gaston Jèze (1904) was a key figure in introducing Duguit's conception of the 'public-service' state into its judgements; while after 1945

Roland Maspetiol (1957) was one of those who applied the ideas of Hauriou. Moreover, important political figures like Michel Debré, Léon Blum, Georges Pompidou and Jean Lecanuet served for varying periods in the Council. The Council of State also provided the leading figures in the early direction of ENA and thereby reinforced the latter's legalistic approach and self-conscious concern with the 'mission' of the state.

Another ubiquitous figure in 'state' societies besides the lawyer–administrator is the lawyer–politician. The principal politicians of the Third Republic were lawyers who were steeped in Roman-law conceptions of an independent public power subject to law: Gambetta, Ferry, Waldeck-Rousseau, Blum. Two important politicians of the Fourth Republic, Edgar Faure and Pierre Mendès-France, continued this tradition. The post-war impact of another lawyer–politician, Debré, was considerable. He was creator, with de Gaulle, of ENA as part of his reformist conception of the state; ENA's continuing intellectual mentor, through the presence there during the 1950s of his collaborator Pierre Racin; architect of the constitution of the Fifth Republic and its first prime minister. René Capitant and Marcel Prélot were other prominent examples of Gaullist lawyer–politicians; both, like Debré, were deeply concerned about the authority of the state. In the Bonn Republic Professors Horst Ehmke and Peter von Oertzen, former students of Rudolf Smend, have been leading figures in the discussion about political planning and policy programmes within the Social Democratic Party from the late 1960s. Their influence was most apparent in the new long-term programme of that party (OR'85).[2]

The role of the faculties of law is strengthened not just by the number of experienced politicians (like Faure and Capitant), senior civil servants and judges who return to take professorships there. Along with the role that their professors play in the administrative courts, this circulation of personnel keeps them in touch with affairs and provides impulses for change that are not present in the faculties of philosophy or letters. The adaptive quality of the teaching of law increases in turn the breadth and richness of courses offered. Pressure for a stronger sociological and political content to administrative training led the nineteenth-century German law faculties to develop statistics (*Statistik*), which was a return to the attempt to found a comprehensive and practical science of the state (*Staatenkunde*) that would provide systematic information for policy-makers, of the kind developed in seventeenth-century Germany by Hermann Conring and Ludwig von Seckendorff.[3] It had its forerunner in Italian work of the sixteenth century and its successor in eighteenth-century Cameralism and in the empirical *Statistik* of Schlözer at Göttingen. Hence economics and political science developed out of the law faculties in Germany; there was not a problem of combining two equally and separately developed subjects, law and social science. The broadening of legal curricula was a product partly of the desire of the law faculties to maintain their privileged position and partly of adaptation through closer contact with practice.

At the same time there was a greater strain between the 'reference groups' of the scholar than is apparent in Anglo-American universities. This strain arose from the tension between the training role of the universities for state service and their critical, philosophic role. In Germany the emphasis on the applied, practical role was apparent in the model provided by the Cameralism of the Prussian University of Halle and the 'common-sense' rationalism taught there in the eighteenth century by Christian Thomasius, the prophet of enlightenment and absolutism, and later by Christian Wolff, a reformer and a more controversial figure. This essentially 'bureaucratic' conception of the scholar contrasted with the 'cultural' model of the scholar that was associated with the Greek classics of eighteenth-century Gottingen and the Idealism of the 1800s and post-1890s. In France the 'bureaucratic' model of the scholar who served the state found its most severe critiques from within Latin Quarter opinion—for example, in the post-1905 attacks on the 'New Sorbonne' and in the late 1960s attack on the new bureaucratic/technocratic state. Even the faculties of letters and of science in Paris were heavily involved in training *lycée* teachers, especially the elite core of *École Normale Supérieure* students. Their teaching was, therefore, constrained by *lycée* subjects and state examinations. The 'useful' knowledge imparted in Germany through Cameralism in the eighteenth century and positivist conceptions of the *Rechtsstaat* in the nineteenth and twentieth centuries remained a source of strain between governments, which wanted a more practical and relevant approach, and universities (as well as within the universities themselves).

There was a constant tension between law faculties, whose prestige depended on their elite-training function, and faculties of philosophy or letters. The 'mandarin' or 'cultural' wing of the intelligentsia found its home in the latter. It was, for example, from the philosophy faculties of Jena and later Berlin that the optimism of the *Kulturstaat* (cultural state) emerged. Fichte, the originator of this conception, and then Hegel and Schelling reflected the cultural revival of late eighteenth-century Germany (notable in Göttingen and Weimar). They attempted to link political philosophy to the concerns of artists and poets like Schiller and Hölderlin rather than to those of the bureaucracy. The state's sublime function was to assist in realizing the comprehensive educational ideal of *Bildung,* the forming of the whole personality by intellectual values (Bruford, 1975).[4] This ideal of 'pure' learning, which was outlined by Wilhelm von Humboldt and became the central one in the German cultural tradition, was dependent on the notion of an 'inner' freedom that would enable the cultivation of a 'higher' timeless self. The theory of the *Kulturstaat* was preoccupied with metaphysics rather than epistemology and emphasized the achievement of harmony through a synthesis that placed the particular in the context of the 'whole' (Ringer, 1969). Its theorists were concerned to determine the state's essence, which was defined in the moral and spiritual categories of *Geist,* categories that were to provide a universally acceptable set of purposes for the state. The result was a vague, elevated level of political discourse that was clearer about what it opposed than about what it stood for and that had, in Nietzsche's words, 'a weakness for noble poses' and an inability to sustain 'any kind of philosphical abstemiousness or scepticism' (Bruford, 1975, p. 170). There was little interest in empirical research and in the kind of sustained political and economic analysis that is concerned with the practical difficulties of building consensus and with the nature and limits of political tactics and techniques. Emphasis on the 'whole' and on 'spirit' reflected a search for moral certainty and a yearning to escape from painful dilemmas. Such an outlook generated an indifference to reality and a willingness to entertain the sort of illusion that contains the seeds of irresponsibility. Only against this background of deep tensions within the German university created by the question of the proper character of the intellectual's role can the extraordinary complexity and polemics of German theories of the state be fully appreciated. German universities combined the conception of the *Kulturstaat,* which emphasized the detachment of 'pure' learning (*Bildung*) and which encouraged a 'merciless moralizing' by its preoccupation with the 'whole' and with 'spirit', with the 'practical' learning of the Halle model and the law faculties. In addition, and in large part as a reaction, there was a tradition of radical demystification or debunking of orthodox Idealism. Much less typical, and forced out by intellectual polemics, was the spirit of scholarly caution and precision apparent in the work of Friedrich Meinecke, Tönnies and Max Weber. It was, of course, Weber who made a celebrated attack on the 'priestly' role claimed by German intellectuals, a role that had been inspired by

Idealism's search for ultimate values and synthesis, in favour of a more analytical and technical role.

In the University of Paris, at the centre of the French educational system, there have been considerable differences between the faculty of law and the faculty of letters, with the latter somewhat more open to the political and ideological currents of the Latin Quarter (Clark, 1973). The distance between them was reflected in the progress of sociology: Émile Durkheim's sociology dominated the faculty of letters rapidly after his appointment in 1902, while somewhat belatedly Gabriel de Tarde's (1909) introspective sociological method had greater influence on the law faculty (through the work of Maurice Hauriou). Their differences were also apparent in the political strains between the 'conservative' law faculty and left-wing-inclined colleagues in letters and science during the establishment of the new university structure between 1969 and 1971. More significant and distinctive has been the tension that has been created by the continuous involvement of the University of Paris in the life of the Latin Quarter and the influence of shifts in the climate of opinion there on the ideological temperature of the University. These shifts are more clearly reflected outside the University, in the *Collège de France,* where, for example, after 1905 Bergson's 'vitalist' influence began to counteract Durkheim's reputation. Parisian culture has formed a remarkably self-sufficient, introverted world, one that has not been deeply involved in international scholarly contacts and has oscillated between Cartesian rationalism and what Clark (1973) calls philosophies of 'spontaneity' which experience on occasion a resurgence in the Latin Quarter. One philosophy of 'spontaneity' was existentialism, with its emphasis on subjectivity. Its influence on the post-1945 University helped to weaken the hold of Kant and Descartes in the faculty of letters. A further example was provided by the so-called 'New Philosophy' which emerged in the 1970s. Writers like Glucksmann (1977) were viscerally anti-*étatiste* and attacked, often in an ironic and witty manner, the influence of the 'great' German philosophers (Fichte, Hegel, Marx and Nietzsche) for their cult of the order and authority of the state, their 'idolatory of reason', and their myth of *le Savoir total.* The unholy alliance of reason and the state in the 'great systems' thinkers was seen as the root cause of twentieth-century barbarities. In fact, the 'New Philosophy' ended up as dizzyingly abstract and as prone to universalize the particular as the theories that it attacked.

Common to France, Germany and Italy has been a competition for a

hold on public opinion between the 'rationalism' and the formal traditions of the universities and the philosophies of 'spontaneity' outside, or
marginal to, the university establishment. There are various examples of
how the universities could be outbidded by other intellectual appeals to
the semi-educated and young: in France Henri Bergson's *élan vitale* at
the *Collège de France* and Sartre's existentialism; in Italy after the First
World War Gabriele D'Annunzio, the heroic 'poet-warrior', advocated a
politics of spiritual transformation that was essentially aesthetic and contemptuous of 'official' Italy; in early twentieth-century Germany a national *völkisch,* anti-Semitic and anti-'modernist' literature and a vulgar
Lebensphilosophie were essentially non-conceptual and stressed immediate experience in opposition to the abstract rationalism of neo-Kantianism. There have always been two totally different and unrelated groups
of intellectuals in Germany: the highly respected, official establishment
of university professors and a volatile and bohemian minority of radicals
(Mann, 1960, p. 495).

Of central importance to the diffusion of particular theories of the state
is the role of academic patrons. Patrons provide grand, programmatic
schemes and place their followers and associates in key positions. One
result of their activities is a pattern of inter-institutional links established
through common membership of an informal coterie which Clark (1973)
refers to as a 'cluster' and which is attached to the patron; another is the development of a homogeneity of social and political views in certain faculties. The competition for academic leadership and the associated patronage
lead in turn to an excess of grand, eclectic and often ponderous theoretical
statements by would-be patrons. Studies of the rise and fall of these clusters
would be enormously helpful to any elucidation of the varying fortunes of
different theories. In France, for example, the influence of Duguit's conception of the 'public-service' state and of his 'school of Bordeaux' was very
dependent on the fate of the cluster that centred on Durkheim, Duguit's
former colleague at Bordeaux. This cluster provides a notable instance of
the audacious and aggressive character of programmatic statements: a very
broad definition of sociology that suggested that all forms of behaviour
could be explained in terms of external and constraining social 'facts'. The
Durkheimians were extraordinarily successful in establishing sociological leadership before 1914. However, with the Great War and Durkheim's
death, the cluster's influence declined rapidly until, after 1945, its dominance ended (Lukes, 1973a). One of the most influential clusters was that

which formed around the jurist Maurice Hauriou, whose disciples like Achille Mestre, Prélot (1957) and Vedel (1949) at the Paris law faculty ensured that generations of jurists were trained in his ideas.[5] By contrast, Carré de Malberg at Strasbourg remained relatively isolated. He was never integrated as a patron into the national system and, like Burckhardt in Switzerland, inspired largely by the excellence of his example. In Prussia during the Weimar period the extremely aggressive and polemical character of rival theories of the state reflected contending clusters: the legal positivists of the Laband school; the 'decisionists' who were disciples of the Bonn jurist Carl Schmitt (1928) and were concerned with the requirements of an effective sovereign power; and the 'integrationists' who were inspired by the Berlin jurist Rudolf Smend (1928) and emphasized the importance of the spiritual content of the state. Ideological factors and moral concerns have continued to complement scholarship as criteria for appointments to key academic posts. Much of the rivalry between Smend and Heller, for example, arose from Smend's view that Heller's appointment to a chair in Berlin in the late 1920s was political in character. In France the rise of Durkheimian sociology and Duguit's theory of the state were linked to Dreyfusard ideology, republicanism and socialism; the counter-attack on the 'New Sorbonne' represented in part right-wing and neo-Catholic reactions to the 'bourgeois' state. Similarly, much German academic writing from the 1890s to the 1930s had a strongly programmatic and polemical character that derived from a preoccupation with the nature of the newly united state and of the social forces, represented by new bourgeois and working-class groups, which pressed upon this state.

Such deep ideological involvement of scholars excited enthusiasm, interest and hatred and lent an organized character to their divisions. Consequently, both the structure and form of continental European scholarship tended to be in sharp contrast to the Anglo-American academic traditions of historiography, law, politics and social science. There were periods of apparent intellectual stability, while one theory of the state was dominant, followed by the turmoil and drama of 'succession crisis', when vacancy in a major post offered an opportunity for new perspectives to be established. In this environment of 'succession crises' the intellectual development of the state could seem to be deeply fractured and characterized by sharp discontinuities, even faddism. Academic patrons were most powerful in centralized university systems like those of France, Italy or Prussia, where there was a vertical mobility pattern and very few central posts which enjoyed an inflated status through appointments accumulated in different institutions. In particular, Sorbonne professors were able to practise a paternalistic style of authority denied even to their German counterparts. Within the decentralized university system of Germany, especially after the abolition of Prussia, the greater opportunities for horizontal mobility restricted the patronage of individual academics and made professional organizations a more important reference point for the scholar.

French theories of the state illustrate well the two themes of dramatic change, which is associated with the succession of clusters and the emergence of new patrons, and the strongly ideological character of scholarly activity. Adhemar Esmein's individualistic theory of the state was suited to the stabilization of the fragile Third Republic and to its secular outlook; while the threat posed to the cluster that surrounded him before 1914 by Duguit reflected a new political awareness of the 'social question' and of the relevance of social science to the creation of a republican morality that would deal with the problem of individualism in modern society. The 'Scelle affair' of 1925 provided an interesting and notable example of the political significance that Latin Quarter opinion attached to contests between rival clusters for academic appointments. In this case of an appointment to the Paris law faculty Georges Scelle, a representative of the Duguit school, was nominated rather than Louis Le Fur, a conservative figure. The appointment was symptomatic of the growing strength and confidence of the Duguit cluster. Consequently, it was bitterly resisted. When, as a result of this controversy, Berthélemy was forced to resign the deanship of the faculty, there was great and active support for him within the Latin Quarter. During the crisis years of the 1930s, when the political and constitutional failings of the Third Republic were once again being assailed from all sides, traditionalists like Joseph Barthélemy (later Minister of Justice in the Vichy regime) and Henri Berthélemy provided 'appropriate' authoritarian theories of the state. After the Liberation an extraordinary dominance was achieved by the institutional theory of the state, which was associated with Hauriou. This rationalist theory sought to avoid the errors of a pragmatic muddling through, which had appeared to characterize the Third Republic, by focusing attention on the purposes of the state as the basis for the design of its institutions. Adherents of the institutional theory like Prélot and Vedel became prominent critics of the Fourth Republic and helped to shape the climate of ideas favourable to the greater autonomy of executive institutions, which was the aim of the Fifth Republic.[6]

The rivalry of patrons does not always mean sharp intellectual opposition, and the succession of clusters does not necessarily bring about dramatic changes of ideas. In Italy, for example, the eminent jurist and later politician Vittorio Emmanuele Orlando (1952) had an extraordinary influence which outlasted a succession of clusters. The influence of his ideas on the autonomy of legal institutions and methods, which derived from Laband, stemmed in large part from the way in which they served a function similar to that in Germany: the justification of a recently created state. His famous pupil, Santi Romano (1901), gave a new rigour and coherence to Italian public law, at first through his skill in developing formal legal concepts and later (1917) by introducing the concept of the institution. The formalism, conceptualism and abstraction that characterized the Romano cluster enabled it to accommodate to Fascism (Romano became president of the *Consiglio di Stato* or Council of State in 1928) and, through its scholars, to dominate post-war Italy. There were other patrons who acted as rivals to Orlando and Romano (notably Roman law scholars such as Vittorio Scialoja and Oreste Ranelletti), but major opposition, in the name of the empirical method and of a political conception of the state and law, did not emerge until the 1960s (Cassesse, 1971). The long dominance of an historical, purist legal science was to be explained partly as a defence against the seductions and risks of Fascism and partly as a product of the impediment of the sociological outlook by Fascism for two decades.

STATE AS ORGANIZING AND INTEGRATING CONCEPT

The vitality and importance of the intellectual tradition of the state is associated with its role as an organizing and integrating concept within fields of study like law, political science, economics, history, pedagogy and administrative science. The idea of the state is a common philosophic reference point within the humanistic sciences: the German notion of *Geisteswissenschaft* incorporates Idealist assumptions that predispose the scholar to take state as an intellectual point of departure. Furthermore, university posts are only a first step in the establishment of new subjects like social science (as the Durkheimians found) or statistics. In the longer run it is usually essential for the state to establish examinations (that is, to exploit the training function of the universities) and posts in secondary education. Academic debate is consequently addressed to the ministerial bureaucracy that adopts curricula for the educational system. The development of individual

subjects is considerably affected by the way in which they are assimi-
lated into existing educational structures and ideas that emphasize the
requirements of the state. For example, economics took on a strongly
institutional and legal emphasis within the faculties of law. Social science
grew up in the French Third Republic and post-1945 Germany allied to
the idea of providing a new public morality through civic training—in
the case of France, of replacing Catholicism by a new secular morality.
The close relationship of both the theory and the practice of education
to the idea of the state found its expression in a moralistic pedagogy that
stressed the authority of the teacher as the interpreter of the great moral
ideas of his time and the community's need for a rigorous 'binding', for
social discipline and 'collective forces'. From very different ideological perspectives Theodor Litt, Georg Kerschensteiner and Jonas Cohn in
Weimar Germany, and Durkheim in pre-1914 France, adopted conceptions of the imperative character of the teacher's role as a moral authority.
According to Durkheim, it was essential that the state should be present
in education to ensure social solidarity ('a sufficient community of ideas
and sentiments'); education must not be abandoned to the 'arbitrariness of
private individuals'. After the famous educational reforms of Jules Ferry
in the 1880s, which were intended, in Ferry's own words, to ensure 'a
certain morality of the State', a new Republican morality (involving a
mixture of Kantian moralism and 'benevolent' science) diffused through
the centralized education system and was reinforced later by the introduction of Durkheim's sociology into the écoles normales. According to
Daniel Halévy 'Durkheim's lecture-course [at the Sorbonne] was the sign
of the insolent capture by a doctrinaire group of the teaching of the state'.
Durkheim's rationalist secular morality (Cartesian in rationalism, Comtian
in science and Kantian in morality) became, along with solidarity, a new
sort of official ideology of the Third Republic in the years before 1914
(Lukes, 1973a, pp. 135, 374).

Both the academic study of, and political debate about, economics in
continental Europe revealed the presence of the state as an organizing
concept in the clearest light. An economic paradigm which emphasized
the market and profitability and was concerned primarily with the micro-
level of economic activity has dominated the Anglo-American tradition of
economics. There have, of course, been important differences within that
tradition: notably between, on the one hand, the philosophic outlook of the
classical theories (Adam Smith and Ricardo) and of the Cambridge School
(John Maynard Keynes, Roy Harrod and Joan Robinson) and, on the other, the

empirical and strongly mathematical interests of American economics. It was, however, much easier to graft this American tradition on to the analytical traditions of English economics than on to continental European economics. The result of the colonization of economics by legal minds and of the training function of the universities was to give a strongly institutional dimension to continental European study of economics and to link that study to philosophical questions about the appropriate character and functions of the state. The approach was at the same time less strictly 'academic' than in the English tradition; it was firmly interlocked with the practical, applied orientation of the universities. There was strong emphasis on public finance (witness the influential nineteenth-century work on the science of public finance by Lorenz von Stein, the Berlin economist Adolf Wagner and the Austrian Albert Schaffle) and on a more systematic involvement (certainly in the teaching of the subject) with policies pursued through institutions and the links of both policies and institutions to economic philosophy. A preference for synthesis was reflected in a critical reception of the 'atomist' character of Anglo-American economics and a preference for placing the latter in a wider framework if it were taken on board. For example, the German theorist of political economy, Friedrich List (1841), argued that the idea of the state stood on a different plane from the economic world of exchange values and therefore was not amenable to the methods of economic science. In his view, orthodox economists offered an incomplete, abstract account of economic activity because they failed to see that the economy was intrinsically a part of the state and that consequently economics had to be political. The state was conceived of as an economic unity and its purpose was 'the harmony of productive powers'. Hence state intervention was inherent in economic life.

Continental European economics went beyond a concern for quantities like demand and supply and for mechanisms like pricing to the qualities of the economic order as the focal point for evaluation and appraisal of specific institutions and policies. Particular proposals were related for reasons of consistency and legitimacy to wider theories about the relationship of state and economy. An attempt was made to mould all the elements of economic and industrial policy to accord with a single concept (the 'social market economy', the 'concerted economy', the *économie dirigée*) which dealt with the nature of the economic 'order' and established the character and objectives of intervention. The emphasis was upon a comprehensive approach which, by stimulating a recognition of economic interdependence, would encourage responsible economic behaviour. Thus the misleadingly titled 'Socialists of the Chair' in late nineteenth-century Germany objected to the timeless abstractions of English economic analysis and to 'economic man' as a social model. In its place they offered an historical approach which stressed the non-economic and institutional context of economic life (Schmoller, 1900–4). Their economic ideas were fitted into an organic conception of the state: in Albert Schaffle's words, 'an organ which concentrates and expresses the whole of social life'. Concern for 'community' and the 'interest of the whole' led them to propagate, through the Social Policy Association (*Verein für Sozialpolitik*), which was founded in 1873, their ideas of an active social policy, in contrast to the views of Treitschke and Ranke who, they feared, would undermine the power of the state by aggravating the problem of dissent.[7] Gustav Schmoller, the Berlin economist, who stood on the conservative side of the Association and glorified monarchy and bureaucracy as the protectors of the 'lower strata' against the higher bourgeoisie, became a kind of university 'pope' who helped his students into important government positions and influenced the development of German social welfare legislation.

Even the post-1945 'social market economy' sustained the traditional German belief in the keywords *Kooperation, Integration* and *Augsleich* as well as an organic conception of society. Against the background of the 'total state' of the Third Reich, with its directed economy (*Lenkungswirtschaft*), there was a desire to re-establish the idea of the distinction between state and society. On the one hand, the heritage of the German (*Ordo*) liberal tradition of the Weimar years led to a stress on the importance of the authority of the state if the development of power structures within the economy were to be prevented. The state's purpose was to provide the basic economic order and the moral framework of economic policy, within which the economic process could unfold automatically. Its functions were the maintenance of the competitive order (through, for example, the 'middle-estate' policy or *Mittelstandspolitik*) and of economic stability (through the autonomy of the *Bundesbank* in the management of monetary policy). Both Eucken and Röpke, perhaps the most important theorists of the 'social market economy', were convinced that a strong independent state, which was able to resist sectional interests, was a prerequisite of a neo-liberal economic system. On the other hand, the liberal conception of the *Ordnungsfunktion* of the state was an attempt at depoliticization by market decision. This conception sought to establish the autonomy of economic activity as the chief function of civil society, to prevent *ad hoc* intrusions of morality into the economic process, and to reduce the influence of politicking on currency management.

In French economics, too, considerable attention was paid to the moral character of economic phenomena and their institutional context. The possibility of radically separating moral from economic phenomena was typically denied. Consequently, the state was seen as the 'guiding force', the 'organizer and regulator of collective existence': it was seen in *dirigiste* theory as 'commanding' and exercising initiative; and in the theory of the 'concerted' economy as minimizing 'collective loss' through the spread of imbalances in an interdependent economy, through the 'collective solidarity' and discipline which arise out of synthetic processes of reasoning characteristic of a centralized process of planning whose decisions are based on 'reliable' information and enable a co-ordination of objectives and resources. It was, of course, scarcely surprising that in both France and Germany particular policy areas (like agriculture in Germany) should fall short of achieving coherence and co-ordination with economic doctrines, or that these doctrines should be controversial (in the 1960s, for example, French economists and certain politicians like Pompidou and Giscard d'Estaing began to favour neo-liberal views, and some German SPD ideologists referred to the need for a developmental role for the state that was dependent on improving its 'steering capacity'). What remained distinctive was the concern for policy consistency in terms of abstract argument. The short-term, pragmatic character of economic policy debate in Britain was apparent in the field of government intervention (which is not geared to a particular principle like that of 'market conformity', as in Germany, or readily accepted, as in France, where the conception of the moral function of the state as economic entrepreneur and manager is historically rooted), and in the field of tax reform and wealth distribution, where in Britain fiscal 'fine tuning' predominated over the attempt to make explicit and to order basic principles. 'State' societies are, in other words (whether one looks at economic policy or education), characterized by a very different context of language in terms of which academic contributions are made and policy measures discussed.

A study of the intellectual tradition of the state can lead all too easily to an exaggeration of the cultural resonance of the idea and, therefore, to an overestimation of its practical impact. In some societies an intellectual concern with the state can become the preserve of a juristic culture, which is separated from the general culture and centred on its own specialized realm of publishing houses and book shops. For example, in Italy jurists in the tradition of Orlando and Romano have been so firmly trapped within their speculations and formal abstractions (which pose as legal 'positivism') that they have lost contact with the practical problems of applying legal norms in a particular cultural and political setting. The divorce between a highly abstract intellectual life and politics was most apparent in agrarian societies like Naples: Vico helped to make it into an eighteenth-century centre of the 'universal' ideas of the Enlightenment; with the mid-nineteenth-century work of De Sanctis and Settembrini it became the centre of the Italian school of Hegelian philosophy; while Benedetto Croce derived from Vico and Hegel an Idealist philosophy of history that was to dominate Italian intellectual life from the eve of the First World War to the mid-twentieth century. Croce preached the political dangers of positivism and of a lack of high-mindedness and stressed that the intellectuals had been the active element in Neapolitan history. According to Gramsci, he became the great 'lay pope' of the intelligentsia (Allum, 1973, p. 82). However, it can be doubted that Neapolitan intellectual life had much meaning in the context of the practical problems that were experienced by those who were dependent for a living on an agrarian society.

The intellectual tradition of the state is not of course, monolithic. In the Netherlands and Sweden, for example, there is an abhorrence of abstract speculation and intellectual 'systems', and a more individualistic style of scholarship is preferred which exhibits a critical 'common sense'. In the nineteenth century the result was a lack of creative power in political ideas but, at the same time, a tolerance of a plurality and incoherence of ideas. Even in France and Germany it should not be assumed that formalized elite training is geared to the implantation of a single, unified theory of the state. A plurality of contending theories of the state coexist, and the individual can choose among them. The student can, in fact, avoid the idea of the state by opting for those law and social science courses that are not directly concerned with the concept. Indeed, the growth of the social sciences and their establishment (for example, in Western Germany from the 1960s) as separate faculties have been seen as an opportunity to escape from the notion of the state. Even then, the intellectual focus tends to be on the demystification of the state.

NOTES

1   The *commissaires* appeal frequently to *la doctrine* when they propose novel solutions to the *Conseil d'État*. Doctrine is not just influential in the preparation of particular judgements. In its efforts to systematize existing judgements by discovering the underlying principles, doctrine makes a contribution to future judgements (Waline, 1957).

2   Wilhelm Hennis (1977), a former pupil of Smend and a former member of the SPD (Smend remained a political conservative), attacked Oertzen (chairman of the party commission which produced the draft programme OR'85) and Ehmke (a vice-chairman of the commission) as exponents of a socialist *Staatslehre* which sought to establish the 'SPD state'. They were encouraging the SPD to move away from the *Rechtstaat* conception of the delimitation and division of the public power towards the 'goal-orientated programme state' (*zielorientierter Programmstaat*) and a preoccupation with its 'steering capacity'. Both Hennis and Böckenförde (1972) stressed that the interest of the Smend school in a material analysis of the state had been at the expense of insight into the formal requirements of order and, in particular, into the importance of the analytical distinction between state and society. The emphasis had been on the elements of will and organization, on the notion of the *Staat als Willensverband* and *Organisation* rather than on that of the *Staat als Ordnung*.

In his inaugural address at Freiburg Professor Ehmke took as his model the 'engaged' academic Karl von Rotteck, leader of the liberal opposition in Baden before 1848. His *Staatslexikon* of the 1830s was a powerful influence in spreading ideas of natural law. The tradition of politically engaged jurists in Baden politics had been continued by Mohl and Bluntschli, Mohl's successor at Heidelberg.

3   Seckendorff's *Fürstenstaat* (1656) had a considerable influence. It drew together ethics, law, economics, finance, policy studies and politics in its discussion of the reforms in Sachsen-Gotha after 1640, the 'model state' in which he was an administrator.

4   The original meaning of *Bildung* derived from Pietist thought. In the process of becoming secularized during the nineteenth century it turned into a formal doctrine of privacy. *Bildung* encouraged a retreat from ordinary life into radical subjectivism; a narrowly aesthetic view of man as an unpolitical being that was most clearly articulated by Thomas Mann (1918); and a blindness to social realities and an overconfident arrogance (Bruford, 1975).

5   The Duguit tradition did not completely disappear: the jurist de Laubadère (1970) and the political scientist Maurice Duverger kept it alive in the post-1945 period.

6   Prélot and Hauriou had been members of the progressive Catholic *Parti Démocrate Populaire* during the inter-war period and had contributed to that party's unusually high quality of discussion about constitutional matters. The party's 1929 congress was devoted to *Réforme de L'État Républicain* and included proposals for greater governmental stability, a strict separation of powers, regional assemblies, administrative decentralization and corporatist

forms of group involvement. This programme moulded the later ideas of the Gaullists, and Prélot himself became a Gaullist in the late 1940s. Another law professor, René Capitant (a left-wing Gaullist), established the Gaullist Union in 1946 to advocate de Gaulle's constitutional proposals for quasi-presidential government, proposals that had been advanced in his famous speech at Bayeux. In 1956 Vedel and Duverger were notable supporters of presidential government. This background, and the fact that even Blum came round to supporting the idea of presidential government after 1940, suggests the error of identifying a common source of opposition to the system of *gouvernement d'assemblée* in the 1936 report of the conservative *Comité technique pour la Réforme constitutionnelle* which had included Barthelemy and the jurist Raphael Alibert, both of whom became Pétain's chief legal advisers.

7   The vigour of supra-party organizations like the *Verein für Sozialpolitik*, and indeed of 'lecture-hall' politics in general, owed much to the disillusionment of liberal intellectuals with the fragmented character of political liberalism in nineteenth-century Germany and their withdrawal from liberal parties whose ideology as parties of the people contrasted so sharply with their alienation as parties of notables from the grass roots.

chapter four | three conceptions of the state: might, law and legitimacy

The term state evokes firstly the idea of power, of effective, controlled, organized power.... Effective power, the state also implies a sovereign power.... The state is defined again as legitimate power.

J. Donnedieu de Vabres (1954, pp. 15–18)

One way of bringing some order into the complexity of theories of the state and of helping to elucidate the concept is by offering an analytical distinction between different types of theory. The usual distinction offered in continental Europe is between socio-political, legal, and philosophical conceptions of the state (Ermacora, 1970). These approaches have been concerned with different problems raised by the existence of the state as an institution or apparatus and have emphasized opposed properties of the phenomenon. While the distinction is useful, it is worth stressing the interdependence of these three approaches. Socio-political and legal approaches are capable of offering prescriptive propositions about the state, just as philosophical approaches can be critical of the adequacy of the descriptive propositions which are contained in socio-political and legal analysis (d'Entrèves, 1967, p. 4).

THE STATE AS MIGHT

The state is not an academy of arts. If it neglects its strengths in order to promote the idealistic aspirations of man, it repudiates its own nature and perishes.

Heinrich von Treitschke (1963, p. 15)

In the continental European view a socio-political perspective on the state involves political 'realism': an interest in 'realities' rather than ideas and in processes and socio-economic factors rather than institutions. There is not the focus on norms, which is characteristic of the legal approach, or on the ontological preoccupations of the philosopher. The concerns are those of Machiavelli: a factual analysis of the state as it is rather than as it ought to be, and the stability, efficacy or effectiveness of rule. This 'realistic' approach offers essentially a theory of the preservation of states, and it was likely to be found appealing in those times and places (like sixteenth-century Italy, seventeenth-century France after the Wars of Religion, and nineteenth-century Germany) in which the fragility of existing or new states was most apparent and the requirement of force most clearly observed. Its thinkers were absorbed with the problem of sheer political survival in the face of external and internal threats. In this context of vulnerability the state emerged, to both its friends and its foes, as an instrument of force or might that was outside and superior to the individual will and concerned to suppress dissent at home and wage successful war abroad. Its symbols were seen to be those of *potentia:* of economic power, weaponry and propaganda. Its incarnation was to be found in the entrepreneur, soldier or manager. Political 'realism' has, in fact, had an extraordinary influence, largely in terms of devaluing the state by reductionism. Although Machiavelli did not use the term *ragion di stato* or the Latin *ratio status,* this political 'realist' was the first to popularize the idea of the state by linking it to the theme of political prudence. Marxism has provided an alternative influential formulation of the 'realistic' view of the state in the nineteenth and twentieth centuries, while the 'repressive' state has formed the essential ingredient of anarchist theories like that of Bakunin (1970) for whom *l'État, c'est le mal.*

The debate about the 'reason of state' reveals how the approach of political 'realism' could be extended into the prescriptive proposition that not only is force the essential characteristic of the state but also its accumulation and effective use the fundamental value of politics. In fact, the vast majority of French and German writers who were concerned with the reason of state in the seventeenth century recoiled before such implications of the doctrine. Where they adopted it they subordinated it to the religious purposes of the state. A secularized concept of prudence which allowed a purely autonomous ethic of state action was likely to lead, as in the case of Pierre Charron, to one's work being placed on the index of prohibited books (Kogel, 1972). Glorification of the state as force, of might as right, reached its high point in the nineteenth-century German *Realpolitik* conception of the

Machtstaat. The *Machtstaat* was in part a 'realistic' response to the circumstances of German unification by force of Prussian arms and to the militaristic spirit of society (embodied in the reserve officer corps and the martial figure of the emperor). While it reflected and inspired talk of colonies, of military preparedness, of a navy to rival Britain's and of the superiority of German *Kultur,* the *Machtstaat* was based as much on fear and pessimism as on aggression and the desire for conflict. According to Field Marshal von Moltke, 'Perpetual peace is a dream and an unlovely one at that, while war is a link in the divine order of the world. In it are developed man's purest virtues, courage, faithfulness to duty and the willingness to make sacrifices. Without war the world would sink in the swamp of materialism.' This glorification of war as a contest of moral energies was captured in Thomas Mann's ironic reference to 'General Dr von Staat'. In fact, many of the theorists who became associated with *Machtstaat* theories were disillusioned reformers. Clausewitz turned from idealistic identification with the Prussian state to revolt against it and, finally, to a disillusioned acceptance and preoccupation with 'realistic' analysis of the efficient use of the power of the state (Paret, 1976). Treitschke began as an anti-Bismarck Saxonian liberal. A further element, which took *Machtstaat* ideas outside the realm of political realism, was the heritage of German Romanticism, with its organic conception of the state as a historical growth and its assertion that man cannot be thought of outside the state. The state was seen as a living, articulate force, a historic individual with a personality and will of its own, a personalized 'whole' that embodied its own unique spirit. This Romantic conception of individuality fused with *Realpolitik* concerns in the work of the historian Treitschke, the most influential exponent of *Machtstaat* ideas. In Treitschke's (1963, p. 14) view, 'the state is the public force for offence and defence', 'a moral force unto itself'.

During the nineteenth and twentieth centuries two theories of the state as force or might have exercised considerable influence. The classical elitist thesis of the Italians Vilfredo Pareto and Gaetano Mosca saw the state as the instrument of a ruling minority that could not be controlled by the majority, whatever the constitutional form. Mosca and Pareto were influenced by the ideas of the Austrian (but Polish-born) sociologist Ludwig Gumplowicz (1881, 1902), who argued that: 'The state is the organized control of the minority over the majority.'[1] An exclusive, coherent, united and self-conscious group used the state to manipulate the 'atomized' masses. The power of this elite rested on its organizational abilities (in the view of Mosca and the

German Robert Michels) or on certain psychological factors that are rooted in human nature (according to Pareto). While these elitists, like Marxism, offered a scientific and 'objective' account of the state, they did so in defence of the political interests and status of the middle class. The elitists offered a counter-ideology to Marx's ideology for the working class by emphasizing the inevitability of a hierarchical structure of society and the dominance of the political over the economic. While they were willing to recognize that state institutions had an independent dynamism which affected the attitudes of those who participated in or otherwise dealt with them, the elitists viewed these institutions as instruments of conspiratorial rule by a minority over the 'mass'.[2]

By contrast, Marxists tended to see the state as a coercive instrument that is used by one economic class (the ruling class) to subjugate another. From this Marxist perspective the state was viewed as a *part* of society. It was the product of class rule at a particular stage of social development, reproduced the relations of production, and would 'wither away' along with class rule. However, Karl Marx also expressed a view of the state as 'alienated' social power, as a creation of society that will come to dominate its creator and will turn into a 'parasitic' growth. Marxism contains, therefore, another perspective: that of the state *versus* society. Unfortunately for later Marxists—and in part related to the basic tension between these two conceptions of the state—Marx failed to offer any coherent or comparative account of the political structure of bourgeois class power (McLellan, 1974; Miliband, 1977). Despite Marxism's enormous practical influence, the very fragmentary views of Marx on the relationship of state to bourgeois society have left it strikingly deficient as a political theory. It seems that Marx did not consider the state as simply an epiphenomenon of more basic economic forces, except in the long run. Indeed, in the *Grundrisse* he claimed that the state as the instrument of class domination could only be found in North America. In two pamphlets, the *Class Struggle in France* (1850) and the *Eighteenth Brumaire of Louis Napoléon* (1852), the French state was viewed less as a committee of the ruling class (in the manner of the *Communist Manifesto* of 1847–8) than as an independent source of power that was supported by the bourgeoisie but at times overrode their wishes in order to preserve the *status quo*. By pointing to the deep divisions within the French ruling class Marx emphasized the weakness of the 'dictatorship of the bourgeoisie'. It is interesting to note how his intellectual preoccupation with the idea of the state receded, after leaving a 'state conscious' continental Europe for Britain, to cede priority to a theoretical analysis of the capitalist mode of production. The combat with Hegel was deferred (rather than renounced); British economic analysis became his central concern. His sense of being in a 'stateless' society was reflected in the view, attributed to Marx, that Britain and the United States would be excluded from the necessity of violent revolution. The flexibility of their institutions, in the absence of the idea of the impersonal state whose 'autonomy' hid the pursuit of dominance by particular economic interests, enabled them to adapt in the required direction.

While Lenin added to the political theory of Marxism a revolutionary strategy and tactics that implicitly recognized the importance of capturing the state 'machine' by violence, his work on the state was polemical rather than analytically rigorous. In particular, he failed to offer an adequate appreciation of the diversity of political conditions which resulted from the opportunities offered by, and constraints built into, the very different institutional expressions of political power within capitalist societies. It was Antonio Gramsci, leader of the Italian Communist Party, who noted that the success of Lenin's strategy in Russia in 1917 was to be understood in terms of a decisive distinction: between societies where integration is provided only by the state as, along with the Church, the sole organized body, and societies in which a variety of private voluntary associations have an existence distinct from that of the state (Hoare and Nowell Smith, 1971): 'In the East, the state was everything, civil society was primitive and unmoulded; in the West, there was a balanced relationship between the state and civil society and when the state trembled the robust structure of civil society was visible.' The vital significance of Gramsci for later Marxist political theorizing on the state lay in his comprehension of the variable relation between state and society. His differences from Lenin illustrated also the effects of national experience and native intellectual traditions on Marxist thought. Lenin was influenced by a Russian tradition of revolutionary thought which fed upon Western ideas; the problems in the relationship between Leninism and 'classical' Marxism emerge from this difference of context. Improvisation was the hallmark of Leninism. Gramsci's humanism was influenced by his early exposure to the historicism and Idealism of Benedetto Croce and the general cultural interests that this encouraged, and by the 'realistic' method of the political analysis of Machiavelli and his growing recognition that Marxism was too immersed in economic categories and did not appear to be working out satisfactorily in political terms. Consequently, Gramsci provided a pioneering attempt to re-examine the relationship of economic 'base' and political 'superstructure'. He recognized, as did Louis Althusser in the 1960s, that Marx had provided two ends of a chain, 'structure' and 'super-structure', but too little analysis of what went on between them. At the same time the Crocian heritage led him to offer a new vision of the role of con-sciousness within the framework of historical materialism (Femia, 1975). Within this framework a range of ideological and political forms were seen as possible and capable of exerting an independent influence. In contrast to the mechanical materialism typified in Lenin's *Materialism and Empirio-Criticism* (1909) and embodied in the Second International, Gramsci elab-orated a voluntarism that was not prepared to see man and his institutions as simply passive factors conditioned by economic structures that had a life of their own. To Marxism his major theoretical contribution was his enlargement of its conception of the state. He recognized that Marxists had concentrated on a narrow conception of the state, which comprised the executive power, administration, courts, police and military. These institu-tions were essentially coercive but, in Gramsci's view, exercised a 'domi-nation' that was important only in exceptional circumstances. His interest was in a broader conception of the state as the ideological superstructure that included education and the Church and maintained its hold over opin-ion and generated consent through the exercise of hegemony. Hegemony referred to a cultural domination of the state that was achieved by moral and intellectual leadership alone. This ideological aspect of the state, its co-optation of the masses by a process of intellectual subordination, was by far the more important aspect of its power. However, the 'non-monolithic' and yet pervasive character of this hegemony suggested new more com-plex forms of revolutionary strategy based on the creative intellectual and requiring a prolonged struggle on the plane of ideas. This revolutionary message gave new inspiration to a frustrated Marxist intelligentsia that was able to find a new legitimacy for its role through his work.

Gramsci's importance lay in his open-mindedness, his empiricist outlook and practical cast of mind, his ability to ask important and provocative political questions (although it cannot be said that he solved many), his widening of the Marxist conception of the state through the idea of hegemony, and his recognition that the state could achieve a degree of formal autonomy from civil society. However, claims that he was the intellectual father of modern Euro-communism, and was benign in his search for a 'humanistic' communist doctrine, represented an exaggeration by later Marxist writers or practitioners who were concerned to find and use past masters as an authority for changes that they wished to introduce (particularly following re-evaluations of Stalinism in the light of the Twentieth CPSU congress). In the fragmentary, disordered and inconclusive political writings of Gramsci it is possible to find, as Santiago Carrillo does, support for a Euro-communist theory of state. Gramsci was, nevertheless, too ambiguous and elusive a figure to be seen as the father of Euro-communism. There is a temptation to read too much into him. Indeed, Gramsci had little to say on the desirable institutions of a socialist state. He did not approach a philosophy of the state, in the sense of allowing for the incorporation of 'progressive' values in the state. For Gramsci the state incorporated a bourgeois hegemony that was a legitimating mask designed to disguise the predatory nature of class domination. It was necessary to 'impose' a new hegemony on the working class. After 1920 the emphasis in his work switched from the role of factory councils and revolution from below to the vanguard party and the primacy of organization and leadership.

Carrillo (1978), the Spanish Communist Party leader, showed a greater willingness to go beyond political economy analysis and came closer to establishing a normative idea of the state. In his view the state was an apparatus available to successive hegemonic groups that were able to mobilize democratic power and use its degree of independence of bourgeois rule to effect substantial reforms. It was possible to conceive of the state as performing an arbitrative role. His writing on the state was, however, as unsystematic as Gramsci's and characterized just as much by its immediacy and passion at the expense of sustained analysis. A French Marxist jurist like Demichel (1978) could admit the distinction between the formal conception of the state which is used to delineate state from society and the material conception according to which the state contains various objective, neutral principles to which the ruling class has committed itself. However, while Demichel argued that the state had an internal logic of its own, he did not construct a normative Marxist theory of the state.

THE STATE AS LAW

The state is a union of an aggregate of men under rightful law.

Immanuel Kant (1797, p. 163)

If socio-political approaches have concentrated on the state as *potentia,* the legal approach saw the state in terms of *potestas.* The state was conceived of as a set of offices (rather than persons) whose rights and duties were laid down very precisely in law. While, as will be seen later, legal scholars have been concerned philosophically with the problem of legitimacy, with the 'quality' of the will of the state, there was a powerful tradition of legal positivism in continental Europe, notably in Austria, Germany and Italy. This tradition was preoccupied with the power (*pouvoir, Gewalt, potere*) of the state, and with the validity and legality of its commands. Its power was seen as impersonal and predictable, exercised according to known or knowable procedures; its symbols were held to be the legally trained official, the judge and the legal scholar. They would ensure that regularity and uniformity in the exercise of power remained the highest values of the state and that the legal order was inviolable. Perhaps the most influential statement of this viewpoint was provided by Friedrich Julius Stahl's famous definition of the *Rechtsstaat* (1846, vol. 2, p. 106): 'The *Rechtsstaat* does most definitely not refer to the purpose and content of the state but only to the form and character of their realization.' In other words, the conception of the *Rechtsstaat* was concerned with the relationship of law to its application rather than to fundamental purposes. While the state was, as Gerber stressed, to be regarded as an 'association of will' (*Willensverband*) and hence had the essential attribute of personality, the nature of that will was not to be tackled by legal theory (von Oertzen, 1962). 'Higher' principles amounted to no more than the will of the state; they were only higher in the sense of being willed by the state. Paul Laband (1901), the famous public lawyer of the German Second Empire, wrote of freeing law 'from the chains of a political doctrine' by an exclusive commitment to the method of formal logic. This loss of a constitutional and political conception of the *Rechtsstaat* found its ultimate expression in the Austrian Hans Kelsen's view that every state was in fact a *Rechtsstaat* and in his definition of the state as 'a King Midas, all that it touches turns to law (*Recht*)'. For Kelsen (1925, p. 44) the origin of law was, scientifically speaking, a fictitious and meaningless problem. By 1932 Carl Schmitt, a devotee of Stahl's view, was able to argue that the *Rechtsstaat* had become a formula into which anything could be fitted and had therefore lost scholarly value; while in 1934 the Nazi-party apologist Hans Frank was able to write about *der deutsche Rechtsstaat Adolf Hitlers*. To the English-speaking world perhaps the best-known expression of the ascendancy of the formal conception of the *Rechtsstaat* was Max Weber's reference to 'the readiness to conform with rules which are formally correct and have been imposed by accepted procedure' as the chief characteristic of authority in the modern world. The state was seen as the expression of rational–legal authority which found its embodiment in bureaucracy as the typical form of organization (Weber, 1956). From such a standpoint it was a short step to the prescriptive proposition that laws should be obeyed because they were law: *Gesetz ist Gesetz*. Legality became the basis of legitimacy. Moral questions were 'merely' matters of ideology or personal opinion and unanswerable by science, which was committed to the ideal of ethical neutrality. Even so, the positivists were not in agreement about the nature of the 'facts' with which they were dealing. Among those concerned with a scientific understanding of law two theories developed: one viewed law as a psychological factum to be apprehended by exploring the inner world of consciousness; the other saw it as a phenomenon of social existence with social causes and effects. By contrast, Kelsen sought to give legal science a purely ideal and analytical character like those of logic and mathematics. It became a normative rather than a natural science, concerned with rules that prescribe right conduct and with the relativity of secular legal values as expressed in the deductive process of 'gradual concretization of the law'. The method of legal science was logical analysis of existing legal material.

Some of the excesses of German and Italian legal positivism were perhaps attributable to a reaction against the strength of established 'schools' like Idealism, Historicism and Natural Law, particularly the latter in Italy, where the ideas of the Roman Catholic Church had always exerted a powerful influence. Indeed, continental European legal history has been one of the rivalries of schools of thought rather than one of specific legal institutions, persons and cases in the English manner of Maitland. Out of these rivalries emerged much of the richness and complexity of the state tradition, for legal theory, the equivalent of English jurisprudence, provided much of the abstract, critical analysis of the nature of political societies, of the role of the state in determining which values were to be embodied in law, and of the character or moral obligation. Legal education was regarded as a wider subject than in England, a general cultural as well as a professional and technical education. A firm distinction was drawn between *Rechtslehre,* a practical science which dealt with litigation and was given much less attention than in England, and *Rechtswissenschaft,* the theoretical science of law which, as philosophy of law, was concerned' with fundamental abstract questions about the state and, as jurisprudence in the continental sense of the term, with concrete problems raised by case law. *Staatsrecht* was one of the most notable achievements of this legal science. The failure to develop English jurisprudence into a similarly important body of knowledge, of major relevance both to practising lawyers and to an abstract understanding of the body politic, is to be understood primarily in terms of the continuity of the common law tradition and the relative lack of impact of ideas of Roman law. There is no attempt in the English term 'law' to follow the Roman distinction between *jus* and *lex* (as there is in the distinctions between French *droit* and *loi* and German *Recht* and *Gesetz*). Law is an ambiguous term which covers both its abstract sense (when one refers to the law or law) and its concrete sense (a law or laws). In the English legal tradition Roman law has been regarded as of some historical interest but not as a complete legal system with contemporary legal validity. The unification of English law was achieved by the king's travelling judges rather than, as in France or Germany, by an academic profession which applied the ideas of Roman law. Consequently, the top jobs in the English legal profession were at the Bar and on the Bench. Recruitment of the Bench from among the more successful of those practising at the Bar reflected a preference for apprenticeship through experience as against theoretical training and confirmed the closed, inward-looking character of a legal world that was centred on the medieval heritage of the Inns of Court. By contrast, the legal scholar based at the university came to hold a position of authority in the continental profession of law and undertook much of the work of English judges. His role was reminiscent of the Roman *jurisprudentes* who had been expected to reflect upon the law and to educate the citizens into accepting changes within it. The judiciary was a public service and, correspondingly, continental European judges adopted an objective and anonymous style and a deductive mode of reasoning which rested on the theory that each decision was no more than the logical interpretation of a *texte*. It was, after all, the state which spoke through the court in interpreting its own legislation. Conversely, English common law accorded the judiciary a central place. Judges explained the law and developed it through argument and counter-argument. They acquired an individualistic, subjective and discursive style. The law appeared as in large part a courtroom game, one whose preoccupation with 'due process' embodied a 'sporting' theory of justice. Maitland remarked once: 'We are often reminded of the cricket match. The judges sit in court, not in order that they may discover the truth, but in order that they may answer the question 'How's that?" (Bell, 1965, p. 86).

The strength of the legal scholar's position in continental Europe arose from two factors. In the first place, the training function of the universities for state service (they produced officials and judges) enabled them to exert a considerable effect on the general outlook of the servants of the state. One needs consider only the extraordinary influence at the University of Halle of two educators of the Prussian administration: Christian Thomasius (1655–1728), the prophet of enlightenment and absolutism, and above all Christian Wolff (1679–1754). Wolff dominated German legal philosophy from 1720 to 1765 and represented the high point of German teaching of natural law. His reformist ideas led him into frequent clashes with the Prussian authorities, stimulated a number of societies that were dedicated to ideas of enlightenment and produced disciples who were largely responsible for Joseph II's reforms in the Hapsburg Empire and for the Prussian *Allgemeines Landrecht* (the first major attempt at codification). The German Enlightenment ideas of Wolff also had an impact in the Netherlands, where from the mid-eighteenth century *Staatsrecht* had begun to emerge as a university subject. Scholars like Trotz and especially Kluit (a pro-Orangist) were influential in educating generations of students in a new critical approach towards Dutch public law and in disseminating ideas of natural law which appealed to Dutch history rather than to abstract reason and which characterized the 'Patriot Period' of the Netherlands in the second half of the century.

Secondly, legal scholars sought to provide a doctrine, a body of concepts that were based on elaborate technical distinctions and would enable lawyers and judges to act with promptness and precision, clarify the deliberations of the law-maker, and bring unity, coherence and order into the legal system. Their authority derived from the rationalist character of a legal system that was constructed around the idea of codification and displayed a preference for logical system over the experience of history, for a strict hierarchy of sources of law with pre-eminence for complete, internally consistent and clear legislation and a distrust of judicial subjectivism, and for a view that justice was only to be obtained through the strict application of known rules. These intensely anti-medieval ideas, which emphasized certainty and order, contrasted with the flexible, empirical and historical character of English law, with its notion of the inherent, equitable power of the judge and with its view of statute law as an intrusion that needed to be limited by a rather strict grammatical interpretation of the precise terms used rather than interpreted by reference to the legislative policy that it embodied. In the continental European tradition law was seen as the articulation of the idea of the state, and the jurist was concerned to provide the general principles, refine the terms, and criticize the specific applications of that law. Perhaps the most extraordinary example of the influence of legal scholars was to be found in the general part of the German Civil Code of 1896, with its formal definitions, clear conceptual distinctions and broad general rules that reflected the work of the Pandectist school of legal thought. Embodied in the German Civil Code were the results both of the attempts of the Historical school of law to derive principles from a study of the development of German law as an expression of the *Volksgeist* and of Bernard Windscheid's *Pandektenrecht* or 'conceptual' jurisprudence, with its concern to systematize Roman law and to establish and organize general concepts at a high level of abstraction. These two scholarly influences distinguished the German Code as a competitive model from France's *Code Napoléon* of 1804, whose elegance and simplicity stemmed from the rationalist attempt to derive principles from 'enlightened' assumptions about human nature. Nevertheless, both codes had in common a text-book style and didactic tone.

A high status for academic law was not, of course, confined to 'state' societies. In the United States, for example, a written constitution and provision for the judicial review of legislation by the Supreme Court led to a much greater practical engagement on the part of the law schools and a more highly developed interest in jurisprudence than in England. However, the American law schools focused their attention almost exclusively upon preparation for the private practice of law and not upon the preparation of public servants. English and American jurisprudence remained, moreover, very different from continental European legal theory in their empirical and utilitarian emphasis. American legal 'realism', which borrowed heavily from a native pragmatism and behaviouralism, diverged from the formal conception of the study of law by focusing on a sociological and psychological understanding of how judges came to create law in the administration of law. The ruling theory of English law derives from the seminal influence of Jeremy Bentham: it combines a legal positivism in its conceptual part (represented by H. L. A. Hart's concern with legal rules rather than principles) with utilitarianism in its normative part. Under the influence of Oxford philosophy Hart contributed an interest in the logical analysis of concepts to unravel confusions (although Hart himself was not a utilitarian where ethics were concerned). What is missing in Anglo-American jurisprudence is a sustained, systematic concern for the coherence of the legal system or for the nature of political authority.

Although continental European law is not to be understood exclusively by reference to the heritage of Roman law, many of the differences between English and continental law are to be explained by their contrasting emotions towards Roman law. In particular, continental European legal theories of the state were the product of the renewed study of Roman law (in the form it had received in Justinian's codification of 527–34). From the twelfth to the sixteenth century the major creative achievements were those of Italy, especially those of the University of Bologna whose lay commentators sought to fashion Roman law into a living body of law to be used for contemporary practical ends. Leadership in legal science passed next to the French legists, who pursued an historical, scientific knowledge of Roman law, and finally, in the nineteenth century, to the German Pandectists who stressed the logical rigour of the Roman mind. Roman law undermined the heritage of feudal ideas and provided some of the basic notions which continue to inform the state tradition of authority. In the medieval mind law and the political community were seen as related but essentially different. Priority was accorded to law, above all to divine and customary law. The decisive contribution of Roman law was the idea that somewhere in the community, whether in the people or in the prince (or in both combined), there existed a supreme will that could alter laws to suit the changing requirements of society. This organ or body was simultaneously higher than the law and conditioned by the law, a paradox that nevertheless appeals to common sense and which theorists such as Jhering and Jellinek attempted to resolve by the notion of 'auto-limitation' (by which the state agrees to bind itself, for example, by a written constitution). The preconditions for the identification of a state were seen to be the existence of a coherent and comprehensive legal system and of a recognizable source of law. Its peculiar character as a political association was to be understood in legal terms, in terms of a *summa potestas,* a Latin phrase that Bodin used interchangeably with sovereignty. This notion had been kept alive in the medieval canon-law concept of the *plenitudo potestatis,* the 'fullness of power', which had been ascribed to the Pope and was now transferred to the secular political world, for example to French kings, to give authority to the new legislative function (d'Entrèves, 1967, p. 97). Under the impact of Roman law, and as a consequence of that law's close links to a vigorous canon law, the political community began to be credited with attributes that were formerly assigned to the Church. Because Roman law lived in a complex relationship of co-operation and conflict with a theocratic conception of kingship it gave to the concept of sovereignty a mystique and majesty.

Roman law appeared of less relevance to a comparatively cohesive English political community; which was already well covered by a body of statute law by the end of the reign of Edward I (1307) and had little need of an elaborate and systematic juristic theory of integration. It was, moreover, associated with an autocratic and theocratic view of government that had little appeal to a society with a strong feudal tradition of limited monarchy. Feudalism had bequeathed a conception of law that was not only flexible and adaptable to the practical exigencies of a changing society but also defended by a well-established and independent judicial profession. Roman concepts of will and of a superior public power were both unnecessary and largely undesired in such a context. English medieval society left a resilient legal inheritance in which law was conceived either as customary or unenacted law which manifested a tacit consent (common law) or as made by joint effort, by explicit consent to statute law (Ullmann, 1975). Law was not given by the will of the king. Consent, implicit or explicit, was its defining quality. Quite simply, Roman law was excluded because the idea of making law had already been firmly established by feudal institutions. The concept of sovereignty was adopted from the French without the superstructure of Roman law and latched on to traditional institutional arrangements.

The early political theorists of sovereignty were concerned not just to make an abstract statement about the character of a new political association but also to identify the locus of sovereignty in a particular person or organ: for Bodin, the monarch; for Thomas Hobbes, the monarch or his assembly; for Johannes Althusius, the people. Bodin's views excited great interest in Germany, where the fragmentation of authority—a consequence of the Thirty Years' War—and religious disunity made the determination of its locus both difficult and important. Hippolithus a Lapide, who supported an aristocratic constitution, found its location in the imperial estates; Dietrich Reinkingk, who upheld a monarchical constitution, identified it with the Holy Roman Emperor; while Johannes Limnaeus combined Bodin's *Herrschersouveränität* with Althusius's *Volkssouveränität* by distinguishing between *die reale Majestät* or real sovereignty, which was enshrined in the community as the highest authority, and *personale Majestät* or the personal sovereignty of the ruler, which was embodied in an office constituted by, and dependent on, the community. This early tendency to identify the notion of sovereignty with a particular institution or organ (*Organsouveränität*) has persisted in Britain, for example in A. V. Dicey's formulation of Crown-in-Parliament (1895). In continental Europe, by contrast, it has given way gradually to an identification of sovereignty with the abstract impersonal state (*Staats-souveränität*) and to its dissociation from any one constitutional form (Jellinek, 1900). Once the notion of an ultimate decision-maker with a final and binding authority was given to an abstract impersonal entity, it was possible to argue that the logic of sovereignty was not violated if powers (for example, legislative and executive, federal and state functions) were separated in the interests of institutional balance. There is nothing in the West German conception of the federal state (*Bundesstaat*) to deny the logic of state or sovereignty.

The Roman tradition also bestowed upon the continental European state its distinction between public and private affairs (*res publica* and *res privata*). Governing was concerned with the care and custody of *res publica,* the common and public interests. Legal rules were accordingly to be divided into public law, which pertained to the impersonal abstract character of the state, and private law, which applied to the relations of private individuals. One example of the continuity of medieval tradition in England is the legacy of a 'personal' concept of power and a confusion of public and private spheres. The absence both of a clearly defined body of public law, with its own principles to guide legislation and administration, and of a distinct system of administrative courts, which are concerned with the elaboration of these principles and their application in the relationship between the individual and the state, has been a distinctive feature of British government in a West European context. Maitland (1901) wrote: 'If I saw in an English newspaper that Mr A. B. had written a book on "public law", my first guess would be that he had been writing about international law.' Administrative courts and the theoretical debate that accompanied them played an important role in the political development of 'state' societies. They became important mechanisms for resolving conflicts in the relationship of ruler to subjects. Their institutionalization and the definition of their purpose reflected changing power relationships in society and were an important focus of debate. The French Council of State was a model, particularly after its reforms of 1872 when it achieved jurisdiction in all litigation that involved public authorities and the citizen, unless a law expressly provided otherwise. As one of the most important institutions in the establishment of republican morality during the Third Republic, it began to annul public acts that were corrupt in form or intent or that involved an illegal or perverted use of administrative discretion (*détournement de pouvoir*). With the expansion of the decree-making power under the Fifth Republic the Council of State became an even more important institution. Germany developed administrative courts more hesitantly and, moreover, did not create a federal court or give the administrative courts the general jurisdiction of the French court until the Bonn Republic. The major theorist of administrative courts was the renowned Berlin jurist and anti-Bismarck liberal parliamentarian, Rudolf von Gneist (1872). He proposed their creation as a 'middle way' between the *Polizeistaat* preferences of governments, which liked to see remedy against the state as a matter of grace, and the *Justizstaat* conception of Otto Bähr (1864) who saw the ordinary courts as defenders of the 'subjective' rights of individuals. In the *Justizstaat* proposal of Bähr the problem was that the state could claim an area of legal autonomy, a claim that was supported by theorists like Laband, and was able to define the area of uncontrolled discretion (*freies Ermessen*) widely. While various states including Prussia and, in a more developed form, Würtemberg created administrative courts, these courts were also constrained by such problems and, above all, by the ascendancy of an apolitical conception of the *Rechtsstaat* which led theorists of the administrative courts to concern themselves with procedural rather than material principles. The importance to continental European liberalism of legal control over the administration reflected a view of the administration as *the* institution that realized the purposes of the state. This view led to an emphasis on the importance of exercising public power in accordance with definite principles. If the state was seen as possessing the inherent power to govern without the need for a detailed statutory grant of power in each instance, the case for a distinct body of administrative law was pressing. England had no such idea of the state, and its law inherited the notion of the inherent powers of the judiciary, which included control of the administration.

Legal theories of the state were concerned with the depersonalization of power, with the distinction between public and private and with the peculiar character of the authority of the state. Law was regarded as the cohesive factor in political association. The state was conceived of as the legal system whose categories provided coherence and consistency in the exercise of power. Relationships were to be

institutionalized rather than personalized; offices were to be clearly delin-
eated in law and became more important than the figures which occupied
them. The central categories of these theories were the institution, the office,
sovereignty, and a capacity for implementation (*Durchsetzungsfähigkeit*).
There was a greater awareness than in the Anglo-American tradition of
the role of the law (as the articulation of the idea of the state) in providing the values which informed conduct. Its normative framework and
the institutions that expressed it were held to be of both theoretical and
practical interest. The dissociation from each other of law, on the one
hand, and politics and administration, on the other, in England reflected
a medieval notion of the Rule of Law which saw the law and the ruler,
though connected, as two different things. Law did not merely depend on
the ruler for its existence but was prior to the ruler. It did not owe its existence simply to a creative act of will but was regarded as one aspect of
the collective life, a set of habits, customs and practices that constrained
the exercise of power. Even the establishment of the idea of sovereignty
in Crown-in-Parliament, while a setback to the common law's medieval
claim to embody a higher law, did not resolve the problem of the fact that
there was no clear determination of the ultimate source of law. There was
no conception of the state to which principles and rules could be attributed, only a proliferating, incoherent maze of statute law complemented by
a judge-made, patchwork, empirical development of common law from
accumulated precedents and 'individualistic' premises. It became difficult
(despite Bentham's influence on legal theory and his contempt for tradition) to entertain the notion of a legal 'system', to hold firm to fundamental principles or to begin to order these in a rational manner.

THE STATE AS LEGITIMACY

*The state is not a work of art and a matter only of calculated, conscious
power politics. but above all an established order, regulated and formed
from within by law, and governed from above by rules which apply to
the co-operation of mankind in general.*

Rudolf Smend (1955, p. 369)

Philosophical theories of the state have been distinguished by their
concern with authority (*autorité, Herrschaft, autorità*), legitimacy and

obligation; with the manner in which authority is to be recognized and constituted and with the values that must inhere in the state if its laws are to appear other than arbitrary. Neither force nor legality have been seen as providing an adequate basis for the right to rule and the duty to obey; force becomes repression, legality arbitrariness. Legitimacy depends upon values that reside beyond positive law: whether in a particular constitutional form that embodies basic principles and procedures to achieve consent; in an ideal of law, whether divine or natural; in a communal sense that emerges, for example, from the role of the state in developing the consciousness of individuals away from particularity; or in certain shared purposes such as security, welfare or happiness. In continental Europe philosophical theories of the state have not only occasioned a rich debate but have also proved somewhat different from those in the Anglo-American tradition.

It is worth giving some considerable attention to the conception of the *Polizeistaat* (police or policy state), partly because it is distinctively continental European, and partly because it has been of great practical significance. The *Polizeistaat* was a strongly moral theory of the state, one that sought to use its machinery for the development of society and the improvement of individuals (Chapman, 1970). Its focus was policy and welfare, hence its close association with the terms *Policeystaat* and *Wohlfahrtsstaat* (Dorwart, 1972). Above all, the *Polizeistaat* lent to the continental European tradition the notion of the administration as 'the state in action', as 'the chief organ of state unity' (Krüger, 1966, p. 80). The term *Polizei* was used to refer to the whole area of internal administration except for the army, diplomacy, finance and justice. Jean Domat (1625–96), who followed earlier work by Le Bret, was the ablest French theorist of the police state. His theory of a state that was responsible for the 'universal policing of society' legitimated comprehensive regulation in terms of an elastic concept of the public interest and was to survive the Revolution by its incorporation in Jacobinism and Bonapartism.[3] Delamare in the eighteenth century and Councillors of State like Aucoc, Macarel (1842) and Vivien (1859) in the nineteenth century were wedded to these ideas, while various schools or special faculties for the teaching of administration in the first half of the nineteenth century, and Boutmy's establishment of the famous *École Libre des Sciences Politiques,* were an attempt to keep this tradition alive in the face of the claims of the law faculties to monopolize the teaching of administration. Until the 1870s the police-state tradition was dominant in France, and even then was not completely displaced. In Germany the conception of the

Polizeistaat found its intellectual embodiment in von Seckendorff's influential *Fürstenstaat,* which provided a comprehensive practical science of the state and drew on policy studies, law, ethics, politics and finance, and in the eighteenth century in Cameralists like J. S. Pütter and J. H. G. von Justi (1755). Cameralism reflected the administrative preoccupations of successive Prussian rulers and their concern to develop a profession-alized and centralized civil service that would be capable of intervening effectively in society. This interest led Frederick William I to establish a chair in Cameralism at Halle in 1727 in order to provide the practical training which his paternal, improving and dedicated administration would require. Accordingly, Cameralism was professionally orientated: it was an administrative science that focused not just on day-to-day aspects of office management, the management of state-owned enterprises and the practi-cal aspects of political economy (finance, statistics, commerce, scientific farming, etc.) but also on the ethical foundations of administrative conduct (Maier, 1966). Although it was concerned with summarizing the substance of the principles that apply to public administration, Cameralism was above all oriented towards economics, had a lasting effect on the applied charac-ter of German economics, and stressed the key importance of mercantilism as an aspect of state-building. The importance of Cameralism lay in its recognition that *Polizei* included both the protective or constabular role and the welfare role of the official. His responsibility for the general man-agement of society and the economy in a technically efficient way was indicated in the Prussian conception of *Wohlfahrtspolizei,* according to which the official had an inherent duty to prescribe as well as prohibit forms of social behaviour.

Its origins in an absolutist age gave the conception of the *Polizeistaat* a repressive character that was apparent, for example, in Justi's desire for a regulation to spell out the age from which deceased children could be mourned for by their parents; in the activities of Fouché as Napoleon's policeman–statesman and the surveillance and brutality that is still associated with the extraordinary system of spies and informers and with the exercise of extensive prerogative police powers in France.[4] On the other hand, it enabled the emergence of the notion of the state as an agency with an inherent responsibility for social welfare.[5] Arguments about social policy were largely dissociated from party or the idea, associated with Benjamin Disraeli and Joseph Chamberlain, that the economically privileged classes should attempt to assuage the disaffections of the less fortunate. When justifying his first social insurance measure before the *Reichstag* in 1881, Bismarck declared that the policy of the state must be one which

> would cultivate the view...among the propertyless classes of the population, those who are the most numerous and the least educated, that the state is not only an institution of necessity but also one of welfare. By recognizable and direct advantages they must be led to look upon the state not as an agency devised solely for the protection of the better-situated classes of society but also as one serving their needs and interests. (Pinson, 1954, p. 241)

The product of this view of the state was not only beneficent and paternal legislation (health insurance in 1883, old-age and invalidity insurance in 1889) but also a sense of responsibility for the welfare of workers within German public agencies. While there was poverty, sickness and misery in a rapidly industrializing Germany, official attitudes both towards them, and towards the relationship of the profit motive to the common good, were very different from those in Britain. A widespread assumption of the appropriateness of state action made it easy for Bismarck's successors, of all political parties, to extend the social insurance schemes, to commit the German state to a large role in housing, and to bestow upon the Weimar Republic a peculiar economic system of mixed ownership in which, in the aggregate, the publicly owned sector was not much smaller than the private. In fact, the nineteenth-century liberal theory of the *Rechtsstaat* was more influential in altering the form and methods of state activity than in limiting its activities to those associated with the notion of the *Ordnungsverwaltung*. The political system of Imperial Germany combined in a complex manner formal elements of the *Rechtsstaat* and the features of an authoritarian and welfare state (*Obrigkeitsstaat* and *Wohlfahrtsstaat*), which was benevolent in social policy and severe in its *Kulturkampf* against the Catholics and in anti-socialist legislation (a severity which, incidentally, was championed by the liberal supporters of Gneist). In the French Third Republic it was the Assembly and not the administration that impeded social policy. Measures of the 1890s which set up workers' delegations, limited the hours of work for women, fixed standards of hygiene, and established pensions and accident insurance were the direct product of the administration. Long before the introduction of universal and compulsory insurance the French state had been administering insurance schemes that covered quite large sections of the population as well as its own employees. Despite the renaissance of a philosophy of economic liberalism in the nineteenth century, the state itself did not surrender any of its existing functions and even acquired a few new ones. As under the *ancien régime* and Napoleon the state was still conceived of as a positive instrument of change. While the conception of the police state did evoke a liberal reaction, which began to have success after 1870, the French conception of the 'public-service' state and the twentieth-century German conception of the 'social state' (*Sozialstaat*) continued its welfare traditions in a democratic context.

Two aspects of the *Polizeistaat* tradition require emphasis: its Roman origin and its effects on the psychology and prestige of the official. The Roman conception of police power involved far more than the notion of a body of men empowered to enforce rules of conduct; it meant the power of the public authorities to regulate affairs in the general interest of the safety and welfare of the population. Common-law jurists have, by contrast, never used the term police state in a neutral, technical sense and have restricted 'police' to its narrow constabular meaning. In the Anglo-American tradition it has been a term appropriated by political commentators for the moral condemnation of tyrannies; most notably, it has been associated by them with the Third Reich. However, in this latter instance the very fact that the political police *Apparat* emerged as the dominant institution at the expense of the notion of the autonomy of state institutions made it very different from the traditional police state: the idea of the state had lost its meaning and relevance to conduct. The *Polizeistaat* tradition has also led to the development of a spirit and style of administration very different from the pragmatic, sceptical, hard-pressed and 'misunderstood' ethos that is traditionally associated with British administration. There is no image of the official as a craftsman or clerk whose virtue resides in practical experience, which is acquired through apprenticeship, rather than in a practical theoretical grasp. British officials have tended not to consider their power and the purposes for which it ought to be used (the latter are provided by Parliament): for a combination of historical and institutional reasons there was an unwillingness to accredit them with an inherent responsibility. The French and German administrative traditions embody a more rationalist view which emphasizes the creative role of the official in society. On the one hand, adapting the model of the Roman Catholic Church to the secular world, the French higher civil service has been viewed as the moral guardian of society, as a 'lay clergy' that is at once intellectual and progressive in its social vision and ideas of management. On the other, France has been seen as the heir, through Napoleon, to the special administrative genius of Rome, a genius that synthesized the paternalism and technical efficiency of 'police power' with the legalism of *l'État de Droit*. Napoleon resurrected the Roman title of prefect to describe his powerful agents in the departments, while the Council of State was regarded as a creative, judicial body akin to the *praetors* of Rome. Both Maurice Hauriou in France and Theodor Mommsen in Germany have stressed the Roman conception of the official as a 'fireman' who protects society from dangers. The very coherence of society itself has been attributed to the administrative system. Consequently, in the words of Michel Debré (1963, p. 251): 'The State is not an employer like others. It is an honour and a vocation to serve the Nation.' The idea of the depersonalization, prestige and devotion of state service was reflected in the legal characterization of the German *Beamte* (higher official) as someone who, by holding an office, entered into a special relationship with the state and thus stood in a privileged relationship with regard to the private citizen.

Roman concepts also informed material (as opposed to formal) theories of the *Rechtsstaat* or *l'État de Droit*. These theories were concerned with the quality of the will of the state, with the idea that there were some fundamental values to which rules and decisions must conform. Historically they arose as an eighteenth- and early nineteenth-century reaction to the enlightened absolutism that was associated with *Polizeistaat* theorists like Justi, and later as a reaction to the moral failure of the legal positivism of the formal conception of the *Rechtsstaat* to offer any resistance to twentieth-century dictators like Hitler and Mussolini, who felt themselves to be bound to nothing. German jurists like Gustav Radbruch (1950), who rejected their earlier legal positivism after 1945, turned to seventeenth- and eighteenth-century theories of the *Rechtsstaat* for inspiration (and, in the case of Radbruch, to the Baden school and its idealistic conception of law as a cultural phenomenon). The fall of the Holy Roman Empire in 1806 was identified by them as a critical turning-point for German theories of the state. During the nineteenth century only relatively isolated figures like Robert von Mohl, Lorenz von Stein or the legal historian Otto von Gierke continued to look back to earlier theories: Gierke to Althusius's writings on natural law, and Mohl and Stein to the Dutchman Hugo Grotius as the father of the *Rechtsstaat*. This post-1945 re-establishment of intellectual ties across a long historical divide represented an attempt to identify the original political components of the *Rechtsstaat* and to rid it of the apolitical implications that it had acquired during the nineteenth century. The eighteenth-century conceptions of the *Rechtsstaat* (the term appears, in fact, to have been first used by Welcker in 1813) had been concerned to establish a *Gesetzesstaat* that would provide legal security and uniformity and would also enshrine subjective public rights in positive law; to achieve a depersonalization of law whereby the association of law with the ruler would be replaced by an idea of law as a superior norm which bound ruler and people equally; and to ensure that legislative power was not exercised arbitrarily by a written constitution, as proposed by Kant, and by participation of the citizens in the legislative process. These anti-absolutist, natural-law ideas were brought together in the work of Ernst Ferdinand Klein, a disciple of Wolff, co-author of the Prussian *Allgemeines Landrecht,* and a thinker who was immensely influential within German intellectual circles in the 1790s. At that time Fichte, Wilhelm von Humboldt (1947) and Kant were preaching the virtues of the conception of the non-interventionist *Nachtwächterstaat* (nightwatchman state), which was committed to *Recht,* over those of the *Polizeistaat,* which was committed to 'happiness'. However, even these writers produced an equivocal political conception of the *Rechtsstaat;* its freedom was essentially freedom from the state through a written constitution rather than freedom to participate in shaping public policy. Later Mohl was to criticize Kant for a 'self-seeking individualism' that accommodated to absolutism. The political dynamism behind the *Rechtsstaat* conception was far stronger in the early nineteenth-century writings of politically active jurists like Rotteck, Welcker, Mohl and Gneist. Indeed, Mohl was to be Minister of Justice of the short-lived Frankfurt Parliament of 1848 and a life-long opponent of Prussia.

The return to a political and philosophical conception of the *Rechtsstaat* after 1945 was associated with institutional developments that appeared to accord a greater role to the judiciary. There was, for example, a greater use by legislatures of 'general clauses' to delegate equitable powers to the judiciary. This recognition of the need for flexibility in applying the law meant, of course, greater judicial discretion in the English manner, but it did not prevent the persistence of different modes of judicial reasoning. The continental European judge remained more concerned with the rationale of a statute in terms of both the logical theory upon which it appeared to rest and the legislative policy that it embodied. More fundamentally, the importance of a material and normative conception of law, of *Willensinhalt*

and not just *Willensform*, was apparent in the supremacy of constitutional principles over the legislature; of written constitutions over civil codes
which had previously served a constitutional function by enshrining respect for private rights; and of new constitutional courts over the ordinary
courts. The most advanced form of this transition towards constitutionalism
was represented by the Federal Constitutional Court in Western Germany.
As it could be formally requested to undertake an abstract review of the
constitutionality of a particular law and was not just dependent (as was
the American Supreme Court) on concrete cases, the new Court played
an active role in the political arena. By contrast, the French Constitutional
Council (after 1958) was a more limited form of essentially non-judicial
review, as indicated by its non-judicial composition and the absence of formal judicial proceedings. Certain kinds of bills must, and others may, be
referred to it by the executive or legislature for decision on their constitutionality. A normative conception of the judicial role and 'general clauses'
led also to a more 'open' jurisprudence and a greater interest in a sociological legal science that demystified the law and concentrated on how institutions and judical actors perceived and solved problems. 'Creative' judges
were more in need of guidance from 'practical' legal rules and principles
rather than of the abstract conceptual system of the Pandectists. While
Jhering's 'jurisprudence of interests' (*Interessen-jurisprudenz*) came at last
into its own, it was complemented by an attempt within legal philosophy to
erect defences against ethical relativism, to return to the neo-Kantian ideas
of Weimar scholars like Rudolf Stammler (1922) who saw law as embodying the universal idea of the justice of natural law.

Despite these developments there remained a greater intellectual controversy about the material *Rechtsstaat* in Austria, Italy and Western
Germany than in France. During the Third Republic, for example, at a time
when legal positivism was dominant in Germany, the two leading French
jurists, Esmein and Duguit, could agree that the basic rights that had been
laid down in the Declaration of the Rights of Man of 1789 were part and
parcel of France's public law even though they were not expressly adopted
in the constitutional laws of 1875. After 1945 the legal positivism of Santi
Romano continued to pervade the literature used in the teaching and practice
of Italian law. In Austria Hans Kelsen's anti-metaphysical conception of
law and the state remained dominant and in the 1960s began to find an
enthusiastic response from Marxists. Kelsen had sought to provide an 'ide-
ologically critical' theory of law that would reveal the ideological character

(that is, the socio-economic context) of traditional legal distinctions like those between public and private law and subjective and objective law. Marxists were also attracted by his view that what stood behind positive law was not the absolute truth of metaphysics or the absolute justice of a natural right but only the 'Gorgon's head of power' (quoted by Römer, 1971, p. 582).

Western Germany was characterized by intellectual disputes that reflected a continuation of the divisions of the Weimar period between Carl Schmitt, Rudolf Smend and the socialist jurist Hermann Heller. Weimar overshadowed public-law discussions. These old divisions were further deepened by personal factors, notably Schmitt's elevation to a chair at the University of Berlin in 1933 and Smend's displacement from there to Göttingen. Schmitt (1963) defended himself; his works were re-published and became standard public-law texts; and his disciples, Ernst Forsthoff (1964) at Heidelberg (who became the major academic patron of the Schmitt school) and Herbert Krüger (1966) at Hamburg, produced other widely-read texts. Smend (1955) taught a famous seminar at Göttingen and was represented intellectually by Ehmke, Hesse and Oertzen, while Heller's influence was apparent in the works of the Marxist jurist Wolfgang Abendroth as well as of Karl Dietrich Bracher and Ernst Fraenkel (see Fraenkel and Bracher, 1957). Although all these theorists shared a political conception of the state in opposition to legal positivism, they differed about the character of the *Rechtsstaat*. One dispute arose from the Schmitt school's adherence to a formal conception of the state. Schmitt's major Weimar contribution had been a non-legal and aggressive conception of politics as a relation between a public and its enemy. Accordingly, the central characteristic of the state was held to be its ability to take decisions to keep the 'existential stranger' in his place and to maintain its own integrity and autonomy. The emphasis was on the decisiveness of the state, on its ability to cope with exceptional situations posed by external threat. Far more important than the issue of who took decisions or how they were taken was the requirement that they should be taken. Schmitt's definition of the sovereign as 'whoever was generally recognized to have the right in exceptional circumstances to take measures that violated the constitution' made it easy for him to accept the Nazi seizure of power and, as a prominent member of the Academy of German Law (created in 1933) and editor of the *Deutsche Juristenzeitung,* to occupy a central place in arguments about the character of the new Nazi state. Schmitt scholars took a narrow, apolitical view of the *Rechtsstaat* in the tradition of

Stahl; in Schmitt's view it contained no implication about the form of polity. Hence it was possible to see Imperial Germany as a *Rechtsstaat*. Krüger (1966, p. 677) spoke of the danger of identifying the *Rechtsstaat*, which was only one criterion for the exercise of authority, with *Staatlichkeit*. The state was presented as a value in itself: it embodied the principle of achievement (*Leistungsprinzip*) and was not to be referred to any other outside values. Political decisions lay beyond legal logic. In Forsthoff's administrative-law text (1966, p. 15) even the activities of the administration were held to be legitimated as the expression of state authority, not as the emanation of legal norms. As Schmitt had earlier, Krüger (1966, p. 43) attacked Althusius's conception of the state as a symbiotic association that was based on trust (*Treue*) and the co-operation of sociable men; Althusius was *ein unstaatlicher Mensch* ('a stateless person', that is, one without the state tradition). The Schmitt school ignored Hobbes's social contract arguments and the individualism that his Leviathan served and found in him the prophet of obedience (*Gehorsam*). The Basic Law of 1949 was criticized for undermining the 'authoritative' state in favour of a 'totalitarian' society. According to Rüdiger Altmann (1968, p. 49), 'Society, not the state, has become totalitarian in Germany.'[6] The Basic Law embodied a 'fanatical' democratization, whilst its basic rights represented a decision for morality and against politics, a 'terror of ethics', and enshrined an asocial individualism which ate at the bones of community (Krüger, 1966, pp. 75 and 535). 'Freedom isolates man, distances him from the state...makes no contribution to the supra-individual order...produces no sense of the state' (Forsthoff, 1966, p. 66). The 'realistic' concerns of Schmitt with power relationships within society rather than the normative power of the constitution brought him closer to a *Machtstaat* position than any other influential twentieth-century German legal theorist. Nevertheless, despite the number of chairs held by Schmitt scholars in the post-war period, the *Zeitgeist* (in the sense of historical experience and institutional arrangements) worked against their influence.[7] More relevant to the practical problems of the Federal Republic was the work of scholars like Konrad Hesse (who in the 1970s was appointed to the Federal Constitutional Court), Ulrich Scheuner (1961) and Ehmke (1962), who followed the lead of Smend in attempting to determine the proper relationship between the *Rechtsstaat* and the political form of the state. West Germany was more receptive to the ideas of the so-called 'Freiburg school' of Hesse (1962b, 1967), ideas that stressed both the material character of the *Rechtsstaat* and the essential 'openness' of the constitution in a democratic society.

A second dispute involved different interpretations of Article 28 of the Basic Law that characterized the Federal Republic as a *sozialer Rechtsstaat*. This political conception of the state had been associated with Heller in the 1920s and his attack on the legal positivism of the Labandists and on Kelsen. On the one hand, Forsthoff (1968) argued that the two elements were irreconcilable: 'half a *Rechtsstaat*' and 'half a *Sozialstaat*' would not produce a *sozialer Rechtsstaat*. In his view the *Rechtsstaat* was a formal legal conception while the *Sozialstaat* was a political conception that referred to the purpose of the state. Implicit in this false combination was the possibility of a crisis for the *Rechtsstaat* as pressures for the remedy of social injustice confronted an essentially static conception of rights. On the other hand, jurists like Ehmke, Hesse, Scheuner and Peter Badura have seen it as a homogeneous conception whose two elements are complementary. The *Sozialstaat* element emphasized the social character of rights like that of property, and its welfare concerns reduced the danger that social tensions would threaten the credibility of the guarantees of the *Rechtsstaat*.

Hegel's philosophic theory of the state differed from that of both the *Rechtsstaat* theorists and the Cameralists. He refused to see the state either simply as a legal unity to be understood by the formalistic *a priori* reasoning typical of Kant or, as Justi had, as a 'welfare machine' that was dedicated to administrative efficiency (Plant, 1973). His view of the state as an ethical community (*sittlich–ethische Lebens-gemeinschaft*) was the product of two concerns: to avoid excessive abstraction by relating the state to social and cultural experience, and to outline in some detail the constitutional form that would enable man to participate in the ethical life and would provide the coherence, integration and stability of institutional arrangements that were essential for the state to function as a rational order. By way of a hereditary monarch above faction, a bureaucracy that was able to pursue universal ends and an assembly of estates, Hegel sought to relate the particularity of group and class to the universality of the state and the development of self-consciousness through the state (Plant, 1973). It was an extraordinarily ambitious theory of the state, which was rooted in a very intricate metaphysics centred on the concept of *Geist* (spirit). The state was an objective manifestation of *Geist* and acquired its meaning and coherence as part of the eternal unfolding of *Geist*. Through participation in the ethical life of the state the individual was able to become a truly free person, one possessed of purposes, reason and will.

Hegel's theory of the state was important in two senses. Along with the earlier work of Fichte and Herder, it represented a break with the epistemological preoccupations of the Enlightenment that had sought objective scientific knowledge. Instead Hegel attempted to provide a completely rational philosophy, one concerned in a critical and normative sense with the nature of the human subject and the subjective meaning of his life as an integral part of some cosmic design. It was essential to have an ontology, an overall picture of objective reality and of the fundamental nature of mind and matter and their interrelationship, as the basis for grasping properly the character of modern reality and the conditions of man's well-being. Hegel's metaphysical preoccupations were indeed closely linked to his practical concern about contemporary social and political problems. He wished to provide a philosophical grasp of the new form of political community which had been expressed in the Napoleonic state and which appeared to offer man an opportunity for greater insight into, and control over, his social environment. Hegel was also anxious about the effects of the new commercial society on the sense of community. The second important aspect of his theory of the state was, therefore, its concern about freedom and community in the modern world. Hegel was a critic of the disintegrating consequences for social, economic and political life of the ideas of radical individualism that had been unleashed by both industrialization and the French Revolution. Whether these ideas took the form of theories of the general will or of utilitarianism, he saw dangers of irrationality in the new 'radical freedom'. He argued that the pursuit of individual self-interest, utilitarianism and egalitarian democracy must be transcended through recognition of 'significant differentiation' and membership of a concrete ethical whole, the 'rational' state. The problem with the liberal–individualistic conception of freedom was that it concentrated its attention on civil society and ignored the state. It focused excessively on the 'self' as pure ego which did as it pleased. This conception of freedom was, in Hegel's view, atomistic and an empty abstraction devoid of (objective) ethical significance. The ethical character of man (*Sittlichkeit*), as opposed to the subjective morality that ensued from man's attempt to create a universal moral order from his own will, could only be established in the context of involvement in the life of the community, one central aspect of which was the state.

Hegel's legacy was twofold: it comprised the idea that the atomistic and polarizing tendencies of civil society could only be offset on the basis of an altruistic commitment to community in which man would find rational, universal values, and the conception of the state as an agency of the ethical life, as a condition of 'rational' freedom for the individual through his participation in the universal ends of the state. The virtues of collective public life and of a social conception of freedom were vividly underlined in his work and, as we shall see, inspired a vast range of thought, from the extremes of conservatism to those of left-wing radicalism. Hegel's later interpreters were, however, very often guilty of taking particular ideas out of the context of his metaphysic. That metaphysic was concerned with the development of the human mind (through labour, property, and the multiplication of wants) towards self-consciousness, and with the importance of political organization for the realization of the potentialities of the human subject. The person was conceived of as a process of self-consciousness and self-realization in a concrete ethical context, that of the state as the expression of the human spirit. It was the task of philosophy to unravel the logic of this process of self-realization and to reflect upon the types or levels, and the mode of interconnection, of communal bonds (legal, social and ethical). Hegel realized that in the large territorial state the problem of integration could no longer be solved intuitively, as in the intimate world of the Greek *polis,* but only by a conceptual grasp that could be provided by philosophy.

One major product of the late eighteenth- and nineteenth-century concern with the sense of community and solidarity was the conception of the 'nation-state'. This idea was the result of marrying a new cultural concept of the nation to an older legal and political concept of the state: the nation referred to a unity of culture that was based typically on common language and literature and a feeling of loyalty for a common land, the state to a unity of legal and political authority. While the earliest theorists of the state like Bodin and Machiavelli were acutely aware that this new political association required a sense of solidarity, particularly in the context of external threats, their work exemplified neither the term nor the meaning of nation. English thought, which was less preoccupied with external threats, carried on using the medieval term *communis regni,* a term that indicated that rulers themselves had sought to encourage the growth of community consciousness. The modern sense of nation was unleashed by the French Revolution and by the intense awareness that Revolution produced of the need to base the state on a more closely knit sense of community. Its problematic character as a concept lay in its ambiguity: its use (for example, in the Declaration of the Rights of Man) as a synonym for political society, for a body of associates who lived equally under a common law, and its use in the sense of nationality. In the nineteenth century it proved difficult to keep these two different meanings of nation distinct.

In France the state itself was concerned to shape a nation out of an extraordinarily diverse society. Conversely, in Germany and Italy a particularistic, patchwork structure of states appeared to stand in sharp contrast to an emerging consciousness of a shared culture based above all on language. This consciousness of nation was primarily a creation of the educated classes, which infused it with their own cultural ideas. A conception of the cultural mission of the state (*Kulturstaat*) combined with a Romantic conception of states as 'individualities' and organic 'wholes' to produce the nineteenth-century German view that the good state embodied a unique national spirit and defended or asserted it on the international plane (Meinecke, 1908; Krieger, 1959). International relations was seen as the story (and history as the study) of the tensions of rival national cultures. This conception of the nation-state was regrettable as the source of both intellectual confusion and violent practical consequences. It was important less for what it said than for what it ignored. By elevating the question of the condition of association in the state to central political importance, the conception of the nation-state ignored or skated over two painfully difficult and controversial issues: the appropriate constitutional form for, and the purposes of, the state. Alternatively, the answers to these two questions could be derived from the importance of establishing the cultural nation as the basis of the state: a 'strong' resolute state that was committed to *Realpolitik* and recognized the overriding importance of military and diplomatic activity. It was the context for the ideas of Treitschke and Schmitt, for the identification of freedom with the unity, independence and self-determination of the nation. After the failure in 1848 to unify the German nation through liberal and parliamentary means the idea of the nation was appropriated by supporters of more traditional, absolutist political forms. In the minds of the intelligentsia external freedom and political unity for the nation began to take precedence over internal struggles for constitutional reform. The violent political struggles of the twentieth century led in turn to a questioning of political nationalism and (with, for example, the division of Germany after 1945) a new snapping of the link between the ideas of state and nation. In Germany the problem of the relationship between these ideas was one of the central themes of the *Ostpolitik* (Eastern policy) that was pursued from the late 1960s. Both German regimes experienced the absence of internal integrative values associated with the 'two states — one nation' formula that emerged from the *Ostpolitik*. Nevertheless, despite growing evidence of development of a distinct West German national consciousness, the Federal Republic felt itself unable, in part for constitutional reasons, to renounce the goal of political unification. It was, however, possible in this altered post-war international context to recognize that the ideas of state and nation had not always been historically associated and that there were other bases of solidarity for the state besides the sense of 'nationhood'.

If the association of the conception of the nation-state with destructive power politics had by the mid-twentieth century reduced its credibility within continental Europe as a legitimating formula for political rule, the conception of the 'technocratic state' appeared more relevant to the problems of industrialized and urbanized societies. It was not a new idea. The first major theorist of the technocratic state had been Henri de Saint-Simon, whose ideas have long had an appeal for the technical schools and corps within French administration. The conception of the technocratic state appeared more attractive in an age when politics was understood to be about 'doing things' and the concern with performance led to the saliency of the criteria of efficiency and effectiveness; when the state itself was deeply involved in economic management and industrial affairs, and questions arose about the capacity of the state apparatus to impose some sort of direction on economic processes and industrial decision-making; and when a common interest in prosperity and in an ever-increasing flow of goods and services made 'growth', 'affluence' and 'economic development' seem generally approved purposes, in terms of which the activities and methods of the state apparatus could be defined. The French idea of technocracy envisaged a 'positive' state that acted as a source of disinterested leadership towards the 'good society' and the 'full man'. This state was to be served by the *technicien*, the trained expert in the applied sciences (such as engineering and economics). He would apply to problems his rationalism and an unbiased larger perspective. In Germany the concept of technocracy was used to refer not only to the power of particular experts over policy but also to a fusion of state and technique (Schelsky, 1965). Rule was seen as passing to an autonomous technique with its own logic and to a technical mode of thought that had been induced by that technique. Politics was no longer concerned with questions about the nature of the state. It sought to push through the requirements of technique by manipulating motives and expectations so that people would be prepared to accept these requirements and by minimizing the adverse consequences of the technical state.

The contentious character of the conception of the technocratic state sprang in part from its basic premise of faith in the ability of technological achievements to make the 'good society' possible. Such a state could be viewed as destructive of the 'quality of life'. Technocracy threatened aesthetic values of culture and environment. It also endangered political and 'emancipatory' values of freedom and participation, for by identifying the state with certain substantive purposes and its 'steering capacity' to achieve them, the concept of technocracy neglected the legal and social character of the state as an association. Furthermore, the conception of the technocratic state appeared to embody a paradox. It encouraged politicization, in the sense that technocracy legitimated the right of the state apparatus to intervene in order to regulate tasks that remained with civil society (the police power) or to take them into the domain of the state apparatus (the public-service function). At the same time the idea of technocracy sought to depoliticize issues. It viewed the partisan pressures and 'ideological' arguments that emanated from society as irrational and disruptive and emphasized technical criteria of efficiency and productivity. Habermas (1973) identified the emergence of a 'manipulative' state which pursued the 'instumental' reason of natural science and did not encourage human enlightenment by facilitating communication and the achievement of greater autonomy and responsibility for the individual. If it is possible to identify elements of *Kulturstaat* and neo-Hegelian thought in this critique, the edifice of the German *Rechtsstaat* underpinned Hennis's (1977) fears about the absence of self-restraint in the 'goal-oriented programme state'. In both the cultural and legal criticisms of the conception of the technocratic state there are elements of caricature, for it is difficult to characterize any one West European state, even France, as the embodiment of just this one doctrine. Nevertheless, the doctrine of technocracy provides an excellent example of how the two aspects of politics can part company: a large or enlarged scope of political rule is accompanied by a reduction in the scope of politicking.

NOTES

1   Gumplowicz, Ratzenhofer and other continental European 'political realists' had a considerable influence on early American social science, notably on Arthur Bentley's *Process of Government,* in which thirty-five pages were devoted to the Austrian jurist Rudolf von Jhering's realistic view that law was the product of power struggles (Aho, 1975). According to Bentley (1908, p. 258): 'The phenomena of government are from start to finish phenomena of force.'

     American sociological jurisprudence has a continental European background. Roscoe Pound was at first influenced by Jhering's view of law as a product of manipulation and competing interests and by the sociologist Albion Small, who was also inspired by German scholarship and for whom 'the whole life process [is] the process of developing, adjusting and satisfying interests'. Nevertheless, Pound remained a vigorous defender of the common law and its hostility to legislation and turned increasingly against continental influences. He saw the common law as providing a setting for inherently *private* contests; public-law questions were treated more as controversies or as games between *private* litigants.

2   The relationship between elite theory and Marxism is complex. On the one hand, elite theorists like Gumplowicz, Mosca and Pareto rejected Marxism's monocausal theory of social development in favour of a stress on the interdependency of factors in historical change. On the other, the debt that is owed by elite theory to Marxism is apparent in Michels's use of Marxist categories like 'ruling class' and 'ideology' against Marxism. Michels's defection from socialism to Fascism and the ability of socialist groups in pre-1914 Italy to move between Marxism and elite theory without much embarrassment underline their common medium of a 'realistic' scientific approach to the state and their shared idea of force as the foundation of the state and of group antagonism as the dynamic of politics (Beetham, 1977).

3   *Police Générale* refers to the power of government to make binding regulations in the interests of public order and legitimates a much wider range of activities for the police in France, as elsewhere on the Continent. 'Police power' is indistinguishable from the authority to govern. It may involve criminal matters or encompass (unlike in Britain or the United States) more general directions such as the supervision of newspapers and films, the control of epidemics, the licensing of building construction, the control of foreigners and the inspection of asylums and certain children's institutions (Bayley, 1975, p. 335). In France the police grant passports, survey dangerous buildings, scrutinize prices and the quality of produce and inspect factory premises—as well as keep a very close watch on political opinions and activities.

4   Bayley (1975, pp. 362–4) considers the factors that have promoted an active role of the police in policy and politics: where popular resistance and social violence accompany state-building, where a political system is unable to accommodate demands for political participation without violence, and where

in certain religious contexts there is a cultural insistence upon right belief.

5   In contrast to the individualism of the American tradition of 'happiness', the continental European, and particularly German, tradition of 'happiness' (*Glückseligkeit*) stresses the welfare of the citizen as essential to the integration of the state. This continental tradition of 'happiness' lies at the root of the conception of the *Wohlfahrtsstaat* (Scheuner, 1977).

6   The concept of the *formierte Gesellschaft* (the 'fully shaped society') was conceived by Altmann and used by Chancellor Ludwig Erhard in the 1965 election campaign. A 'classless' society of competing groups required a strengthening of the authority of the state (*eine autoritäre Demokratie*) and a greater consciousness of the requirements of *das Staatsganze,* of the interdependency of all. Erhard does not seem to have used the term in quite the same way as Altmann. Its appeal to Erhard lay in its vision of a conflict-free society in which political leadership would stand above party and groups. Such a view of politics reinforced his impotence in power conflicts.

7   For critiques of the Schmitt 'school', see Bracher (1968), von der Gablentz (1966) and von Krockow (1965).

However, when the Basic Law was being drafted (1948–9), members of the Parliamentary Council were more familiar with the constitutional ideas of Schmitt than with the work of Heller. For example, they were influenced by Schmitt's proposals on executive–legislative relations, particularly with respect to the procedure for votes of no confidence, as well as by the concept of a 'militant' democracy. Heller's writings were not as easily available at that time or as specific in their detailed institutional proposals as those of Schmitt. They were, therefore, less directly relevant to the drafting of the constitution. Schmitt had been an extraordinarily gifted scholar whose style, comparative knowledge and power of thought astonished and attracted many other jurists who had been unable to see the possible consequences of his conception of sovereignty. Within the Parliamentary Council the chairman of its 'main committee' (*Hauptausschuss*), the SPD jurist and politician Carlo Schmid, was best acquainted with Heller's work. Like Heller earlier, Professor Schmid saw that the SPD could not continue either to ignore the state or to adopt a mechanistic conception of the state. In the 1920s Heller had worked within the SPD to awaken a consciousness of the importance of the concepts of state and nation; he had seen their acceptance as essential to the future of democracy.

chapter five | the historical development of theories of the state

Another method of analysing theories of the state is the historical one of looking at variations over time and at how these variations reflect particular historical experiences and changes within the social structure. In this way it is possible to identify the ideological and social function of these theories by the way in which they are relevant to different social and economic interests. Disputes about their meaning can be related not just to assessments of their inherent logic but also to contrasting social experiences and the interests associated with these experiences. At the same time it is wise to bear in mind that there have been particular periods when intellectuals have sought with increased energy and determination to produce general theories of the state. In early nineteenth-century Germany, for example, the combination of the impact of the French Revolution (Hegel referred to Napoleon as 'this world soul') and a fragmented social, political and religious structure encouraged intellectuals to look for new ideals far removed from contemporary realities. Similarly, the dramatic emergence of a new German state in 1871 produced intellectual efforts to comprehend the character of, and to legitimate, this new phenomenon. In France it was above all the effort to secure the new Republic after 1875 that produced an explosion of general theories of the state, or rather a series of explosions, as the problem of the authority of the republican state was repeatedly posed (1910–14, in the 1930s, and after 1940). These theories were the first major outburst of intense juristic preoccupation with the notion of the state in France since the sixteenth and seventeenth centuries. The Revolution itself did not, in fact, produce any notable juristic discussion on the idea of the state. It was not until Laferrière's text on administrative law in 1887 that a textual analysis that was based on the Civil Code (*loi*) gave way to an interest in *l'État de Droit* and in the principles of public law. Concern with theories of the state has not, therefore, been continuous; intellectuals and practitioners have been content to take particular ideas for granted for long periods without exploring them critically.

It is, in fact, very difficult to divide the history of theories of the state into distinct time periods. The French Revolution of 1789 and the economic model of a commercial and industrial society presented by England in the eighteenth century undoubtedly combined to suggest a clear breaking-point in development. One can speak of an 'early modern' or transitional period, which was very extensive in time and stretched from the end of the fifteenth century to 1789. It was the period of dispute between a patrimonial conception of the state (*Fürstenstaat*) and the conception of the *Ständestaat;* of a view of the state as an object rather than as a legal personality; of the gradual, incoherent emergence of those characteristics that were to be combined into the notion of the abstract, impersonal state of the nineteenth century; and, above all, of debate about the proper locus of the new sovereignty. The seminal models were the personalized state of the French *ancien régime* (in the seventeenth century) and the bureaucratic, Cameralist state of Prussia (in the eighteenth century).[1] It would appear that the theoretical innovators of the new idea of the state were the French legists who followed earlier Italian impulses. Germany was, by contrast, happy to rely upon imported ideas and to engage in the very difficult task of applying them to an extremely particularistic political order in which medieval ideas and institutions proved more tenacious than in France (although even Bodin did not wish to get rid of estates, guilds and corporations, which he saw as invaluable means of political consultation). The influence of the French legists had been established as early as the reign of Philip the Fair. As Bartolists who were strongly committed to Roman-law ideas, as Gallicans and members of the *politique* 'party' during the Wars of Religion, they were centralizers and exponents of the claims of monarchy. Charles Du Moulin was a key figure, the first to attempt to codify customary law by applying Roman-law principles and to break with feudal ideas by stressing that all subjects were in a direct and equal relationship to the king. Bodin's concept of the sovereignty of the monarch, who was constrained by the limits of divine, natural and fundamental law, was developed by Pierre de L'Hommeau and Charles Loyseau into a more rigid, divine-right and absolutist form; by Cardin Le Bret, a councillor of state and intimate of Richelieu, into the ideal of the voluntary self-limitation of a ruler who was dedicated to a Christian 'reason of state'; and finally by Domat into the ideal of the absolute state in which the personal interests of the monarch were to be subordinated to the general good of the state. Under the influence of Roman law the conception of kingship became more and more of an abstraction. The idea that the authority of the state existed of itself was reflected in the remark attributed to Louis XIII: 'It is not I who speak, it is my state'. However, it remained a personal state and therefore deeply ambiguous. It was possible to interpret Louis XIII's remark or the famous *L'État, c'est moi* that was attributed, probably falsely (Hartung, 1961), to Louis XIV as either a claim for personal power ('I am the will of the state') or an obligation to act in the interests of the state regardless of personal views.

By transferring the locus of the idea of sovereignty from monarch to nation the French Revolution both carried over from the *ancien régime* the 'one and indivisible' character of that sovereignty, the notion of a unitary state that was subject to a comprehensive code of standardized rules, and enabled the emergence of the concept of the abstract impersonal state. While patrimonial ideas lingered under the Bourbon Restoration, the major nineteenth-century problem had become how institutionally to embody or represent the idea of the sovereignty of the nation. One model was *l'État Liberal,* which was advocated by Abbé Sieyès and contained in the monarchical constitution of 1791. Its emphasis on the individual was reflected in the Declaration of the Rights of Man; its institutional conception was apparent in the idea that the deputies represented the nation because, by the act of constitution, the nation had invested its powers in the Assembly. The reputation of this model was, however, to suffer from its later association with the July monarchy. A more successful 'Assembly-orientated' model was that of *l'État Jacobin,* which was inspired by Rousseau, advocated by Marat and Robespierre and contained in the constitution of 1793. It was essentially an 'anti-intermediary' philosophy that equated representation with delegation (all public functionaries were delegates of the people), stressed the direct relationship between the individual and the state, and emphasized a central monopoly of rationality. The principal requirement was an identity of the will of the delegates and the general will of the nation. Alexis de Tocqueville, Hippolyte Taine, Félicité de Lamennais and Ernest Renan were powerful nineteenth-century critics of the centralization and mysticism that were enshrined in Jacobin ideas. Centralization was also a key characteristic of the third model, the Napoleonic *État Césarien.* This Roman model emphasized hierarchical imperatives, with authority flowing from above and confidence coming from below, and the concentration of authority at all levels in individuals who were to assume personal responsibility. The state was seen as a machinery set up by the nation to regulate and administer matters of a general and public concern. As the Napoleonic model sought to institutionalize heroic leadership and stressed depoliticization as the precondition of rational action, it tended to reassert itself at times of crisis when change seemed overdue. Its legacy was notable in the fields of administration, police and the Civil Code.

A central feature of the nineteenth- and twentieth-century theories of the state was the problem of how to give institutional expression to the general ideas that were contained within the 'modern' impersonal and abstract state. It was a period of experimentation with new institutions. The complexity of the 'modern' period was further reinforced by the conflict between liberal individualist theories of the state, which emphasized the importance of the state/society distinction, and proponents of the 'social' state who, because they recognized the realities of group power, especially in the economy, and the need to do something about the new 'social question', began to see less value in traditional views of sovereignty and the state/society distinction. There were also differences of view about the character of the state: between those who stressed that bureaucratic impersonality was indispensable to the functioning of an advanced economy that depended on an extensive division of labour (*Staat als Anstalt*) and those who advocated a participatory conception of liberty (*Staat als Genossenschaft*); between those who were concerned with the state as a body politic or mode of association (*Staat als Ordnung*), with the values according to which its authority should be exercised and the purposes that it should pursue, and those who conceived of the state more narrowly as a rational organization or apparatus for the effective 'steering' of social development (*Staat als Organisation* or *Apparat*). What has been typical of the 'modern' period has been the complex coexistence of these different theoretical perspectives. Whilst one can speak, say, of the rise of the 'social' state from the 1870s and of twentieth-century interest in both the *Staat als Organisation,* which parallels the development of managerial views within society, and the *Staat als Genossenschaft,* which was associated with democratization throughout society, it is important to underline the continuing importance of the other perspectives. For example, the governmental instability of the Third and Fourth French Republics focused theoretical attention on the authority and power of the French state. Similarly, the failures of the Weimar Republic and the horrific experience of the Third Reich led post-war German theorists to renew their concern for the *Staat als Ordnung.*

It is possible to bring some order into these disputed theories and to gain some insight into their historical variation by showing how they spring out of ideologies which themselves are related to changes in social structure (Miller, 1976). Theories of the state have been formulated against the background of certain assumptions and beliefs both about how society functions and about the standards by which conduct should be judged. Behind theories of the state are certain abstract models of society in terms of which their historical and social relevance is established. Particular conceptions of society have fascinated individual theorists of the state. They have either embraced or felt repelled by models of society which they believe have existed (and perhaps need to be rediscovered), do exist (and need to be defended against their enemies or displaced for a new model), or might exist in the future. It does not, however, follow that a single theory of the state will be associated with a particular model of society: within the confines of the model will emerge a type of theorizing, and within that type a competition of theories.

SOCIETY AS AN HIERARCHICAL ORDER

The notion of society as an hierarchical order, as composed of different and unequal ranks which are bound together by reciprocal interest and mutual obligation, had its most powerful effect on theories of the state from the sixteenth to the early nineteenth centuries. These theories agreed in emphasizing the importance of a paternal state to protect the social order and the traditional rights which attached to one's 'station in life'. They had also in common a pessimistic conception of human nature, above all a fear of the anarchy and destruction that could follow from the 'self-interested' individual who was detached from the bonds of a well ordered society. One product of these background assumptions was the theory of the patrimonial state of bureaucratic absolutism. This theory, which was propounded by Du Moulin, Bodin and later, in divine-right terms, by Bossuet, sought to destroy the political order of feudalism. However, the new notion of the king and his subjects was still interpreted by these theorists in the context of a hierarchical model of society in which the privileges of the nobility remained an essential prop of the social order.[2] The hierarchical social order was given a more explicit political defence in theories of the *Ständestaat*. In sixteenth-century France provincial jurists like Claude de Seyssel and Guy Coquille elaborated the conception of the state as a composite society of 'pyramidal' social groups; each occupied a particular position in the hierarchical structure and performed a specific function necessary to the life of the whole. *Ständestaat* conceptions had an even firmer grip on Germany. They were popularized by the radical Protestant jurist Hippolithus a Lapide in the seventeenth century and became a central element in the German Enlightenment (for example, in the political writings of Leibniz). These political ideas, based on a hierarchical social order, were to be revived later by some of the writers who reacted against the fragmentation and social dislocation that were associated with the new commercial and industrial society. German Romantic theorists such as Adam Müller (1922), Novalis and the Schlegel brothers retained the organic metaphor of *Ständestaat* theories but offered an idealization of the state as a hierarchical order that enabled a living integration of opposites. 'Past-mindedness' was also apparent in the two major prophets of the Restoration monarchy in France, Joseph de Maistre and Louis de Bonald, who returned to the seventeenth-century theocratic claims of Bossuet, to the notion of a God-dependent, hierarchically structured world. The German jurist Max von Seydel (1873) and the economist Gustav Schmoller held on to patrimonial conceptions in the nineteenth century, while towards the end of that century French Social Catholics like Albert de Mun and La Tour du Pin, both of whom had been shocked by the experience of the Paris Commune, revived traditional 'corporatist' ideas in order to counteract the materialism and anarchy of capitalism and the threat of atheistic communism. Othmar Spann (1921), the Austrian social scientist and cultural pessimist, was undoubtedly the most extraordinary and influential exponent of *Ständestaat* notions in the 1920s. He emphasized the hierarchical principle of 'quality' as the alternative to the class and mass society that was associated with the principle of equality.[3]

THE INDIVIDUALISTIC CONCEPTION OF SOCIETY

The 'unhistorical' character of theories of the patrimonial state and *Ständestaat,* in the sense of their inability to face up to the social changes of the nineteenth and twentieth centuries, did reduce their appeal and importance. An individualistic conception of society arose as a reaction to the constraints that were imposed by a static view of rights and a hierarchical view of relationships upon the emergence of a market economy. This conception was premised upon the notion that individuals should be rewarded for effort and achievement and that status and office should be open to competition. Society was composed of a multitude of autonomous individuals who possessed and expressed their free will. The central issue which divided theories of the state based on this model of society was whether what was of social and political value was to be determined by the individual's autonomous exercise of his free will or by the individual's use of his free will (and reason) to determine absolute values that have an objective existence of their own. Despite this important dispute, these theories shared an optimistic conception of man, viewed the state as a legal phenomenon and personality, as both a depersonalization of power and a subject or carrier of rights and duties, and reflected an ascendant middle class.

One variant of these theories was the formalistic, 'subjectivist' conception of the liberal state in which the state was essentially an 'association of will' (*Willensverband*). Its most influential exponents were the French jurists Adhémar Esmein (1909), a legal historian, and Charles Beudant (1920) in the late nineteenth and early twentieth centuries, and the German jurists Friedrich von Gerber (1865) and Paul Laband (1901) in the nineteenth century. The French theorists produced a political conception of the liberal state that drew on the earlier political ideas of Sieyès, Benjamin Constant and Guizot and reflected in part ideas of Radical individualism associated with 'Alain' (Émile Chartier). After the Dreyfus affair these ideas acquired a new political importance. Esmein followed Sieyès's view that the public power (the state) existed only in the interests of the individuals who composed society. It was the juridical personification of the nation that willed certain values into existence (*l'État-nation*), not just an organ of the nation. The source of all law was the individual, who was, in Esmein's view, the only real, free and responsible being; the rights of the individual were prior and superior to the state, whose only absolute value was the liberty of the individual. Order depended on the assumption of rational conduct on the part of the individual: it was a premise that he would not give up his liberties, that he would respect the rights of others and, indeed, that he would put value on public order. The *État de Droit* was to be neutral in the struggle of opinions, while the sovereignty of the nation became an essentially formal concept and was constituted, according to Esmein, by the majority. With the exception of the requirement that the state was to be based on the rights of the individual, Esmein adopted a morally eclectic position, an essentially empirical and pragmatic attitude towards values.

This moral relativism was even more extreme in the apolitical conception of the liberal state as a body of positive law put forward by Gerber and Laband. Its liberalism was reflected in Gerber's non-patrimonial conception of the state as the highest juristic personality that represented the people and was distinct from the person of the ruler (monarch and government were simply organs of the state).[4] It was also apparent in the emphasis on the distinction between society, which was the realm of economic motivation and was to be understood by the methods of sociology and economics, and the state, which was the realm of impersonality and regulation and was to be understood exclusively in terms of law. The emergence of German legal positivism paralleled both the defeat of political liberalism in 1848 and its submergence in the process of unification by force of arms and the defeat of the moral and political concept of the *Bürger* (citizen), which was to be found in the earlier work of Mohl and Stein, by the economic concept of the prosperous *Bourgeois* (Smend, 1955, p. 309). Its success was attributable in part to the fact that it suited the conservative character of the Second Empire and its interest in maintaining the *status quo,* and in part, to its avoidance of contemporary controversy about the appropriate purposes of the state between the advocates of *die gute Polizei,* the beneficial police power, and the exponents of the *Nachtwächterstaat* in the tradition of Wilhelm von Humboldt (1947).

The other variant of the liberal theory of the state objected to the extreme subjectivism and voluntarism of these formal theories. Its fear of assigning primacy to 'public opinion' and its idea that the state presupposes the law were best expressed in Germany by liberal jurists like Otto von Gierke (1883), the bitter opponent of Laband and the Pandectists, and Rudolf Stammler (1922), a neo-Kantian opponent of the legal positivists in the Weimar years; in France by such eminent jurists as Julien Bonnecase (1928), Antoine Pillet, Raymond Saleilles (1922), Francois Gény (1930), Louis Le Fur (1937) and Maurice Hauriou (1923). In their view the liberal state was based on an objective, universal moral order that was accessible to reason. Its values were not empirical and contingent but bore a rational relationship to objective principles. Consequently, the concept of the sovereignty of the nation was given a positive content and an objective character by the French jurists; the state was not simply neutral. Man was characterized by a 'social individualism'; he possessed a capacity and a willingness to associate in institutions with others. It was above all through institutions that the importance of the rational coherence of moral ideas was expressed and social cohesion safeguarded (Renard, 1939). Institutions offset the fallibility of the free will of the individual and raised his horizons and vision above the selfish pursuit of private interests or desires. Such an approach insisted on the idealism and 'aristocratic' character of law, on the view that the mainspring of human efforts was the attempt to realize a good greater than that which already existed. This theory of the state had its precursors in the natural-law ideas of the Stoic philosophers, the work of Thomas Aquinas and the seventeenth-century work of Grotius and Pufendorf. Natural law had, however, fallen into some discredit in the nineteenth century, when it was held to be too vague and general as a theory to be acceptable or satisfactory as a guide for conduct. Saleilles (1922) and his disciple Gény blamed the influence of Rousseau, with his equivocal attitude to natural law, and the Revolutionary idea of the sovereignty of the nation for introducing the conditions for a tyranny of opinion. In their view the state was a moral, spiritual and natural phenomenon which informed the consciousness of the individual by being internalized within his conscience. It was not simply a convenient fiction or external constraint. The state was seen as a necessity, which arose out of the fallibility of man, as opposed to an artefact. It was no longer just a *Willensverband* which created law but also a rational institution which ascertained and recorded the law. The emphasis was upon the legislator who served the law rather than upon the idea of the law at the service of the legislator. During the twentieth century these natural-law ideas came to dominate French theories of the state, although shorn of their earlier association with the notion of a social contract. They accorded, as we shall see, with the Catholic social outlook of jurists and the replacement of the individualist by the 'personalist' outlook on man. In Germany, by contrast, it took a drastic historical experience to revive these ideas.

SOCIETY AS COMMUNITY

Both variants of the theory of the liberal state were premised on a 'conflict model' of society and had an appeal for those who feared the emergence of the state either as an *Apparat* that was engaged in managing an enterprise or as an *Anstalt* of bureaucratic offices that administered rules. There was, however, an alternative model of society that generated different theories. The 'communitarian' model of society stressed solidarity between persons and was based on the optimistic assumption that men were prepared to co-operate altruistically in both taking and carrying out collective decisions. Man was held to have important needs that could be satisfied only in and by the community. Theories of the state associated with this social model emphasized the problem of community and the importance of the state for moral discipline. Both the major theories that dealt with the state as an ethical community were concerned about the enervating effects on the person of social fragmentation, which was caused by the market economy, and 'machine' models or technical 'rationality models' of state and society.

A distaste for conceptions of the state as an artefact formed to serve clearly delimited ends, for conceptions of a 'timeless' and 'lifeless' state based on *a priori* reasoning, was most evident in theories of the historical state. The historical approach sought to ground its views on state, society and nation within a distinct cosmology, a comprehensive conception of man and his place in the evolving universal order. While its view of the state as a process of growth led to organic analogies, this approach differed from that of the German Romantics in concentrating on the diversity and conflict to be found within that process. The state was not simply to be understood through the categories of the jurist or the Cameralist but as a community that was held together by spiritual ties, themselves the product of a shared heritage. Rousseau was a precursor of the historical approach, but its first major formulation was Herder's *Kulturstaat*, based on the *Volk*. Hegel, Marx and the jurist Savigny were the leading representatives of the nineteenth-century German 'historical' school; and the Frankfurt School provided a twentieth-century continuation of its themes. In Hegel's view the state had arisen by necessity out of the system of needs but was able, through its institutions, to provide individuals with universal ends. Man reconciled his particular subjective will and the universal will by finding rational values within his own community through engagement in practical activity. In other words, the institutions of the state offered the possibility of developing the self-consciousness of human minds within a more universal objective framework. Moral principles were not to be discovered by a process of self-reflection on the part of the individual but in the concrete, continuing life of the community, in the logic of experience.

Theorists of the social state were prone to regard Hegel's solution to the problem of community and moral discipline as abstract and mystical. Their response to the austere individualism of Kant and the utilitarianism of the classical liberal economists was social scientific. Once again the organic analogy emphasized that the individual was an integral part of the society into which he was born and that if the individual became isolated from that society he diminished himself. However, that society was to be understood 'realistically' both through rational clarification of the basic social entities and through observation. The result was a demystification of the state. The conception of the social state was to be found in the work of Tönnies (1887) and Schäffle (1875) in Germany and Durkheim (Lukes, 1973a, p. 268) and Duguit (1911) in France, in their reaction to the emergence of the 'social question' on the political agenda and to the new importance of organized groups, notably the trade unions. Tönnies saw in the modern bureaucratic state the most dangerous form of rationalization in modern life, the destruction of community and the erosion of individual creativity. His solution of moral integration through occupational associations was close to that of Durkheim. At first Durkheim viewed the state as little more than the 'agent of the sovereign authority', which reflected and articulated the *conscience collective,* the system of beliefs and sentiments within society. Later he continued to view it as essentially deliberative, 'the very organ of social thought', which thought and acted instead of, and on behalf of, society. However, he began to see it as intervening more actively to liberate the individual personality by deploying 'energies proportionate to those it must counterbalance', as 'the organ *par excellence* of moral discipline'. In order both to liberate the individual from the state and to safeguard the idea of the autonomy of the state there would need to be vast new occupational associations, which were to be attached to, but distinct from, the state itself. These new corporations would become the fundamental political unit and would enact industrial legislation, provide certain services, regulate disputes and act as 'a source of life *sui generis'.*

The view of the state in terms of function rather than of authority, power or ethical purpose found a more elaborate expression in Duguit's controversial theory. French theorists (like Hauriou) of the liberal state as objective morality were to follow the introspective sociology of Gabriel Tarde, Durkheim's most respected contemporary critic. Tarde (1909) was a methodological individualist; he argued that everything in society was to be explained in terms of the properties of individuals who were themselves a function of autochthonous creation. His work finds its reflection in Hauriou's view that social phenomena, including the state, were immanent in the consciousness of men (rather than external and constraining social facts as Durkheim argued) and in his stress on imagination, inventiveness, contingency and the conceptual life of man. Whereas Hauriou pursued a metaphysical realism and neo-Thomism that related social science to other subjects, Duguit took up an anti-metaphysical positivism, one that was concerned with moral issues but refused to admit the metaphysic (Gény, vol. 2, p. 270). Duguit's approach was scientific, empirical and objective, initially more stringent than Durkheim's: his nominalism was apparent in his rejection of Durkheim's concept of the *conscience collective*. However, after 1901 and under the influence of Hauriou Duguit began to give more recognition to the role of consciousness. The starting-point of Duguit's work was his famous attack on the mystification and absolutism that had been introduced into French public life by the Revolution's 'divinization' of the nation and by its attribution of sovereignty to the state, which the Revolution saw as the embodiment of the nation. After the Revolution France had been left with a 'regal' concept of the state; the tyrannical principle of absolutist democracy had replaced that of absolutist monarchy. Unintelligible mystification of the state was also the product of the influential political ideas of Kant, Hegel and, above all, Rousseau who was, in Duguit's view, the father of 'Jacobin despotism' and 'Caesarian dictatorship'. Outside France his enemies were German juristic theories of the state (notably Gerber's individualistic idea of the *Willensmacht* of the state and Jellinek's thesis of the auto-limitation of the state) and the Austrian legal positivist Kelsen's view of the state as a system of abstract norms. Kelsen's formal neo-Kantian conception of the state as an organization of legal norms could not do justice to the pluralistic character of social facts and failed to recognize that different legal organizations arose because of differences in those social facts. Duguit's state was pre-eminently an empirical social community rather than an abstract legal organization. It was the realism of Anglo-American ideas that attracted Duguit, and he was himself to have a greater influence in the United States and Britain than any other French jurist of his generation. Duguit attacked four major contemporary French ideas that were represented primarily in the work of Esmein: that of the autonomous individual (Duguit favoured a social conception of man, for 'man does not exist anterior to society'); that of the 'absolute', one and indivisible sovereign state with the right to command; that of the personality of the state as a subject of law; and that of the identification of state with law in the Roman tradition. The result of the notion that law was the creation of the state was a 'fetishism' of the law. Law was, in his view, the spontaneous creation of society. It was to be understood in sociological terms as a social phenomenon rather than in terms of the formulae of *lois* and of metaphysical questions about the will of the state. Although the law was a living and therefore transitory reality, it was an objective reality. However, the law did not depend on the notion of a sovereign will. Duguit emphasized the extra-legal or social sanction of law. The state was seen as only there to observe the law and to ensure its observance by others. Duguit took the idea of social law from the ideas of an objective natural law in the work of Grotius and Pufendorf but dropped their metaphysics and authoritative perspective in favour of an experimental attitude towards law.

In his concern to establish the legitimacy of the state on a new basis he ignored metaphysical questions about the origins of public power and devoted himself to a consideration of the function that the state served. The basis of authority was found in society and its fundamental purpose, social solidarity. State action that was not designed to promote social solidarity was arbitrary and ought to be resisted. The state was, in his view, just an organ or *Apparat,* which served a particular function in society, and the product of a simple division of labour. Duguit produced a pragmatic conception of the state as society politically organized, as more the product than the producer of social solidarity. Its chief function was to protect and extend that solidarity. The idea of social solidarity was extremely influential in the period 1900–14 as a philosophy of social legislation. While Durkheim held the 'solidarist' movement to be too narrow in its concerns, Duguit found in solidarity both an adequate moral principle, which synthesized individualism and collectivism, and a principle of social organization, which recognized the importance of the vitality of society and especially of its new associations as the most reliable limitation on the exercise of public power. Solidarity led to the conception of a positive state, which intervened on behalf of common needs and reparative justice, and of its treasury as a friendly society fund for the benefit of citizens. Duguit's definition of the state substituted the notion of public service for that of sovereignty. The state was seen as a public-service corporation that functioned according to the objective law, a law that was independent of the state and reflected subjective social sentiments. His judicial pluralism was reinforced by an emphasis, borrowed from Durkheim, on the central importance of professional associations for social solidarity. He went on to advocate a form of syndicalist federalism.

For a number of reasons Duguit's ideas were to prove very controversial and the idea was to gain strength that although he was a very intelligent critic of traditional notions, he was also a vulgarizer. The height of his influence from 1918 into the 1930s coincided with a period when a crisis of regime appeared to many observers to be turning into a crisis of the liberal state itself. Duguit was criticized for attacking the myths of the sovereign nation and of the personality of the state without providing an alternative principle of authority that would provide a satisfactory basic myth for the beleaguered Third Republic. His myopic realism and the reduction of the notion of the state to what it did (and, even then, his failure to encompass all that it did) appeared destructive. Liberal theorists of the state like Joseph Barthélemy (1933) and Henri Berthélemy (1933) lost confidence in the idea that the state was a moral personification of the sovereign nation. For Barthélemy this notion had only been a useful myth in the struggle first against the monarchy and then against class conflict. They became essentially pragmatic theorists of the state. Barthélemy reacted against a heightened fear of anarchic tendencies in French liberalism by stressing the pedagogic function of the state and the central role of the school. Eventually both theorists, like Henri Chardon (1926), an eminent Councillor of State, adopted the conception of the state as an impartial administration by disinterested technicians who were dedicated to criteria of public utility. In their view politics had been allowed to block the motor of social life, the process of the competent, devoted, honest and rational administrative resolution of problems. Monarchist jurists such as Marcel de La Bigne de Villeneuve (1929 and 1931) and later neo-Fascist theorists of the state like Roger Bonnard (1939) used Duguit's demolition of liberal concepts. Duguit's ideas attracted primarily the many public servants of a socialist political outlook right up to the 1940s. The attraction of socialism for public officials lay in the syndicalist conception of the state. There was, however, a failure to develop a serious and influential socialist theory of the state that went much beyond an economic analysis. Before 1914 what socialist theories there were tended to use the language of Radical individualism or Sorelian syndicalism. After 1918 socialist ideas began to use, and be infected by, Duguit's work. Although Duguit had a more benign view of the state and was concerned to avoid conflicts, socialist theorists like André Mater, Paul

Louis and Maxine Leroy (1918) found in his attack on the notion of the 'regal' omnicompetence of the state and the 'tyranny' of the sovereign nation an excellent weapon with which to discredit the state itself from an anti-*étatiste* perspective. By 1927 Blum had adopted Duguit's view of the state as a federation of public services. This extraordinarily diverse use of Duguit's work to shatter established myths led to the accusation that he was an 'anarchist of the chair'. Georges Gurvitch (1932, p. 152), theorist of social law and disciple of Duguit, appeared to epitomize the 'enfeeblement' of the state when he wrote: 'In judicial life the state is like a small lake profoundly lost in the immense sea of law [*droit*] which surrounds it on all sides.' Georges Burdeau (1949, p. 303), a disciple of Hauriou, pursued a very different and less clumsy analogy: 'The State is a summit from which one can only re-descend.'

The fundamental difference between Duguit, on the one hand, and Esmein, Hauriou and Burdeau on the other, resided in Duguit's notion that what is real is observable. Burdeau and Hauriou saw the state as an abstract and subjective representation. In their view the most important realities were fictions or myths that were created by the human mind and reflected its imaginative and creative power. Duguit's mistake was to ignore the element of personality, which is the essential difference between the social and natural worlds. For Duguit fictions like the sovereign state were elaborate hoaxes, the product of fantasy; they were not real because they could not be observed. The most extraordinary aspect of the French debate was the process of reaction and counter-reaction, in which both sides took up positions that were difficult to sustain. One side was in danger of forgetting that there might be more to reality than concepts and of thinking that something existed because it was thought; the other ignored the importance of myths in sustaining political integration and stimulating political action.

While theories of the historical state and the social state have had an appeal because they appeared to relate to modern social conditions, they have not had a particularly secure hold on the minds of intellectuals. One reason why they have not been more widely adopted is that the appeal of the assumptions contained in the individualist conception of society persisted. The liberal theory of the state as objective morality has shown a remarkable resilience and has proved able in the twentieth century to take over from a voluntaristic theory of the liberal state that had been under serious attack. Moreover, in the conception of *der soziale Rechtsstaat* an attempt was made to make a broader ideological appeal by combining a concern for need, an important criterion of the communitarian conception of society, with a recognition of the importance both of reward for effort in a competitive society and of a framework of order in which individuals could pursue their personally defined goals.

THE IDEA OF THE STATE AND ACADEMIC
SELF-INTEREST

When looking at the ideological background of theories of the state it is well to bear in mind that intellectuals have their own distinctive professional self-interests which shape their basic attitudes towards the state. Nowhere is this process of academic self-interest better reflected than in Germany's so-called *Revolution des Geistes* which began around about 1800. During the eighteenth century German universities had been through a period of expansion, reform and reinvigoration compared with their British or French equivalents. There was the foundation of Halle (1694), then Göttingen (1734), and finally Berlin (1810), with Fichte as its first rector. Berlin acquired the name of the 'First Guards Regiment of Learning'. The emergence of a new and self-confident intellectual elite was reflected in the rapid development of *Kulturstaat* theories and in the emergence of academics as the definers of national ideals (Ringer, 1969). At first *Kulturstaat* theories represented an aggressive critique of the dominance of the landed nobility and a claim for the tremendous public responsibility of higher education. The ideology of a state that was committed to learning was embraced by faculties of philosophy and its Idealism gave a unique character to the German humanistic disciplines. Similarly, the theories of the *Rechtsstaat* were embraced by the faculties of law, for they offered an ideology which supported the role of the faculties as the interpreters of the law of the state and the trainers of the servants of that state.

When social realities changed with industrialization and the status of academics was recognized, both ideologies became more defensive as academics reacted to new threats from below. They began to sense that they were living through a prolonged crisis, engendered by a fundamental discordance between formalized thought and practical, rapidly changing life. In this context the transcendental Idealism of neo-Kantianism, with its pursuit of a pure notion of rational truth, attracted many academics who hungered for a world-view that would reaffirm their role. The form of neo-Kantianism that most influenced the character of thought about the *Rechtsstaat* was that of the Marburg school of Hermann Cohen and Paul Natorp.[5] This school's Idealist conception that truth could only be attained by the pure 'philosophical sciences' of logic and mathematics had a powerful effect on the highly formalized nature of late nineteenth-century *Rechtsstaat* theory and on Kelsen. After 1890 *Kulturstaat* ideas underwent a dramatic new development, one that was later accelerated by the experience of the First World War, of the revolution of 1918–19 and of the Weimar period. The intellectual source of this change was the revival of Kantian ethics by the Baden or Heidelberg school. In their search for a philosophy of culture that was based on absolute transcendental values the neo-Kantians Heinrich Rickert and Wilhelm Windelband returned to the tradition of Idealism and emphasized once again the interpretative role of the philosopher as the discoverer of norms and values. They began a debate about the character of the *Geisteswissenschaften* (their term was *Kulturwissenschaften*) that was continued by such eminent figures as Wilhelm Dilthey and Max Weber. From this debate emerged a new appreciation of the role of the state in counteracting the threat to *Kultur* that was posed by the 'materialistic' and 'positivist' tendencies unleashed by industrialization, 'machine' technology and 'mass' democracy with 'its politics of interest'. In philosophy the trend was away from epistemology to metaphysics; from the relativism of historicism to a substantive philosophy of culture; from a materialistic and deterministic positivism to Idealism. German *Kultur* was opposed both to French civilization, with its rationalism and democratic and egalitarian spirit, and to the 'trader's spirit' and political economy of England, with its egoism and acquisitiveness. A combination of neo-Hegelian and Romantic ideas led on to a view that the conception of the *Kulturstaat* was essential to spiritual renewal. It would provide a synthesis and 'wholeness' and keep the political order free from the new economic class interests.

Underlying the vagueness and ambiguity of these terms was a recognition by intellectuals that the rise of competitive elites—the 'utilitarian' industrial magnates and technicians, the trade unions and the political parties—threatened to displace them as the 'bearers of culture' and to reduce the state to a want-satisfying machine. The intellectuals feared the effects of a decline of the 'non-economic' middle class. Max Weber was very critical of the 'priestly' role that was claimed by intellectuals. Nevertheless, he suspected also that the new bourgeoisie, which he saw as the essential basis of the state, would be too attracted to an 'instrumental rationality'

(*Zweckrationalität*) to pursue a progressive, altruistic politics of moral conviction (*Wertrationalität*). For Weber the central requirement of the German state was a secure middle class with sufficient idealism to bridge the enormous gap between a disenchanted working class and the old elite. His brother Alfred Weber (1925) wrote of the crisis of the modern idea of the state, which had been brought about by a combination of the Versailles Treaty, Bolshevism, Fascism and the political pre-eminence of economic forces. The German state itself had become a *Scheinstaat,* an *Ersatzstaat.* Sensing a division between *Geist* and politics, he spoke of the 'plight of the intellectuals' and of the need for cultural renewal. In a wider-ranging analysis Max Scheler (1925) stressed the need for a new intellectual elite that was to be committed to 'the knowledge of salvation' and would combat the anti-intellectualism that threatened to engulf German *Kultur.* He looked forward to an evolution of the state as the expression of perfect solidarity, a *Gesamtperson* or collective personality. The intellectuals were, therefore, identifying themselves and their threatened interests with the idea of the state. Practically they could observe that new elites were acting as 'counter-patrons' to the administration and that the administration was departing from its old aloof, impartial stance. The result was in large part an emotional reaction, an outburst of 'cultural pessimism' which reached its peak in the Weimar period and was to be carried into the Bonn Republic by right-wing theorists like Arnold Gehlen (1956) and Hans Freyer and by the Frankfurt School. Theorists of the Frankfurt School kept open intellectual lines to Weimar, notably in their critique of the political and academic ascendancy of the model of technical rationality which reduced the intellect to an instrumental role and lured it away from a critical humanistic role. In fact, the ideological exhaustion of Germany between 1945 and the 1960s and the socio-political consequences of the 'economic miracle' were not conducive to a new outpouring of theories of the *Kulturstaat.* It was its language that lingered. A similar perception of intellectual decline was apparent (although not felt so acutely) in the France of the 1950s and 1960s. The technocratic ideology of the early Fifth Republic and its gradual conversion to neo-liberalism led to a more utilitarian, pragmatic conception of the state, one whose roots were in the technical *grandes écoles* rather than in the Sorbonne. It seemed a long way from the 'republic of professors' (the Third Republic), when intellectuals had been politically engaged and influential, particularly over the Dreyfus affair, and had played a major role in establishing the ideology of the 'republican' state. In both countries it was really the faculties of philosophy (or letters) that had faltered as centres of theorizing on the state. The prestige of the law faculties was secured in Germany by revitalized theories of the *Rechtsstaat,* and in France by Hauriou's and Renard's institutional theory which offered to the jurists a critical and constructive role, one that stressed the importance of judicial doctrine for interpreting and ordering institutional relationships with reference to fundamental purposes.

NOTES

1   Clark (1958) stresses that the 'pattern state' during the seventeenth-century period of state-building was the Bourbon monarchy of France and argues that internal political arrangements were greatly influenced by a costly military revolution that affected armaments, strategy and tactics in the century after 1560 and by the effects of war.

2   More recently even the literature on the French *ancien régime* has begun to distinguish between the 'rhetoric' of absolutism and the 'reality' of provincialism, resistance and the problem of revolts. Mousnier (1970) sees French society as one of 'orders' based on function, with vertical lines of loyalty exemplifying the continuing vitality of traditional society, whilst Goubert (1969) views absolutism as a process, a continuing dialogue between forces.

French society was fundamentally aristocratic and provincial. It was founded on the values of hierarchy and privilege, glued together by family connections and local solidarities, and nourished by patronage. There was no simple linear development to the patrimonial polity but a dynamic system of compromise and bargaining between monarchs and elites. Both shared a hierarchical model of society and feared the poor. If the thirty or so intendants who were established at the provincial level by Richelieu were professional administrators, more typical were the tax farmers and revenue contractors whose method of operation was far from bureaucratic in the modern sense. The monarch was engaged as much in manipulating old ways and arrangements as in enforcing new institutions and methods of government; he was as much a prisoner as an arbiter of the various religious, financial, judicial and military offices which encircled him. For a useful survey of the state of scholarship, see Kierstead (1975) and Salmon (1975).

3   The *Ständestaat* continued to provide a model for conservatives, for Catholics who were inspired by the papal encyclicals of 1891 and 1931, for Fascists and even for some syndicalists—for all those who perceived a crisis of parliamentary democracy and saw the roots of that crisis in political organization on the basis of parties and classes. Such ideas were influential after 1918 in Austria, Italy, Spain and Portugal.

4   Gerber was recognized by his contemporaries as the founder of a new epoch

in *Staatsrecht*. He defined *Staatsrecht* as *'die Lehre vom Staatswillen'*; the state was viewed as a legal person, capable of action, possessing a real power of will that was provided by the moral consciousness of the people. His rationalistic *Staatsrecht* was neo-Kantian in manner and based on the model of the Pandectists. Besides his chair at the University of Leipzig, Gerber was for a long period education minister, and then prime minister, of Saxony.

5   The grip of neo-Kantianism was difficult to avoid. In his realistic account of law the extremely influential, late-nineteenth-century, Göttingen jurist Jhering protested against a 'mathematical' rationalism that conceived of law as a system of immutable rules rather than as a dynamic historical process of social evolution and the expression of shifting relations between social interests. His emphasis on the social function of law was a great inspiration to later sociological jurisprudence, notably in Scandinavia and the United States. However, when it came to constructing the principles of legal organization and legislation, Jhering fell back into the pursuit of a rationalist science of purposes (*die Lehre vom Zweck im Recht*). A formal abstract rationalism was even more apparent in his account of the state as a 'thing-in-itself', creating law and protecting rights and, as a force of irresistible constraint, imposing limitations upon itself (Hallis, 1930).

chapter six | a comparison of theories of the state in france and germany

Another method of bringing some order into the complexity of theorizing about the state is to identify enduring differences in the 'national character' of these theories. There are important variations across political systems which need to be identified. Equally, there are hazards in isolating particular elements within a complex, internally variegated intellectual tradition, however distinctive that tradition may be, and using them to explain individual theories of the state. Each theory weaves together in its own way diverse strands within that tradition and embodies, moreover, the intentions of its author. It may also find stimulation outside the confines of the native tradition.

The argument for concentrating on two cases, France and Germany, is not just based on the difficulties of comparing national traditions of political theory. France and Germany served as 'modernity' models within continental Europe, and the pattern of diffusion of conceptions of the state across frontiers suggests both their intellectual dominance and the competitive character of the two models. For example, in Italy, French political and legal ideas were influential in the early nineteenth century but ceded pride of place to German ideas (Hegelianism, Laband and the Pandectists) after unification when the circumstances and problems of Germany and Italy seemed so similar. Foreign ideas were, nevertheless, usually accepted into the native intellectual tradition only after considerable reservation and amendment, for intellectual styles tended to reflect, in part, wider cultural attitudes.[1] In the case of the Netherlands William I was deeply influenced by late eighteenth-century German conceptions of the state. Jan Rudolf Thorbecke was the most outstanding Dutch politician of the nineteenth century and the major architect of the political reforms of the 1840s.[2] His *Notes on the Constitution* (1839) indicated the influence of German historicism and *Kulturstaat* conceptions through Savigny and Krause respectively. Later the pro-German Opzoomer (1873, 1854) produced a doctrinaire liberal view of the state, while the didactic philosopher Bolland made use of Hegelian ideas. However, the influence of Opzoomer and Bolland was not extensive, and Thorbecke displayed in his politics that critical common sense which has been so typical of the Dutch tradition. The French impact on Belgium was, in fact, greater than the German impact on the Netherlands. From the 1880s the University of Louvain was a centre of the development of neo-Thomist ideas. Nevertheless, when it came to political theorizing the French-speaking intelligentsia of Belgium borrowed from French theories of the state, particularly those theories of natural law that were associated with neo-Thomism (Dabin, 1957). In Sweden theories of the state have also been largely imported. During the nineteenth century C. J. Boström lectured on the Hegelian conception of the state at Uppsala University. Boëthius and Kjellén (1924) produced conservative German conceptions of a paternalist state. Although the concept of the state was widely known and used, there was little sustained interest in general theories of the state. One reason was Sweden's long history as a nation: there was not the same search for a theme of unity as in Germany. Another reason was to be found in the influence of the Uppsala school of philosophy: the 'value nihilism' of Hägerström and his disciples could be described as an indigenous variety of positivism. It engendered an interest in realistic theories of law and the state and a sociological form of jurisprudence. Sweden has continued to have a pragmatic conception of the state.[3]

Until the 1860s France was the model that Spain pursued, and it remained the one whose effects on institutions have been most deeply felt. The new Bourbon dynasty after 1713 initiated French ideas of reform from above as a way of overcoming Catholic traditionalism. Charles III's 'enlightened absolutism' (1759–88), which was supported by the so-called 'generation of 1760', was the high point of bureaucratic reforms. Spain's nineteenth-century liberals were much attracted by France and were to be responsible finally for pushing through the eighteenth-century conception of the centralized state that was to impose uniformity through a rational administration. In the 1860s the extraordinary phenomenon of 'Krausism' emerged. The ideas of a relatively minor German Idealist philosopher, Krause, were introduced by Sanz del Rió. This philosophy of 'mystical modernism' accorded a priestly role to the intellectuals, who were to be the source of national regeneration through the new sense of moral purpose that they were to bestow on the state. It was, of course, popular among intellectuals as a claim for academic freedom against a theocratic conception of the state. In 1875 the Free Institute of Education was founded in Madrid to propagate Krausism. Its influence was reflected in the social concerns of the Liberal Party, in a humanistic socialism like that of Fernando de los Ríos and, above all, in the Republic of 1931. In the case of Greece the idea of the state entered into political and legal discussion with the accession to the throne of a Bavarian, King Otto, in 1833. As Bavaria had been strongly influenced by France, French as well as German administrative ideas were adopted. Later there followed an interest in their legal theories of the state. At the School of Political Sciences, where public servants are given their training, Michael Stassinopoulos (1954) and Vezanis concentrated after the Second World War on teaching, respectively, French and German theories of the state. Stassinopoulos was also an eminent member, and later president, of the Council of State.

In Spain and Greece, as well in Italy and the Netherlands, there was intellectual disagreement in the late nineteenth and early twentieth centuries between those inspired by French individualist theories and those inspired by German organic theories of the state. Nevertheless, these countries were not passive recipients of such theories (Switzerland is discussed in n. 4). The earlier example of the revolution in the Netherlands between 1789 and 1813 is instructive. The reforms of state and the centralized administration that was modelled on French ideas represented a decisive watershed in Dutch history, one upon which the new monarchy of William I built. There was, however, an important continuity, in the sense that these ideas were adopted by forces for change that had been gaining ground in Dutch society during the eighteenth century (Schama, 1977). A concept of the abstract, impersonal state was not just dependent on importing French or German political ideas, and, as the examples of Italy and Spain suggest, such ideas could be received differently by different sections of society.

INTELLECTUAL TRADITION: SIMILARITIES AND CROSS-FERTILIZATION

A comparison of French and German theories of the state must recognize what they share as intellectual traditions. They have in common a heritage of ideas of Roman law and an historical experience of the leading role of the public bureaucracy. More importantly in this context they are dominated by a distinct view of philosophy. Philosophy is expected to provide a general orientation in the confusing world of life, to help solve juristic and sociological difficulties associated with the idea of the state. The result is a metaphysical urge to reflect critically on ontological assumptions, to enlighten and to educate by destroying baseless beliefs, and a subsequent tendency to self-conscious, laborious and even 'agonized' theorizing. There is, above all, an abhorrence of inconsistency and a passion for synthesis and systematization. This magisterial motive to achieve completeness and comprehensiveness was most apparent in German Romanticism and, later, critical theory. It was also an aspect of the preoccupation of German thinkers like Fichte, Herder and Dilthey with the notion of *Kultur* that refers to the interconnected values of a community. Marx's search for a unity of theory and practice is another example of the magisterial motive. An ambitious eclecticism was also apparent in the theoretical work on the state of Gény, Hauriou and Burdeau, who pursued an integrative ideal that sought to synthesize philosophy, politics, sociology, history and law. Philosophers have rarely been concerned, to the exclusion of all else, with technical logic (Frege was an exception) or with 'psychologism' (again, Freud and the Gestalt School were exceptions).

Both philosophical traditions concentrated, from the eighteenth century onwards, on morality as a manifestation of reason, on an 'active' notion of man who was seen to be capable of moral action and on a view of knowledge and action as inextricably intertwined. In part reflecting its Protestant background, the German tradition had an enduring conception of individual possibility: there was a stress in the literature on *Bildung* on man as a subject of self-education, and in critical theory on man as having a 'natural' interest in emancipation. Positivism did not capture philosophy and theories of the state in France. The continuing strength of the Idealist tradition was apparent in the work of Bodin, Domat, Esmein, Gény, Saleilles and Hauriou. Even those who were inspired by the positivist Comte tended to have their reservations about him. For example, Durkheim represented more the traditions of Cartesianism and neo-Kantianism than the tradition of positivism. During the eighteenth century, under the influence of René Descartes' dualism, French philosophy shifted towards voluntarism. The human problem was seen to reside in the drama associated with the attempt of an autonomous self, which was possessed of reason and will, to confront and seek to shape as best it

could an objective, 'cold' and resistant world. It was an intellectual tradition that proved hostile to economic materialism. The emphasis was on the
contribution of mind, which tries to order reality into a meaningful whole,
on *représentations* (states of mind) as an independent reality.

The strength of the Idealist outlook was reflected in a philosophical tradition of attachment to abstract ideas, and in particular of neo-Kantianism
(p. 150), in social science. There was also a tradition of esoteric but highly charged methodological disputes: between Schmoller and the Weber
brothers in the *Verein für Sozialpolitik* before 1914; in the *Staatslehre*
disputes of the 1920s between, on the one hand, the legal positivists and,
on the other, the different positions of Heller, Schmitt and Smend; in the
Methodenstreit of the 1960s between Habermas and the positivists; and,
of course, in the running battle between Idealists and those influenced by
positivism in France. These polemical arguments had non-academic roots
in the passions that were aroused by two questions: how one should regard the fundamental economic, social and political changes at work, and
how one should conceive of the form and purposes of a state that was to
be able to meet the challenge of these changes. At best, this philosophical
concern with the state could yield an impression of extraordinary insight, power and command of argument and could establish fascinating
views of past and present contradictions. At worst, it could produce ob-
scurantism and charlatanism, verbal pomposity and assertion, and polemics dressed up as theory. Even in the impressive theorizing of Herder,
Hegel and Habermas there was a thinness of argument about how the
kind of political order which they desired was to be established. Perhaps
the greatest contribution of the continental European philosophical
tradition was its awareness of change in the meaning of fundamental concepts. It was prepared to accept that the idea of the state could not be
divorced from historical variations in social structure (Schindler, 1932;
Kägi, 1945). Alexis de Tocqueville, Léon Duguit, Maurice Hauriou and
Raymond Aron in France and Hegel, the Frankfurt School, Gehlen and
the Freiburg school of jurists in Germany were united by the importance
of the idea of social change in their theories, an idea which, despite the
work of Spencer, Maine and Hobhouse, is not as strongly represented
in the British intellectual tradition. This difference from the essentially
static and timeless quality of F. H. Bradley's Absolute or of later British
analytical philosophy reflected, perhaps, an experience of the sudden and
violent character of social and political change within these two societies.

In addition to a similarity of philosophical concern, there has been an element of cross-fertilization between the two traditions. The influence of French ideas in Germany was apparent in the seventeenth century, with the reception of the work of Bodin and Loyseau, and in the eighteenth century, aided by the emergence of French as the 'universal' language, with the popularity in German courts of French culture and the interest in Enlightenment ideas of reason and nature. In the early nineteenth century von Mohl (1859) and von Stein (1850), both of whom were exponents of a 'realistic' social scientific view of the state, were greatly influenced by French ideas. Similarly, much later Carré de Malberg (1920) was to turn to German ideas on sovereignty, and to the work of Jellinek in particular, in his reappraisal of the basic ideas that informed French theories of the state. It was, however, German Jews like Heine, Marx and Adorno who represented the high point of openness to French ideas. Marx (as a schoolboy) was exposed to the ideas of Saint-Simon before those of Hegel. Indeed, Marxism and French positivism had in common their descent from the Saint-Simon 'school', notably in the notion of history as a developmental process that was subject to invariable laws. The tensions between the positivist and dialectical aspects of Marxism reflected its legacy from Saint-Simon (France) as well as Hegel (Germany). By the late nineteenth century Durkheim was commenting favourably on the greater social sensibility of German theorists and on the organic analogy of the state that was pursued by the so-called 'socialists of the chair' like Schäffle and Wagner. The most influential German theorist during (and particularly at the end of) the nineteenth century was Kant, who was interpreted for a French audience by Charles Renouvier. An Idealist rationalism that combined Kant and Descartes prevailed in various forms between 1880 and 1920 and profoundly affected theories of the state. It was not until the 1930s that the entrance of Hegel, and of German Idealism in general, into French intellectual life produced important consequences.

The phenomenon of cross-fertilization, of the import of foreign ideas, is in part to be explained by the fact that the native tradition was failing to provide insight into contemporary problems. The French 'return' to Hegel in the 1930s was followed in the post-war period by the emergence of Marx as a central figure for the first time. Marx was, nevertheless, interpreted within the terms of the French intellectual tradition and in particular of the two opposed political reactions within the French Communist Party to the crisis of de-Stalinization after 1956. On the one hand, there was the success among intellectuals of Marxist humanism. Roger Garaudy's Marxism was based on an anthropological conception of man, viewing Marxism as a doctrine of human freedom that was concerned with overcoming man's 'alienation'. By contrast, Sartre's Marxism, which began from the existentialist premise that existence comes before essence, argued that the problem of freedom was 'authenticity'—man's commitment to his subjectivity and to his responsibility for decision. Their anti-Leninist and Cartesian perspective emphasized the active and creative role of man in shaping concrete historical situations and rejected 'economism'. On the other hand, there was in the 1960s Louis Althusser's politically motivated counter-attack on this Idealistic 'moralism' and the 'cult of personality' that it engendered. Althusser represented the positivist outlook, although many positivists would feel uncomfortable with the primacy that he attaches to politics. Above all, his mission was to expunge Hegel from Marx. Marxism was viewed as a scientific enterprise that was important for its epistemological novelty. Althusser fitted Marx into the structuralist perspective by arguing that Marx had begun to develop an analysis of the formal structure of relationships within 'systems' that moved autonomously. Marxism became the search for the underlying abstract and universal properties of social and political phenomena, for the reality that was hidden behind the contingent complexity of experience. Nevertheless, Althusser's view that ideologies were central and had a force and logic of their own led him also to reject economic determinism. The French Communist Party had preferred to avoid too much official reference to the state. Now it became embroiled in a Marxist debate about strategy for transformation of the state, which extended beyond the party, particularly after the departure of Garaudy, and which for the first time played a major role in French intellectual theories of the state. The Party was embarrassed first by Garaudy's and Sartre's calls for a more open and experimental Marxism, later by Althusser's argument that a party that could not transform itself through a concrete critical analysis, and that had even taken on the mechanical, manipulative attributes of the bourgeois state apparatus, was quite unable to transform that state.

INTELLECTUAL TRADITION: DIVERGENCE

Despite these examples of cross-fertilization between the French and German intellectual traditions, the differences remained considerable.

After 1806 German thinkers turned against the 'crass materialism' and positivism of the French Enlightenment, while after 1871 French thinkers, who generally admired the German model of scholarship, turned against German Romanticism, against Hegel as 'anti-liberal' and against the juristic theories of Gerber and Jellinek, especially Jellinek's notion of the 'auto-limitation' of the state. A central difference was the effect of the French Revolution, which bestowed on French theories of the state the idea of the sovereignty of the nation, of *l'État-nation*. By contrast, in Germany patrimonial ideas lingered into the nineteenth century and gave way gradually (for example, in Gerber) to a view of the nation as an organ of the sovereign state, one that in Jellinek's view determined as it willed the extent of its own powers. More typical of France was Renard's (1930, p. 152) notion that 'the state is only a secondary phenomenon that addresses itself to a primary phenomenon: the nation'. Maspetiol and Renard, members of the Hauriou 'school', agreed that the state had only the authority of its mission; it was an *imperium* that served the *res publica*. The abstract notion of the nation, which was part of the Jacobin language that has so infected French debates about the state, was nevertheless a cause of considerable dispute. Carré de Malberg (1920) offered a major critique of received ideas by following a distinction, which he found in the work of Jellinek, between the *puissance étatique* or *Staatsgewalt* (public power) and the sovereignty of the nation. He argued that the sovereign nation did not create the public power but rather legitimated it and determined the conditions of the exercise of that power particularly through the constitution. The sovereign defined the idea of law; the *puissance étatique* expressed in institutional terms (organs) the force of this idea; while the 'governors', the third aspect of the state and the source of initiative, directed the *puissance étatique* and ensured its compatibility with the will of the sovereign. Carré de Malberg was an original and important figure who stressed the importance of the organs through which public power was expressed and through which the unity of that power was safeguarded. If the idea of law was essential to direct and legitimate public power, public power was necessary to give effect to law. The state was seen as a phenomenon of domination that was concerned to reduce the resistance of individuals rather than, as Duguit suggested, to achieve their collaboration. Carré de Malberg's notion of the authoritative state was to have a considerable influence in twentieth-century France.

Another important critique of the nineteenth-century French idea of the nation was provided by Hauriou (1923). He rejected the idea that the nation delegated its sovereignty to the Assembly, whose sovereignty was an emanation of the nation. In Hauriou's view sovereignty had been 'nationalized' by the Revolution. However, the exercise of the power of government had not been bestowed on the nation and, therefore, was not an emanation of the nation; it had an anterior existence. Esmein's idea of the identification of the state and nation (*État-nation*) put the individual at the mercy of the state. It was necessary to see the nation as having an existence apart from the state within civil society. Hauriou emphasized that the 'constitution' of civil society was at least as important to liberty as the constitution of the state.

Despite this debate about the concept of the nation in French theories of the state, it remained an important reference point of debate. The dominant view was that the nation referred to an abstract and indivisible collectivity but, as 'the succession of human generations', was not to be identified with popular sovereignty. According to Carré de Malberg, the electorate was an organ of the nation and was limited to the function of choosing and controlling members of the Assembly.

Another difference between French and German theories of the state lay in the treatment of the idea of individualism. Individualism has dominated French theories of the state, as the pained reaction to Durkheim's 'social realism' and his emphasis on the variability and complexity of human nature indicated. The nineteenth-century liberal theory of the state assigned an absolute value to the autonomous individual and his free will. This intense individualism found a powerful body of support in classical humanism, Roman law, revolutionary sentiment and, above all, the abstract individualism of eighteenth-century thought and its cosmopolitan view of an immutable human nature. An important contribution of nineteenth-century radical liberal theory was a durable concept of liberty, a human sensibility, and a sense of the nobility, isolation and vulnerability of the individual. It was also associated with an instinctive distrust of authority; in the view of its critics it was an 'anarchistic' attitude.

Twentieth-century French theories of the state have reacted against the excesses of the view that liberty is the principle of the state and have based themselves on a negative view of *individualisme*. Indeed, Lukes (1973b) has suggested that the term *individualisme* was primarily pejorative and grew out of a nineteenth-century reaction to the isolation and social dissolution that appeared to have been engendered by the French Revolution and, earlier, by the Enlightenment. This reaction found its foremost expression in the work of de Maistre, Saint-Simon, Constant and Tocqueville. The emphasis has subsequently been upon the need to strengthen the power and authority of the state so that it can provide unity of direction and act as 'the creator of homogeneity' (Maspetiol, 1957). Carré de Malberg offered the first major theoretical statement by a jurist of the fear of a disintegration of the public power, of the inadequacy of the Assembly as a source of unified action and of the need to reinforce the executive. René Hubert in the 1920s, Louis Le Fur in the 1930s and Debré in the 1940s and 1950s stressed the principle of the authority of the state, which was not in opposition to, but was a condition of, liberty. Both the state and the individual were seen as related to a higher law through which they found integration. The mechanism of this integration was the conscience, from which springs an objective morality which transcends time and place, state and individual. Individualism was qualified by the notion of an objective morality as the basis of authority. Debré (1947, p. 9) provided the most passionate expression of the dangers to liberty of a feeble state that was 'dying by assassination': 'the chief enemy has become the degradation and the agony of power'. In doing so he reflected the *Zeitgeist* in theories of the state. Hauriou had argued with great effect against Duguit, claiming that the state was not to be defined in terms of a goal or a function. It was not viewed simply as a provider of services or a 'need-satisfying' machine. The state embodied public power in the service of an idea of law. When Hauriou argued that the individual and society were dualisms and the one was not reducible to the other, he was rejecting both Esmein's individual and Duguit's social man in favour of a 'social individualism'.

German ideas of individualism were conditioned by two major influences. The first of these was the tradition of *Innerlichkeit,* which stressed that the individual should find his fulfilment, his unique 'individuality' (a Romantic idea that came into use from the 1840s), in the pursuit of personal truth. This divorce of individualism from the notion of engagement in practical matters has been traced back to eighteenth-century Pietist doctrine, which emphasized inner conviction, the value and sanctity of the individual soul, and the idea of education as a means of furthering the autonomous and integral growth of a unique personality (Bruford, 1975). An austere asocial individualism was implicit in the notion of *Bildung,* of personal culture and pure learning, as the principal vocation of man. Another source of this divorce was, as we shall see, the social and political conditions in which the German Enlightenment took place. The tradition of *Innerlichkeit* did not encourage intellectual attitudes that favoured the bourgeoisie and their engagement in civil society or that were likely to generate realistic political proposals. It tended either to look to a strong directive state as an antidote to, or even to supercede, civil society or, as in the case of the anarchic individualism of Max Stirner, to lose faith in the possibility of a secure public morality and to suggest that values were simply relative to the intentions of individual egos.

A second influence on the German idea of individualism was the organic conception of state that ascribed 'individuality' to the state, through which the individual achieved self-fulfilment. Durkheim stressed the acute sense of the importance of collective life in the German intellectual tradition and related this sense to the organic metaphor that saw the individual as an integral part of society and suggested that his value and dignity depended on his integration within that society. By contrast, a cultural conception of the state, which had been implicit in Rousseau's notion of the general will as a social bond, had languished in nineteenth-century France. The state was viewed there as a vast machine which repressed a multitude of unsociable individuals (Lukes, 1973a, p. 89). In Germany Herder's metaphor of the organism and his historical awareness had not only been adopted by the Romantics but also deeply infected the historical school of jurisprudence that was associated with F. C. von Savigny. The notion that the personality was first and foremost fulfilled in and through the state, which represented what Krüger (1966, p. 5) called 'das Bessere Ich' (the better self), could have very different political implications. These implications depended upon whether emphasis was on the notion of participation in the universality of the state (as was the case with Heller) or on the notion of obedience to a state that embodied and defined its own morality (as was the case with Krüger). There was, however, until after 1945, an absence of the framework of natural law from which had emerged the French idea of 'social individualism', the idea that neither the individual nor the state was an absolute value.

Neither the French nor the German intellectual tradition was homogeneous or even coherent, but there were some important differences in their approach to the state. French theories of the state were strongly influenced by what Pascal called *l'esprit géométrique,* the concern to arrive at a rational understanding of the world as an object. *L'esprit de finesse* represented a parallel tradition of intuitive thought and introspective moralism, which emphasized consciousness as the basis of knowledge and the world as a 'lived' experience through which man made or created himself. This latter current of thought, which ran from Montaigne through Bergson to the post-1945 existentialists, was not particularly interested in the state or, indeed, in conceptual knowledge in general. *L'esprit géométrique* was associated above all with Cartesianism, the 'cult of distinct ideas' (Durkheim), and positivism. Cartesianism combined a passion for ideas with an extraordinary lucidity of thought, an idea of using reason for practical purposes with a formal concern for clarity of definition and logical reasoning. Much of its inspiration was drawn from the classical ideals of ordered unity and harmony. The remarkable influence of this native rationalism was the product of its diffusion from the *École Polytechnique* into the administration and the military, from the *École Normale Supérieure* into the national educational system and from the law faculties that were the centres of theorizing on the state. Another manifestation of *l'esprit géométrique* was positivism, which was an extraordinarily optimistic theory of social improvement by the discovery of laws of social life analogous to those of nature. Positivism was inspired by the materialism of Condillac, given its first clear formulation by Saint-Simon, and eventually transformed by Comte into a new religion of humanity that sought to replace classical metaphysics by a new secular morality based on science. Such ambitions distinguished it from the 'value-free' perspective and quantitative concerns of modern behaviouralism. Much of the lasting appeal of positivism came from its promise of a form of socialism that dispensed with the notion of class conflict. While it lacked a practical political outlet till the enthusiasm for technocracy of the Fifth French Republic, positivism's intellectual influence was apparent in the 'scientific rationalism' of Durkheim and Duguit. Although neither was a dogmatic positivist, they were unwilling, in contrast to the Hauriou school, to posit a faculty of reason that was independent of natural or social causes as necessary to the establishment of a good society and state. The Hauriou school, for whom reason was logically prior to society and the state, attacked the neo-positivists for conflating the individual's ability to reason and his moral sense. This argument about the status of reason was probably the central one within *l'esprit géométrique* and French theories of the state.

Although the French and German Enlightenment shared an interest in reason and nature, it is possible to identify in the very different character of the German Enlightenment the roots of later Idealism, Romanticism and *Kulturstaat* ideology (Kelly, 1969). The German Enlightenment was a product of the great tensions within eighteenth-century Germany between religion and reason, feudalism and absolutism, a native culture and a cosmopolitan French culture that was centred on the princely courts. Despite the emergence of Cameralism and secular ideas of natural law, scholasticism remained much stronger than in France, whether in the form of the Aristotelianism of the Protestant states or the Thomism of the Catholic states. Its view of man as a disinterested observer of a reality outside himself was different from that of French Cartesianism. Political thinkers like Leibniz and Wolff were concerned to unite scholasticism with natural science, and it was not until Kant that the idea of man as a thinking subject gained a firm hold. Debate within the German Enlightenment centred on religion and the attempt to restate it in terms of a rational world order; the Enlightenment represented an attempt to modernize, rather than to be a critique of, Protestantism. It drew on Leibniz's concept of 'contextual harmony' as an alternative both to Cartesianism and to British empiricism and offered a view of the world as a harmonious conjunction of a variety of discrete and spontaneous elements. The central concern of the German Enlightenment was to reconcile a rationalist search for simple, universal truths with the spirituality and the personalized character of Protestant Pietism. Pietism led on to an ethical idea of education and the notion of the *Bildungstaat,* which was animated by a spiritual ideal through which the inner life of man would be enriched. It is notable that of the works of the French Enlightenment the most widely read in Germany was Rousseau's *Émile.* Besides its discussions on education, this work contained an implicit ethical position of withdrawal from, rather than direct opposition to, a corrupt political system. The German Enlightenment was not associated with a tradition of radical social criticism and practical political concerns from which later generations could draw sustenance: 'While in France philosophy and despotism lived in a state of armed truce, the German Enlightenment was paternalistic and authoritarian' (Kelly, 1969, p. 76). In the context of government oppression of 'atheism' or radical critiques, and of the association of revolutionary ideas with anti-patriotism and the chaos of the Terror in the 1790s, there was a retreat from reality to 'pure' thought, to *Innerlichkeit.* Another major legacy of the Enlightenment was the historical consciousness and, above all, a 'past-mindedness' that was to appeal to later Romantics and found its expression in the attempt of Enlightenment thinkers to revive the *Ständestaat* constitution. Reason and spirit were reconciled by 'historicizing' the concept of reason: reason contained a spiritual element that was striving through history towards self-fulfilment.

The heritage of the German Enlightenment was not *l'esprit géométrique* but Romanticism and historicism. The Romantics took certain German Enlightenment ideas, like 'past-mindedness' and a view of the state as a historical growth, but rejected the supremacy of reason in favour of a radical aesthetic individualism, super-rational ties to nature, emotion, intuition and, occasionally, a sloppy mysticism and a curiously nihilistic quality. They represented 'uprooted' middle-class figures who had no political faith in what was a weak middle class and looked instead to reform imposed from above. Their idealization of the state as something inherently undefinable, because beyond the grasp of finite minds, was to form a part of the German intellectual tradition and to distinguish it further from the French.

The historical school that was initiated by Herder, Hegel and Savigny was to leave an extraordinarily complex legacy. It viewed history as an all-embracing process in which a historical subject attained its essence and in which particular phenomena were only to be understood in relation to a historical 'whole'. Hegel was a seminal figure, but largely because of his very intricate and laborious metaphysics he was used rather than understood. He was very difficult to interpret, partly because he was a philosopher of change who believed that ideas did not have a fixed eternal meaning, and partly because of the synthesizing character of his work and his fondness for making qualifications within elaborate arguments. Later writers tended to elevate certain aspects of Hegel's work to central importance or to pick out particular errors, inconsistencies or vagueness. In both cases they lost sight of his philosophy as a whole.

Despite the fact that during his lifetime he was attacked for writings incompatible with the principles of the Prussian state and the Hohenzollern dynasty, Hegel's ideas were co-opted by right-wing theorists of the state from Constantin Rössler's *System der Staatslehre* (1857) and Max von Seydel (1873) in nineteenth-century Germany to Krüger in the 1960s (Lübbe, 1962). In their works the state was clothed with Hegelian dignity as a spiritual phenomenon, as an ethical community that expressed the 'better self' and restrained and corrected civil society. At the same time, and in contrast to Hegel, a bureaucratic conception of the state was offered: *Amt* (office) with its values of impersonality, reliability and continuity was identified as the embodiment of the 'better self'. The state was regarded as a rational artifact, a massive organization of offices. Hence the official emerged as the state, office as the concrete realization of its moral purpose. Whereas Hegel emphasized the importance of bringing state and civil society into a close relationship, these writers stressed the importance of a distance between them.

The socialist left (Moses Hess, Marx and Lassalle, for example) took up Hegel's dialectic as a technique to be used in critical analysis, as a method of discovering and specifying the contradictory character of reality, the positive and negative aspects of whatever was under scrutiny (Löwith, 1962). It was 'in the grasping of opposites in their unity or of the positive in the negative' that speculative thought consisted. While Marx 'corrected' Hegel on the relationship of state to civil society by 'demystifying' him, he did not break with Hegel. Marx's criticisms gave the impression that he differed from Hegel more than in fact he did. From Hegel he grasped both the idea of universality (although Marx's universal force was not the state) that absorbs all particular individuality and the theory that labour in the broadest sense was man's essence in the world. The powerful impact of Hegel on German Marxism was apparent in the early work of Karl Korsch and the Hungarian Georg Lukács (who was influential in Germany and for whom the proletariat was the carrier of historical consciousness). Above all, it was the Frankfurt School that took up Marx's ontological interests and historical materialism, with its concern to portray the interaction between theory and practice, between conscious activity and the material conditions of existence. In rejecting the dialectical materialism, which had followed from Engels' positivist interpretation of Marx and had been popularized by Soviet Marxists, they stressed that matter or the relations of material production did not determine social and political change. The Frankfurt School went back to the Enlightenment tradition of Kant and the idea that critique or 'oppositional' thinking was the essential activity of practical reason. They also returned to Hegel as an offshoot of that tradition, to the idea of emancipation from the constraint of coercive illusions and of the self as having a natural 'will to reason' which is itself liberating. Critical theory was therefore very different from the positivist tradition of French left-wing thought. It entailed a process of self-reflection that questioned the objectivity of objects of experience and the idea of an 'emancipatory' social science that was involved not just with epistemological problems but also with the problematic condition of the social world. The 'Utopian will' of critical theory gave it an imposing grandeur as a philosophical statement. Its notions that self-reflective reason was a 'natural' aspect of man and that such reason had an emancipatory value in and of itself remained, nevertheless, very questionable bases for philosophy or political practice. Many of its weaknesses stemmed from a failure to focus on the basic problem of how its ideas were to be translated into the everyday.

A more general effect of Hegel and the historical consciousness on both the left and the right in Germany was an anxiety about the future, a sense that there were no longer any intellectual or moral certainties, only the danger of an anarchy of values. In fact, Hegel and Marx were not as worried about this problem because they held the philosopher to be in a privileged position and able to avoid relativism by his insight into the logic of the historical process. Their successors often had less faith in the possibility of such insights. A cultural pessimism, a sense of the impending end of history as it had been known, recurred amongst the Young Hegelians of the 1830s and 1840s like Bruno Bauer, Moses Hess, Arnold Ruge and Max Stirner; after the First World War in the popular work of Oswald Spengler (1924) and his idea of an increasingly beleaguered state, no longer able to provide a spiritual community through which man could develop his individuality and moral essence, and in the Hegelian–Marxist phase of Lukács and his notion of a crisis of culture in bourgeois society; in Gehlen's (1956) idea of the residual state (*Reststaat*), immersed in an undifferentiated 'mass' society; and in the reliance of the Frankfurt School on cultural criticism rather than on a particular political programme or party. The crisis of culture was the crisis of an idea of the state that was committed to the ideal of *Bildung* and was being undermined by the materialism of civil society. This aspect of the Hegelian heritage was unfortunate for German intellectual history, in the sense that it encouraged a debilitating fatalism.

Left-wing German *Staatslehre* was deeply influenced by Hegelianism. Heller's *Staatslehre* (1963), first published in 1934, exemplified the extent to which German social democracy had been infected by Hegel through Lassalle, its creator and leader during the first heroic years, and August Bebel, its great organizer. Heller rescued the idea of the state from Marxism by arguing that society was inherently incapable of self-organization and needed an activist state as 'the independent organization and activation of territorial–social co-operation'. The state was viewed as a social formation in which fact and value, will and norm, were inextricably interwoven in a dialectical relationship. It was only to be understood by synthesizing the normative character of *Staatsrechtslehre* (legal theories of the state) with the empiricism of political science. This idea of a dialectical *Staatslehre* was revived again in the 1970s by the German jurist Dieter Suhr (1975) who drew also on the earlier works of the eminent Swiss jurists Dietrich Schindler (1932) and Werner Kägi (1945). Their analysis of the 'constitutional state' did not look at the normative written constitution and its approximation to reality on the ground that such an approach tends to lead to the view

that constitutions and ideas are inadequate guides to conduct. They emphasized the dialectical, dynamic relationship of interdependence between
theory (the constitutional norms of the state) and practice (the reality of
political conduct). Constitutions were seen to live and develop in time, being applied, interpreted and revised. The approach was comprehensive and
extraordinarily complex. It focused upon consciousness and its relationship to both the constitution and social structure, upon the 'multi-dimen-
sionality' of thought and, like the Freiburg school of jurists (for example,
Fiedler, 1972), upon the openness of the constitution and its need to embody contradictions and to act as a catalyst by providing the basic logic
and grammar of politics, without pre-empting too much of its actual vocabulary. 'Emancipatory' social development was only possible in a state
that was based on recognition of the dialectic, that accepted dissent and
dialogue and recognized the creative character of contradictions. Above
all, practice was to be seen as a challenge to the development of theory; it
was important to be willing to adjust one's intellectual framework rather
than to insist that practice be adjusted to fit theory. The style of argument
was non-dogmatic and very flexible, for the emphasis was upon self-reflection and a 'trial-by-error' approach to truth. Its central problem was
that of the dialectical method itself: the absence of rigorous standards by
which the worth of dialectical analysis could be evaluated. This approach
encouraged a tendency for 'reach' to exceed 'grasp' and a leaning towards
a moral relativism that made choice among competing rationally defensi-
ble conclusions difficult.

While both French and German intellectual traditions of the state have
looked outside the confines of their own historical experience for inspiration, an essential difference between them lies in the kind of model to
which each has aspired. For example, France has been fascinated by the
Roman model. This phenomenon is explicable by reference to France's
earlier reception of Roman law, the traditional educational dominance
of the Jesuits, and the fact that France is a Roman Catholic country and
has a Romance language. Peyrefitte (1976) has suggested that a love of
centralized power, within the Communist Party as well as the state, was
nurtured by both Catholicism and a Latin heritage of 'Caesarism without
Caesar'. By contrast, German thinkers began at the turn of the nineteenth
century to look to the Greek model of the *polis,* which Hegel referred
to as that 'paradise of the human spirit'. The turn to Greek culture as
the key to true 'German-ness' was as an alternative to the French, and

therefore, Latin, influence in German courts of the eighteenth century. It inspired the humanistic ideals of *Bildung* which by 1815 had come to dominate *Gymnasium* education. A major factor in the appeal of Greek culture was the extraordinary influence on German intellectuals like Herder and Hegel of the research of J. J. Winckelmann. The Greek ideal of the whole man was compared with the fragmentation of the individual personality in Germany (a fragmentation which Kant was held to have encouraged), the communal mores of the *polis* to contemporary religious, political and cultural divisions. Herder and Hegel were concerned to restore harmony to personal experience, to recreate the whole man in an integrated, cohesive political community. Their theories of the state were theories of social relations in a broad sense and inaugurated a German concern for the state as a cultural rather than a 'mechanical' concept.

Both intellectual traditions of the state were also deeply influenced by different religious conceptions. The German Enlightenment was mainly a Protestant phenomenon, and its theories of the state reflected in part at least a secularization of Pietist ideas that emphasized inwardness and personal truth. Even more obvious was the impact of Roman Catholic ideas on French theories of the state, particularly with the revival of Catholic social thought at the end of the nineteenth century. This religious dimension remained strong, for after 1945 the French Catholic Church emphasized a more active social role. During the twentieth century two important Catholic ideas came to dominate French theories of the state. 'Personalism' emerged out of the late nineteenth-century attack on the subjectivism of liberal individualism by philosophers like Renouvier and jurists like Bonnecase. It drew a distinction between the concept of man as individual (*individu*) and the concept of man as person (*personne*), between a materialistic and an 'absolutist' view of individuality, which focused on the 'selfish' ego as the centre of all things, and a spiritual view of personality as the creative, 'unified' self which realized freedom and goodness through its sociability, openness and generous character. Man was at the same time an individual and a social being. Through its exaggeration of individualism French liberalism had created a danger of anarchy and moral disintegration; by denying the internal life of man in favour of seeing him in terms of social relationships the positivists and Marxists had 'deformed' man. Personalism was a central tenet of the Hauriou school and of institutional theory. A second major influence came from Catholic ideas of natural law. These ideas were revived and broke away from the earlier medieval and clerical—but now 'Rousseau-tainted'—notion of the social contract. The idea that the authority of the state rested upon respect for fundamental human values and recognition of their universal and objective character came to dominate French theories of the state. However, theorists like Saleilles, Gény, Debré and Hauriou had a 'realistic' perspective on natural law. They refused to 'canonize' law by identifying certain moral principles as commands to the legislature. Instead these theorists emphasized the importance of the sense of responsibility and competence of men in specific situations to the realization of such principles. The approach of natural law rejected the moral relativism of American socio-psychological analyses of authority; it saw authority as a matter not just of how one proceeded but rather of the ends to which one's conduct was directed. The proper concern of theories of the state was the rational analysis of moral values.

It is against this religious background that the failure of legal positivism to make the same impact in France as in Germany is to be understood. Of the major French theorists of the state Carré de Malberg and Charles Eisenmann (1939) came closest to adopting the legal positivist position. Their reservations were, nevertheless, significant. Although Carré de Malberg (1920) claimed that, as a jurist, he was an agnostic who was not concerned with questions about the legitimacy of public power, he refused to make the radical separation of morality and law to be found in Kelsen. Carré de Malberg stressed the importance of the moral ideas on which the state rested and claimed, moreover, that these ideas were to be found outside the state. However, the jurist was not directly concerned with moral ideas but with the state as a reality, a 'complex fact' that was independent of law in its origin but, once in existence, was inseparably connected with the judicial order. Carré de Malberg was unable to suspend his Christian morality. The state was not the only source of law. It was limited not just by Jellinek's concept of auto-limitation, which described voluntary self-restraint by the state, but above all by objective moral principles that were enshrined in the conscience of the individual. He differed from Kelsen also in his refusal to see the state as an abstract, 'pure' system of unified norms. These norms were the expression of competition and conflict between different social and economic forces. Moreover, it was important to recognize the power and constraint of the state. The origins of the state were, according to Carré de Malberg, in force not law. He saw the state as a unified system of organs rather than of norms, as a material organization of con-straint (*la puissance dominatrice*) and not simply a spiritual phenomenon.

THE DEBATE ABOUT METHODOLOGY AND POLITICAL SCIENCE

The French intellectual tradition, unlike the German, has been character-ized by the enduring strength of a political conception of the state.[4] This political perspective was partly the product of the revival of natural-law ideas by Saleilles and Gény and partly the consequence of the broaden-ing of public-law perspectives through the influence of sociologists like Durkheim on Duguit and Tarde on Hauriou. From Gény through Hauriou to Burdeau there has been an 'integrative' approach to the state, one that combines philosophy, history, political science and sociology with law. This eclecticism has been motivated by a concern for reflection on fundamental values and for synthesis, as well as by a desire to match academically what was recognized to be the complex multi-dimensional character of the state. Some jurists, like Jean Rivero, have argued that the 'realistic' methods of observation of political science, which were recom-mended by neo-positivists like Maurice Duverger and André de Laubadère (1970), who followed in the tradition of Duguit, were in danger of sacrific-ing these larger concerns: others, like Burdeau, have seen political science as a systematic normative science that is both analytical and interpreta-tive and is concerned to establish the coherence of the 'political universe'. According to Burdeau, the 'political universe' is magical and non-rational, a mental cosmogony that is more akin to the 'universe' of poetry or religion than to the observable physical world. The greater willingness of French jurists to embrace political science has in part reflected their interest in the state as power and in its capacity for action in the service of ethical values, an interest that was stimulated by the political experiences of the Third and Fourth Republics. For example, Burdeau saw power (following Carré de Malberg) and the idea of law (following Hauriou) as the unifying concepts of the state; they were mutually dependent and gave life to each other. The state was viewed as institutionalized power, both force and idea, and legitimated by the law which it served.

Germany's more controversial and esoteric debate about methods of studying the state reflected fundamental disagreements not just between the proponents and opponents of a political conception of the state but also among those who advocated a political perspective. Although the comprehensive term *Staatslehre* was in use by the middle of the eighteenth century, its distinction from *Staatsrecht* was already being made in August von Schlözer's treatise (1793). In the early nineteenth century it was possible to identify, in the works of Romeo Maurenbrecher (1837) and especially of H. A. Zachariae (1841–5), a *Staatsrechtslehre* that sought to develop a common German *Staatsrecht*. Meanwhile, the works of Constantin Rössler, Robert von Mohl (1859) and J. K. Bluntschli (1875), Mohl's successor at Heidelberg, kept alive a comparative and empirical *Staatslehre* with a strong emphasis on constitutions and the formulation of general concepts. The birth of a self-confident and successful *Staatsrechtslehre* dated really from Gerber's (1865) and Laband's (1901) elevation of public law to a juristic discipline akin to private law. Their exclusively legal conception of the state meant the loss of philosophical, historical and social perspectives, of that integrated concept of the political and that concern for *both* state and society that had been apparent in the studies of von Mohl, von Stein and Bluntschli. Only a few writers, like Gustav Ratzenhofer (1893), followed von Mohl's political analysis of the state as a social reality. In the view of the legal positivists the proper field of concern of social science was society, not the state. The birth of modern *Staatslehre* dated from the publication of Jellinek's (1900) famous *Allgemeine Staatslehre*. Influenced by the ethical neo-Kantianism of his colleague Windelband, Jellinek advocated a dualistic *Staatslehre:* a *Rechtslehre* that dealt with the state as a legal institution and used juristic methods to analyse norms; and a *Soziallehre* that was concerned with the state as a social organization and employed empirical methods to investigate social reality. *Staatsrechtslehre* was to become a part of *Staatslehre*. This idea of the two aspects of the state helped to enrich legal perspectives, but at the same time, as Smend and Heller were to complain, it eventually obliterated the notion of the state as a unity. It was possible for the disciples of Laband and Meyer to continue their activities relatively untouched. They offered a view of the 'authoritative' state as *Herrschaftsgewalt* and an anthropomorphic picture of the personality and will of the state. By contrast, Jellinek's colleague at Heidelberg, Max Weber (1956), attempted to provide a *Soziallehre* of the state.

In the 1920s there was an assault on both Jellinek's dualistic *Staatslehre* and legal positivism. The revival of interest in Idealism and the humanistic sciences within the faculties of philosophy began to influence the faculties of law and notably the Berlin jurist Smend (Kaufmann, 1921). From the faculties of philosophy emerged an attack on the philosophical roots of legal positivism, on the formal rationalism of 'pure thought' which had been induced by the neo-Kantianism of the Marburg 'school' and its emphasis on mathematics and mechanics as models of knowledge. This Idealist revival and subsequent broadening of theoretical interest coincided with a troubled period of uncertainty, and fragmentation of views, about the character of the new republican state. The major representatives of legal positivism—like Gerhard Anschütz, Kelsen and Richard Thoma (Anschütz and Thoma, 1930, 1932)—were now liberal defenders of the Weimar Republic. They saw in positivism an insulation against critiques of the new regime, a foreclosing of questions that had earlier assisted the Second Empire. In Anschütz's view, although the Weimar Republic was not sufficiently centralized, it was more truly a state than the Second Empire because it rested on the idea of the unity and impersonality of the *Volk* and not just on the agreement of princes. There was, however, a new division within legal positivism. Both Anschütz and Kelsen rejected Jellinek's dualistic *Staatslehre* in favour of a purely juristic conception of the state. However, whereas Anschütz saw the state as a sovereign entity and personified it in the tradition of Laband (1901) and of his own predecessor in the chair at Heidelberg, Georg Meyer (1899), Kelsen made a radical identification of the idea of the state with the positive legal order. The state was viewed as simply the expression of the logical completeness and inner consistency of that order. Such opponents of the legal positivists as Heller, Schmitt (1928), Smend (1928) and Heinrich Triepel (1927) attacked Jellinek also for making it possible to continue to see the state in such narrowly legal terms. For Smend the state was a sociological reality whose central requirement was spiritual integration and which was to be understood by the phenomenological methods of the humanistic sciences; for Schmitt (1932) it was a political reality whose central requirement was a capability of decision and which needed to be understood as a system of power relationships.

Before 1918 the extraordinary dominance of legal positivism was in large part to be explained by the comparatively small importance of constitutional law in Germany, by the limited number of material problems of constitutional law that arose, and by the absence of the stimulus of competition from a system of 'judicial review' of the constitutionality of political measures. The Weimar constitution did not introduce judicial review. Nevertheless, the critique of positivism in the 1920s was a practical juristic response to the changed circumstances after 1918, in particular the emergence of a greater number of specific constitutional issues than before. *Staatslehre* displayed a new interest in constitutional questions and moved away from a static view of the constitution as a collection of fixed norms to a view of the 'living constitution' and of constitutional law as different from other branches of law because it required greater attention to extra-legal factors. In this context writers like Kaufmann (1921), Smend and Triepel sought to integrate old and 'modern' and to make it easier for traditional groups, which were orientated towards a monarchical conception of the state, to accept, or live with, the new democratic conception of the state. The 'anti-positivists' varied both in their style and in their ambitions for synthesis. What they had in common was the topical character of their work. Under the influence of the Baden school of ethical neo-Kantianism and, to some extent, of Theodor Litt's *Lebensphilosophie,* Smend pursued a broad, fluid and dialectical approach that was very different from the formalized *Rechtsstaat* outlook of Schmitt and later of Forsthoff. In Smend's *Integrationslehre* the emphasis was on the constitution as a method of securing a unified and effective formation of the political will. Its individual elements (for example, head of state, basic rights, electoral system, symbols of state) represented factors of integration; their value was determined by whether and how they fulfilled their task of integration. In particular, the Smend school followed Wilhelm Dilthey's demand for 'vitalized learning': for a practical approach that would uncover the historical texture of life as a subjective experience in order to gain greater insight into material problems, while avoiding the disdain for analytical concepts and unqualified faith in intuition of Bergson and Nietzsche. Rejecting the logical objectivism of the Marburg school, the Berlin philosopher Dilthey had emphasized the concept of life, 'the totality of inner experience as it is lived'. Historical understanding involved an analysis of world views as the basic structures of human thought. The elasticity of Smend's central concepts did, however, generate doubts about the suitability of his *Integrationslehre* as the basis for a theory of constitutional law or, indeed, for a fruitful political theory. Smend's post-war disciples, who attended his famous seminar at Göttingen, were prone to forget that during the 1920s his preoccupation with harmony led him to subordinate the *Staatsbürger* (a key concept in Smend's work) to the requirements of integration rather than to sense, like the Swiss jurist Dietrich Schindler (1932), the importance of the critical role and of the personal responsibility of the citizen. Heller's style was even more polemical and his outlook even more topical than those of Smend, for some time his colleague in Berlin. Moreover, he sought to synthesize the new variety of methodologies that had been recognized by Jellinek's earlier reorganization of *Staatslehre* by creating a 'third way', one that, as we have seen, would avoid the extremes of historical and philosophical speculation, on the one hand, and a crude empiricism, on the other. The concept of organization became central to Heller's *Staatslehre* (1963) and suggested his departure from a formal view of the state as an institution that guaranteed 'orderly' relationships towards a functional view of the state as an 'action-centre'. A combination of a comprehensive, but apparently systematic, outlook with the dynamic conception of a *sozialer Rechtsstaat* made Heller's work especially attractive to many German political scientists after 1945. Similarly numerous postwar *Staatsrechtler* drew inspiration from, and displayed an often uncritical respect for, Smend whose critique of positivism was more geared to specifically juristic concerns. His work appeared to be revisable to suit new circumstances in which judicial review and the practical importance of constitutional issues were firmly established and, moreover, to offer an opportunity for a dynamic, politically conscious and material analysis of these issues.

Many of the opponents of legal positivism during the Weimar Republic seemed to have concentrated on a 'realistic' analysis which, it was later argued, had discredited the importance and efficacy of constitutions. If Schmitt had 'debased' the idea of the state, had reduced debate to the posing of questions about effectiveness, Kelsen's brand of legal positivism had reduced the notion of the state by denying to it personality. The Third Reich saw the demise of the idea of the state. As a reaction there was after 1945 a new intensity of preoccupation with the authority of the state. *Staatsrechtslehre* re-emphasized its normative character, its concern to understand institutions and the processes by which norms acquired influence over conduct. Its function was, in Konrad Hesse's (1959) famous formulation, to strengthen the normative power of the constitution. At the same time *Staatsrechtslehre* became less narrowly legalistic and expanded its interests to encompass in particular the issue of the relationship between state and society. The Smend school, which was centred on Göttingen, pioneered a concern for building social change and politicization into the theory of the state. This broader, open perspective became associated with the influential Freiburg school which included Hesse, Ehmke and Peter Häberle (1970). For the Freiburg school, and also for the Bonn jurist Ulrich Scheuner, the focus of interest in their 'republican' constitutional theory was the concept of *das Öffentliche* or *die Öffentlichkeit* and the old idea of *res publica:* they were used to suggest an *Überwindung* (overcoming) of the separation of state and society, and a view of the state as, in Scheuner's words, 'the centre of internal pacification and social foresight'. The unified will of the state was seen as a continuous political problem and Gerber's relegation of it to the status of an assumption rejected. In the context of this competition the new political science began life with a crisis of identity, in part related to the question of whether it should be located in the faculty of law or that of philosophy. Some political scientists, like the Mannheim school, looked to the United States and sought a distinctive empirical method, which was not necessarily much concerned with the idea of the state. However, prominent representatives of political science like Bergstraesser, von der Gablentz, Hennis, Landshut, Maier, Oberndörfer, Sontheimer and Voegelin sought to define the nature of political science by reference to the lessons of the failure of a positivist and formalistic conception of the state in 1933. For them political science was an *Ordnungswissenschaft,* which attempted to identify the ordering principles of the state. They returned to the period from Althusius to Kant, to the comprehensive and universalistic conception of the state that was characteristic of the seventeenth and eighteenth centuries. Politics was an aspect of practical moral philosophy; integrated in a synoptic fashion anthropological, historical, economic and social factors; was committed to a methodological pluralism; and, above all, had a deep interconnection with law because of the identity of the object (the state) being studied.

During the 1960s the interest of political science in the philosophy of the state gave way to a new socio-economic analysis which emphasized that the state was not the key site of politics. Under the influence of American behaviouralism and, especially, of the revival of Marxism a clearer distinction began to emerge between *Staatsrechtslehre* and political science. At the same time the appearance of a new journal, *Der Staat,* in 1962 heralded a rebirth of *Staatslehre* within the law faculties. *Der Staat* was programmatic in conception and claimed to be *eine Stätte der Staatsbesinnigung* (an abode of state-consciousness). The re-emergence of *Staatslehre* coincided with a period of doubt about the viability of liberal democracy occasioned by the rise of both the neo-Nazi National Democratic Party and the mainly university-based and neo-Marxist Extra-Parliamentary Opposition. These challenges to existing institutions drew forth a new appeal to the idea of the state and an expression of fear of the political consequences if a clear idea of the state as the principle of order was lost at the very time when collective arrangements were becoming increasingly complex, influential and more difficult to manage. For example, Forsthoff complained that there were only 'memories of the state'. In their new texts on *Staatslehre* Krüger (1966), who wrote from an authoritarian 'Hegelian' position, and Herzog (1971, p. 181), who adopted a more pragmatic position, could agree on the need to re-emphasize the sovereignty of the state and to encourage the emergence of an independent 'strong' state. For both the danger was not so much the arbitrary, powerful state as the 'total society'. This new *Staatslehre* provoked a methodological debate. Herzog (1971, p. 25) spoke of a group of 'state sciences' (history, social science, economics, law) and tried to give his approach an anthropological basis in the work of Konrad Lorenz. *Staatslehre* was in his view a normative and critical science rather than an empirical and practical one. It dealt with a normative subject, the state, and in the process 'used' empirical research. Despite their eclecticism and concern with new topics like organized groups, media and the economy (that is, the relationship of state and society), both Herzog and Krüger emphasized that the idea of the unity of the state was ultimately provided by the normative ordering of law. Social science was regarded as of assistance to law, which remained the integrating discipline. Their judicial rather than sociological inclinations were apparent in the central categories of analysis like institution, office, sovereignty and implementation, and in their normative conception of politics as an activity that was translated into legal norms and was to be judged according to these norms (which always related back to the notion of the state as the source and generator of the legal order). Other jurists like Ulrich Scheuner criticized this excessively static view of the unity of the state because it underplayed the problems of political power and of its formation and use. Scheuner advocated a more political view of the state as a *process* of integration which aimed to achieve co-operation. In opposition, traditional jurists such as Wilhelm Henke and Helmut Quaritsch (1970) stressed the need to see the state as an authority structure. The state was regarded as public power that was expressed in the legal form of offices and as such could be comprehended by a juristic *Staatslehre* that was committed to a distinctive juristic method. As opposed to the empirical, inductive method, the juristic method ordered empirical material in relation to general concepts and refined these concepts in the light of the changing character of that material. A juristic *Staatslehre* established the relations between persons and objects not in causal or functional terms but in terms of justice. In their view both Jellinek's dualistic approach and the eclecticism of modern *Staatslehre,* which emphasized the ontological, political and juristic aspects of the state, were in danger of failing to offer a clear definition of the state and of 'disintegrating' a unitary entity.

The debate about method and the relationship of law and social science to the idea of the state is reflected in the great difficulties which have beset administrative science (*science administrative* or *Verwaltungslehre*) in France, Germany and Italy since its revival in the early 1960s. Unlike Britain or the United States, none of these countries has doubted that public administration is a distinct subject in its own right. As early as 1603 Johannes Althusius (1948, p. 36) expressed the 'modern' view: 'The administration is the bond which holds the state together. It is the living spirit which guides, orders and directs to the public good the multitudinous functions of the human community.' Lorenz von Stein (1865–8) justified his *Verwaltungslehre* by reference to the central importance of the theory of public administration to the resolution of the emerging 'social problem'. His *Verwaltungslehre* was an ambitious, encyclopaedic attempt to integrate the science of the state (*Staatswissenschaft*) with legal science (*Rechtswissenschaft*). There is then a tradition of analysing public administration as an aspect of the idea of the state and of its changing functions—such as regulation, service provision, and planning. As the subject of public administration was taught academically, often by practitioners, to trainee civil servants or potential entrants (this was not the case in Britain), the method of studying it became an important issue. The problem for administrative science was dissociation from law rather than, as in Britain or the United States, from general administrative theory that incorporated business studies. This problem of dissociation from the *Rechtsstaat* helps to explain the debate about whether public administration was the study of the administrative sciences (*Verwaltungswissenschaften*), which included administrative law, politics, history, sociology and management science, or whether it was necessary to distinguish between administrative law (*Verwaltungsrechtswissenschaft*) and administrative science. By the early twentieth century German and French administrative law had been developed, as a result of Otto Mayer's (1895–6) classic two-volume treatise and the monumental works of Laferrière and of Jèze (1904), into a sophisticated body of knowledge, one that comprised a systematic body of general principles and related them to such specific topics as finance and the police.

The importance of administrative law was underlined by Mayer's definition of the administration as 'the activity of the state in the fulfilment of its
purposes'. Until the 1960s it dominated the earlier *staatswissenschaftliche
Methode* of Mohl (1832) and Stein, both of whom had followed the practical concerns of Cameralism. Continental European administrative science, like administrative law, remained an education *for* and not just *about*
public administration. Moreover, in contrast to Anglo-American administrative theory, which had a behaviouralist emphasis or factual outlook,
it maintained both a strong philosophical dimension, which focused on
the purpose of the state, and an inability to divorce itself from law and
from a recognition that the distinctive organization and procedure of public administration derived from public law.[5] The problem of administrative
science was that the social sciences were felt to be ill-disposed, because of
their internal controversies, to establishing any kind of unity of knowledge
(*Lehre*) and unable, because of the 'behavioural persuasion' of many of
their adherents, to understand what was distinctive and unique about *state*
administration. The interest of jurists in studying the norms of the state
appeared to make their work far more relevant to public administration.
Furthermore, the objective of continental European administrative law—
to determine the sum of public-law norms that regulate the institutions
and activities of the administration and the relationships of individuals
and groups to the administration —appeared nobler than that of its Anglo-
American counterpart.

The problems of relating law and social science in the study of the idea
of the state were considerable, especially in Germany. These methodological disputes were also remarkably self-contained. Outside influence—
like that of the French jurists on Otto Mayer, of German Hegelianism
and Marxism successively on French intellectuals, of American social
science on French and German intellectuals after 1945—was drawn
into a native intellectual culture (in the case of France, into a tradition
of abstract rationalism) and transformed. While France and, to a greater
extent, Germany lost their intellectual self-confidence and self-sufficiency
after 1945 and developed a distaste for historical speculation, the new
enthusiasm for American behaviouralism was applied to their traditional
intellectual concerns and clothed in older intellectual mannerisms. For
example, French and German social scientists continued to be fascinated
by the problem of authority: although they drew more frequently on
American sociological studies of group leadership and of interpersonal
and intergroup relations, they tended to reject the idea of spontaneous

social organisation and consensus. Dahrendorf (1959) began by arguing that the fundamental characteristic of modern society was 'imperatively co-ordinated associations' and the relations of super- and sub-ordination which derived from them; while Crozier (1964) stressed the close relationship between the French pattern of bureaucratic authority, which combined an historically derived absolutism with the universalism of Cartesian rationalism, and the insistence on personal autonomy and freedom from interference. Both these writers, like Raymond Aron and Alain Touraine, wrote against the background of a liberal concern about the inheritance of the idea of the bureaucratic state. With the general reaction against behaviouralism and functionalism, from the 1960s the native intellectual traditions of philosophical politics began to re-emerge more clearly: for example, in the clash between Habermas and Hennis in Germany over the 'legitimation crisis' of the state. It is easy to overlook the extent to which even modern German scholars in the 1950s found answers to their problems within their own intellectual history, notably in the period from Althusius to Kant. Nevertheless, the immediate effect of the ideological exhaustion generated by war and the requirements of reconstruction, and of the altered balance of international power after 1945, was to produce in France and Germany a more confused intellectual picture, a new uncertainty about the appropriateness of historical understanding and occasionally, as in the work of Arnold Gehlen or Werner Weber (1951), a prickly self-defence against outside influence. There was less interest in general theories of the state, a disconnection of theories of the state from philosophy (in Germany owing to the disrepute of theories of the *Kulturstaat,* in France owing to the philosophical vogue of existentialism and later structuralism, only the latter of which had much concern for the idea of the state) and a continuing crisis of identity for social scientists because the intellectual ground that they sought to occupy was already taken up by others.

NOTES

1   Whatever the influence of foreign models, institutions like administrative courts take root also as part of the special circumstances of individual countries. For example, the administrative jurisdiction of Sweden is somewhat different from that of other continental states, in that a separate administrative court did not emerge till 1909.

2   In Denmark the great nineteenth-century jurist and statesman Anders Sandøe
     Ørsted had a much greater influence on all aspects of law. He made a very
     deliberate and eclectic use of foreign law, in particular of German legal ideas
     (and of French ideas in so far as they were channelled through Germany).
     Ørsted's enthusiasm for the German historical school of Savigny, a school
     that preached respect for law as part of a heritage, made him sensitive to the
     need for the application of foreign law to be tempered by a sympathy for the
     national legal order.

3   Legal science in Sweden retained an idealistic and religious character until
     the end of the nineteenth century, attributable partly to the influential phi-
     losopher Christofer Jacob Boström (1797–1866), the so-called 'Plato of
     Sweden', and partly to the influence of German universities where many
     Swedish jurists studied. The radical change in the first half of the twentieth
     century was the product of the Uppsala 'school' of law which attacked ideas
     of natural law and all varieties of legal positivism, idealistic or sociological.
     Axel Hägerström argued that basic legal concepts of Roman law had their
     origin in primitive magic rites and that there was no worldly reality behind
     abstract concepts. His successor at Uppsala, the Social Democratic politi-
     cian and jurist Vilhelm Lunstedt, advocated the criterion of social welfare
     (everything that is good for the common production of wealth and common
     exchange of commodities: in other words, security in economic enterprise) as
     a practical guide in designing institutions and legal rules. At Lund the jurist
     Karl Olivecrona offered a realistic account of the state as the monopoly of or-
     ganized force. Although these positivists (and their counterparts in Denmark,
     Alf Ross, Knud Illum, and in Norway, Torstein Eckhoff and Vilhelm Aubert)
     referred frequently to English analytical jurisprudence and American legal
     realism, their work was embedded in continental European legal arguments.
     They were influenced by the earlier work of the Danish jurist Ørsted and of
     the German jurist Rudolf Jhering, who had rejected the idealism of principles
     in favour of making human needs and interests the basis of legal philosophy.
     The product of this naturalistic jurisprudence was a realistic and pragmatic
     (although not egotistic) approach to law and the state, both of which were
     considered to be instruments or machinery for the satisfaction of wants and
     needs. However the emphasis was very much on needs. Correspondingly,
     jurists became concerned with the 'public-service' state.

4   Similarly the French-language part of Switzerland displayed a greater inter-
     est in social science (e.g. at the universities of Geneva and Lausanne) than
     the German-speaking part. This concern for unmasking the 'reality' of the
     Swiss political process may of course reflect the minority position of the
     French language rather than the 'outside' influence of French literature. The
     legalistic and historical preoccupation with the idea of the state has been
     stronger in the German-speaking part (Schindler, 1975). However, a tradition
     of direct democracy and the practice of the referendum have given a specifi-
     cally Swiss character to *Staatsrechtslehre*: a concern for the qualities of the
     Staatsbürger, a central concept in the work of Max Imboden (1945); and an
     interest in a political analysis of specific material questions of policy, as in
     the work of eminent jurists like Hans Huber (1939), Werner Kägi (1945) and
     Dietrich Schindler (1932).

5   However, until the post-1945 period British administrative studies were characterized more by an ethical concern that reflected the influence of earlier philosophical Idealism. Even then there was little inclination to tie specific topics together by reference to a systematic body of general principles. Such studies were not concerned with the unitary character of the 'public power'.

chapter seven | the word 'state' in the british intellectual tradition

In the last quarter of the nineteenth and the early years of the twentieth century the idea of the state exercised some influence over both the American and the British study of politics. There was, for example, a selective but important reception of German scholarship in American social and political thought: John Dewey began as a Hegelian; Arthur Bentley studied under Wagner and Schmoller; the American Economics Association was modelled on the *Verein für Sozialpolitik* (Aho, 1975). The monumental works of T. D. Woolsey (1878) and Woodrow Wilson (1889) displayed an interest in German *Staatslehre* and reflected their concern as Progressives that the very basis of American government was being undermined by corruption and that, consequently, a return to fundamental principles about the nature of the state and its proper ends was necessary. Such attempts to transplant European 'state legalism' into the American context were, however, to produce the kind of arid formal–legal studies that were to be such an easy target for Bentley and his followers. Their 'realistic' theory of group processes was influenced by German *Realpolitik* literature but, after translation into a native, optimistic, liberal faith in reason and science, was much more attuned to the peculiar nuances of American political culture. In fact, American social science remained very introverted and essentially pragmatic in philosophical outlook and favoured the individual as the basic unit of analysis. Its major concern was with interaction among individuals, who were seen to create society, rather than with institutions as both constraints on and definers of the character of individuals.[1] The survey analysis of Paul Lazarsfeld and the structural/functionalism of Talcott Parsons illustrated the ahistorical and non-institutional interests of this social science (although Parsons's *The Structure of Social Action* was intended to defeat individualism and to make the European sociological tradition available to American readers). Even when the United States imported academic refugees from continental Europe it took on board logical positivism, which was itself a reaction against continental European metaphysics, and the elite theories of Michels, Mosca and Pareto rather than the historical and theoretical traditions of Idealism. In so far as American social science developed a radical outlook, this took the native form of a populist critique of established authority, a critique that both embodied a Lockean view of government as a trust that is to serve the community as beneficiary and drew on a tradition of the open frontier and man against the 'system'.

It was somewhat less easy to banish the term state from theoretical discussion in Britain although, as in the United States, it was difficult to recognize the state as an institution of rule. The emergence of socialism with the rise of the Labour Party produced some philosophical concern about the nature of the state, which appeared deficient to early socialists both as a form of political association and in terms of its functions. There was an interest in the individual's relation to the state and in the justification of state activity. The early British socialists were not, however, divided between anti-*étatiste* Marxists and *étatiste* neo-Hegelians or Jacobins. More important were the influences of Saint-Simon's notion of solidarity and of T. H. Green's passionate concern about social problems and his vision of the universe as a living, evolving organism permeated by subjectivity. Both influences were apparent in Ramsay MacDonald's conception of the state as the organ of the democratically expressed and moral will of the community rather than as an aspect of the class struggle. A rather different and important strand in British socialism was represented in the writings of R. H. Tawney who continued John Ruskin's and William Morris's cultural and moral criticism of industrialism. His humanitarian vision of socialism as fellowship was rooted in a historical analysis very different from that of Marx and in a cultural perspective that attacked the materialism of acquisitive capitalism as opposed to the state itself. The reference point in Tawney's rejection of the class divisions of capitalist society was a backward, nostalgic look at medieval Christian values that emphasized craft, guild and profession, the ideals of service and community and organization with respect to social function. Nevertheless, from the Webbs onwards, and particularly after 1918, socialism was increasingly associated with an instrumental and mechanical view of the state. Moral reformers and revolutionaries were squeezed out by the Fabians' materialism which appeared more

directly relevant to problems of war, mass unemployment and class antagonism. Their ideas were also effectively transmitted through a network
of institutions like the Fabian Society, the *New Statesman* and the London
School of Economics. Whether optimism about historical progress reflected a faith in certain moral imperatives or in a beneficient science, socialism
did not develop a coherent theory of state power. Indeed, in a European
context, the term state was given comparatively little attention. Restraint
from employing the term represented in part a recognition of its prevailing pejorative use, in part its lack of cultural resonance. In the absence of
the idea of the abstract, impersonal state and its embodiment in certain
institutional arrangements, and with the attraction of the elasticity of representative institutions, there developed a parliamentary rather than state
socialism, which was well adapted to the libertarian tradition of the political culture, with its high value on individual freedom and distrust of all
forms of power. Those socialist intellectuals who were European-minded
adopted, with often very different shades of emphasis, the communal and
managerial elements of continental theories without exploring their juristic
background. On the one hand, writers like H. R. G. Greaves used state to
refer to a public communal association, a form of beneficial self-help organization that was concerned to promote a humane and rational distribution of the fruits of industry. On the other, C. A. R. Crosland (1956), whose
view of socialism was also indebted to Tawney, meant by 'statism' little
more than the supremacy of the political world over the economic world
and a benevolent attitude towards governmental intervention that was seen
as directive and managerial.

The search for the use of the term state in British political theory leads
immediately to Thomas Hobbes and to the 'metaphysical' conservatives.
Leviathan (1651) stands out in British political philosophy as the creation
of a system with an imaginative power comparable with that of Hegel.
This work, along with that of Bodin, Machiavelli and later Hegel, did
more to stimulate continental European state theorizing than any other.
One reason was Hobbes's claim to be the first to see the importance of
the body politic as a type of corporation, an artificial 'person' in the law,
which enjoyed both permanence and sovereignty and acted as an authorized representative. The notion of the corporation was taken from Roman
law. In the Preface to the Latin edition Hobbes says: 'This great Leviathan,
which is called the State, is a work of art; it is an artificial man made for
the protection and salvation of the natural man, to whom it is superior in

grandeur and power.' By contrast, as Maitland emphasized, Locke's 'trust conception' of government, which rejected the notion of government as an independent party confronting and contracting with the community, was rooted in the English law of equity. Even Hobbes's theory of contract was formulated in the continental European terms of positive law rather than with reference to the common law. Hobbes attacked the independent prescriptive rights of irresponsible petty authorities and groups like Churches, which he saw as the source of contemporary disorders. Nevertheless, he has often been misunderstood by state theorists like Carl Schmitt who have 'used' him. At the foundation of Hobbes's political philosophy was an individualism quite different from that of Hegel or Schmitt and a concern with the 'representative' rather than anything like Rousseau's 'general will'. Hobbes may have attacked those who claimed too much for liberty; he was equally against those who claimed too much for authority.

The 'metaphysical' conservatism of Burke, Coleridge and Stephen recognized the need for authority and viewed politics as a moral activity. Hence they attached considerable importance to the term state, which formed a central element in their attempt to elaborate an 'independently premeditated' theory of conservatism. While the Tory tradition was distinctive in its positive view of the state, its metaphysics remained peculiarly English. S. T. Coleridge's (1829) conception of the state was primarily concerned with the balance or equilibrium of opposing interests and the need for a stronger cultural role for the 'National Church'. Edmund Burke admitted no real distinction between state and society. He conceived of the state as 'society in its moral guise', as a 'work of art' which expressed the values of a community and included, in particular, the institutions of Court and Church. The rule of reason in public affairs was only guaranteed when the landed aristocracy presided over both state and society: in other words, the state was the instrument of the aristocracy, itself the embodiment of wisdom. The state had a special cultural function of upholding the moral order and the traditions of conduct upon which that order rested. It was not the creator of the moral order. The state performed its cultural function in a regulatory fashion (directed at preserving the sanctity of landed property) rather than by providing services for the general welfare (Harris, 1972). For this reason Burke, though a Whig, is often seen as part of the conservative rather than the Tory tradition (this distinction was made by Disraeli in the 1840s). When Tories reflected on the notion of the state, they saw it as the creation of society and society as always superior to the state. Their use of the term state did not qualify their preoccupation with diversity, with the importance of independent social institutions as a guarantee of a multiplicity of centres of power. Moreover, their metaphysical approach did not succeed in displacing the empirical tradition of 'analytical' conservatism. Although David Hume, Henry Maine and Michael Oakeshott shared the Tory concern for moderation and balance, they viewed conservatism as essentially a unique historical phenomenon that had emerged from, and was to be understood in terms of, a particular context. The sceptical and pragmatic characteristics of this approach, its emphasis on contingency and individualism, produced an 'anti-statism'.[2] To the historical ambivalence about the state within British conservatism was added, from the mid-1880s, the creed of 'self-help' and 'free enterprise' of the manufacturing interest that transferred from the Liberal Party. From this latter perspective the state was seen as an 'alien' machine that was needed only for essential services. The consequence was a considerable intellectual muddle in the Conservative Party about the state and particularly about its relationship to the economy. Its theorists, who have been few and not typically welcomed, have preferred to avoid questions about the nature of the state and to concentrate on the leadership class and its functions—for example, in the manner of Disraeli's 'natural' aristocracy, which was to encompass 'brains', industry and land and to be committed to the 'national idea'.

Before the 1870s Idealism was mainly fashionable among literary figures who rejected eighteenth-century rationalism and empirical philosophy in favour of inward, imaginative consciousness and philosophical first principles. Its adherents, the most influential of whom was Coleridge, were predisposed to reflect on the proper constitution of the state. It was through educationalists like Thomas and Matthew Arnold that the ontological concerns of the 'Germano–Coleridgean doctrine' (John Stuart Mill's phrase) were disseminated in opposition to the utilitarianism and materialist metaphysics of Jeremy Bentham and James Mill. Their conception of the state developed from a religious perspective to which the state was subordinated, from the poetic sensibility of literary intellects and from a many-sided European outlook. While these literary Idealists have been characterized as conservatives, they sought fundamental reforms through which the spirit of the state, one of 'moral partnership', would balance the spirit of commerce. Their particular horror was the ethos of middle-class nonconformity, with its sectarian and narrow outlook. For Coleridge the state was a co-operative partnership or spiritual organism whose coherence and mission was to be provided by the 'National Clerisy': while for Matthew Arnold (1869) its special function of culture would offset the anarchy that was implicit in the 'faith in machinery' and in liberalism by providing educational means (notably state secondary education) to attain human perfection as an 'internal condition'. Matthew Arnold's conception of the state as the organ and repository of the 'collective best-self' represented an English equivalent to continental European views that saw in the strong state the necessary agency for *Geist,* for the spiritual development upon which the health and strength of different societies depended.

During the period from about 1880 to about 1910 philosophical Idealism enjoyed considerable success within technical philosophy (principally at Oxford) and had an influence upon political leaders like Herbert Asquith, R. B. Haldane and Alfred Milner, social reformers like William Beveridge and Arnold Toynbee, and public servants, many of whom were educated in Oxford liberalism. This success was attributable to a number of factors. First, it fitted in with an English evangelical tradition of philanthropic humanitarianism and with the earnestness, zeal and 'moral thoughtfulness' that had already been broadcast widely by Idealist, religiously minded literary figures from Coleridge to the Arnolds (Richter, 1964). The religious and anti-materialistic impulse behind the new interest in Hegel was very apparent in J. H. Stirling's *The Secret of Hegel* (1865) and Edward Caird's influential *Hegel* (1883). Moreover, Scottish scholars, traditionally more European and didactic in outlook, played a notable part in its dissemination. Another factor was the emergence of fundamental doubt about the premises of society and politics from the 1860s. The appeal of Idealism was increased by its provision of a theoretical justification for the kind of collectivist policies that interested reformers who shared T. H. Green's passionate concern for the social problems that had been induced by industrialization. A further factor was the revival of Platonism at Oxford and a rebirth of interest in a somewhat romanticized and idealised Greek *polis.* Hegel was important because he too had looked to the model of the *polis* in order to restore some sense of that wholeness and integrity of the human personality that had been lost with the division of labour of the modern world. A philosophical understanding of the state was felt to be necessary if men were to recapture the full meaning of citizenship and community, to find some non-divisive cultural form as a basis of social integration. In fact, Green was influenced as much by Aristotle and Kant as by Hegel. Green sought to reintroduce the concept of community into liberalism and to divorce it from utilitarianism. For him the state was the essential agent for the achievement of the common good based on the common will. Its purpose was to promote the 'good life' of its citizens and to develop the moral nature of man, which was ultimately shaped by the quality of the community in which he lived. Such ideas infiltrated the Fabian Society and were to influence the new Labour Party, particularly as many of the Liberal intelligentsia crossed over to Labour. The Hegelian character of philosophical Idealism was stronger in the work of Bernard Bosanquet and D. G. Ritchie, who more forcefully made the distinction between the 'real' interests of citizens (which were not in conflict) and their immediately 'felt' private interests (which do tend to be in conflict). Thus Bosanquet (1899) argued that the ideal state should seek to further the 'real' interest of citizens rather than their own perceived interests, and should thereby overcome the 'repellent isolation' of the individual. In addition he conceived of the state as a moral person, one that did not possess a fictional character but was an ideal fact realized in the concrete life of its citizens.[3] On the whole, however, British Idealists tended to neglect the theoretical and substantive problems of history in favour of a fundamentally teleological approach that celebrated moral and often religious virtues.

British Idealism, unlike its counterpart in Germany, was not part of an intellectual culture suffused with its categories. It remained divorced from, and hence did not generate, significant sociological theory (Collini, 1978). The new sociology departed from Idealism primarily over its neo-Hegelian account of the state. Thus L. T. Hobhouse (1918) sought to demolish the ideas of the general will and the 'universal'. The state is only 'one of the ways in which individuals are grouped.... To confuse the state with society and political with moral obligation is the central fallacy of the metaphysical theory of the state' (Hobhouse, 1918, p. 77; Collini, 1976). With the twentieth century the view of the state contained within philosophical Idealism came under a formidable assault (Lindsay, 1914), so that Ernest Barker (1915) could write: 'the State has generally been discredited in England'. One reason for the demise of Idealism lay in growing doubts that a political theory that was dedicated to free and rational discussion of 'enlightened' minds and rejected the language of party, majority or class could deal with the intense sectional conflict that plagued Edwardian England and spelt the end of its self-assurance, respect for proper procedure and willingness to compromise on the basis of reasonable discussion. The violent and emotional outbursts associated with the power of the new trade unions, women's suffrage, reform of the Lords and the issue of Ulster led young scholars like Harold Laski (1919) to seek a new world view, one that involved him in a preoccupation with a 'realistic', demystifying theory of the state in the context of the general problem of authority in modern society. Another factor was the growing disrepute of German ideas during and after the Great War. Some theorists like Laski turned to France, notably to the sociological jurisprudence of Duguit: others, like F. W. Maitland earlier, took an interest in those German theorists such as Gierke who appeared as critics of the German tradition of the state. In fact, unlike the Pluralists, Gierke (1915) spoke of the sovereign will of the state and of the state as the highest *Machtverband.*

Out of these changes emerged English Pluralism. Pluralism had a curious relationship to Idealism (Nicholls, 1975). The Pluralists frequently used Idealist arguments in their attack on the individualism of Herbert Spencer and the utilitarianism of Bentham. Some of the Pluralists, like Barker and Lindsay, were later to move closer to the Idealist position. Even the most vociferous opponents of the Idealist conception of the state like Laski (and, outside Pluralism, like Hobhouse) were indebted to Idealism for their 'social liberalism' and for T. H. Green's concept of freedom as 'a positive power of doing or enjoying something worth doing or enjoying, and that, too, something that we do or enjoy in common with others'. Agreement between the Pluralists centred on a recognition of the importance of groups and the importance of limiting the claims of the state. Maitland pointed to France, where 'we may see the pulverising, macadamizing tendency in all its glory, working from century to century, reducing to impotence, and then to nullity, all that intervenes between Man and the State' (quoted in Nicholls, 1975). The enemy was the continental European 'concession' theory of corporations which represented institutions as creatures of sovereign legal enactment. Influenced by Gierke's doctrine of the inherent rights of groups, Maitland argued that institutions ought to be acknowledged as legal persons, which existed independently of state recognition and were logically prior to, rather than created by, the state. Liberty could only be guaranteed by a dispersal of power in society, by confining the state to a regulative role of maintaining a framework of order in which people as individuals and groups could follow self-chosen paths. Groups would act as agencies of 'social co-ordination' through horizontal relations of adjustment and exchange. This view of groups was premised on an economic model of relationships rather than on a political model that would have emphasized vertical relationships based on the imperative authority of the state. Laski spoke of a pluralistic state which consisted of 'a series of co-ordinate groups the purposes of which may be antithetic' and which was replacing the hierarchical structure and 'mystic monism' of the sovereign state. By liberating the diversity of society from the state and demystifying the state the Pluralists hoped to remove the state from contestation. The process of demystification of the 'coercive' authority of the state was assisted by their reading of Duguit's demolition of the sovereign state in France in favour of a 'federalized' society. In this functionally decentralized society the dependence of the state on other associations was recognized, while the law was seen to emerge from the interplay of social institutions rather than to be simply an imperative expression of public authority. Philosophical Idealism was attacked for its view of the state as 'a kind of divine institution' which possessed moral sovereignty against which there could be no rights.

Despite these agreements, there was no generally agreed theory of the state among the Pluralists (Nicholls, 1975). J. N. Figgis, an Anglican priest, put forward a more monistic view of the state as a *communitas communitatum* akin to the medieval empire. G. D. H. Cole, who provided a link with the Guild Socialists, envisaged society as a complex of self-governing functional associations that were to be co-ordinated by a 'federal body' rather than the state.[4] Laski revealed the inconsistent views that a single theorist could hold about the state; in his writings systematic speculation and reliable commentary on continental European debates about the state gave way to political commentary on changing events (Deane, 1955). Unlike Figgis or Lindsay he began by viewing the state as just one among many groups in society, a group that differed only in that its basis was 'territorial' rather than 'functional'. During his Pluralist period (approximately 1914–24) Laski could also write of the state as 'a great public-service corporation' (the influence of Duguit) and even as essential for the 'highest life of its members' (the influence of Green). By 1925 he recognized that the state differed in kind and not merely in degree from other associations. The state was 'the keystone of the social arch' and 'the final co-ordinating factor in the community'. It protected men as 'undifferentiated persons' and 'centres of universal decision' and was pre-eminent over other groups which represented men as producers. This new view of the state reflected the influence of Fabianism and the new hopes aroused by the Labour Party as a party of government in 1924. Similarly, the collapse of the second Labour government in 1931 led Laski (1935) at last to accept the sovereignty and coercive character of the state and to see it as the instrument of capitalism, the state's activities maintaining a particular system of class relations. The common thread in Laski's work, and what distinguished him from later writers, was that he continued to think in broad terms about the state and to look at the problem of authority in the context of economic and political change.

There was more in common between the English Pluralists and Idealists than is commonly recognized. First, Idealists were more willing to admit pluralism than many Pluralists recognized. The problem of the French system of government was, for Hegel as well as for Maitland and Laski, in large part the result of the weakness of the right of association. While the state was in Hegel's view the precondition of the realization of a universal normative order, personal autonomy (particularly in economic activity) remained a fundamental value. Indeed, he criticized Prussia for concentrating too much power at the centre. Similarly, for Green the state was only one aspect of the work of moral liberation; it was the 'community of communities', an adjustment centre for individual and group claims. Among Pluralists Figgis and Lindsay adhered to a monistic view of the state, while Laski moved closer towards this view over time. Second, when viewed from a wider European context, neither set of English theorists was aggressive or militant. Theorists like Green, Cole, Hobhouse and the Webbs were not the centre of polemics like Durkheim or Weber. A revival of interest in theories of the state did not generate revolutionary or counter-revolutionary theories and tightly organized bands of theorists. There was no perceived need to offer elaborate theoretical justifications, in terms of an open-ended system of ideas, for the solution to contemporary problems associated with the political and social structure. The impression was one of a loose eclecticism, of *bricolage*. British theorists came from a receptive elite that was, for historical reasons outlined earlier, accessible to ideas of reforms. Consequently, there was a remarkable continuity of assumptions among intellectuals, a relative indifference to theoretical disputes elsewhere and a tolerance for theoretical and ethical muddle. The basic differences resided in the Pluralists' rejection both of the sovereignty of the state and of the notion that its authority was absolutely binding because it embodied the general will—and therefore the 'real' will—of all citizens, with which their 'true' interests could not conflict. However, as Barker (1915) recognized, by creating a new individualism ('our individuals are becoming groups') Pluralism had savaged the

196 | the state tradition in western europe

case for focusing on the term state. The major new challenge to its relevance was a flowering of independent-minded groups which could shelter and prosper under the English legal device of the trust. Thus they avoided the continental European and Romanist idea that their legal existence derived from a concession by the state and that consequently their juristic personality was a fiction. This group power in part superceded, and in part drew sustenance from, an older English nonconformist spirit of 'soul-liberty' and a political economy of economic individualism.

STATE AND POLITICAL SCIENCE: AFTER IDEALISM AND PLURALISM

Philosophical theories of the liberal democratic state continued to be produced by such writers as Barker (1942), Lindsay (1943) and MacIver (1926) as a reaction to the 'ethical state', to twentieth-century disillusion with the German 'connection' and to the challenges posed by group power. However, these theories suffered from a rapid questioning of their assumptions about the active, well informed, rational and participative citizen from empirical theories of the political process. In political science there was a general retreat from concern with normative questions about the nature and purposes of the state, a retreat that was facilitated in Britain and the United States by the state's absence as a formal legal institution that could not escape recognition. The term state was rarely used within empirical political science. For example, in studies of power political scientists preferred to refer to elites rather than to the state and to consider whether there was a 'power elite' or competitive elites. American and British Marxists who were concerned to identify a 'ruling class' spoke more consistently of the state. They reflected the continental European origins of Marxism. In their view the state was a repressive or 'inhuman' collectivity that was vaguely defined. Miliband's (1969) 'state system' referred to all public institutions except parties and organized groups; for Gamble (1974) the state expressed 'the particular priorities of the prevailing politics of power' and covered 'the general social, economic and political arrangements that are found in a community'. When British or American political scientists looked at the same problems as their continental European colleagues they tended to do so differently. There was no strong native tradition of cultural criticism, of concern with the problem of legitimacy and the nature of authority, or of theorizing on the character of institutions. From the dominant philosophical tradition and a widely shared social liberalism which sought an enlightened social policy emerged a British preoccupation with inequality rather than authority and a predisposition towards 'common-sense' empirical inquiry that took institutions for granted and was content either to describe their mechanics and working or to explore the experience of groups and individuals with them. British political science had a firmer grounding in history and philosophy than its American counterpart (reflecting the training of its earliest practitioners): the former meant a preoccupation with stylistic brilliance (history as art form) and with documentary evidence that emphasized the contingent complexity and contradictions of life, and the discrimination of detail, and made theory appear hazardous, tentative, even impossible; the latter involved an analytical precision in the definition of terms, which led T. D. Weldon (1953), for example, to see questions about the state as unprofitable or misleading, as well as skills in logical combat and a critical concern with criteria of explanation, models and standards of evidence. The result was a scepticism about general explanation and a distrust of metaphysics, a preference for handling specific, detailed concepts (sometimes for 'concept-knocking') and, above all, a concern to safeguard a gentlemanly style that allowed a plurality of approaches while preventing the formation of rigid schools of thought. American 'modern' political science was put to the test of utility by the British, with survey analysis doing somewhat better than functionalism and general systems theory, both of which were attacked for loose concepts and superficial propositions. However, in the absence of continental European Roman law and a written constitution, there was no competition from, or need to take account of, public-law texts preoccupied with the nature of the state, its personality and its functions. British political science continued to direct its attention to usage and the informal aspects of politics. Constitutional theorists viewed state as an inherently puzzling and unclear concept for defining the terms on which political authority ought to be exercised. In their view confusion resulted from running together separate questions about the international personality of the state, the source of law in the community, the nature of the executive power and the authority of the majority. Marshall (1971) argued that reference to the sovereign state could lead to confusion about the precise locus of sovereignty and a failure to dissect the state into its sovereign (legislative) and non-sovereign (executive government) aspects. Theorists of the state would, of course, stress the importance of seeing the connections between related questions, point to their own tradition of preoccupation with dissection of the state into its constituent elements and argue the importance of establishing some unity among the diverse institutions that comprise the 'public power'.

When in the 1960s frustration with the gradualism of social liberalism emerged on the left, there was for the first time since the 1880s a significant importation of concepts from continental European scholarship: Gramsci's hegemony, Althusser's structuralism and Habermas's critical theory. A new concern for the state, in the context particularly of its hegemony, affected sociology more than political science. Indeed, the continental European intellectual background of sociology in Marx and Weber—and, Nisbet (1967) would argue, in the 'conservative' reaction of de Bonald and de Maistre to the social, political and ideological consequences of industrialization—influenced the language in which that subject has been conducted. The lack of much interest in state in political science was associated with the modest role of theories of bureaucracy and Marxism. It was at times of doubt about the premises of society and politics that there was an interest in identifying the nature of the British state. Intellectually it was impossible for social scientists not to address themselves to some conception of the state, whether a realistic account of the state apparatus or a philosophical conception of the fundamental principles of the state. At such times of doubt Marxists and anarchists sought to 'unmask' the state, while liberals or 'reactionaries' engaged in a new rationalist preoccupation with establishing a consistency of basic principles. Libertarians from Spencer (1884) to Nozick (1975) on the 'nightwatchman' or 'limited' state have used the term state in the context of their fears about the individual's liberty. Nevertheless, in its wider failure to integrate political philosophy into the general body of philosophy Anglo-American liberalism revealed its utilitarianism rather than the influence of Kant or Hegel. It was in danger of adopting an impoverished view of human nature, an essentially atomistic conception of man as voter in an electoral system or consumer in a market system, and of overlooking the need to expand imagination and establish a sense of civic duty through a theory of political education and culture. While the Americans Rawls (1972) and Nozick felt the need to protect liberalism from attack by the left, their notions of justice and rights were distinct from the idea that the state should define the nature of the good life. Nozick emphasized 'free exchange' and 'free consent', with the state protecting only property and persons; while Rawls relied heavily on technical arguments drawn from economics in elaborating his two principles of justice, the libertarian and the egalitarian. Rawls did not develop the theory of the state that underlay his method of arriving at these principles. What emerged was a strongly economic model of political man as a possessive and 'maximizing' individualist and of society as a series of market relations.

STATE AND PHILOSOPHY

In order to understand why the British approach to politics has concerned itself less with the requirements of a coherent pattern of authority and more with specific issues and discrete institutions and the detailed analysis of functions and powers, it is necessary to look beyond the absence of Roman law to the ethnocentric character of the philosophical tradition. Specific cultures or national communities appear to produce different ways of writing philosophy. These differences are related in some part to the degree to which a language lends itself to the kind of abstraction which, for example, *Staatslehre* reveals and in large part to historical experience and the extent to which this experience exhibits a more or less stable identity over centuries and the threat of foreign domination. The British neo-Hegelians came under attack primarily from Cambridge—in the name of 'common sense' and literal language (Henry Sidgwick and G. E. Moore), science (Bertrand Russell) and 'ordinary' language (Ludwig Wittgenstein). Oxford itself was dominated successively by the Realism of John Cook Wilson, which had a passive conception of knowledge according to which the philosopher observed objects whose existence was independent of the mind; the logical positivism of A. J. Ayer, which dismissed metaphysics for science; and the 'use' of language of J. L. Austin. For Austin as for Wittgenstein philosophy was essentially an activity of liberation from false and oversimplifying theories. This twentieth-century preoccupation with logical analysis, natural science and language was valuable in stimulating self-criticism and in lending clarity of ideas and rigour of method to Anglo-American philosophy. It was also very much in the tradition of the material mode of British empiricism and of Bentham's 'method of detail', which consisted in breaking every question into pieces before attempting to solve it and resolving abstractions into their constituent parts. The result was a radical, demystifying nominalism that had little use for the idea of the state, which tended to be regarded by logical positivists as a 'meaningless' concept and by analytical philosophers as a source of confusing questions. It was precisely because particular abstract concepts like state were torn from their wider context of ontological argument and because their 'reality' was denied that they lost their meaning. In fact, this analytical tradition was not directly interested in ontology; whatever ontological interests it had (and often its exponents professed to be 'ontology-free') emerged from its concentration on the problem of knowledge and theory of perception rather than from a concern with commitment, culture, community and change, with giving men a sense of the unity, interconnectedness and meaningfulness of the world. The Anglo-American rejection of Hegelian Idealism was very different from its earlier repudiation on the Continent by figures like Kierkegaard and Nietzsche, who had concentrated on its ethical, historical and political aspects. This new attack concentrated on the technical aspects of the Hegelian system which, interestingly, had also preoccupied British neo-Hegelians like Bradley, with his timeless, immobile (and hence non-Hegelian) Absolute. Indeed, British philosophers tended to discuss the difference between Idealism and Realism in terms of perception: Realists regarded material objects as existing independently of perception; Idealists argued that they existed only as objects of perception. In the process they misunderstood continental European Idealism, for which to be 'real' was to be a member of a 'rational system', the nature of whose parts was only intelligible in so far as the system as a whole was understood, a system that was both ideal and spiritual. One reason for this misunderstanding was that British Idealists themselves were interested more in the epistemological than in the ontological aspects of Idealism.

A metaphysical interest in the concept of the state in continental Europe was part of the attempt to formulate a coherent world view that would be adequate to the conduct of life and in which the whole person would be adjusted to his complex environment. The test of such theories of the state was coherence and elegance in the elucidation and defence of interconnected principles as well as correspondence to facts. This coherence, elegance and correspondence would in turn furnish a basis for meaningful commitment. As a higher-order, generalizing concept, state was suited to a wholeness and comprehensiveness of philosophical vision and to a philosophical conception and practice of politics. By contrast, the Anglo-American philosophical tradition appeared to do little to enrich intellectual and cultural life. Its technical skills produced a certain scholasticism and a concern for problems that appeared to be of limited social and political relevance. On the one hand, it avoided the monistic political 'theology' and hostility to open politicking of the continental European state tradition at its worst. On the other, it failed to provide that fusion of sense of mission with dedication to public service which was the state tradition at its best. The combination of an analytical, conceptual approach with a history-of-ideas perspective, both of which were so typical of British political philosophy, encouraged reflection on, even revelry in, the plurality of values and of perceptions of reality. They led to rejection of 'the optimistic view...that all good things must be compatible' (Berlin, 1978). Political philosophers devoted considerable attention to particular concepts like democracy, equality, liberty and social justice but not to an overarching concept of rule like state with reference to which these might be related. Nevertheless, whatever its intellectual failures (and, as this chapter has shown, it was not a self-contained, insular tradition), the Anglo-American philosophical outlook had a moral basis in a view of freedom as civility, as a practice of mutual respect and tolerance for diversity and individuality. It was a view that found a vivid expression in the work of a European-minded English scholar like Michael Oakeshott (1975). Compared to continental Europe, political ideas and practice in Britain exhibited a greater faith in the creative nature, vitality and resilience of a variegated civil society and in civic humanism, rooted in a practice of civility, as the source of standards in public life.

NOTES

1   Alexis de Tocqueville's famous *Democracy in America* (1873) is a charac-teristically continental European reaction to the American democratic soci-ety and its central values of equality and individualism: the basic problem is how to create a sense of public concern in a society that fosters private rather than civic virtues.

2   Michael Oakeshott seems to fall into this category of conservatism. Nevertheless, he is difficult to categorize, for his acquaintance with German Idealism and European-wide outlook (like that of his predecessor at the London School of Economics, Harold Laski) led him to a continuing con-cern with the character of the state as a political association (Oakeshott, 1975).

3   Bosanquet (1899) begins by defining the state as an aspect of organized social life, its outward organization (p. 7). More generally, the state is seen

as including and absorbing all other institutions. It is identified with the whole of society, as 'the fly-wheel of life' (p. 152) and 'the operative criticism of all institutions' (p. 150).

> The State, as thus conceived, is not merely the political fabric....But it includes the entire hierarchy of institutions by which life is determined, from the family to the trade, and from the trade to the Church and the University (p. 150).

4   The Guild Socialist method of dispersing public power attracted the philosopher Bertrand Russell who described the state in 1916 as representing a principle antagonistic to creativeness and individuality (Barker, 1978, p. 100). He followed Hilaire Belloc's popular *The Servile State* (1912) in arguing that socialism was in danger of creating servitude. Welfare reforms would increase the dependence of the worker in place of bringing about the sort of fundamental change in the distribution of property that was the precondition of his independence and self-sufficiency.

part iii
state as an ideal type and as a
'problem-defining' concept

chapter eight | state as a tool of analysis

If one wishes to study the birth of a conception of the world which has never been systematically expounded by its founder...search for the Leitmotiv, *for the rhythm of thought as it develops should be more important than that for single casual affirmations and isolated aphorisms.*

Antonio Gramsci (Hoare and Nowell Smith, 1971, pp. 382–3)

The idea of the state has acquired a complex of meanings in the context of diverse historical experiences and frameworks of ideas. It may be tempting to rest content with outlining the concept's various usages or to agree with the German Romantic Adam Müller (1922) that the state defies definition because it is entirely beyond the grasp of finite minds, that indefinability is the hallmark of the idea of the state. State is a 'problem-defining' concept in the sense that it involves a normative preoccupation with the proper mode of exercising public authority. It is neither simply an empirically identifiable object that can be comprehended in terms of particular buildings or people nor just a pattern of power relations that can be detected and described. As a normative ordering, its motivating force is that of ideas, its peculiarity the compulsion that underlies this ordering. The notion of the state offers a mental picture of the political world in terms of which individuals and groups can communicate with one another: it affects entire intellectual processes—what questions are raised and what answers presented. Hence it is not the kind of concept that appeals to those empirical theorists who stress the importance of 'operationalizing' concepts in the sense of discovering their empirical correlatives.

The use of a concept like state in different historical, intellectual and cultural traditions might suggest that it eludes definition. However, the search for greater precision, for systematic refinement of concepts, is necessary if the use of language is to avoid association with political rhetoric and if we are to sharpen our perception of phenomena. Concepts need to be made rigorous in order to be relevant to both political philosophy and comparative analysis. The danger with formal definitions is that in the pursuit of 'correctness' they can imply that it is possible to give a 'trouble-free' description of a phenomenon; in other words, that the phenomenon in question has definite boundaries. Definitions are important, not least in order that the marginal is not confused with the central, but they need to be sufficiently loose or 'open-textured' to incorporate some complexity, ambiguity and change and to be filled out in different ways.

Underlying the variety of theorizing on the state it is possible to identify a catalogue of common features which amount to a concept of the state and which, moreover, derive their coherence from a rationalist conception of the technical requirements of an 'ordered' society. *Besides referring to an entity or actor in the arena of international politics, state is a highly generalizing, integrating and legitimating concept that identifies the leading values of the political community with reference to which authority is to be exercised; emphasizes the distinctive character and unity of the 'public power' compared with civil society; focuses on the need for depersonalization of the exercise of that power; finds its embodiment in one or more institutions and one or more public purposes which thereby acquire a special ethos and prestige and an association with the public interest or general welfare; and produces a socio-cultural awareness of (and sometimes dissociation from) the unique and superior nature of the state itself.* The definition incorporates the three aspects of the state: its functions as a legal conception which attributes a distinct personality to a particular institution or complex of institutions; as a political conception which establishes the unique character of, and the guiding principles for, the exercise of public power; and as a sociological conception which refers both to an institution endowed with a remarkable coercive power and to a special type of communal bond capable of generating sentiments of affect and disaffection.

So formal a construction seeks to avoid offering detailed moral advice about, for example, how to arrive at a substantive theory of the state, which would have reference to such values as liberty, justice and democracy; about how to adjudicate between competing theories of the state (although it does suggest that in some political theories, like Fascism, the state may be less important than other concepts); or about whether or not one should be disaffected from a particular state. Nevertheless, the definition is not value-free. Its emphasis on depersonalization and on the distinction between state and society indicates liberal as well as rationalist foundations, which would suggest the inadequacies of, for example, aesthetic theories like that of Adam Müller, of Gentile's 'totalitarian' state or of Carl Schmitt's *Führerstaat*. The difficulty with their attempts to define the concept of the state lies in an unwillingness to delimit it. If the definition that is offered here does not have an ecumenical appeal, it identifies ideas and disputes that cannot be ignored. The definition embodies a set of logically related ideas that can be said to represent a political theory in its own right. It stresses in particular the vital connections between legal authority, political power and community, and the importance of making these connections in political theory. At the same time the definition serves a heuristic purpose as an ideal-type construction that can help to identify important qualitative similarities and dissimilarities between forms of conduct in different political systems by making intelligible the subjective meaning of conduct—that is, of political life 'as it is lived'. This perspective does not discount the importance of objective phenomena in favour of idealism in understanding conduct or even require abandonment of the view that ultimately all ideas are sociologically anchored. It recognizes that ideas about reality, purpose and method associated with the state provide a framework within which individuals consider their responses to political events and set parameters to what is perceived as politically desirable or possible. The idea of the state has been associated with a distinct set of attitudes towards authority, power and community. Caution is, of course, required in tracing the political and administrative implications of such an idea. State is *one* idea motivating conduct and, moreover, conduct is shaped by external forces of social structure, economic circumstances and political events as well as by 'internalized' ideas and institutional constraints.

While the state may be basically an institution of enforced cooperation, which involves an irreducible residue of constraint, as a political concept it is viewed as much more. The idea of the state provides a basis for social order by identifying the need for the 'public power' that furnishes an ultimate decision-maker whose decisions are final and binding and/or undertakes a special mission on behalf of society. By establishing the notion of the unique character of public authority in terms of sovereignty and/or function it prevents attempts to understand that authority and the nature of political obligation with reference to the behaviour and standards that obtain in civil society. The idea of the state encourages also a sense of community by identifying a common set of principles and a clear statement of the nature of public functions as the basis for collective action. In other words, it represents a form of collective life in which power is institutionalized and legitimated rather than being reliant on brute force. Legitimation is provided in part by the importance of procedure (wholly, in the view of some) and in part by a sense of purpose, a dedication to preserving certain substantive principles. Clearly, then, the notion of the state is important as a unifying formula capable of integrating a number of concepts (sovereignty, force, power, law, government, public interest, etc.). A characteristic of many theories of the state is that they focus on one of these related concepts and confuse the state with that concept. What unifies the state as a set of ideas is its emphasis on the importance of authority and relations of authority, whatever the form of government, as the basis of community. Democracy is one form of the state and one which, from the perspective of the notion of the state, ought not to cancel out the effectiveness of the public power by suppressing the idea of the state. Representation does not create the public power or the idea of law but takes its place alongside them (Burdeau, 1949–57, vol. 6, p. 211; Herzog, 1971, p. 204). Indeed, German theorists (for example, Kruger, 1966; Schmitt, 1928) have given the concept of representation a wider meaning than is conventional in English-language usage. Representation becomes a central element of the larger idea of the state and finds its expression in an institution or set of offices that stand apart in order to represent and give presence to the whole and to act on its behalf. The idea of the state is dedicated to the value of reason, placed at the service of a set of public norms that are to be guaranteed against violation by individuals who are attempting to satisfy egoistic wants. Its grandeur as an institution lies in its authority, but equally power (though not a good in itself) is a necessary basis of its action.

STATE AS A GENERALIZING, INTEGRATING AND LEGITIMATING CONCEPT

When the state is characterized as the most integrated form of political society, an emphasis is being placed on its association with the ideas of collectivity and the general good, on its combination of a socio-cultural with a legal dimension. As a summating concept state stresses the interdependency and integration of institutions as opposed to the structural differentiation typical of 'civil' society and so beloved of modern Anglo-American political science. Consequently, it is to be distinguished from the more limited concepts of government and Crown. Government can be used in a restricted sense to refer to the men in executive authority at a particular time, and in a broader sense to denote 'continuing legal organs and machinery' (the nearest it comes to the concept of the state) or the need for some form of rule. In all these senses government is necessary; a state tradition is not. State is a concept of a universalistic nature that endows the 'public power' with a unique 'mission' (whether *Ordnungspolitik* or *soziale Gestaltung*—that is, whether providing a framework of 'order' or 'shaping' society) and links government into a wider institutional context as part of one collectivity.

The English-language concept of government is, in fact, broader in its meaning than its French and German equivalents, *gouvernement* and *Regierung*, which are subordinated to, and understood in the context of, the idea of the state. Without the notion of the state it has to serve more functions. In the seventeenth century the idea emerged that government was exercised by monarch and Parliament, subject to the trust of civil society; government combined the notions of leadership and responsiveness. By the nineteenth century government became, unlike that in France or Germany, a strongly instrumental concept related to a narrow idea of representation (witness J. S. Mill's concern with 'representative government'), which focused on the manner of selection of elected representatives, and to civil society of which it was increasingly seen as a function. In an organizational sense it came to be identified with particular persons (ministers). By contrast, the French concept of *gouvernement* did not develop into a key concept of political thought. After 1789 it was limited to the executive and used to express the idea that the unity of the state required a gradation as well as a separation of powers in order to ensure a primacy of the executive if paralysis were to be avoided. This view was reflected in the Fifth Republic's notion of *gouvernement présidentiel;* the powers of the President were to some extent independent of the Assembly. Originally the German concept of *Regierung* was associated with the person of the ruler; *Regierungslehre* identified itself with an anti-democratic, monarchical principle. As theorists of *Staatsrecht* from Gerber (1865) to Jellinek (1900) broke down the patrimonial principle and were influenced by French usage, *Regierung* began to be seen as an organ of the state, an aspect of the executive power providing leadership and control, as distinct from *Verwaltung* (administration). This traditional idea of *Regierung* as an autonomous area of 'political' or of extra-statutory action, distinct from the other functions of the state, was continued in *Staatslehre,* but the Basic Law and the Federal Constitutional Court spoke of it in a narrow, organizational sense rather than in terms of any special comprehensive function.

If, as Maitland (1901) suggested, the idea of the Crown was used in Britain as a substitute for the theory of the state to denote the fount of executive authority, it has remained both narrower in scope and theoretically underdeveloped. Rooted in the concept of kingship, of personal authority (and immunity from the courts), the Crown has proved difficult to develop as a legal and political concept that refers to a corporate entity in which powers of a particular kind are invested; this is partly because it has mixed public and private interests in a confusing manner, and partly for the historical reason that its implications were feared by powerful local and parliamentary interests that had benefited from the seventeenth-century settlement. The idea of the Cabinet as the monarchy in commission, of Ministers of the Crown (exercising royal prerogatives) being advised by servants of the Crown (the civil service), undoubtedly confers a certain mystique, cohesion, continuity and independence on central government, even a certain normative role on the administrator in the 'Whitehall' view of the constitution (Birch, 1968). However, its other consequences are secretive government, in which confidentiality acquires a supreme value and is used to justify and reinforce the secrecy that is a product of hierarchical organisation *per se;* prerogative powers, exercised by ministers outside the control of the courts; a private, often obscure Whitehall language that rapidly demoralizes the outsider; a concentration of formal responsibility at the top, expressed in the conventions of ministerial responsibility; the anonymity of the administrator and his collectivist ethic, his preference for government by committee rather than personal responsibility; and a narrow conception of administrative responsibility focusing all attention on the minister rather than on an obligation to the community that is being served. Internal values and norms within the administration have crystallized out of a concept of private personal service, of a passive advisory role, of solidarity within a closed community, rather than out of a philosophy of its functions within a larger collectivity. It has proved impossible to develop a notion of the inherent responsibilities of the official as the embodiment of the state; to emphasize the personal responsibility of the official in law; or to locate personal responsibility, in the managerial sense of accountability for results, in an orderly manner within the administration. The concept of the Crown has not generated any theory about the relationships among institutions in an extensive sense or about the relations between government and the individual. It has also proved a source of confusion about, for example, the identification of Crown services and those organizations that share in the sovereign immunity of the Crown's servants.

The narrowness of the concept of the Crown is apparent when contrasted with the French conception of the unitary state or the German conception of the *Bundesstaat* (federal state). French local authorities and public enterprises are seen as agents of the administrative decentralization of public services, as branches of the state in a relationship of hierarchical subordination to central government. If centralization is France's expression of the notion of the unitary state, the conception of the 'unitary' *Bundesstaatis* seen as a different method of achieving institutional integration through the co-ordination of autonomous units on the basis of *bundesfreundliches Verhalten* or loyal conduct to the federation (Hesse, 1962a). Unlike the separated jurisdictions of American federalism, the conception of the *Bundesstaat* supports an interlocking of politics, a diffusion of responsibilities, with direct participation of state (*Land*) governments within the federal legislative process through the powerful *Bundesrat* and execution of most federal laws by the state administrations. West Germany's federal system is based on a tradition of ideas of *Gouvernmentalismus* (the executive outlook) and *Sachlichkeit* (expertise), on an intricate network of horizontal and vertical co-ordination of autonomous units, which network gives privileged contacts to executives and is deeply influenced by bureaucratic mores and strategies of co-operation. In Britain the emphasis is on ideas that support institutional autonomy: the divorce between the provision of central services at the local level and local self-government (with no executive at the local level like the French prefect who fuses the administration of local and central policies); the autonomy of the law; the absence of a strong training function within higher education to produce 'state-created' elites (on France, see Suleiman, 1979); the reliance on a vast network of independent advisory and consultative bodies to initiate proposals for change as opposed to an attempt to draw them more firmly into the administrative orbit (cf. British Royal Commissions and Swedish committees of inquiry; the French modernization commissions and Britain's National Economic Development Council (NEDC) machinery); and the autonomy of the administration in its own internal self-management, especially in respect of personnel policy. The Crown, local authorities, public corporations and the growing comet's tail of *ad hoc* bodies represent distinct entities within an 'unstructured' pluralism of government. The subsequent fragmentation reflects one view of how liberty is best safeguarded. Activities of public agencies are considered in relation to discrete statutes rather than, as the French Council of State would stress, in relation to an idea of the inherent functions of the state and to a body of public law relating to the state and its organs. The emphasis has been on 'arms'-length' relationships, on the problem of ensuring the independence of local authorities and public corporations, instead of on the problem of the weakness of the centre. In the absence of an integrating concept, of a body of principles in terms of which particular institutions are interrelated and of the idea of institutions as organs of the state, there has been a piecemeal approach to institutional reform and an indifference or hostility to questions about how coherently authority is exercised. Little attention has been paid to how particular reforms (Parliament, the civil service, devolution, local government, administrative regionalism) relate to one another as aspects of a coherent whole, and there is little interest in tying proposals together in terms of an overall theory of the state, its authority and functions. For example, the public corporation is established in such a way that ministerial intervention generates friction. There is no notion of its property as state property (it is the proprietor of its own assets), of its employees as part of an integrated public service or of its policies as aspects of state policy. They are seen as independent bodies with their own problems, not as part of a single system; the powers of the minister are delimited (like those of a super-trustee) and his controls are exercised 'externally'.

State is also a legitimating concept. Its component institutions and individuals are seen as elements in a wider collectivity, a political community whose coherence and unity is established by the explicit identification, articulation and ordering of certain principles or norms; in other words, a constitution is essential as the expression of the idea of the coherence of the state. Continental European constitutions have had a systematic and rational character, compared with those of much of the English-speaking world which have been premised on a scepticism about the search for coherence.[1] Within the continental tradition there have, nevertheless, been certain differences of view about the nature of constitutions. In the dominant French view (represented by

Hauriou) the constitution did not give birth to the idea of the state as a legal phenomenon. The constitution expressed the dominant idea of law (or synthesized competing ideas, for example about the value of the individual), organized the idea of the unity of the state, and defined its organs, their functions and their relationships to one another in order to ensure the expression and realisation of a collective will. There was, however, nothing exceptional about the origins of the state. As idea and institution the state emerged gradually. Its legal existence was the product of an elitist process of foundation of a social 'organism' and of attachment of others. The constitution made explicit what existed already. Furthermore, the state was not regarded as the source of all law. From Gény to Hauriou French jurists were critical of the belief that strictly legal methods of controlling the state could be satisfactory. For example, Gény (1927–30) saw the state itself as an ambivalent phenomenon expressing both the idealism of justice and the competition of material forces. This essentially 'realistic' and limited view of consitutions contrasted with a more idealistic German attitude in which, according to Jellinek (1900), the constitution gave birth to the juristic idea of the state. When combined with the Roman-law tradition and the idea of deducing the one 'right' answer from the all-embracing system of legal norms (in contrast to the adversary tradition of American and English law) the constitution acquired an imperative character and policy became very judicialized. There was an attempt to bring constitutional text and social and political reality into agreement, either through an 'activism' concerned to force reality into line with the constitution or through constant pressure for constitutional amendment to ensure that the written document reflected reality (Hennis, 1968). Such formalism was associated with a fear that the constitution was being undermined and with disenchantment either with reality or with the constitution. One aspect of this imperative character was the notion of constitutional mandate under which certain changes were a positive requirement of the constitution. The constitution was seen as a kind of political programme containing particular substantive goals (for example, the 'right to work', derived from the *Sozialstaat* principle of the constitution) that had to be legislated into existence. It was not just a general framework establishing a minimum consensus about certain principles that set the general direction and guided the form of competitive political argument. There was, furthermore, a discomfort about, even intolerance of, apparent inconsistency within the constitution (for instance, between Article 21 of the Basic Law, which legitimated the central role of political parties, and Article 38, which asserted the rights of the individual parliamentarian).

THE IDEA OF THE STATE AND DEPERSONALIZED
POWER: THE CASE OF FASCISM

Two major products of 'state' societies have been theories of bureaucracy and theories of the institution. To Max Weber the essential feature of the modern state was the rational–legal authority structure embodied in bureaucracy as the typical form of organization. Nineteenth-century German interest in the concept of bureaucracy was related to attempts to evolve a 'science' of the state and, in particular, to comprehend the 'bureau system' instituted by the Stein–Hardenberg reforms in Prussian administration, with its emphasis on unity, concentration and decisiveness (Albrow, 1970). At the same time there were polemical outbursts against its inefficiencies and its association with rule by officials. Both strands met in the work of Weber: on the one hand, he identified bureaucracy with formal rationality, with an intrinsically rational procedure that involved the expert application of rules based on respect for science, logic and calculation; on the other, and with particular reference to his practical political interests as a liberal, he feared the effects of the power of the official and recognized that it did not guarantee material rationality. However, both his central theoretical concerns—*Verband* (organization), *Ordnung* (rules as a factor in social conduct) and *Herrschaft* (authority)—and his emphasis on the values of order, continuity, precision, predictability and impersonality in the exercise of authority reflected a state tradition of political thought. By contrast, in Britain and the United States bureaucracy was conceived of as a foreign concept referring to 'rule by officials' rather than 'rational organization' and, when imported, was used in a pejorative way to characterize the power of public administration in society. A preoccupation with bureaucractic 'dysfunctions' by American 'post-Weberians' and a stress on informal organization and social psychology reflected a value system pledged more to individualistic values and responsiveness than to social solidarity, regulation and control. Similarly, the 'New Public Administration' exemplified a concern with strengthening participative values and the 'inner-directed' orientation of the official at the expense of hierarchy and integration (Marini, 1971).

The general concern with precision and explicitness of social organization and with the formal logic of collective action was also apparent
in theories of the institution and in their vitality and degree of intellectual refinement compared with the rather shallow treatment of institutions
in the Anglo-American tradition. In so far as Anglo-American theorists
viewed institutions as important, they saw them either in descriptive terms
as 'machinery' or in structural-functional terms as 'self-regulating' social
systems. This greater consciousness of institutions of continental European
theorists was intimately associated with the idea of the state and found
its expression in two major approaches: the *Naturlehre* of Gehlen (1956),
a German social scientist and philosopher, and Schelsky (1965) and the
Geisteslehre of Hauriou (1906), Renard (1933) and Romano (1917).
Gehlen's naturalistic view of institutions was extraordinarily conservative
and embedded in a characteristically German pessimism about cultural decline. Human progress was seen as the slow march from instinct to institutions. Institutions were an *Instinktersatz* (a substitute for instinct) and, like
instincts, possessed the character of objective and regulatory forces with
a logic of their own (*Eigengesetzlichkeit*) and channelling conduct into
predetermined channels. The importance of institutions was established in
this cultural/anthropological view by reference to the basic biological requirements of man for survival. In the work of Gehlen, more than in that
of Schelsky, the point of departure was an abstract picture of man's needs
rather than an historical, sociological or economic approach. The purposes
of institutions confronted man as impersonal and objective, unburdened
him of complexity and 'subjectivity', of the need to engage in critical
reflection and to establish self-direction, and provided personal security
and stability through mutual subordination to a framework of rules. For
Schelsky institutions were the precondition of rational thought and action;
reflection was the quality of institutional leadership rather than of man in
general. Underlying this strongly monistic theory of institutions was the
idea of an opposition between social action and individual thought and
an essentially passive view of man as an isolated, manipulated individual
without a capacity for reason or for critical reflection that could transcend
a concern for the gratification of egoistic and 'parasitic' needs. From such
an extreme perspective it was easy to see in modern developments a weakening of the authority of institutions and the emergence of problems of
political obligation. A heightened self-consciousness of the individual and
an interest in self-expression threatened to reduce insight into the function

of institutions in satisfying what had become trivial needs to man and to generate a view of institutions as 'oppressive' and 'restrictive' rather than as instruments of cultural advance.

In Italy the eminent jurist Santi Romano, president of the *Consiglio di Stato* (Council of State) for fifteen years from 1928, turned the institution into a central concept of the teaching and practice of public law. He took French ideas and fitted them into a legal positivism that derived from Germany and that was content to describe and classify 'normative facts' rather than to evaluate norms. For Romano the institution had two components: a permanent organization, by which it could be immediately recognized, and an 'internal' legal order of norms and procedures. The state was defined as a superior legal order that contained other legal orders centred on organizations internal to the state. The Romano school, which concentrated its attention on analysis of these 'internal' legal orders, was left with a considerable problem by this pluralistic view of the state: what degree of 'autonomy' did these 'internal' legal orders within the state possess?

From the French Idealist perspective, institutions were the fundamental social phenomenon; they established social solidarity by reconciling the subjective will of the individual with objective ideas and values. The central element of the institution was 'communion in an idea' (Renard) detached from the person or persons who conceived it; the two other elements were the organizational power (its organs and procedures) devoted to this idea and the sense of community associated with adherence to its realization. This emphasis on the motivating power of ideas through institutions found its inspiration in the rationalism of neo-Thomism and its first influential statement in Hauriou's view of the state as 'the institution of institutions' (supporting, that is, a variety of institutions within itself). According to Hauriou, the idea of the state was rooted in 'the indeterminacy of the political domain' and differed from its goals or functions, which were part of the domain of administrative determination. The institutionalization of its power produced an objective 'auto-limitation' of the state. It was Renard who developed the idea of the institution. He saw the institution as a judicial organism that possessed its own personality and generated a distinct legal system. Hence society was composed of a plurality of legal systems. Whereas Hauriou had spoken of 'consent constructed round an idea', Renard emphasized the 'authoritative structure' of the institution. The state was viewed as an institution that served three ideas: the 'political' idea, which involved changing definitions of purpose; the 'governmental' idea, which was represented by the constitution or form of rule shaping its organization; and the idea of the 'nation'. State and law were not, therefore, simply material realities; their existence and character could only be confirmed by reference to the ideas of those who conceived them. The fragility of this theory lay primarily in its 'harmonious' assumption of allegiance to universal values. It failed to identify the difference between the recognition of a normative expectation (which may require external incentives and sanctions to realize) and an internalized moral commitment to uphold a norm.

This concern with the philosophy that institutions are supposed to embody and the need to understand conduct in an institutional context, which involves enduring relationships of a normative and impersonal character, is not strongly represented in the Anglo-American tradition. The language of institutional reform has been one of machinery, one well adapted to a concern with how *efficiently* government *reacts* to changes in its environment and how *smoothly* business is expedited (that is, how conflict-free the process is). The term institutional reform usually lends a spurious distinction to what amounts to little more than reorganization of structures or new processes of decision. Internal criteria of 'good' organization and management tend to take precedence over a rationalist concern with the fundamental political values involved in institutional design. A deductive style of argument gives way to a preference for collecting evidence and a view that the best solution will suggest itself from that evidence. The improvisation and expediency that have characterized British reforms are apparent if proposals for devolution or changes in field administration of central services are contrasted with the way in which French debates about regionalism and the prefectoral system have been based on a coherent theory of the 'one and indivisible' Republic.

The idea of the state lends to a complex of institutions the appearance of a certain coherence, by providing them with certain common substantive purposes, and authoritativeness, by emphasizing the importance of constraints (in the form of procedures and rules) in order to ensure binding decisions of common concern. It is difficult to begin to understand conduct within these institutions without reference to the idea of the state. For example, the self-confidence, prestige and judicial independence of the French Council of State is founded on its conception of itself as an institution at the apex of the republican state, one that embodies a unique purpose, the establishment and guardianship of the principles of *l'État de Droit*. Similarly, post-war institutional innovations like ENA and the French Planning Commission cannot be defined exhaustively in factual terms; they represent an attempt to proselytize 'modernizing' values as part of a conception of coherent, purposive state action. Many of the differences between public-service training at ENA and the British Civil Service College, and between French planning and the British NEDC system, reflect the existence in France of a philosophy of the state as an integrative conception and underline the problems of exporting institutions into a very different historical, ideological and cultural context. Another example of the institutional expression of state values is the *Bundesrat,* the powerful upper chamber in Bonn which has an absolute veto over proposals affecting the administrative, financial or territorial interests of the states (that is, most proposals). Its membership, drawn from state governments and mandated by each separately, might be expected to produce both intense parochialism and its use primarily as a party instrument of opposition. Both dangers are offset by its conception of its institutional purpose—that of a federal organ concerned to defend the idea of the *Bundesstaat* (federal state). This idea broadens its concerns; it turns attention away from a narrow defence of states' rights and forms a basis for criticism of the way in which the (partisan) conduct of particular members at certain times fails to live up to its values. The emphasis on being part of a coherent whole contrasts with the strongly pluralistic British tradition of thinking about discrete institutions and suggests that federal arrangements in Britain, in the absence of a strong, unifying, intellectual formula, would be likely to generate 'zero-sum' rather than co-operative political strategies.

Another feature of 'state' societies is the fascination of jurists with the different character of institutions that form part of the state and the nature of their legal personality. French jurists have been concerned with the differences between 'person-institutions' like the state itself and 'thing-institutions' such as marriage or the rule of law and have also sought to distinguish between the 'police power' and the *service public* of the state. Attention has focused in particular on the different institutional forms according to which the public services could be organized (for an excellent discussion see Rolland, 1938). The essential element of *service public* was its disinterested character for it referred to activities that were directed at the satisfaction of a general interest. Direct provision of such services was either *en régie,* part of the general services of the state but with separate accounts, or by administrative decentralization to *établissements publics* (public institutions) like universities, chambers of commerce and hospitals. An *établissement public* was a detached branch of the general services of the state, one that had a separate legal personality and financial autonomy.

In Germany the major work on the various types of institutions that comprise the state was by the celebrated administrative jurist Otto Mayer (1895–6), who was in turn much influenced by the French Council of State's refinement of the concept of *service public*. Mayer cleared away a heritage of conceptual confusion and imprecision about the *Anstalt* and *Körperschaft*. The *Körperschaft* was a body of persons that was legally constituted as an artifical person and over which government control was an 'external affair'. Its defining quality was its membership, in other words it associational character. Examples are provided by local authorities, the industrial and commercial chambers, and the churches. By contrast, the *Anstalt* was a subordinate but distinct branch of the general services of the state. Legal personality attached to certain designated physical assets that were being used to perform particular duties. The *Anstalt* possessed a hierarchical administrative structure that served 'users' but exercised a distinctive *Anstaltsgewalt* over those 'users'. Examples include the federal railways (*Bundesbahn*) and other public enterprises. However, in certain cases, like public libraries, there is no attribution of legal personality because the *Anstalt* is not noticeably independent in its management. If the personality of the *Anstalt* was by common consent a juristic conception that was created by positive law, the personality of the *Körperschaft* constituted, it was sometimes argued, an objective reality that pre-existed positive law. The argument that associations had a *de facto* personality was usually based on Otto von Gierke's Germanistic and anti-Roman idea that the state recognized, but did not create, legal associations. Their activities were superintended by the state. The classification of institutions has important practical implications. For instance, one controversy has concerned the category of institution into which the universities fall. They appear to be in an ambiguous position. The tendency to view universities legally as a *Körperschaft* is accompanied by the recognition that their lack of autonomy over finance and personnel makes them akin to an *Anstalt*.

To jurists the determination of what kind of institution the state itself was seemed of profound importance. With exceptions, like the ultra-conservative jurist von Seydel, the nineteenth century saw a general retreat from the notion of the state as a tangible object, a notion that was associated with patrimonial political ideas, towards the idea of the state as a legal subject or ideal unity that was carrier of its own rights and duties. The notion of juristic person was transferred from private to public law. As a juristic person the state could, in Jellinek's (1900) view, be subsumed within the concept of the *Körperschaft*. The state was the *Gebietskörperschaft* (territorial association) that possessed an inherent superiority of will. By contrast, nineteenth-century jurists like Rotteck, Stahl, Zachariae and Gierke had seen the state as both association and *Anstalt* (though the concept of the *Anstalt* was employed by them with little precision). Otto Mayer, the jurist who gave a new clarity to the notion of the *Anstalt,* was also more inclined to see the state as an *Anstalt* with (and here he did not differ greatly from Jellinek) the distinctive quality of an *Überperson.*

In this context it is worth considering the relationship between the idea of the state as depersonalized power and Fascism. A *leitmotif* of the idea of the state has been a fear of the power of man over man. If in the Anglo-American intellectual tradition pluralism has been seen as the best check on personal power, the state tradition has emphasized the need for permanent legal machinery to regulate and administer matters of general public concern. Consequently, the state tradition of authority has had an ambivalent relationship with Fascism (see also p. 59). Fascism's exaltation of the political over the economic and cultural made it likely that Fascist thought, more than Marxism, would generate a concern with the idea of the state. Thus Robert Michels, a member of one of the three new faculties of political science founded by Mussolini to confer intellectual respectability on the Italian Fascist state, argued that under Fascism 'the prestige of the state has been elevated to the supreme place'. His 'scientific' work borrowed the concepts of elite, passive mass and organizing myth (expounded earlier by Mosca and Pareto) both to spread the climate of disillusion with democracy and to provide a legitimating formula for the Fascist state (Beetham, 1977). More frequently used as a legitimating formula, largely because it was linked to the academic dominance of Idealism in Italy, was Gentile's neo-Hegelian *stato etico* (ethical state) in which 'the state is the very personality of the individual' whose rights and duties could not be conceived of apart from it. Mussolini's early conceptions of the state had been confused, ranging from anti-statist views to his espousal of the 'Manchestrian state' as opposed to the collectivist state. However, after 1921 he adopted Gentile as the major ideologist of Fascism and referred to the 'integral' or 'totalitarian' state: 'everything within the state, nothing outside the state, and nothing against the state'. The state was seen as the juridical incarnation of the nation (or race, a politically rather than (as in

Nazism) biologically defined category); it referred to the moral order which provided the continuity of this historic community. Mussolini differed from Gentile's emphasis on the pedagogical functions of the state as the embodiment of the universal rational will in his idea of developing civic virtue by a disciplinarian approach based on non-rational appeals to elementary myths (Gregor, 1969). Partly related to Mussolini's interest in the articulation of Fascist doctrine (he wrote in 1932 that the political conception of the state must be fundamentally 'a conception of life'), Italian Fascism had by the early 1930s produced a more distinct (albeit still loosely organized) conception of the nationalist–imperialist state than German National Socialism was ever to achieve.

A number of factors combined, nevertheless, to make it unlikely that Fascism would ever develop a clear conception of the state that would inform the conduct of its leadership. First, there was the extraordinarily eclectic character of Fascist ideology, its different elements (reactionary conservatism, imperialist nationalism, race, socialism) being available for combination in a variety of ways. National Socialism was, for example, more preoccupied with a *völkisch* ideology which combined nationalist and 'biological' racial ideas than with the notion of the state. Certain conservative *Staatslehrer* sought at first to legitimate the new regime by applying the old liberal terminology of the state to it: Forsthoff referred to it as a 'total state'; Carl Schmitt called it a *staatsbetonter Rechtsstaat* (a *Rechtsstaat* emphasizing the state) and even more ambiguously a 'tripartition of political unity' into state, movement and people. Schmitt went on to contrast the 'concrete' character of the *Führerstaat,* in which the will of the leader was the source of justice, with the abstraction of the *Rechtsstaat.* Fascism and National Socialism remained, however, basically anti-theoretical and anti-intellectual in character. They sought intellectual legitimation, whether in scientific or in idealist terms, for an 'actionism', intuitionism and irrationalism that derived from the essential idea of a mobilized rather than ordered society. Many Fascists resisted an identification with Gentile's philosophical system, and even those who supported him tolerated him as an apologist rather than exalted him as a creative thinker. Fascism contained Gentile's ideas but remained distinct from them. Above all, both Hitler and Mussolini were power-hungry opportunists, who were prepared to use the idea of the state as one tactical ploy in the pursuit of power but remained distrustful of purely technical instruments and were more attracted by the cult of the hero. The Third Reich's formula of *ein*

Volk, ein Reich, ein Führer left little room for the idea of the state. Indeed, as the embodiment of formal rationality and impersonality, the notion of the state could make no lasting appeal to Fascism and its institutions could only become increasingly irrelevant to the exercise of power (hence the failure of Frick as Hitler's Interior Minister in his efforts to claim a decisive place for the bureaucracy in the consolidation of the new regime).

Both the Fascist and the National Socialist regimes remained essentially ambiguous and enigmatic, resting on a conception of the state that remained very vague and on ill-defined formulas concerning the unity of party and state. The result was confusion, especially between party and state, which produced both an inability to create durable, functioning political systems and problems associated with the interpretation of their character. Although confirmed as a public-law institution that was 'the representative of the German state idea and indissolubly linked to the state', the NSDAP's lack of the necessary administrative and technical skills and internal centrifugal tendencies frustrated the party's ambitions to become the directing centre of the new integrated system. Unclear institutional ideas led to complex problems of organization and personnel and a jurisdictional chaos of party and state agencies (exacerbated by the rise of the SS).[2] In both Germany and Italy the only common factor was loyalty to the superior role of a leader who ruled over both movement and state but whose contempt for the legal profession, vacillation at crucial moments or deliberate encouragement of divisiveness prevented him from acting as an integrator in an institutional sense. By 1943 Mussolini was admitting that Fascist Italy had been *de facto* a dual state comprising a revolutionary party elite (represented by the Grand Council of Fascism) and traditional elements based on the monarchy (represented by the Council of Ministers).

THE IDEA OF THE STATE: INSTITUTION AND PURPOSE

It is not possible in a general definition to identify the idea of the state with a particular institution or purpose. In the case of France and Germany, for example, the notion of the state has traditionally been used to describe some or all of the institutions operating in the area of the executive power. One is tempted to identify it with the public bureaucracy. However, the idea of the impersonal state emerged in seventeenth- and early eighteenth-century Russia without a proper professional bureaucracy, and in Spain during the same period bureaucratic methods became prominent without a concept of the modern state (Sherman, 1974, p. 55). In Sweden the idea of the state has been used extensively to refer to all the institutions that comprise central government (including Parliament) as opposed to local government. Its use in the Bonn Republic with various other terms (*Rechtsstaat, Bundesstaat, Parteienstaat*) suggests a wide range of views about the institutional reference points of the concept of the state—although, notably, there is no theory of the *Parlamentsstaat*. There is variation not only in the institutions with which the idea of the state is associated (monarch, central government as a whole, bureaucracy, military, the law, the parties) but also in the breadth of definition of these institutions. A similar range of variation is also apparent in definitions of the purpose of the state: from the regulative ideal of *Ordnungspolitik* to the interventionism of *soziale Gestaltungspolitik;* from the aggrandisement of power of the *Machtstaat* to the emphasis (as in the work of Carré de Malberg or the post-war French philosopher Eric Weil) on the pedagogic or cultural mission of the 'educative state' as the basis of social morality. Whereas the institutional reference point of the conception of the *Machtstaat* was clear, the *soziale Gestaltungspolitik* of the conception of the *Polizeistaat*, for example, could take very different institutional forms: the paternalist bureaucracy of Prussia, Joseph II's creation of an efficient bureaucracy paralleled by a secret police organization for Austria and Fouche's elevation of the police, particularly the 'high police', to the position of 'moral sensors' of society in Napoleonic France (Chapman, 1970).

One typical characteristic of discussions of the purpose of the state is the stress (for example, Debré, 1947) on the importance of the 'sense of mission' and moral conception in the leadership of the state rather than just its managerial capacity and grasp of *technique*. Institutions acquire from their identification with the idea of the state an elevated sense of purpose, and even when these purposes are defined narrowly (as in the case of *Ordnungspolitik*) they tend to be interpreted expansively. At the same time this identification produces powerful institutional constraints. For example, the conception of the *Machtstaat* was associated with the notion that the Imperial German army was identical to, not simply a servant of, the state and owed direct allegiance to the Kaiser as its *Kriegesherr*. According to General von Lüttwitz in August 1919: 'Today, as yesterday, the army remains the basis of authority in the State' (Craig, 1964, p. 342). This idea found its institutionalization in the emperor's 'military cabinet', the insulation of the army from wider political accountability and the legally privileged position of officers (including immunity from the civil courts) who regarded themselves as an unchallengeably superior social order (*Stand*). However, despite bitter anti-parliamentary and anti-socialist attitudes within the army, its political interventions were inhibited by the paramount importance of preserving its aloofness, autonomy and privileges. As the embodiment of the idea of the state it sought to maintain a commitment to *Überparteilichkeit* and preferred to work 'behind the scenes'. The cult of discipline and legality was to prove stronger than its anti-parliamentarianism, despite departures from this tradition, as in the 'silent dictatorship' of Hindenburg and Ludendorff in 1916–18, the Kapp *putsch* of 1920 and the intrigues of von Schleicher after 1930 (Craig, 1964).

Political conduct is shaped by the degree to which state values and norms are institutionally concentrated or diffused in a particular political system. France represents a case of institutional concentration; the bureaucracy is the repository of the state tradition. Consequently, France's constitutional and political development after 1789 has been one of persistent antagonism between representative institutions (emphasizing the role of the deputy and distrust of public authority) and the idea of the state, with periods when the representative system has been limited or even suspended. Political parties have been seen traditionally in negative terms as spokesmen of interests and ideologies rather than as providing leadership for the executive power. The state tradition has been associated with the idea of a zone of authority independent of the Assembly and the parties and interest groups (the so-called 'intermediaries'). De Gaulle's ambition to turn the French state into 'a decisive, ambitious and active institution expressing and serving only the national interest' found its expression in bureaucratic reforms (the establishment of ENA and the planning system in his post-war government, the reassertion of the executive supremacy of the regional and departmental prefects in 1964) and in the 'controlled' parliamentary system of the Fifth Republic. During the Fifth Republic a series of developments seemed to suggest the replacement by a *République des Fonctionnaires* of the *République des Députés:* the bestowal of increased powers of decree on the executive; the ubiquity of the *grands corps,* who occupied posts as ministers, members of the increasingly powerful ministerial 'cabinets' which advised ministers and co-ordinated departments or, through *pantouflage,* as senior executives in industrial corporations; and increasing politicization of the civil service. In Burdeau's view *l'État gestionnaire* or *fonctionnel,* which was committed to calculation and the coherence and rationalism of planning and found its legitimacy in performance, was taking over from the political competition for power characteristic of *l'État conflictuel.* Conflict about basic human purposes was giving way to conflict about matters of economic rationality (for example, the criteria of investment).

There is much exaggeration in this picture of the *République des Fonctionnaires.* The administration is far from being a coherent whole at the service of technocratic planners (with some 1,200 fiercely independent corps); there are great divisions amongst the technocrats themselves; there is no real evidence of greater cohesion of policies than under the Fourth Republic; and politicization of the civil service is not new and has not turned it into a Gaullist instrument. Indeed, it could be argued that constitutional arrangements (which relaxed parliamentary pressures on ministers), the growing significance of 'cabinets', the new importance of the Presidential Office and the Prime Minister's Office, and the emergence of a majority party facilitated political control by creating a more cohesive executive (Suleiman, 1974). However, within this new framework the position of the *grands corps* as the major representatives of the idea of the state was strengthened. They appeared self-confidently imperialistic. Through the principle of *détachement* their members (only a quarter of the Finance Inspectorate works within the corps at any one time) took on seemingly incompatible roles: in administration (as 'cabinet' members and directors), in politics (as ministers and parliamentarians), in both public and private industry, and in financial institutions. The pivotal role of 'cabinets' to their ministers reflected the closed nature of corps and divisions, the distant and mistrustful relationship between division directors (the so-called 'Parisian barons') and ministers. Directors continued to see themselves as 'guiding' the ministers and as 'communicating' policy to groups rather than as negotiating their substance. They were protecting the autonomy of the administrative system from intruders, from the particularism of ministers and deputies. As technicians or managers, directors had a monopoly over a domain, in which they possessed their own body of authority (legalism) and applied rational standards in the general interest (technocracy). In the context of such ideas and of struggles for colonization of posts between corps (limiting the minister's choice of directors) there were plenty of opportunities for battles with ministers.

At the same time a capacity for public leadership and initiative exists within the French bureaucracy, a capacity to formulate and sustain a policy through to implementation, albeit with some notable failures and reverses like the *Plan Calcul* which was designed to rescue the computer industry (Hayward, 1973). There is in some instances a willingness to impose the technically 'correct' solution on recalcitrant interests, to exercise bureaucratic power somewhat abrasively. This resort to formalized methods of control (price controls, etc.) has been associated with tendencies to 'direct action' which can, as in May 1968, 'undo' the controls. The 'domination-crisis' syndrome has, however, been the subject of growing criticism. On the one hand, there have been political demands for participation and decentralization to remove responsibilities from the remote, impersonal state apparatus, partly to combat *incivisme* and partly to remedy the inefficiencies of centralization. On the other, doubts have emerged about the capacity of the centralized state apparatus to handle the problems of an increasingly complex industrialized society that has been subjected to new competitive pressures from the international market, with membership of the European Economic Community, American 'domination', trans-national corporations and a more assertive Third World. The new economic liberalism of Georges Pompidou, Jacques Chaban Delmas and Giscard d'Estaing has had a modest conception of national planning, has preferred voluntary contractual agreements in government–industry relations to the imposition of bureaucratically defined objectives on private interests by statutory obligation, and has designated the state's role as essentially subsidiary within processes of structural change in the economy.

The political controversy about the autonomous and centralized bureaucratic state in France contrasts with the dispersal of responsibilities and the integration of party and state that is characteristic of the West German conceptions of the *Bundesstaat* and *Parteienstaat*. These two conceptions combined to suggest the institutional diffusion of state values and norms in the Federal Republic and supported a greater reliance on informal, socially consensual modes of problem-solving in which the bureaucracy could be seen to share power with other 'state-conscious' elites. The institutions which were held to embody the idea of the state were able to represent, more accurately than in France, the basic cleavages of society, a fact which had consequences for their ability to implement agreements relatively smoothly. If the *Bundesstaat* reflects a German tradition, *Parteienstaat* is a more recent term. During the Weimar Republic *Parteienstaat* was used pejoratively in the context of discussion about 'the crisis of the party state'. It referred to the 'divisiveness' and 'irresponsibility' that the parties had introduced into public life. After 1945 various factors combined to facilitate the integration of the ideas of party and state on a scale not achieved in France or during the Weimar Republic: the circumstances of the origin of the new Republic, which included the displacement of traditional elites and the discrediting of traditional institutions during the Nazi period; constitutional recognition of the role of the parties in the very first article of the Basic Law which dealt with the new Republic's political institutions; and the political development of a more concentrated party system in the 1950s as Adenauer's Christian Democratic Party pioneered the model of the 'catch-all' party (*Volkspartei*). With the Weimar experience in mind and confronted on this occasion by a power vacuum, the parties moved pre-emptively after 1945 to forestall the rise of counter-elites by penetrating other institutions. The conception of the *Parteienstaat* referred to the presence of partisans in key positions of the state apparatus. It did not necessarily mean the replacement of liberal parliamentarianism by instructed party delegates, as was suggested by Leibholz, nor did it imply that the problems of party government had been overcome (Dyson, 1977). The parties established themselves from the outset as the major channel of career advancement; *Parteibuch* (party membership) became a major criterion of appointment to, and promotion within, the permanent bureaucracy. Reconstruction of the bureaucracy, even if on traditional lines, was therefore guided by the party system. Party elites identified themselves with the state, and interest-group leaders sought to legitimize their own substantial power by emulating its values and norms and stressing their social responsibility (no doubt often in a dissimulating manner) in order to gain official status and public approval. The dissemination of state values and norms, of a 'public-regarding' ethic, took place. At the same time neo-liberalism in economic affairs combined with the legalism of the *Rechtsstaat*, and with recent historical memories, to introduce a greater modesty into the exercise of executive power than in France. Nevertheless, its exercise was facilitated, unlike in Britain, by values and styles in the political process that emphasized shared responsibility and *Sachlichkeit*. Symptomatic of this institutional diffusion of the state has been the greater integration of *Beamte* (higher officials), the traditional embodiment of the state idea, into the political process. On the one hand, their dominant presence within the parties and parliaments has transformed these institutions, notably through their organizational and policy skills. On the other, increasing party politicization of the public service has reflected the attempt by the parties to confirm their formal ascendancy.

Party and bureaucracy are fused in the idea of the state. There is criticism of the *Parteienstaat:* the left bemoans the effects of the idea of the state on internal party democracy and resents the didactic style of party leadership; the right decries the effects of the parties on the traditional conception of the bureaucratic state; while liberal intellectuals fear that dominance of party perspectives will restrict the horizons of political debate and will generate 'excess' pressures for democratization at the expense of the bureaucratic ethic. Above all, in a society that has been used to the identification of the idea of the state and bureaucracy there is much confusion about the implications of so profound a transformation of the institutional reference points of the concept of the state. The implications of the conception of the *Parteienstaat* are much broader than those of the English term party government: it involves a distinct sense of mission of the *staatstragende* parties, a concern for their institutional capability to discharge their functions (apparent in the party research institutions and in the Party Law of 1967, which recognized and regulated state finance for their electoral activities and endowed them with such broad functions as political education and 'influencing political development'), and the integrative role of *Parteibuch* in smoothing relationships between institutions. In Britain, in the absence of a state tradition that legitimates an inherent role for the executive power autonomous of Parliament, an enormous responsibility has traditionally fallen on elected representatives and the parties into which they are organized as instruments of direction. And yet in the debate about the problems of British government in the post-1945 period comparatively little attention was paid to the ability of British parties to provide 'strong' government by, for example, thinking in programmatic terms and developing their grasp of technical policy arguments and their skills in managing the executive machine. Both Germany's Party Law and France's bureaucratic reforms (unlike Britain's piecemeal reforms) concentrated on improving the capability of the central institutions of state to undertake their mission. The very notion of a 'mission' in public affairs appeared alien to the British view of politics.

THE ANALYTICAL DISTINCTION BETWEEN STATE AND CIVIL SOCIETY: MARXISM AND THE IDEA OF THE STATE

The idea of a distinction between state and civil society is the precondition of the state's ability to take a disinterested view of the public interest. From this conceptual distinction flows the unique honour of serving the state and the strenuous obligations imposed on those who serve it. Hence, where the notion of the state is equated with bureaucracy the bureaucratic state can be seen not just as a 'tyranny' of officials but also as a 'tyranny' over officials. The differentiation and self-regulation of society are contrasted with the idea of the unity of the state, which is dedicated to rationalism and the importance of consciously designed procedures in decision-making and enables man to become conscious of universal values and interests. It is possible to identify two basic approaches to the definition of the state/society distinction. Sociological theories take an essentially utilitarian view of the state and see it either as a 'sub-system' of society, which is distinguished by the special character of its functions, or, like MacIver (1926), as an association of people (as opposed to a community) who act in unison for certain common ends. For MacIver the state is an agency of social control that regulates 'the outstanding external relationships of men in society'. Durkheim and Duguit emphasized the special character of its function; Duguit, for example, focused on public service as its *raison d'être*. The prevailing view has, however, been represented by philosophic and juristic theories that thought of the state as an immanent intelligence, directing social change, rather than as a social agency. The distinction between state and society rested on the notion of the unique quality of its authority, its sovereignty. Thus French jurists like Hauriou, Maspetiol and Renard stressed the divine origins of its authority and the sacred character of public power.

Hegel and Marx paid considerable attention to this conceptual distinction, but the distinction itself predated them. The separation between 'social' and 'political' can be traced back to Aquinas, while the concepts of state and society could be taken from Montesquieu, who was in turn indebted to the Italian legal theorist Giovanni V. Gravina (who drew on Roman law). However, discussion of the idea of the state as distinct from society really began with economists. They conceived of society as the area of 'particularity' that provided self-regulating mechanisms for the satisfaction of material needs. According to the French writer J. B. Say, economic science focused on society as a circular process of exchange and was a social rather than a political science. From economists came the notion that society produced the state but was not identical with it. As economists and sociologists specialized in society, so jurists specialized in the idea of the state. Indeed, Raymond Aron (1968) has argued that there was an intimate connection between the analytical separation of state and society and the historical separation of sociology from traditional political theory. Amongst jurists there emerged two opposed views. For theorists like René Hubert (1926) the authority of the state emanated from society. The state's principle and function was solidarity; it expressed in its 'synthetic unity' all the particular forces that flow from society. By contrast, Bertrand de Jouvenel (1945) saw the state as the product of power that was artificial or manufactured.

British political thought showed little interest in the question of the distinctive character of the 'public power' (which was an unfamiliar term) or in the idea of a unitary public interest transcending particular loyalties. Institutional reform succumbed easily to 'managerialism'. A cult of economic efficiency, represented by ideas of rational resource planning and 'economies of scale', and a concern for structures and techniques rather than institutional doctrine infected proposals for civil service reform as well as for the reform of the central machinery of government, local government and the National Health Service. The standards with reference to which institutional reforms were evaluated were increasingly derived from the industrial corporation: management theory acted as the mechanism for this transfer of values. Institutional reforms displayed a loss of philosophical and constitutional sensibility, an absence of interest in the rational analysis of political values, and a concern for technical criteria rather than for legitimation.

The idea of the state stands in complete contrast to the notion of political institutions as neutral 'transformatory' structures processing 'inputs' (demands and supports) from the system's environment into 'outputs'. Input–output models of the political system consider political activities as simply 'a system of behaviour embedded in an environment to the influences of which the political system itself is exposed and in turn reacts' (Easton, 1965, p. 18). Such a perspective avoids the character of the ideas embedded in institutions and their influence on conduct. In theories of the state the requirements of 'authoritative' decisions take precedence over the input side of politics (the articulation and aggregation of interests). Those entrusted with the exercise of public power are expected to adopt a more didactic approach, rooted in the identification of general interests. The state tradition has focused on the 'authoritative' generation as well as the allocation of values and on the essentially political concept of institution, on the presumption that the rational analysis of values is central to politics and that there is some relation between what actually happens and what is intended. There is a resistance to economic

theories of politics (Downs, 1957) in which the political process is reduced to a market, with the 'maximizing' individual as the centre of the
political universe; to cybernetic models of the political system (Deutsch,
1963) in which the decision-making process is seen in terms of the mechanical language of information flows (channels, load, feedback, etc.);
and to group theory (Bentley, 1908) in which government is held simply to mediate among contending groups and to be composed itself of a
number of interacting groups which represent a microcosm of external social processes. American behaviouralism, in its preoccupation with empirically accessible factors as determinants of conduct, led to a 'realistic'
and essentially non-critical analysis of political phenomena that did not
allow for any qualitatively distinct characteristics of the idea of the state.
Both politics and administration were to be understood in terms of propositions about the psychology of individuals and the sociology of groups
rather than of doctrines about the state and its (political) purpose through
which an attempt is made to bind people together (often unwillingly). For
theories of the state the central problem is to keep 'parochial' attachments
within limits in order to promote and safeguard public purposes. The typical answer was found in the normative ordering provided by institutions.
For behaviouralism ideas were to be understood in their sociological and
psychological context rather than in terms of independent criteria of judge-
ment sustained by institutions. The resistance to empirical methods in
societies with a state tradition reflected a view that the kind of precise,
quantifiable variables with which these methods were concerned were
of limited relevance to the central problems of politics. Continental texts
on public administration emphasized a philosophical perspective which
saw state administration as *sui generis* in contrast to Anglo-American approaches (whether behaviouralist or descriptive–analytical) which shared
an essentially workman-like, practical conception of an administrative
system they were prepared to dissect. At its worst, hostility to objective
analysis in the continental tradition went along with a pronounced conservatism from theorists who, unlike those in Britain or the United States,
were themselves part of a state that they sanctified. One important consequence was the development of a 'counter-literature', a polemical approach that sought to strip the state of its halo. Theories of the state have
not, therefore, been associated with analysis of politics in purely functional terms or with an instrumental conception of government as a process through which individual and group interests are pursued. According
to *Brockhaus* (the German equivalent of the *Encyclopaedia Britannica*),

the basis of all theories of the state must be that 'the state is no mere tool or "machine" for the pursuit of individual or group interests... it is a phenomenon in its own right, the standing and value of which rests upon the fact that it is a manifestation of a concept of the state transcending the individual'. The state is seen as a unique collectivity whose dignity and value reside in its embodiment of an impersonal and comprehensive set of moral ideas that have an existence apart from the conflicts and fluctuations of social and political life. This aloofness and embodiment of the principle of neutrality have found their expression in three decisions of the West German Federal Constitutional Court which characterized the state as 'the home of all citizens (*Staatsbürger*) without respect of persons' (BVerfGE 12, 4; 19, 1; 19, 216).

Emphasis on the notion of the distinctiveness of the state has a number of important institutional implications. One of the most obvious is a process of elite training which is concerned to inculcate state consciousness. In Germany and Sweden, for example, there is a tradition of government influence on the content of certain aspects of university education (and the separate technical universities) through its participation in setting the state examinations which, notably in law, are the traditional passport to the public service. This pre-entry, but vocationally relevant, training for the public service differs from that in France, where the state has established its own very eminent higher education system parallel to the universities, the *grandes écoles,* concerned with inculcating a respect for *technique,* for marrying practical technical skills with cultural awareness and literacy. The *École Polytechnique* and the other great technical schools supply the 'technical' corps and produce a sort of mafia of state-trained engineers encompassing government and industry, while the *École Nationale d'Administration* provides post-university training for the highly competitive entry examinations into the *grands corps.* The character of the continental engineer was formed in the context of state institutions, of state recognition of the importance of developing and using technical skills (with reference also to external threats, open land frontiers and defence requirements). In Britain, by contrast, the 'profession' (essentially a medieval legacy and associated with clerics, doctors and lawyers) became the model for the engineer as for other middle-class groups. The self-governing, inward-looking and disinterested outlook of the profession that offered a particular type of advice was substituted for the managerial and entrepreneurial ethic of the continental engineer trained for state service.

Another manifestation of the notion of the distinctiveness of the state was the attempt to distinguish between government and administration (*Regierung* and *Verwaltung*) in order to safeguard the creative values of the first and the regularity and order (objectivity) of the second. One possible explanation for this conceptual distinction is the historical one that in the age of absolutism 'government' was the political level: in other words, the distinction was equivalent to the politics/administration distinction. Now, in a democratic age, German writers distinguish between *Politik, Regierung* and *Verwaltung*. In Germany and Sweden the distinction is given an institutional expression: there is administrative decentralization in Germany either to dependent agencies (*nachgeordnete Behörde*) or to the state district administrations (*Bezirksregierungen*) and in Sweden to the boards and county governors. These agencies are expected to operate autonomously and to take their own decisions subject to control of the courts.

A third manifestation is the theoretical distinction between public and private law. There are notorious and growing difficulties in drawing this distinction, given the variety of criteria that can be applied and the emergence of new types of organizations (for example, in planning) that mix public and private interests.[3] Nevertheless, it has proved of great technical value in imposing some order on the complex, diverse rules that make up the legal order and in providing a source of richness of judicial categories applicable to persons, goods and acts. Certain jurists like Duguit and Kelsen have opposed its 'autocratic' implications (that is, the notion that government and governed are not subject to the same legal principles), but the overwhelming view has been that the distinction was of political value in providing a better guarantee of individual liberties. There is, therefore, a separate body of public law (incorporating constitutional, administrative and financial law) which regulates in considerable detail the organization, rights and duties of government and administration, and establishes the special status, privileges and obligations of the public official. A separate system of administrative courts is concerned with developing its general principles and legal categories, which attempt to take account of the inherent differences of position between public authorities and private individuals. Above all, an effort is made to maintain a rational and elegant synthesis of public law by relating judgements to principles derived from a coherent and evolving philosophy. In Britain, by contrast, constitutional theory is not a phrase in general use; constitutional law is not really a technical term in law for it is difficult, in the context of so much reliance on diverse types of conventions, to determine where the boundaries of constitutional law lie. Administrative remedies have been evolved by the ordinary courts in a piecemeal fashion without clear recognition of the special character and needs of public law as a separate legal discipline. Even official reviews, like the Donoughmore Committee on Ministers' Powers in 1932 and the Franks Committee on Administrative Tribunals and Inquiries in 1957, have failed to concentrate on general principles, to link their proposals to philosophical considerations about the sovereign and non-sovereign aspects of the state. A characteristically medieval confusion of public and private responsibility remains. The common-law system is caught up in a web of medieval government immunities and concepts which have not permitted the evolution of a coherent body of public law.

Emphasis on the notion of the distinctiveness of the state could also have important policy implications. In France, for example, the corporate claims of the Churches and the trade unions were rejected in a manner not found in Britain. Émile Combes' virulent anticlericalism led him to write: 'There are and there can be no rights except the rights of the State and there is and can be no other authority than the authority of the Republic.' The issue of state aid for private education was interpreted by its opponents as a Catholic threat to the autonomy and primacy of the state's role in education, itself the precondition of a cohesive society. At the local level the issue manifested itself in the traditional conflict between the village schoolmaster, who represented the secularism of the republican state, and the priest. Similarly, Bismarck's *Kulturkampf* against the Roman Catholic Church reflected the claims of the state for unity and autonomy.

The issue of the distinctiveness of state from society was the major preoccupation of Marxist theories of the state. With the 1960s there emerged a new Marxist interest in 'realistic' analysis of the 'autonomy' of the state and a greater willingness to accord a 'relative' autonomy to the state.[4] This renaissance of Marxist theorizing on the state and the shift from a view of the state as mere superstructure or 'heavenly facade' had numerous roots: in the translation of Gramsci's writings; in a recognition that the nature of the state had changed in 'late' or 'advanced' capitalism; in a sense that an optimistic liberalism was not providing a credible interpretation of contemporary politics or insight into the character of new economic problems (Marxism, as above all a theory of and against capitalism, revived at times when capitalism appeared in profound or novel crisis); and in a recognition that Marxism was itself deficient as a political theory. Nicos Poulantzas

(1974) argued, for example, that the 'economism' of the Second International and of the Third International after Lenin had led to a failure to develop Marxist theories of the state and hence to an unpreparedness for the Fascism of the 1920s and 1930s. Rejection of mechanistic and reductionist explanations, which treated the state as an epiphenomenon, in favour of exploring the interaction of political and ideological with economic structures could be justified by reference to the 'classics'. Thus, Engels had written: 'The economic situation is the basis, but the various elements of the superstructure... also exercise their influence upon the course of the historical struggle and in many cases preponderate in determining their form.'[5] On such foundations Louis Althusser made his famous, but oddly ambiguous, distinction between determination and dominance. Although the material mode of production furnished the conditions of any structure, it was possible, and indeed probable, that in a given situation something else would be dominant within it. In other words, the material determined, except where it did not. Under the influence of Horkheimer and Adorno the Frankfurt School had parted much earlier, and in a way that Althusser was not to do, from scientific analysis of the forces and relations of production. For example, Habermas rejected early on in his work the possibility of a revolution of the proletariat and saw the motive force of social development in technology rather than class relations. In his view the state presided in an active manner over capitalist society.

Continental European Marxism produced two major approaches to the study of the relative autonomy of the state. Both rejected the conception that the state was an instrument of domination by a single, unified class and the thesis of 'state monopoly capitalism' according to which the state was the agent of the monopolies. The structuralist approach of Althusser and Poulantzas denied explicitly the possibility of historical explanation and indeed argued that Gramsci had been too profoundly influenced by Hegel. Their structuralism was based upon an attack on the illusion of subjectivity, the view that men were subjects and hence stood in opposition to Sartre's project for an 'existential' Marxism and Garaudy's humanistic Marxism. The latter were criticized for making a number of Marx's crucial concepts so vague as to render them of dubious use in rigorous economic and political analysis. Marx's major breakthrough had been methodological: the emergence in his work of a scientific study of structures and their objective relations. This 'scientific' Marxism (as opposed to the 'ideological' Marxism of both the younger Marx before the 'epistemological break' in 1845 and, more recently, of the Frankfurt School) was anti-empiricist. It was concerned with the study of elementary reified wholes, rather than empirical and historical processes, and with establishing formal sets of relations between elements. For Poulantzas (1973) the state was a 'unifying social formation' that contained numerous contradictions. Although the state was to be understood primarily in terms of its class function, as 'the condensation of a class relation', the economically dominant class was not necessarily dominant on the political scene even as a source of recruitment to the state apparatus. Instead there was a kind of pluralism in which several classes or class 'fractions' exercised political power and the state balanced, reconciled and organized the different social forces of a given 'social formation'. The state was viewed as 'internal' to the class struggle and, therefore, responsive to working-class pressures as well as capitalist demands. While the state was a site for class struggle, its pre-eminent role was maintaining the unity and cohesion of the 'social formation'. However, it remained a 'capitalist state' (the structuralists' term), which elaborated the political struggles of capital (for example, between financial, monopoly and non-monopoly capital) and organized its hegemony. Its relative autonomy did not involve a capacity to oppose and arbitrate between different capital interests from an independent perspective simply because the state was seen as in no sense external to, and separate from, the class structure. Thus, although he argued that it was possible for the bureaucracy to become a 'relatively autonomous social force', it could not be held to have a will or power of its own to impose its own policies.

Critical theory in the tradition of the Frankfurt School was prepared to recognize that the state was itself a source of power and rejected the notion that its policy was externally determined by objective structures. Emphasis was historical rather than analytical; it was on the historical character of the state as a changing entity and on its concrete empirical character within the 'totality of society' and the 'historical whole'. In this view the state remained fundamentally concerned with the general interests of capitalist enterprise and capital accumulation. However, Habermas (1973) and Offe (1972) concentrated on how the expanded functions of the state (involving new 'stabilisation', 'corrective' and 'compensatory' functions) had produced a new relationship between base and superstructure in advanced capitalist society. Enlargement of the public sector, which utilized more resources (for welfare policies and 'infrastructural' provision, for instance) and replaced market by political decisions (for example, with the 'managed' economy and environmental policies), reduced the freedom of individual 'capitals' and the scope for capital accumulation. The state emerged increasingly as an actor that played off particular 'capitals' against each other (for instance, industry against industry) by identifying the very different interests contained within the capitalist system and by attempting to reconcile the demands of the electorate with the needs of capital accumulation. It was, nevertheless, a fragile state, which was dependent on its capacity for crisis management. In the first place, there was the danger that the economic restrictions imposed by a capitalist economy could lead to a 'fiscal crisis' of the state. Maintenance of capital accumulation through lower taxes clashed with the state's need for higher revenue to support its other functions like counteracting unemployment, poverty and economic stagnation. There was, furthermore, the danger of a 'legitimation crisis' as the accumulation-supporting state had to legitimize itself to an electorate whose demands for expenditure were not being met and which perceived a 'crisis of rationality' in the failure of the state to match the expansion of its functions with greater control over the economic process. Offe attempted a functional rather than an institutional definition of the capitalist state. Essentially, this state did not defend the interests of one class but the common interests of all members of the capitalist class society in a particular framework of rules and social relationships that assisted accumulation. Unlike the work of Poulantzas, in which the economic functions of the state, particularly its role in capital accumulation, were neglected, the capitalist state was defined in terms of its relationship to the accumulation process. It was regarded as having four characteristics: exclusion from accumulation because of the dominance of private ownership; its 'maintenance' function for accumulation; its dependence for resources upon accumulation and hence its institutional self-interest in this process; and its reliance on 'legitimation' through a variety of participative mechanisms in order to 'conceal' its nature as a capitalist state. For Offe the central problem of the state was the absence of an effective strategy for reconciling these four functions: hence the 'crisis of crisis management' and the state's search (through corporatist devices and policy planning) for new methods to increase its limited potential for the resolution of conflicts.

It is illuminating to compare these two approaches with British Marxism. Some professional sociologists like Hindess and Hirst have looked to structuralism as a useful professional paradigm, but otherwise interest in Althusser, notably in the *New Left Review,* has been distant and critical. The sober empiricist outlook of Gramsci has been better suited to the Anglo-Saxon intellectual climate. Structural analysis was attacked for its impenetrable concepts and pretentious aridities, for a 'theological', over-abstract and formalistic approach that had too little respect for empirical research (Thompson, 1978). While the Marxist humanism of the Frankfurt School was *prima face* more attractive, its ponderousness, 'density' and allusiveness, combined with absence of a 'rigorous' analysis of social and political reality, diminished its influence. British Marxism has been characterized by eclecticism, historical argument sensitive to the ambiguities and subtleties of history, emphasis on the complex relations between ideas and social movements and a concern with a cultural perspective that delves into the more intimate areas of life and work and recognizes, for example, the existence of rival value systems in public life. Perry Anderson and Tom Nairn exhibited an idiosyncratic empiricism that underlined the difficulty of, and the relativity and caution required in, political analysis.[6] Interested in detailed studies of national peculiarities and the subtle aspects of class, they stressed the developmental uniqueness of the British 'state', the absence both of a bourgeois revolution to establish the idea of an abstract, impersonal state and of a bureaucratic and military apparatus to enable a reaction of the state itself against society (Nairn, 1977). As far as the theory of the state was concerned, the major contribution was the 'instrumental' approach of Miliband (1969). He neglected objective structures and the functions of the state in favour of an analysis of the nature of the ruling class in terms of its social biography. The emphasis was on group manipulation unrelated to a structural context or the 'historical whole'. As the social origins of agents of the state apparatus and the motivations of individuals who composed social groups and the state were assumed to be central, his work relied on empirical data about interpersonal connections between members of the dominant economic class and the state apparatus. When Poulantzas (1969) attacked him for depending on 'bourgeois' social science, he was, of course, recognizing that Miliband was part of an Anglo-American intellectual world whose intellectual traditions were very different from the native rationalism and positivism that informed his own work. Miliband (1977, p. 68) was prepared to qualify his approach not only by recognizing that the state could act as an agency of reform but also by emphasizing that 'the relation of the "ruling class" to the state is always and in all circumstances *bound* to be problematic'.

Marxist theories of the state have been helpful in stimulating interest in political economy. However, even as political economy they leave much to be desired. Political economy needs to bring out the very different possibilities in the relationship of the state and the economy: how, for example, the room for manoeuvre of the state apparatus depends on the surplus to be allocated and the resource base of the public sector. The state itself may intervene to support a dependent capitalist development or, alternatively, to plan and control the economy, particularly the allocation of the surplus. In the latter instance it may allocate the surplus in the interests of domestic and foreign capital; at the other extreme it may take over the means of production as part of the process of transferring power (however nominally) to the masses, or intervene to replace the bourgeoisie, thereby acquiring a degree of class autonomy even if benefiting mainly the middle classes and organized labour.

The empiricism of Miliband is indeed limiting, distracting attention from the less visible aspects of politics. At the same time structuralism and critical theory have got bogged down in arid, vague, opaque abstractions and never precisely specify how far economic forces shape political life. In the case of structuralism there is the problem of how adequately to relate infrastructure and superstructure without the dialectical understanding that it explicitly rejects. Its stress on capitalism's functional requirements leaves little room for explanations of class-conscious actions and generates the kind of extended, un-illuminating, abstract categories exhibited in the work of Poulantzas. Above all, these approaches share two basic features: state action is theoretically pre-defined as being in the long-term interest of capitalist relations of production; and the state is held to be important in terms of its function rather than of its specific institutional forms and the limitations that they impose. Marx had originally criticized the state for not meeting certain ethical demands that he viewed as central to the working-class movement. Whether the state was seen as an instrument of class rule (as part of society) or as a parasitic growth (in opposition to society), it was an aspect of man's alienation. Out of his critique emerged a normative theory of a 'non-state' society. However, the concern with the state was later submerged in a critical analysis of capitalism by means of a critique of those concepts that could be shown to be germane to capitalism. Marxism's legacy has been neglect of the idea of the state or 'realistic', explanatory theories of the state that seek to understand its functions in terms of power relationships within the capitalist economy. Neither in the Marxist tradition nor in new Marxist theories of the state is there a normative conception of the state as an institution whose ideals shape the manner in which public authority is exercised, or a recognition that underlying the conceptual distinction between state and society is an emphasis on the importance of imagination and reflection in politics. There is an unwillingness to see economic means as only one basis of power or as one that can be shaped in accordance with distinctive state purposes and interests; to appreciate that conscious adherence to absolute, eternal ideals and to traditional principles and modes of reasoning can act as a powerful check on class interests; or to work out the implications of the view that conscious and imaginative political action, and not just objective forces, will determine whether legitimation and fiscal crises cause the breakdown of the 'capitalist state'. The issue of the political weight of the top economic class is a relative question, the answer to which cannot ignore the institutions that embody the idea of the state. In Marxist theory the notion of comprehending conduct in terms of the institutional expression of ideals is subordinated by definition to attention to social biography, objective structural conditions or the functions of the state in capital accumulation.

Many of the limitations of Marxist theories of the state stem from the way in which Marxism embraces one aspect of the origins of the state at the expense of others. The state is seen as a response to man's increasing recognition of his capacity to control nature. It is a form of economic union that is designed to allow property to exist and to encourage material production. Little, if any, attention is paid to the notion of the state as a constitutional structure which is a moral response to man's experience of the horrors of religious civil war (Forsyth, forthcoming) and which, as a moral force for social harmony, can become integrator and humanizer, and not just external manager or regulator, of the society that had emerged from the industrial and French revolutions (Stein, 1850). Lorenz von Stein, for example, took a narrow view of the science of society (*Gesellschaftslehre*); it remained a subsection of the more important science of the state (*Staatswissenschaft*). It was necessary but insufficient to investigate the 'real state' by the methods of *Gesellschaftslehre*, to examine the means by which the class struggle of society invaded the domain of the state apparatus itself and state power became misused in the interest of the upper class. Far more important, in Stein's view, was the determination of the conditions for the 'ideal' state, one which stands outside the class struggle as the personification of the general will (for Stein a constitutional and 'social' monarchy which favours and promotes the interests of the lower classes).

Theories dealing with the nature of the autonomy of the state face the basic problem of how to delineate the constantly changing relationship of society and the state itself. The danger of imposing rigid theoretical frameworks on a discussion of this issue is that the complex dialectical relationship between them is ignored, and the subtle tensions between the ambitions of the state apparatus and the very real limitations imposed by the structure of society are not recognized. It is easy to underestimate the complexity of social structures. The state itself cannot be neatly separated from the society of which it is the product but which, in turn, it informs and shapes; indeed, it is permeated by the assumptions of the age (about hierarchy, tradition, the basis of reward, for example). Debate between structuralists who argue that conduct is determined and actionists who stress voluntarism obscures the constantly varying relations over space and time between the constraints of economic and social structure and the possibilities available to human agents in institutional frameworks. Constraints differ from one situation to another. Twentieth-century legal and philosophical theories of the state have moved towards a more pragmatic view of the relationship between state and society, one emphasizing the continuous problems associated with giving each its due and enabling a mediation between office and citizen. For example, Carré de Malberg (1920) saw them as different but not autonomous. While the state apparatus was inspired by principles of justice and reason, social forces carried 'partiality' and emotion into its heart. In themselves, the state and the legal system were not, therefore, infallible means by which to realize moral conduct which depended on the conscience of the individual. Herzog (1971) rejected the idea of the relationship as one between superior and subordinate; the relationship between state and society was viewed as paradoxical, one of both domination and service. The state, an 'external steering system' that embodied distinctive procedures, was needed to 'correct' and complement society, to act as 'the better conscience of society'. At the same time its activities were dependent on acceptance in society. For Herzog the impossibility of precise delineation did not erode the importance of the analytical distinction between state and society. In the context of an analysis of the dangers of the enfeeblement of the state apparatus as its economic tasks grew and it found itself subordinated to, rather than regulating and controlling, the 'industrial–economic' process Böckenförde (1972) provided an influential restatement of the state/society distinction. According to Böckenförde, the state was a social working unit that was related functionally to society but needed to be organizationally independent of society. There was a gradual shift from the conception (represented by Jellinek) that the state was an external phenomenon with its own unique will towards either the view (like Gény's) that the state was a reality of the judicial order, an abstract aspect of society that served an objective reason, or the view (like that of Adolf Arndt, the SPD 'crown' jurist) that state and society were two different aspects of one and the same reality, a democratic polity, whose members could claim that it was 'their' state.

The issue of state and pluralism became central for post-war theories of the state. A basic agreement on the need to prevent the tendency of society to decompose produced a variety of responses: Prélot wanted to integrate corporate groups into the state itself in order to assign responsibility to them; Maspetiol feared that excessive extension of the state's responsibilities would enfeeble its exercise of power; while Burdeau, who stressed the antinomy of state and pluralism, sought institutional means of ensuring that the public power would be able to transcend the turbulence of social forces and preserve its unity (Halbecq, 1965, p. 554). In Germany, too, anxiety about the possibility of a *Verbändestaat* began to replace the *Parteienstaat* discussions that had so animated the Weimar Republic. Organized groups, much more integrated and professional than those in France, were heavily involved in the exercise of public functions, while the success of government's economic policy depended on the collective bargaining of the *Sozialpartner* (social partners). By the mid-1970s there was a widespread desire to make the internal policy-making processes of the groups a public matter. The Liberal Party (FDP) expressed an interest in a *Verbändegesetz* (a law concerning organized groups) akin to the Party Law of 1967: its purpose would be to strengthen the position of the individual *vis-à-vis* the group and to establish a legal requirement to pursue the common good. Adoption of similar ideas in the Christian Democratic Party's (CDU) Mannheim Declaration of 1975 and in the Social Democrat's long-term programme (OR'85) reflected a concern for the 'steering capacity' of the state apparatus and an attempt to increase the decision-making capacity and to strengthen the arbitrative role of the state.[7] More generally, corporatism has been seen as a method of integrating the state itself and organized groups. By recognizing certain groups and bringing them into a privileged, stable relationship of 'collusion' in particular policy areas the state apparatus would be able to imbue them with the idea of reciprocal interdependence and mutual rights and obligations. The basic difficulty was seen to be to establish a balance between the state apparatus and society, for the conception of the *Sozialstaat* could be interpreted to suggest both a *Verstaatlichung der Gesellschaft* (a spread of statism to society) and a *Vergesellschaftung des Staates* (a socialization of the state).

THE IDEA OF THE STATE AS A SOCIO-CULTURAL PHENOMENON

A major theme in continental European theories is that the state is more than simply the system of legal norms, the embodiment of sovereign authority or a collection of public services. It is viewed as a socio-cultural phenomenon, an expression of 'modernity'. As such, the state is conceived of as a form of *Gesellschaft;* it possesses the characteristics of a deliberately created, formal and complex organization dedicated to a specific end or function (Poggi, 1978). The state is held to be the product of an advanced and sophisticated process of social differentiation and of what some Germans have liked to call *Wille zum Staat* (the will to put a state into being). For Max Weber its rational–legal authority structure reflected the 'rationalization of the world'. At the same time there was an unwillingness to see the state as just a convenience or contrivance.

Hegel was the first modern thinker to explore systematically the connection between culture and politics established in Montesquieu's work. His conception of the state as an ethical community related civil and political institutions and attitudes to dominant cultural forces. In his view the categories of *Geist* (the culture of a country or period) and *Bildung* (the process of moulding minds and characters with its contents) determined the two dimensions of political life: the structure of institutions, law and other social arrangements, and the subjective sentiments of men. On the one hand, he recognized that the unity of the state was differentiated and man-made (unlike the simple and natural unity of the *polis* where politics and culture had found a coherence centred on public affairs) and saw increasingly the importance of the 'subjective' freedom and particularity of society. On the other, identification with, and consciousness of, the state as an ethical community was the condition of that 'inner harmony', 'happy consciousness' and identity of public and private ends that is 'real' freedom. This non-utilitarian, non-instrumental conception of the state was also apparent in Heller's (1963) argument that: 'By his will or otherwise the individual finds himself implicated in the state with vitally significant levels of his whole being.... The state organization reaches deep into the personal existence of man, forms his being....' Similar viewpoints were put forward by twentieth-century French theorists like Debré, Jouvenel and Weil. According to Debré (1947, p. 30): 'The state is not an inert body but a living being, because it is the expression of a community living like a person, living like a family: the nation.'

Drawing on the work of Jellinek, and influenced by Hegelian as well as neo-Kantian thought, Max Weber identified two aspects of the state besides its territorial character. The state was seen as an *Apparat* that depended on *staatspolitische* groups like the army and civil service. These groups, concerned with the power, prestige and integrity of the state, were in danger of generating *Machtstaat* conceptions. The state was viewed also as a community, a *Staatsvolk,* in which *kulturpolitische* groups like teachers, writers, artists and journalists sought to promote and maintain cultural values (for Weber, associated with the nation). While Weber argued that the power of the state had intrinsic value, he stressed its responsibility as a means to the realization of the values associated with *Kultur* (like 'rationality', one of his frequent terms). The values of *Kultur* were not identified with the idea of the state; they resided in the nation, an example of a *Gemeinschaft* (Beetham, 1974). However, though the state was seen as a *Gesellschaft,* an association developed consciously for particular purposes, it was deeply and inextricably involved with realising sentiments of solidarity. The problem of reconciling *Herrschaft* (domination) and *Genossenschaft* (fellowship) has been a central one for theories of the state and has given rise to a concern for what Germans call *Staatspflege.* Cultivation or encouragement of state-consciousness (*Staatsbewusstsein*) is supposed to be the purpose of political education, of public buildings, of memorials and festivals and even of the constitution. Machin (1977, p. 110) has emphasized the importance of the 'presence', style and symbolism that surrounds the French prefect as the representative of the state. From an idealistic (and sometimes romantic) perspective the state was often viewed as a new source of community in a modern differentiated society of utilitarian relations; it provided a spiritual bond that would transform capitalists and workers alike into servants of 'the whole'. Schmoller looked back to the conception of the socially conscious, paternalist and bureaucratic state; Weber looked forward (less hopefully) to bourgeois altruism, to leadership by an individual who would ensure dominance of the political over the bureaucratic and the 'class-related' economic.

The effects of an historical and intellectual tradition of the state on socio-political attitudes are complex and important. The idea of the state can be a source of both high effective commitment (notably at elite levels where there is more intense socialization of its values) and strong disaffection. Empirical research has shown little interest in discovering whether actors in political events and 'ordinary' people are conscious of the state and, if so, with what consistency and meaning they use the term (but see Allum, 1973). There are clearly differences in degree of cultural disposition to recognize the idea of the state and in the saliency and nature of cognition and affect at elite and mass levels. The saliency of state-consciousness is likely to be reinforced, for example, in those instances like France where the state itself has acted as a primary agency of nation-building, giving form to and amplifying a common experience of solidarity. One would also expect the nature of that consciousness to be shaped by the character of the relationship between the idea of the state and the type of society (see Chapter 2). Another important factor is the relationship between the idea of the state and discord. There is not, however, a simple determinate relationship between the two. On the one hand, state-building appears to be a conscious product of the recognition of the dangers of social strife (as in seventeenth-century France). The idea of the state is often adopted as an integrative phenomenon (as, for example, by Italy after unification). However, in Sweden state-building was partly a product of external threat and partly a practical, pragmatic response to specific problems of government. No attempt was made to give grand theoretical expression to the requirements of state-building. On the other hand, state-building and 'stateness' may themselves generate dissent, reflected, for example, in a marked antipathy to *étatisme*. The idea of the state and its expression can have marked effects on the character of political opposition; it provokes the emergence of centralized structures, aggressive styles (a more 'virulent' Marxism, for instance) and a theoretical concern with the demystification of the ideology of the state. There is a willingness to engage in direct action, as in May 1968 in France, and extra-parliamentary opposition, as in West Germany in the late 1960s, directed against the state itself. 'Anti-system' oppositions on both left and right become more highly structured than in Britain and the United States where, in the absence of the idea and institution of the state as an object of disaffection, there are fewer problems associated with assimilating dissent.

It is instructive to compare the importance for British trade unions of the Trades Union Congress Parliamentary Committee during the

Lib./Lab. period in pre-1914 Britain with the wide gulf that opened up between, on the one hand, French parliamentary parties and, on the other, trade unions influenced by the revolutionary syndicalism of Pelloutier and Sorel. Force and violence have played a prominent role within French democratic movements compared with the parliamentary habits of Britain. The French labour movement evolved in the context of a state apparatus whose 'repressiveness' seemed apparent in the Le Chapelier Law, which forbade the right of association, and in the Napoleonic Penal Code of 1810. Even after the Waldeck-Rousseau Law of 1884 it was possible for the state to continue regulating union development. The effect, combined with memories of the great battles of 1848 and 1871, was to confirm the hostility of the workers to the 'bourgeois' state. From its origins before Marx, French socialism was divided between the *étatisme* of Louis Blanc and the anti-*étatisme* of Proudhon and Blanqui which could be traced back to Babeuf in the 1790s. Besides this influence from bohemian, romantic insurrectionists like Babeuf and Blanqui there were the ideas of the anarchist Bakunin, hero of revolutionary uprisings all over Europe.[8] Syndicalists were influenced by his notion of state and society as opposite principles: the state was viewed as repressive and artificial, the negation of all liberty; society embodied harmonious relationships, freedom and true dignity. The French state represented faith in intellect and reason, in the ideas of Descartes, Voltaire, Saint-Simon and Comte. Correspondingly, political opposition was influenced by anti-intellectualism and Romanticism, by the revolt against reason in favour of intuition, impulse and existence (Ridley, 1970). Thus Sorel, himself a product of the *École Polytechnique,* struggled against the individualism and rationalism of the state itself. Seeing it as an association of intellectuals, what Thibaudet called the *République des Professeurs,* he demanded a true workers' movement without socialist intellectuals like the neo-Hegelian Lassalle in Germany or the neo-Kantian Jaurès in France. In his view these intellectuals were too preoccupied with state power. For Sorel (1950) the state was the agency of effective social control and, consequently, the contested prize in every historic instance of social conflict. Its explicit function was the exercise of force, and 'the object of force is to impose a certain social order in which the minority governs'. Syndicalism was, then, a revolt not merely against the idea of the state as the guardian of bourgeois interests but against the state apparatus as such. In that sense it was anarchistic, emphasizing in Sorel's concepts of violence and myth (for the working class, of the general strike) an economic rather than a political idea of revolution. Moreover, a shared perception of the crisis of the bourgeois state after 1906 gave royalists like Charles Maurras, Catholic corporatists (from those influenced by the anti-Semitism of Édouard Drumont to those influenced by the social teachings of La Tour du Pin), and revolutionary syndicalists like Édouard Berth something (however negative) in common: a strong anti-capitalism and a disgust with the bourgeois state. Georges Valois intended to unite Maurras and Sorel, the monarchy and the working class against this common enemy. The product was the *Cercle Proudhon* which brought together, for a time, royalists and syndicalists.

The idea of the state influences the character of political opposition in some interesting ways. The nature of its effect will, nevertheless, vary with the institutional referents of the notion of the state (whether it is identified narrowly with the bureaucracy or, more broadly, seen to incorporate representative institutions) and with the nature of the regime itself (its representative character, centralization, scope for freedom of association, etc.) Furthermore, class critiques of the bourgeois or 'capitalist' state are only one aspect of disaffection with the state itself. Another form of attack, which may or may not be related to class analysis, is the radical democratic critique of the hierarchical implications of the state apparatus and its claims to embody a unique purpose or peculiar form of authority. This argument for participation as the central value of politics is likely to be associated with a critique of the state as part of a general concern about the 'anomie' and 'disintegration' of modern social life. From Tönnies to the New Left the state has been characterized as the most dangerous form of impersonality, which is destroying social and political creativity and needs to be offset or replaced by new forms of solidarity in society itself (for example, workers' associations).

Exploration of British political language reveals very little state-consciousness. When the term is used to refer to certain political objects it contains ironical or pejorative overtones. One needs, of course, to distinguish between approving, 'neutral' and deprecatory use of, for example, *Parteienstaat* or *Verbändestaat* in continental discussions. In Britain, however, it is difficult to come across approving or neutral uses of the term. Many are proud of the British 'welfare state', but compared with its continental equivalents like *Sozialstaat* it not only has a narrower economic meaning but also implies a relationship of dependence and a lack of personal responsibility and initiative. In contrast to the continental European tradition of the 'social state' it has proved more difficult in the British context to extend the concept of citizenship (in so far as this concept can be said to exist at all in Britain) to incorporate social and economic rights. 'Police state' or 'corporate state' are almost exclusively used to denote loss of freedom: 'law and order' or 'tripartism' are the preferred British terms but their meaning is much more restricted. In the absence of the idea of the state as a cultural symbol the emphasis falls on the Crown as the focus of shared rituals and ceremony, pomp and theatricality. The monarchy as person and institution represents an exclusively cultural symbol of unity, one that is able to defuse ideological and class conflicts by representing the traditional affective ties of community. By contrast, as the cultural expression of a distinct set of political ideas, the notion of the state may prove a more divisive symbol of community.

In important ways empire served also as a collective inspiration for unity in a multi-national British society where, apart from the Crown, there was no clearly articulated ideology of the Union. However, there was only vague, confused thought about the empire that was acquired more by accident and good fortune than by conscious design. The technique of indirect rule used during the unification of England and of the United Kingdom itself was extended to empire: a preference for 'informal' empire, for rule through a co-opted civilian patriciate, for collaborators and clientelism, rather than for centralized, bureaucratic and militarized rule (Bulpitt, 1978). In contrast to Britain's narrowly legal, imperial unity and reliance on internal mechanisms of self-government, the unitary *étatiste* tradition of France led it at first to a policy of assimilation in the Roman tradition. Colonial people were to become French citizens by acquiring French civilization. With extension of the empire this policy was modified to a more limited one of association. A native elite was to be transformed into French citizens and to administer the colonies on behalf of, or rather as, France. The French empire was a reflection of the idea of the state.

In the absence of the idea of the state British elite culture displays a reluctance to give leadership, undertake development functions or exploit technical knowledge. These deep inhibitions about exercising 'public power' are the product in part of a liberal ideology that emphasizes diffusion of authority rather than the importance of instruments of state policy and in part of the absence of a Roman-law tradition which lends a rationalist, technical and authoritative style to administration. There is an addiction to crisis avoidance and group consent rather than the self-confidence that comes from the notion of the indivisible, unitary character of 'public power' and its inherent right to regulate in the general interest. Unwillingness to plan is associated with a liberal distrust of government that purports to identify the needs of the community before the community itself has recognized them. Societies with a state tradition have a view of 'public power' that enables a more creative use of crisis, a view that is in large part a reaction to past experiences of crisis. The remarkable aspect of British elite socialization is its association with society rather than the state. It is an essentially informal, unregulated process which creates an old boy network. This network represents the impact on the British power structure of social institutions like the public schools and Oxbridge as opposed to that of the idea and institution of the state. As the notion of the state and its requirements did not help to shape educational curricula and methods, these social institutions were able to generate their own higher-education ideology in the nineteenth century, and one that was legitimized by the civil service reforms of the 1870s (Armstrong, 1973). The intelligentsia based on these institutions was to play a decisive role. It possessed neither the obsequiousness and 'placemanship' of a bureaucratic, state-conscious intelligentsia nor the rebelliousness of a state-alienated, 'free-floating' intelligentsia. Conforming critically, its criticisms were generally directed at industrial and commercial values. Its educational formula helped forge an accommodation of landed gentry and industrial bourgeoisie by emphasizing the creation of the 'gentleman' rather than the technician.

The character of class attitudes in Britain was also influenced by the absence of the idea of the state. On the one hand, there was not the phenomenon of disaffection from a powerful 'repressive' state apparatus whose autonomy of the holders of economic power could be questioned if existing elites sought to identify their interests with those of the state itself. The seventeenth-century settlement was seen to confirm the historic rights of 'free-born' Englishmen and to have created a political system that was adaptable, even perhaps accessible. On the other hand, the absence of bold initiative on the part of government helped to cement polarization in the industrial and political systems. Social policy appeared to be a matter of concessions based on class compromise rather than flowing from, and achieving coherence in terms of, a conception of the inherent responsibility of the state to provide public services and a framework of regulation for conduct. Accordingly, experience of a relatively 'unbridled' capitalism gave it a bad reputation, created a powerful and isolated working-class culture and undermined willingness to co-operate both in industry and in politics. Britain acquired a peculiar class structure: the obstinacy and distrust associated with attitudes of 'them' and 'us' were not directed at the state but at bastions of privilege and exclusiveness associated with society.

NOTES

1   The abstract, rational character of continental European constitutions appears to contrast with the nature of the American constitution. 'Independence' forced the Americans, unlike the English, to give formal justification to the rights of the individual in terms of abstract, universal, natural law. Nevertheless, in practice these rights were seen as historic rights in the tradition of English dissent (and common law). In contrast to the abstract proclamations of continental constitutions, the emphasis was on continuity and the practical character of statements of rights.

2   On the 'institutional Darwinism' of the Third Reich, see Schoenbaum (1966); on the negative role of the NSDAP and failure to establish clearcut party primacy except in isolated instances, see Orlow (1973).

On the dualism of the regime which combined 'prerogative-state' features as a response to the Nazi political movement with the legalism of the *Normenstaat,* see Fraenkel (1941). For a different view, that the permanent remodelling of institutions and an unregulated pluralism of new agencies make an answer to the question about the nature of the Nazi regime impossible, see Mommsen (1966).

3   Jurists have stressed that a clear delineation of state and society depends upon a definition of the juristic persons of public law. A simple criterion like the exercise of sovereign power has proved increasingly inadequate in the context of new agencies (especially in planning) that seek to 'concert' their actions with private interests. Demichel (1978) offered three criteria (without clarifying whether one or all three were necessary to qualify as a juristic person in public law): the organization is financed exclusively by the state; the state 'controls' the organization; and/or the organization is pledged to the principle of 'state neutrality'.

4   It must be emphasized that Marxist recognition of the need to revise the theory of the state in the light of changing circumstances produced an earlier recognition of the relative autonomy of the state. From the 1890s to 1934 the 'Austro-Marxists' developed an outlook (distinct from that of the Frankfurt School) that reflected their personal political engagement in the Austrian socialist movement and the native strength of positivism. Their outlook derived from Kant and Mach as well as from Marx and found its expression in an empirical sociology that challenged the formal rationalism of Kelsen's legal positivism. Otto Brunner (who symbolized the Austrian Socialist Party between 1920 and 1934) argued that the growing complexity of the class structure meant that the state could no longer act as an

instrument of class dictatorship and that there was an 'equilibrium between class forces' by which the relative autonomy of the state was enhanced. Its actions might be deflected in one direction or another by various political forces. According to Karl Renner in 1916, state penetration of the economy had an independent dynamism that was transforming capitalist society. Renner, the intellectual representative of the party after 1945, went on to develop a view of the state as a socially necessary device for rule and to advocate the idea of the *sozialer Rechtsstaat* (Bottomore and Goode, 1978).

5   According to Engels (quoted in Miliband, 1977, p. 81): 'By way of exception, however [to the state as instrument of domination of the ruling class], periods occur in which the warring classes balance each other so nearly that the state power, as ostensible mediator, acquires, for the moment, a certain degree of independence of both.' He went on to produce a formidable list of exceptions: the absolute monarchies of the seventeenth and eighteenth centuries, France's First and Second Empires and Bismarck's German Empire.

6   For a sophisticated Marxist analysis of the absolutist state, see Anderson (1974). He focuses on the connections between absolutism and the interests of the nobility, but in a Marxist fashion his class analysis precludes recognition of the independent role of the monarchy as an institution in its own right.

7   These two documents illustrated the different CDU and SPD conceptions of the state and their different reasons for strengthening it. The CDU tended towards the traditional view of a neutral state that stands over the particular interests of society and guards the general interest, the SPD towards the idea of a democratically organized state (expressed in the Freiburg 'school' and by Adolf Arndt) which is the only available instrument for major social innovation and is, moreover, able to express unorganized interests. Both parties emphasized the notion of a division of labour in the democratic process between the parties as the foundation and organizers of the general interest (the state) and the groups (*Verbände*) which pursue particularistic interests.

8   Anarchism did not flourish in the British labour movement and became no more than an important subsidiary element during periods of industrial unrest (Quail, 1978). It did not produce theorists of the eminence and notoriety of Bakunin and Proudhon, 'philosophers' of action like Blanqui who inspired by deed rather than word, or the same passion for violence and, occasionally, nihilism. British anarchism rested on an idealism of free association and voluntary co-operation, a society organized without coercion and hierarchy.

chapter nine | the idea of the state and democracy

Compatibility between the unity of power (the state) and the dualism government–opposition (democracy) is the serious problem of the democratic state.

Michel Debré (1947, p. 202)

This study has attempted to define state as an ideal type in order to unravel some of the complexity which surrounds the word and its use and to gain a clearer insight into the way in which its features derived originally from the rationalistic search for political order. It is also necessary to offer a critical analysis of the positive and negative aspects of state as a theoretical term, to look at all its facets and recognize that it has functioned simultaneously as both a 'problem-solving' and 'problem-creating' concept. State is a descriptive/evaluative term that refers to a range of features in political life and puts them into some kind of ideological perspective. The concept of the state involves considerable ambiguity. The state itself, to which the concept refers, is not just a legal apparatus that is designed to hold off threats to public order. In addition it defines 'disorder', creates 'disorder' and presses its right to suppress that 'disorder'. There is therefore no consensus that to talk about the state is to talk in a commendatory way; and if the concept state is used in a commendatory manner, there is no consensus either about what precisely is being commended in terms of empirically detectable features of political life (what are its institutional reference points?) or about what is distinctive about the state (its force, sovereignty or function?). State is a contested concept and, therefore, involves problems of meaning and application. These problems are

made more difficult by the absence of a clear principle that would identify the source of contest: for example, does the issue of whether the state
is to be understood in terms of its force, sovereignty or function arise
from within the concept of the state itself or from contending values and
perspectives that are external to the concept? State is an 'open-textured'
concept whose boundaries are disputed or ignored.

There are different views about the scope of the concept. For Duguit
the state is simply an overt and therefore observable phenomenon, an
Apparat whose individual agents can be identified; for Hauriou it is a
'superior' instrument of control, one that imposes itself by overt and
covert means; while for Gramsci it is hegemonic and reduces possibilities of dissent by manipulating in a comprehensive manner beliefs and
perceptions of self-interest. In addition to the problematic character of
the power of the state, the nature of its relationship to society has evoked
very different views about the scope of the concept. German theorists like
Hegel and French theorists such as Hauriou and Saleilles have seen the
state as society envisaged as a whole (thus Scelle held it to be the most
integrated and elevated form of political society); others have viewed it as
society envisaged under a certain aspect (for example, as a reality of the
judicial order); while Duguit has identified it as just a specific grouping
of society. There are also differences in the kind of questions asked of the
concept, differences that depend on the cognitive interests of the theorist. In the positivist and technocratic perspectives the state is regarded in
instrumental terms as a device for the control of nature. Weber and others
inspired by Dilthey and the *Kulturstaat* tradition thought of the state as a
device for consensus through mutual communication of shared meanings,
a device for comprehending the world. Those in the Hegelian tradition
saw the state as offering the possibility of a critical, emancipatory self-
reflection as a result of which man could attain autonomy, responsibility
and consensus. State is an 'open-ended' concept that will support a variety
of rationally sustainable arguments.

The formal definition of the state that has been proposed in this
study does not represent a consensus meaning or a core descriptive
meaning of the concept. It has not been formulated as a neutral,
'value-free' definition that is supposed to avoid normative and
ideological engagement, for characterizing societies is intimately
connected with appraising them. As an ideal type it offers a continental
European representation of what a perfectly formally ordered society

would look like. There is a range of views of the state from various ideological positions, views that are indissolubly linked to contrasting conceptions of human nature. A determinate and specific conception of the state can only arise from within such a position. When the formal concept of the state is interpreted, it is likely to yield numerous irreconcilable views of the state, views that are closely related to conservative, liberal, social democratic and Marxist varieties of political thought and that are embodied in different forms of social life.

STATE AS A 'PROBLEM-CREATING' CONCEPT

The reputation of concepts can suffer from the past company that they have kept. The idea of the state has attracted writers who feared the 'modernity' that was associated with industrialization and urbanization—the alienation, loss of identity and social disintegration of 'mass' society. They saw in the notion of the state the guarantee of a politics of civility, one that would defend the traditional values of *Gemeinschaft* (hierarchy, mutual dependence, deference). In the light of such a literature, which was prominent in Germany from the 1880s to the early 1930s (for example, Spann 1921; Spengler, 1924) and continued to appear (for example, Weber, 1951; Hamel, 1971 and 1974), it was scarcely surprising that the idea of the state appeared the antithesis to liberal democracy, the embodiment of the authoritarian mentality. The historical evidence provided by the collapse of the Weimar Republic and of Austria's First Republic in the early 1930s, as well as the long-standing difficulties that beset the French Third Republic, seemed to confirm this view. Equally important, this view fitted in with the peculiar liberal ideology of the Anglo-American tradition in which the priority afforded to individualistic and group interests and to fragmentation of power over collective interests appeared diametrically opposed to the notion of the state. Anglo-American distrust of the concept of the state was heightened by the effects of two world wars.

The theme of this chapter is that there is no historically inevitable or logical relationship between adherence to a concept of the state and rejection of democracy, that they are, in important ways, mutually reinforcing. Nevertheless, it would be foolish to overlook the peculiar kind of problems that have beset 'state' societies. In the first place, the state tradition is replete with internal disputes which can be traced back to its ideological ambiguity, its openness to reformulation and reinterpretation. As Edmund Burke noted: 'In the word *State* I conceive there is much ambiguity. The state is sometimes used to signify the *whole commonwealth,* comprehending all its orders, with the several privileges belonging to each. Sometimes it signifies only the higher and ruling part of the commonwealth, which we commonly call *the Government.*' Correspondingly, a central dispute in German intellectual history has been about the relationship between, and the relative weight of, *Staat als Herrschaft* (domination) and an *Apparat* of power on the one hand and, on the other, *Staat als Genossenschaft* (association or fellowship) in which the stress is upon communal identification as a *Staatsnation* (see the different views of Krüger, 1966, and von der Gablentz, 1965). The constitutive elements of the idea of the state are relatively fluid, in the sense that they can be combined with diverse other values (nationalism, socialism, democracy, authoritarianism) to achieve various ideological formulations. The issues which surrounded its reinterpretation to suit the changing circumstances and new perceptions of democratization proved a source of faction: some (for example, Forsthoff, 1971) wished to use traditional doctrine for the purposes of formal control in order to drive out new forms of dissent; others (for example, Herzog, 1971) preferred a non-commital, ambivalent stance; while Häberle (1970) and Suhr (1975) sought a more creative ideological shift. As a source of such conflicts the idea of the state could undermine the very search for community and for the depoliticization of the essential bases of community that it was supposed to promote. In other words, its achievement of depoliticization remained conditional upon a degree of comparative satisfaction with the condition of the polity.

An attempt to identify the common, formal dimensions of the concept through an analysis of its usage will not eliminate continuing metaphysical disputes about the nature and function of state as a highly generalizing concept. The sheer variability and complexity that are contained within the state tradition have made attempts to define in simple terms the 'uniqueness' of the state problematic and prone to reductionism: to Marx it was the repressive instrument of the ruling economic class; to Weber, the monopoly of the legitimate use of coercion; to Durkheim, the organ of moral discipline, one that thought and acted on behalf of society; to Austin, the embodiment of sovereignty; to Duguit, a great 'public-service' corporation; to Bendix and Lipset, the formal institutions for the distribution and exercise of power. One major dispute concerned the purposes of the state which, in empirical terms, proved wide and various over space and time: from the 'Malthusian' state of the Third to the 'modernizing' state of the Fifth French Republic; from the paternal 'welfare state' of Imperial Germany to the participatory 'social state' of the Federal Republic. While German scholars have distinguished between the three 'state purposes' of law, might and welfare, they have disagreed about their relative importance. A state tradition is not necessarily associated with 'bigger' government than is to be found in 'stateless' societies or with fewer limits (material or procedural) on collective action. It is, however, accompanied by a widespread sense of the legitimacy of public action (action that is independent of party ideology) and by a willingness to define 'public power' as distinctive and to exercise it authoritatively. The idea of the state institutionalizes a concern with particular purposes in a vivid way and lends prestige to them by endowing the instruments of these purposes with a distinctive character and significance beyond the requirements of political accountability—as the embodiment of reason and public service applied to a general interest that is more than the sum of partisan interests. Similar characteristics are apparent within the culture of the elite bearers of the state tradition—a sense of independence, prestige and unique purpose. Historically and comparatively speaking, *Ordnungspolitik* has been the central purpose of the state as idea and institution; the 'regulatory' state is legitimized by the need for a framework of 'order' for society. Democratization and the pressures of an industrialized society have produced both the twentieth-century conception of the 'public-service' state (which is seen, to a considerable extent, as an extension of *Ordnungspolitik*) and, much more controversially, the shift towards a conception of a 'developmental' role for the state in shaping social and economic development.

A further dispute arose from different views on the 'proper' institutional expression of state norms and from reactions against the conception and practice of the *Verwaltungsstaat*. The traditional association of the idea of the state with the administration reflected Napoleon's creation of the modern administrative state as the machinery established by the sovereign nation for its own government and the management of its public services. Officials were no longer private agents but instruments of a 'public power'. They were personally responsible for their actions and applied technical criteria of effective management. The administration formed an ideal basis for the notion of the depersonalization of state power (Oppenheimer, 1926), while the concept of the state appealed to cherished administrative ideals of (and self-interest in) autonomy and professional distinctiveness. In other words, the concept of state was tuned to the professional interests of increasingly important administrative groups (and related academic groups) which became carriers of its values. Thus in Germany the conception of the *Rechtsstaat* served, from one point of view, as a legitimation of official autonomy; from another, as an ideology of group self-interest. Law and legal training formed an ideal basis for the claim to depersonalization of administrative power. Other elite groups sought also legitimation for their professional interests in the concept of the state: the military in the *Machtstaat*, the academic elite in the *Kulturstaat*. The different forms of identification of these traditional groups with the notion of the state reflected in part, and also exacerbated, problems of political accommodation to the emerging social forces that were generated by industrialization, technological progress and urbanization.

This historical process of identification of traditional elites with the idea of the state has led Anglo-American and even some continental European theorists to assume an inevitable opposition between the notion of the state and democracy and, consequently, to identify democracy with 'statelessness'. The two ideas have been regarded as either incompatible or subordinate one to another. Bracher (1968, p. 2) writes with reference to German history:

In every case except that of 1945 the concept of the state has been clearly accorded priority over that of democracy. The decisions of 1848 and 1866–71, the formation of the 'semi-democracy' of 1918 and finally the proclamations of solidarity of 1914 and 1933 all illustrated the preference accorded to the organization and efficiency of the state over the requirements and desires of the individual and of society.

Non-political or only narrowly political conceptions of the *Kulturstaat, Machtstaat* and *Rechtsstaat,* which emphasized community, power, order and efficiency, left room for only a restricted idea of freedom that stressed unity and integration over the political liberty of the individual, the supreme right of the state against the individual. These views, which were developed as a self-conscious reaction to English and, particularly, French Revolutionary ideas, put a great strain on the concept of freedom. By contrast, the French Third Republic was gradually (but not completely) able to capture the state apparatus itself and to establish a political conception of the 'republican state'. It was, however, much less successful in curbing the independence of the administration; there remained a gap between the idea of 'divisive' parties which operated through the Assembly and the 'unity' of the administration, with its more absolutist modes of thought.

The political weaknesses of the concept of the state have been a source of fragility to 'state' societies. On the one hand, its emphasis on the development of a logical system of efficient public institutions which were characterized by their autonomy and coherence produced a degree of administrative institutionalization and executive competence that was functional to good government. On the other, these very characteristics of autonomy and coherence led to a downgrading of the prestige of participative mechanisms that were concerned to increase the adaptability of administrative institutions but at the same time threatened to reduce their autonomy and coherence and to increase their internal complexity and hence problems of management. Political institutionalization tended to fall behind administrative institutionalization. As a result, 'state' societies were vulnerable to direct action and 'surge movements' (Kesselman, 1967). They did not have what Weber referred to as the greater 'elasticity' of the Anglo-American democracies. Defenders of the state administration emphasized the importance of depoliticization, so that the effectiveness of government would not be undermined by an 'overloading' produced by the combination of increased political demands with the cross-pressures of group interest (Maspetiol, 1957). Consequently, institutional arrangements could fail to incorporate the kind of responsiveness to changing expectations that allows for the maintenance of political consent. 'State' societies became vulnerable to changes within the 'input' side of politics, particularly the emergence of new social forces and ideologies. Examples were provided by the attack that was unleashed on the 'bureaucratic state' by a sudden amalgam of disenchanted interests in France in May 1968; by the attack that emerged during the period of the Grand Coalition in Western Germany (1966–9) on the 'state of the established parties' from the Extra-Parliamentary Opposition; by a nervousness about wildcat strikes in those societies like Western Germany where the fragility of institutional arrangements for 'social partnership' has proved apparent; and in the 1970s by the political ecology movement with its concern about the nuclear and technocratic state. France has been pictured in terms of the coexistence of 'limited authoritarianism' with 'potential insurrection against authority' (Hoffmann, 1963). The product has been mounting pressure of an extra-institutional and often violent nature that leads on to revolutionary crisis as a creative and reforming force. While Western Germany has been more successful in developing participative mechanisms, delicate problems arise in all 'state' societies from the need to maintain some sort of balance between, on the one hand, interest articulation and aggregation mechanisms and, on the other, the de-politicizing character of the idea of the state.

Traditionally the state tradition was associated with a rather narrow definition of the functions of political parties and legislatures. The legislature was specialized in the legislative and budgetary functions through its committee system, while the parties were seen to be articulators of sectional interests rather than aggregators of interests. Emphasis on the autonomy of the executive power made for great difficulties in the establishment of parliamentary government. Even when it was established there was not the same fusion of executive and legislative powers as was to be found in Britain: continuing autonomous administration by boards subject to the law led to a very delimited idea of ministerial responsibility in Sweden, while both the Netherlands and France's Fifth Republic operated an 'incompatability rule' and recruited a sizeable proportion of ministers from the public service. In Sweden, the Netherlands and Belgium reference was to the two 'powers of the state' (*statsmakter* in Swedish): on the one hand, the legislative power, which was exercised by Parliament and embodied the 'democratic' principle through free elections; on the other, the executive power, which rested on the 'authoritarian' principle and was expressed in the hierarchy of offices (for example, in the Netherlands this hierarchy extended from monarch through provincial governor to municipal burgomaster, the latter two being appointed by the central government). The roles of parties and legislatures have, therefore, rested on quite different theoretical premises from those of their Anglo-American equivalents. In Britain and the United States the notion of party competition for office, and assumption of responsibility in office, is deeply rooted. The French conception of the 'one and indivisible' republic served by contrast to downgrade parties as 'sectional' institutions (intermediaries). However, the revolutionary origins of the French Assembly gave it a legitimacy that proved more difficult to secure in Prussia or Imperial Germany where the *Reichstag* and political parties faced the entrenched role and ideological legitimacy of both the bureaucracy and the military. As in France, elections of parliaments were not elections of governments, and parties were oriented to particular clienteles rather than to the requirements of majority government. The result was unstable coalition government that was characterized by political opportunism, a phenomenon falsely attributed either to proportional representation and multipartism (typically by Anglo-American scholars) or to the 'odious' role of parties (typically by continental European scholars). It was less often recognized that this instability reflected a weakness of party that was generated by institutional arrangements. Only with the Bonn Republic and the Fifth French Republic have elections emerged as a choice between alternative governing formations. Parties, much more in Austria and Western Germany than France, have served to accommodate the state apparatus and society and have thereby emerged as stabilizing factors (Dyson, 1977). The legacy of distrust of bureaucratic claims to autonomy does, however, find its expression in a deep party 'penetration' that influences appointments and promotions within the public bureaucracy. The notion of an autonomous executive power as opposed to one that emanated from, or was an agent of, the legislature had another implication for the role of the legislature. It meant that control over the use of executive power passed to administrative courts whose creation of a coherent system of public law proved a potent source of principles for the state.

The state tradition has exhibited other political weaknesses. In the first place, an emphasis on the disciplining requirements of political rule can lead to a neglect of the importance of vigorous 'politicking' for political morality. A one-sided view of politics encourages a belief in the possibility and desirability of a unified theory of the state as the precondition of political morality. Intolerance of dissent and conflict is associated with an unwillingness to accept the ambiguity of politics (Gallie, 1973). There are political risks involved in adherence to a coherent system of impersonal ideas about rule that are held to possess a peculiar binding force on the community. The result can be an unwillingness to accommodate new interests and a growing detachment from reality or a perceived requirement to force the world to conform to its pattern of ideas. Absolutist modes of thought, which insist on the internal logic of a system of ideas rather than assessing its costs, which pursue deductive processes of inference from basic premises to the point of dogmatic perfectionism, and which express a belief in the need for a unified theory of political rule are hostile to the liberal democratic method and the sensitive accommodation of interests. The danger lies in an apolitical conception of the state, which sees the state as a substitute for the activity of politics and is committed to an abstract cult of human values, or in a political conception of the state, which identifies politics with an activity of providing political order and ignores politicking. Political activity, indeed the ambiguous character of politics, cannot be wholly comprehended within the parameters provided by the idea of the state. A further political problem that is associated with the state tradition is produced by the tension between, on the one hand, its formal rationalism and depersonalization and, on the other, the Romantic conceptions that have sometimes issued from a concern with the character of its uniqueness and primacy. The heritage of political naivety and unreality bequeathed by German Romanticism has done much to discredit state as a concept.

The state tradition has also been accompanied by the development of a 'service' mentality of rigid self-effacement amongst its agents and, as a response to this cultural phenomenon, an obsessive intellectual interest in the problem of 'self'. The arts as well as social and political theories reflect the problems of individuality that appear to beset 'state' societies. One should beware of reducing the fluidity and multivalency of art by offering a simple-minded explanation of its character. The form and subject matter of art are affected by national traditions, such as the revolutionary tradition in France, as well as by a whole series of concrete social and political phenomena and events (like war, defeat, occupation, industrialization, urbanization and new political movements). Nevertheless, experience and observation of the weight and logic of abstract, impersonal, institutional arrangements in 'state' societies have an impact on the psychological environment of the artist. The international appeal of twentieth-century French Dadaism, surrealism and existentialism was based on a horrified reaction to the senselessness of war. However, the strongly programmatic manner and radical subjectivity of the continental European literary revolt owed much to the character of European societies. For example, French surrealism was the product of a very introverted artistic community which produced polemical manifestos in a manner that contrasted sharply with the gentleness and absence of fervent intensity of their British counterparts. It had its precursors in the poetic revolt of the French symbolists against a literary establishment that was centred on the official academies of art and hence formed a quasi-public institution devoted to dignified prose, wit and clear reasoning (Egbert, 1970). Artists came to enjoy political eminence or prestige, whether as 'officialized' artists or an *avant-garde* alienated from the official establishment. One common and powerful artistic motif has been the spiritual hollowness (Thomas Mann), the illusory character (Franz Kafka) and the 'viscous' or 'slimy' nature (Jean-Paul Sartre) of the external, 'respectable' world of impersonal functions and duties, in which man is a thing in a world of things and experiences 'inauthenticity' (Martin Heidegger) or what Sartre called *la nausée*. This fascination of the artist with 'inwardness' and his tortured relationship to the world of routine and efficiency were heightened by the impact of Sigmund Freud. His psychoanalysis was essentially a doctrine of the private man who was defending himself against public encroachments. Man's freedom was a psychic condition, the product of a struggle for inward self-mastery against the binding commitments of community. As an anti-authoritarian viewpoint, which saw salvation in strengthening the individual ego rather than in any constructive social theory, Freudianism represented as powerful an attack on the hollowness of state idealism as Marxism. Freud appeared to see the morality of the state as a mere rationalization of passion. A closer reading of Freud reveals an ambivalence in his view of the state: on the one hand, he provided a pejorative analysis of the state as a fearsome Juggernaut which crushed the vulnerable solitary conscience; on the other, he saw the state as a moral teacher and cultural guardian which confronted a rabble in need of strong leadership (Rieff, 1966). Freud's work, like the early work of Marx, illustrates the saturation of continental European thought by the concept of the state and, in the German-speaking world, by the Hegelian view of the state as the highest form of secular community. The artistic community registers similar problems of coming to terms with this state tradition—which may help explain the appeal to its members of these two thinkers.

The difficult relationship between intellectuals and the concept of the state was captured in the work of Friedrich Nietzsche. For Nietzsche the state was the haven of the 'Philistines', of the cult of normality. The Prussian state had perverted education by elevating the ideal of the 'useful official' above that of the 'complete man'. 'Culture and the state ... are antagonists. ... The one lives off the other, the one thrives at the expense of the other. All great cultural epochs are epochs of political decline' (Nietzsche, quoted in Holling-dale, 1973). D'Annunzio exhibited his contempt for official Italy at Fiume with even more practical effect and was joined by Mussolini for whom: 'The state is a tremendous machine that swallows living men and regurgitates dead ciphers...this is the great malediction that struck mankind...to create, over the centuries, the state, to find itself overcome, annihilated!' The French symbolist poet Paul Valéry gave eloquent expression to a characteristic mixture of fear and contempt amongst intellectuals in attitudes to the state:

The state is a huge, terrible, feeble being. Cyclops with notorious power and clumsiness, monstrous child of force and law, which have bred into it their contradictions. It lives only through a mob of small men who make its sluggish hands and feet move awkwardly and its great glass eye sees only *centimes* and milliards.

At the same time internal or external threats could lead intellectuals to take a different view of the state. For example, Valery recognised that: 'if the state is strong, it crushes us. If it is feeble, we perish'. In the early nineteenth century the German Romantic poet Novalis eulogised the idea of the state thus:

> The state should be visible everywhere.... The state is too little known to us. There should be heralds of the state, preachers of patriotism. The more spiritual the state is, the more it approaches the poetical, the more joyfully will every citizen, out of love for the beautiful great individual, limit his demand and be ready to make the necessary sacrifices.... Everything can become beautiful art.

The public and problematic role of the intelligentsia is one example of the tensions that beset 'state' societies. Another example is provided by the debate in France about the so-called 'stalemate' society, a term that has been derived from Stanley Hoffman's (1963) analysis of the Third Republic, popularized by Michel Crozier (1970) and adopted by the new Prime Minister Jacques Chaban-Delmas in 1969. The debate about the inefficiencies of the bureaucratic state has been associated with a whole series of 'anti-France' books which have praised the virtues of Anglo-American pluralism and decentralization and have identified the roots of French conservatism in the excessive role played by this centralized state. The French state is viewed as combining technocratic arrogance in certain elite corps with a pervasive bureaucratic inefficiency. This literature can be seen as part of a wider political attack on the centralized state, an attack that found its clearest expression in the events of May 1968. The thesis of the 'stalemate' society identifies the causes of France's long periods of *immobilisme,* which are punctuated by political crises and the emergence of charismatic leaders to push through 'overdue' reforms, in the dominance of an 'administrative model of action' whose style of authority is highly formalistic and hierarchical. The dominance of this model and its failure to handle effectively much more than routine matters are further explained in terms of highly ambivalent cultural attitudes towards authority: a desire to avoid face-to-face conflict by entrusting decisions to a higher authority complemented by an attempt to defend individualism behind a barricade of rules and social groupings which serve to neutralise the power of the centre. These cultural attitudes and the style of authority associated with them do not encourage negotiation and bargaining as methods of pragmatic, incremental resolution of policy, and they open up an enormous gap between authority and power. The case is overstated, in part because it views bureaucratic and non-bureaucratic modes of decision-making as rigid polar opposites. The opponents of the bureaucratic state ignore the ills of interest-group pluralism, which has been seen as a major source of stalemate in Anglo-American societies, as well as France's remarkable post-war development which stands up to any comparison. Moreover, in isolation the model gives a somewhat distorted picture of French patterns of decision-making and change: it overlooks the effects of institutionalized leadership, notably the presidency as a device for breaking stalemates under the Fifth Republic, and the amount of pluralistic bargaining that does exist. The debate, nevertheless, provides some valuable insights into the character of an administrative state whose methods of bringing about change (a combination of a regulatory interventionist administration, which claims a monopoly of rationality, with periodic crisis) are different from those of Britain or the United States.

An example of the problems of assimilating dissent in 'state' societies is provided by the West German debate, in which the intelligentsia has been much involved, about the so-called Radicals' Decree of 1972. The federal and state governments sought to exclude members of 'extremist' political organizations from entering or remaining in the public service. The intention was to counteract the strategy of 'marching through the institutions', which had been advocated by the Extra-Parliamentary Opposition as a more effective way of counteracting the hegemony of the state than electoral strategy. For some observers the new critical analysis of an excessively rigid and depoliticized West German political system which had emerged out of the neo-Marxist revival of the 1960s offered bright hopes of a democratization of society; for others it involved the revival of a cultural pessimism rather than a new, constructive, critical engagement; mystification and theoretical rigidity rather than a new realism; an activism and Utopianism arising out of dogmatic political principles rather than balanced political argument. Both views involved gross oversimplification that was the product of generalization from one aspect of a complicated left-wing spectrum. Historical factors influenced the character of the issue: elements of continuity in post-war Germany generated an 'anxiety syndrome' on the left about the right-wing potential in the political culture; while the comparative newness of the regime, memories of the fate of the Weimar Republic, and ideological competition from the East led to an insecurity at elite levels, an inability to establish a relaxed attitude to dissent and a preference for a 'militant' democracy. It was, however, the state tradition that shaped the form the issue took by making the problem continuously and politically visible, by creating an atmosphere of insecurity and pressures for intellectual conformity, and by confirming to left-wingers their view of a 'repressive' state that was resorting once again to *Angst* and the *Freund/Feind* distinction as methods of politics. The absence of a characteristically British flexibility in dealing with the problem is related to the enormous scope of the public service, which incorporates a vast variety of groups—for example, teachers at all levels (including university), railway and postal personnel, federal, state and local government employees—into the common requirements and detailed regulations of public-service law without making a distinction between those who exercise 'sovereign' functions and those who do not. Consequently, in the context of the idea of the state, the antagonism between the claims of the state itself to loyal service and the right to dissent is much more apparant. Second, the preference of the conception of the *Rechtsstaat* for a legal resolution of problems is reflected in the perfectionist search for tight legal regulation of the problem and the important role of the administrative courts in providing legal redress for aggrieved public-service applicants. Finally, the process of party 'penetration' of administrative institutions creates a danger that the established parties may begin to see it as 'their' state, so that criticism of them becomes criticism of the state itself; career prospects may become bound up with party loyalty.

Controversy has focused particularly on the meaning and implications of the depoliticizing character of the idea of the state—depoliticizing in two senses. Because it rests on the importance of the analytical distinction between state and society, the concept of the state defines and delimits the proper scope of political rule. There are, however, contrasting views about the importance of this distinction and about where and how it should be drawn. Second, state is a concept of political rule that defines the proper scope of politicking. It suggests that in certain policy areas like the law, administrative organization or currency management methods other than those of interest accommodation are appropriate to the harmonization of conflicting views. There are different conceptions of theproper scope of politicking. Individual theorists, therefore, have taken more or less political views of the state, which could be politicizing in one sense, for example by suggesting an extension of the area of political rule, and simultaneously depoliticizing in another sense, by advocating a reduction of politicking.

One source of a perceived threat to the individual from the authoritarian implications of the idea of the state is the emphasis on the notion of the state as 'the most integrated form of political society'. This emphasis creates an impression of internal homogeneity and of a systematic web of interconnections in politics. It becomes possible to see each part of society as dominated by the state in the interests of the total system. The result is an intellectual outlook which attributes the impotence of the individual to a well organized system of social and political control rather than to the accidental character of life and the complex interplay of diverse forces.

The authoritarian implications of the state tradition follow from the assumption that the concept of the state or a particular theory of the state offer a 'master idea' in terms of which politics is, or ought to be, fully understood and conducted. This assumption stems from a single preoccupation in politics and lends an impression of consistency and coherence to politics. Politics no longer appears to be a variegated network of parallels and contrasts, and the moral sense that one expects from a concept of political rule is no longer submerged in the texture of political life. The pattern of political thought is overschematic, the moral vision too heavily insistent. There is a tendency to proceed from the abstract to the concrete and to have too little patience with the untidiness of politicking. Political situations are evolved intellectually from the moral consciousness and are only indirectly the product of observation. A rigid definition of the requirements of citizenship and consequent intolerance for diversity replaces a willingness to accept that political rule can, and should, be characterized by an interweaving of themes. The search for a unitary theory of political rule accompanies a tendency to argue that moral principles are contingent on effective political rule and to view these principles as an emanation of the idea of the state. There is a reluctance to recognize that the counterpart in political ideas to a vigorously politicking society of competing interests is a variety of theories about the proper character of political rule, and that a vigorously politicking society, which implies a tolerance for a plurality of values and of perceptions of reality, is as much a precondition of political morality as the abstract commands of the state.

Much of the elevated moral tone of continental European politics stems from a highly developed awareness of the logically independent character of political rule and politicking and of the need, which has been reinforced by experience of challenge to existing institutions, to discipline politicking by emphasis on the requirements of political rule. However, a prescriptive disposition to belittle politicking has discouraged attempts both to map the interaction between different theories of the state and to analyse their complex relationship to institutional arrangements and political practice as legitimating formulae. In the case of the Bonn Republic (Dyson, 1979) it would be helpful to compare and contrast the changing roles of politicizing theories like the *Parteienstaat* and the *Sozialstaat* (which have acted as legitimating formulae for party 'penetration' of public institutions and for participation) with depoliticizing theories like the neo-liberal state (which endows the Federal Bank with autonomy in currency management) and the *Rechtsstaat* (from which follows the major role of the Federal Constitutional Court in the resolution of partisan conflicts). German academic life has, nevertheless, been rent by a polemical dispute whose origins reside in an unwillingness to tolerate complexity and ambiguity in ideas of political rule. On the one hand, there have been those like Offe (1972) who have emphasized the importance of the 'steering capacity' of the state—that is, of its capacity, in terms of either technique or mobilization of popular support, to effect its distinctive purposes in the face of the restrictions that are presented by powerful social and economic interests. An egalitarian society is viewed as dependent on a 'strong' state (Ritter, 1973). On the other hand, Böckenförde (1976) and Hennis (1977) have seen the state as a framework of order. Its legitimacy derives from the conditions in terms of which it rules rather than from goal effectiveness. The conception of the 'active' state whose characteristics follow from a requirement to conceive of and implement programmes is premised on a faith in the creative nature of politics and is justified by reference to the social-state postulate of the Basic Law and the constitutionalization of the parties. By contrast, the conception of the neo-liberal *Rechtsstaat* expresses a view of the repressive as opposed to the rationally benevolent nature of politics. The characteristics of the state are seen to follow from a requirement of depoliticization, of reducing the scope of both political rule and politicking. Political argument takes on a dangerously restricted form once the logically independent character of these two aspects of political rule is held to imply that they are mutually exclusive. Perfectly proper and vitally important questions about the proper relationship between them are obscured.

One of the major tasks in politics is to ensure that arguments, demands and actions acquire prestige in so far as they express shared principles of political rule. This task is fraught with difficulties. It involves the political problem of how to reconcile the relativism that is implicit in politicking, in the complex interplay of interests which are seeking satisfaction of their wants, with the requirement for a rational ordering and integration of norms of political rule as the basis of an orderly society. If relativism conveys the idea of moderation and tolerance, it is in danger of promoting aimlessness, petty self-seeking and exploitation. If the normativism and rationalism of the idea of the state offer the sense of purpose and hierarchy of values of a public philosophy, their appeal to an ultimate standard can appear authoritarian and may offend against the notion of reasonableness. The German *Rechtsstaat* tradition exhibits the extremes of response to this political problem, either through a flight into relativism in the notion of political rule itself or through the imposition of the strait-jacket of a public philosophy on politicking. If political morality is endangered in Britain by a relativism that derives from a loss of insight into the requirements of political rule (Johnson, 1977), it is threatened in Germany by an inherited lack of respect for politicking and by an over-reliance on the normativism and rationalism of the idea of the state. The vagaries of historical experience make the achievement of balance between both faces of politics (political rule and politicking) and an underlying tolerance for political ambiguity a rare and unlikely achievement for any political system. In the absence of this balance there is a basis for political anxiety whose nature will depend on the direction in which the balance tilts.

The dangers in the German intellectual tradition of the state were clearly and presciently noted at the end of the eighteenth century by the poet and philosopher Friedrich Schiller. A disciple of Kant and of his concept of moral freedom, Schiller argued that in the new age of reason man had awakened out of his 'sensuous slumber', induced by dependence on nature, only to find himself in the state. The problem of this age was to 'transform the work of necessity (*Notstaat* or *Naturstaat*) into a work of his free choice'. However, Schiller also recognized the authoritarian character and barbaric implications of an Idealist enthusiasm for principles and the absolute rule of law. He pleaded for variety, for recognition in political theory of the sensuous and natural as well as moral character of man. 'The state should honour, not only the objective and the generic, but also the subjective and specific character in individuals' (quoted in Miller, 1970, pp. 65 and 107–8).

The same threat was identified in the twentieth century by the Italian liberal philosopher Benedetto Croce as a result of his bitter and protracted dispute with Giovanni Gentile, the philosopher of actual Idealism and first president of the National Fascist Institute of Culture. Gentile held a completely social and historical view of morality in which the state was identified with the moral conscience (Harris, 1960). As Croce emphasized, the product of such a view was an intellectual despotism that could find Fascism attractive. Moreover, Gentile's 'actualism', which sought to achieve a unity of theory and practice by arguing that nothing is real except the pure and creative act of thought, led to a confusion of the transcendental state (the ideal of a morally responsible person) with the empirical state and hence to the absence of moral barriers against Fascism. The intellectual ease with which Gentile welcomed Fascism suggests a possible element of continuity between the state tradition and Fascism once that tradition succumbs to an intellectual despotism and a confusion of ideal and real.

By contrast, Croce saw the real state as embodying different ideal tendencies, economic and ethical, both of which were aspects of spirit. It was not identical either with power (the economic or utilitarian state) or with morality (the ethical state). On the one hand, and here Croce reflected both his reading of Machiavelli and his view of Italian political life, 'the State does not revolve in the world of ethics' (Croce, 1945, p. 177). Politicians, who practice the art of directing selfish interests and passions, were obliged to cheat and deceive the public. Gentile found in this utilitarian conception of the state a denial of spirit and therefore of moral life. On the other hand, and here Croce approximated to Gentile, 'the State...is...the greatest of all ethical institutions, and virtually the sum of them all' (Croce, 1945, p. 160). Politicians were also obliged to justify their actions and recommendations to themselves as well as to others in ethical terms. However, Croce was concerned to emphasize that Gentile's doctrine of the ethical state, its identification of conscience and the state, could only generate an idolatory of the state, a 'governmental conception of morality', one that found it difficult to conceive of the moral life as embracing both those who govern and their adversaries. Although he gave less time to an examination of the misery that had been generated by the theory and practice of 'Machiavellism', by the view of the autonomy of the state which is beyond good and evil (Croce, 1925, p. 60), Croce was deeply aware of the tragic dilemma that he was revealing within the state tradition.

STATE AS A 'PROBLEM-SOLVING' CONCEPT

In the light of these various historical problems associated with the notion of the state it is scarcely surprising that the issue of reconciling the idea of the state and democracy should have greatly troubled continental European intellectuals. A notable example of this concern was provided by the attempts of liberals like Gerhard Anschütz and Alfred Weber at Heidelberg to transfer the notion of an autonomous and objective (*sachlich*) sovereign power from the bureaucratic monarchy to the new regime of the Weimar Republic. Perhaps the most persuasive analysis of the issue during the Weimar period came from Richard Thoma (1923). In his view, democracy embodied the principles of equality and majority rule and was concerned to establish partnership rather than to provide government. The danger of an exclusive political commitment to it was the withering away of the notion of the state and a neglect of the requirements of collective action. To Thoma the state was

> an association of people…and a person in law; everything which normally appears as government is merely the application of the authority transferred to the various organs. In this, therefore, the personality of the state must be the ruling factor, and this is relatively less fictional under a democracy than under any other form of government.

It was, in other words, essential to synthesize the requirements of collective action with those of partnership, not to see them as ranged against one another or as subordinated one to the other.

The concept of the state carries few implications about the form of polity. It is articulated as a body of values, powers, procedures and offices and represents a concern for logic and order in collective arrangements. Its emphasis is upon the autonomous exercise of public authority under law rather than participation or 'citizen competence'; upon the unity of such authority, a monism that suggests the distinctive character of public affairs; upon technical criteria and the professionalism of bureaucratic mores rather than group conflict and adjustment; and upon an essentially moral, substantive concept of the public interest that is not viewed as simply emerging from a pluralist process in which groups openly compete. The state is seen as an agent or trustee whose authority is not merely derived from the 'majority' or the 'popular will'. This idea of agency or trusteeship is based on the premises that the public cannot do, and does not want to do, everything; that there is a difference between private taste and opinion and public principles that can and should be rationally ordered and integrated;

that order is dependent on a hierarchy of values in public affairs; and that interests are not simply additive. The state tradition is concerned with the framework of values within which public life should be conducted and with the effective exercise of public authority in the pursuit of those values. It is a rationalist construction that is not easily and neatly reconcilable with, but arguably gives some added strength to, the democratic tradition. Democratic mechanisms of political choice and institutional balance are in danger of becoming meaningless unless accompanied by a capacity for strong collective action on the part of those chosen to rule—for example, in order to effect modernization in a 'stagnant' society or to redress social inequalities. Public authority and the structure of collective action need to represent more than a reflection of ephemeral majorities and pluralistic pressures if an extreme relativism in values is to be avoided and if the value of imaginative reflection is to be admitted in public affairs.

There are variations between 'stateless' societies. The American liberal tradition is profoundly individualistic and anti-bureaucratic; it begins with the autonomous individual and with a populist belief that all authority emanates from the people. A dispersal of public power was seen as necessary in order to maintain the supremacy of the popular will and to protect the individual. The result was administrative fragmentation and a competitive system of government, which seemed more satisfactorily explicable in terms of theories of the economic market and egoistic behaviour and which, moreover, suggested a capacity for 'veto' politics by the powerful, organized groups and a *status quo* pattern of politics. As Brian Barry (1965, p. 272) argues: 'The result (intended or actual) of a power-diffusing system is to raise a series of obstacles to changes in the *status quo* or collective expenditures, thus raising the price (in terms of bargaining costs) of getting collective action.' Although the British tradition of the Crown is a limited one compared with that of the state, it gives a unity and independent authority to government that is absent in the American context and qualifies any attempt to analyse its politics in terms of group theory. Despite the great differences between the paternalistic Tory tradition and modern social democracy, both have combined to inject support for the values of collective action, the public interest and trust in government as beneficial. There is clearly a danger of exaggerating the similarities between 'stateless' societies and of failing to see the ideological factors that have produced European-type 'big government' in Britain. Nevertheless, in a European context these ideological factors appear different and more partisan in Britain where the idea of the inherent responsibilities of the state has not taken root. Britain is characterized by the heritage of liberalism that is important not so much in the form of the modern Liberal Party as in its percolation through the manufacturing interest into the Conservative Party after 1886 and because of the later shift of many of its intellectuals into the new Labour Party. Moreover two Liberals, Keynes and Beveridge, provided the intellectual basis of the post-1945 consensus on the managed economy and the welfare state. The heritage of liberalism has been a widespread and profound ambivalence about the role of government. Considerable government intervention combines with a hesitancy about the use of its authority; a sense of the 'necessity' of collective action is accompanied by scepticism about its desirability or utility (Shonfield, 1965; Hayward, 1975).

The effective exercise of public authority depends on a prior capacity to determine the public interest and the maintenance of public respect for government as beneficial: in other words, on a disposition to approve of collective action. Both characteristics are not strongly represented in the American political tradition (Sharpe, 1973) and are only ambiguously present in the British. In 'state' societies the need for a relationship of trust between professional officials and the governed is derived from the notion of the inherent responsibilities of the state, a notion that in turn supports ideas of the lofty character of public service. A state tradition emphasizes a distinct realm of objective criteria for decision-making rather than an American-style, individualistic adaptation of service provision, with its associated possibilities of corruption and decline in the social prestige of public-service values. In Britain the Crown tradition may have lent to the central administration characteristics of objectivity and disinterestedness and an aloofness (rather than a social prestige) that fortifies public acceptance of its probity. However, the Crown does not extend into local government. Within the English local authority, unlike in central government, authority is seen to emanate solely from the elected representatives in council. The sphere of political intervention and its relationship to administrative criteria are accordingly less clearly defined and understood. Moreover, there is no notion of central government and local government as organs of the state in a hierarchical relationship. In France state officials, notably the prefects who are responsible for the co-ordination of state services at the departmental level and for tutelage of local communes, exhibit distrust of local councils and rely on the mayors, who are themselves state officials as well as locally elected dignitaries. An attempt is made to safeguard administrative autonomy *vis-à-vis* local political pressures by co-opting them, where politically possible, into the working of the state apparatus. Reality is, of course, more untidy. The administrative collusion of mayors and prefects and the mayor's use of his personal political weight in Paris are indicators of the importance of local influences in French politics and their ability to frustrate centralized initiatives (Kesselman, 1967). In Western Germany the self-governing functions and delegated state tasks of the local authority are increasingly difficult to distinguish. Germans refer to a *Mischverwaltung* in which the relationship of mayors or local executives to state officials becomes closer and more politically significant to them than their relationship to the local council. The role of the local authority as an organ or extended arm of the state gives to local executives an important monopoly of information that reinforces their independence of council and their capacity to take a wider view. This concern with a hierarchy of organs and a pattern of normative integration contrasts with the overriding importance attached by Anglo-American ideas of local self-government to local community interests, the virtues of pluralism, and lay participation and control. Such ideas, in terms of which local institutions have been organized, have discouraged trust of the local official and have created an environment in which there is a comparatively low political consciousness of the importance of public-service values. The resulting proliferation of 'whirlpools of interest' has produced a pluralistic stagnation at the local level that further diminishes trust.

The legitimating function of the concept of the state finds its clearest expression in the emphasis on the unitary character of the public interest. This concept is one which Anglo-American scholars tend to reject as a source of vague generality and confusion. One reason for doing so is the nominalist argument that ideas like 'interest', 'purpose' or 'will' can only refer meaningfully to discrete, observable entities like the individual or, more arguably, the group. By contrast, the state tradition holds that 'things held in common' (words, concepts, purposes, interests) are an essential basis of civilized social life. It is characteristic of the English analytical tradition and of American pragmatism and behaviouralism that they should either conclude that concepts which are not readily definable in terms of consensus meanings or core descriptive meanings are unimportant or practically irrelevant, or prefer to concentrate on the use of such terms by specific publics as a rationalization for self-interested proposals. In so far as there is a concern for the public interest it tends to be treated restrictively as an aggregative concept that is individualistic in basis and concerned with the satisfaction of expressed wants. Emphasis in the 'interest-group' literature is upon how to discover and ensure articulation of these wants. Much less attention is paid to problems of political education, of how to clarify people's awareness of their wants and make these consistent and enlightened in terms of a sense of public duty and of intrinsic, rather than derived, public need. An inclination to concentrate on individual or group 'self-interest' (satisfaction of expressed wants) involves an assumption that 'self-interest' is more precise and objective. The concept of self-interest is, nevertheless, problematic and raises difficult issues of the frame of reference (with what is the self to be identified—with higher wage rises for oneself or with stable monetary values for all?), of time perspective (the issue of 'deferred gratification') and of equity (distribution on the basis of rank, desert or need?). Interest remains a normative concept whose interpretation is endlessly debatable. The prevailing Anglo-American view is not that the public interest is an ethical criterion for which men strive, a prior standard by which the claims of competing interests might be evaluated in a disinterested and rationalist manner. It is a *post hoc* label for the compromise product of their bargaining. An ethical criterion is rejected as 'autocratic', 'aristocratic' or 'technocratic' rather than accepted as an essential 'life hypothesis' of a pluralistic society which needs both a source of inspiration and normative integration (however indefinite) beyond the pursuit of private 'egoistic' interests and an antidote to a relativism in values. At a minimum it is a 'spur to conscience and deliberation', a general standard of fraternity to be injected into policy evaluation. However difficult it may be to define the public interest objectively in particular situations, it is not necessary to deny the concept a substantive meaning which transcends a respect for certain procedural requirements of democratic decision and the compromises emerging from group conflict (Barry, 1965). It is possible to identify net interests common to all members of society, a collective self-interest subject to reinterpretation by which individuals will prefer not to pursue their 'egoistic' interests in order that others will not inflict damage on them by pursuing theirs. Individuals consent, for example, to be bound by the restraints of traffic regulations because greater long-term safety for all results. A state tradition is associated with a highly developed consciousness of collective self-interest, which is reflected in a willingness to regulate social, and especially economic, relationships in considerable detail: the classic examples are provided by organized groups like the

Swedish LO (trade union federation) which become quasi-public-management agencies and by the chambers of commerce and agriculture which act as agencies of delegated state administration. In Austria, where there is also a chamber of labour, these chambers are corporations of public law, with obligatory membership for certain persons or organizations. They are bureaucratic in character, enjoy manifold institutional linkages with the state apparatus and provide a range of educational and cultural activities. There is also a willingness to identify a public interest in the provision of certain services (witness the long history of public utilities and of the concern to protect third-party interests) which cannot be guaranteed by individuals or groups acting on their own. The notion of public benefit or need excludes the application of criteria of profitability even to services with an economic character. Analogy with private commercial enterprise and with the market is less frequently used. If the British formula of the public corporation has been a source of endless muddles, continental European public enterprises have tended to be understood in public-law terms as aspects of state administration, thereby avoiding their 'contamination' by private-law concepts like the public trust. Finally, the idea of collective self-interest comprises the need to protect and promote the public interest of consumers against the sectional interests of well organized producer groups.

Underlying the concept of the public interest is the notion of a distinction between public and private and of generality as opposed to particularity. Hence it is central to the state tradition. The state is seen as the institutional embodiment of a concern with the identification and realization of public interests, with the rational analysis of norms in a disinterested and benevolent manner. Even in 'state' societies there exists a complex of informal networks through which certain groups are favoured. Such collusion appears to fragment the state apparatus itself and to distort perceptions of the public interest (Machin, 1977). Nevertheless, the intellectual respectability of the concept and its institutional embodiment remain a precondition of the attempt to realize it: how successfully will depend upon a variety of conditions, internal (like the strength of socialization into the norms of the state) and external (like the degree of fragmentation of the interest-group structure) to the state itself.

The credibility of the public interest as a guiding principle of collective action is dependent on more than a state tradition. Certain conditions are necessary if it is to become possible to establish confidence in political mechanisms and their capacity to identify genuinely 'public' interests: the rule of law, accountability for the exercise of power, and a democratic framework for political choice of the kind that provides comprehensive representation and creates the institutional conditions for the emergence of a political statesmanship that will be able to synthesize interests creatively. American and British political scientists have been prepared to accept that the public interest involves some kind of comprehensive jurisdiction (like the American President or the British administrative class) as an umpire within sectional disputes, and that the balancing and aggregation of group interests must allow for 'indirectly created' interests that emerge from proposals. This concern with the concept of the public interest as a problem of the distribution of want satisfaction is, however, utilitarian and represents an additive approach to interests. By contrast, the concept of the state draws attention to the notion of the public welfare, to certain intrinsic (rather than derived) public needs. These needs are rooted in widely and continuously shared interests (for example, in peace, law and order, education, the avoidance of inflationary boom or of recession) and arise out of organic developments and shared purposes. Their rationale is to provide the conditions necessary for an effective and 'proper' functioning of the community, whether in terms of cultural or of physical well-being. They find their expression in certain purposes (like modernization in France or currency stability in West Germany) which cannot be defined simply as the end-product of compromise amongst sectional interests. The purpose may not be universally appreciated (witness the French Poujadists' anti-modernism) or held with equal intensity by different groups. In practice it may be compromised with particular interests. Nevertheless, its institutional embodiment in the state itself (as in the French Planning Commission and the West German *Bundes-bank*) expresses its overriding priority, a preference for objectivity in its management by attaining a measure of depoliticization (in the sense of remoteness from politicking) and a willingness to pursue the purpose authoritatively. As a result, the process of exchange between viewpoints represented by sectional interests and the public interest is very different in nature. There is a strong cultural disposition to think in terms of defining and supporting collective requirements.

While the substance of the public interest will vary with value judgements and social developments, its essence lies in an approach that emphasizes collective rationality and logic based on an ordering of norms; the search for more objective (*sachlich*) discussion; the role of creative intelligence as opposed to mere arbitration in public affairs; a spirit of 'other-regardingness' or fraternity; an awareness of society's 'seamless web' and the constant impulse to trace things as far as possible before acting; and a priority for generally shared needs and interests. In 'state' societies cultural dispositions combine with integrative institutional values to affect profoundly the organization and conduct of interest groups. Where they are co-opted through administrative recognition (as in Austria or West Germany) broad-based, highly professional and densely organized groups which are able to aggregate interests in terms of 'statesman-like' perspectives are encouraged. Management of public affairs passes to an elite cartel which straddles the boundaries of the public and private spheres. The pluralistic process is infused with considerations of the public interest. In the case of France, where the public interest is identified with the notion of bureaucratic autonomy and initiative, sectional groups are either recognized as 'respectable' and 'professional', and thereby enter into relationships of administrative collusion with the state apparatus, or characterized as 'irresponsible', in which case their conduct ranges from compliance to arouse bureaucratic respect at one extreme to direct action as a response to frustration at the other. The pluralistic structure fragments into extraordinary complexity, has serious problems of legitimacy and encourages administrative tactics of 'divide and rule'. 'State' societies possess a capacity to transcend interpersonal and intergroup comparisons that focus on relativities: either a concern with 'public goods', like faster growth, price stability or full employment, is directly built into the calculations of those who exercise potentially disruptive power or those entrusted with these 'public goods' are prepared to exercise their authority in a more abrasive and determined fashion.

Awareness of the positive side of the state tradition has not been completely absent amongst British reformers. In the nineteenth century the administrative reformer Edwin Chadwick sought to model his bureaucratic and centralizing approach on France and Coleridge found inspiration in German Idealism. Members of the 'National Efficiency Movement', like Lord Haldane, in the early years of the twentieth century looked to the German state which was, in their view, based on the idea of science as its principle of order and sought to disseminate that idea through its system of state education. The nineteenth-century educationalist Matthew Arnold (1869) contrasted the atomistic and mechanical modes of thought of liberal Britain with a German conception of the state that combined efficiency (a scientific idea) with a moral and creative function (a 'spiritual' idea). In the absence of the idea of 'the nation in its collective and corporate character, entrusted with stringent powers for the general advantage, and controlling individual wills in the name of an interest wider than that of individuals' there was 'anarchy', 'dislike of authority' and 'the worship of freedom in and for itself'. Nevertheless, the perspectives of Anglo-American political thought and its characteristic judgements of the continental European state tradition as politically autocratic have remained narrow and parochial. A constitutional tradition, which is expressed in the supremacy of law over government and in the qualification of majority rule by a concern for individual and minority rights, mechanisms of popular choice based on free competitive elections and the legitimacy of opposition, and recognition of political pluralism are necessary but not sufficient conditions for a viable democratic form of government. The political, as opposed to legal positivist, conception of the state was concerned with a theory of 'responsible' government that did not reduce government to the 'will of all' (Rousseau's term) and thereby make the majority or consensus the criterion of the good. Responsibility meant not just political 'answerability' but moral reliability: an ability to distinguish right and wrong, rationally to analyse, order, integrate and defend the norms of community life, and to direct one's conduct by recognizing a rational value order. The emphasis is upon the moral character of 'public power', its necessity and beneficial potential, and the need for an independence of will in government and a capacity to avoid subservience to special interests, so that 'public power' can be exercised to redistribute resources and reduce the 'natural' inequalities that result from the functioning of society. Theories of democratization which stress the ethical values of participation are related to broader questions about the conditions of rational and effective executive action instead of being pursued in isolation. The result is, in one sense, depoliticizing; priority is accorded to questions about the requirements of political rule rather than to competitive-interest politicking. The state tradition rests upon the belief that it is important for the individual that collective action can be undertaken to effect purposive change in social and economic arrangements—in other words, that tradition is not indifferent to the effects on the individual of the exercise of public power. Good government depends on a capacity for collective action as well as control of that action and on a respect for impersonal public-service values. Considerable scope remains for dispute about what kind of capacity and what sort of public-service values are needed.

The character of continental European politics has been shaped by the different patterns of accommodation of the idea of the state and democracy in 'state' societies. It is possible to identify three major patterns. First, there is the French pattern, in which representative institutions and state institutions are seen as two different and coexisting conceptions of how the democratic notion of the sovereignty of the people is to be expressed. This 'solution' preserves a considerable distance and tension between the two sets of institutions, and because the question of the appropriate balance between them is left open means that fundamental constitutional argument remains at the centre of politics. A second pattern is the Dutch and Swedish, where the representative and executive institutions are seen as the two 'poles' or 'powers' of the state. While there remains a distance between both institutions, a co-operative working relationship is emphasized by an extensive view (in institutional terms) of the state which subsumes both. Finally, there is the Austrian and West German pattern, which involves a more complete merging to produce 'public-service' democracies in which a large presence of officials in the composition of both parties and parliaments is complemented by a party 'penetration' of the bureaucracy. They are viewed as 'party states'. The parties are the agencies of integration of the idea of the state and democracy and perform a more elevated, moral and didactic role than is suggested by the British notion of 'party government'. Despite different patterns of historical development and of pluralistic relations, these societies share common points of philosophical departure. They are also characterized by the phenomenon of the 'politician–technician'; the distinction between politicians and administrative technicians loses its force as the parties seek out the kind of personnel able to impose a political will on the bureaucracy and as the technicians become party activists.

Judgements about the stability and effectiveness of 'state' societies must be qualified by further emphasis on the historical problems associated with the state tradition. The relationship between 'stateness' and stability and effectiveness is complex and problematic for a variety of reasons: the primitive state of the concepts of stability and effectiveness when applied to political as opposed to mechanical systems (for example, judgements of stability depend on the indicators applied—longevity of regime, governments, ministers or policy?—and judgements of effectiveness are shaped by the policy areas selected and by the difficulty of evolving and applying measures of assessment); the weakness of theories of political stability which have identified a vast range of political, economic and socio-cultural variables but have established only weak correlations with stability; and the variety of meanings attached to the concept of the state (for example, is one referring to a political or a non-political conception of the state?). Inter-war Austria, the Weimar Republic, the French Third and Fourth Republics are evidence of a negative relationship; Austria's Second Republic, Western Germany and, less persuasively, the French Fifth Republic appear to confirm a positive relationship. One important factor (in addition to the lessons of past experience, a more benign economic climate, etc.) in making comprehensible these variations is the different terms on which the idea of the state and democracy have (or have not) been accommodated and, in particular, the extent to which the values of the state tradition have been interpreted in terms of a wide range of social interests. The complex of environmental, political and personal factors which can disturb stability and effectiveness and the ambivalent heritage of the state tradition make general judgements about the stability and effectiveness of 'state' and 'stateless' societies very provisional and rapidly historical. It is not so much a case of one type of society being more vulnerable than another but rather of their being fragile in different ways.

The vulnerability of democratic societies without a state tradition has already been suggested: it lies in a poverty of government that fudges issues of purpose in favour of registering political pressures and maintains an unending faith in the virtues of 'muddling through'. There is a tendency to interpret chronic failures of political performance and inability to exercise public authority effectively in terms other than those of institutional crisis (or if in terms of institutional crisis, typically only in a restricted managerial sense). In Britain an attempt is made to avoid a fundamental reappraisal of institutions, in the sense of considering their interrelationships and the philosophies which they embody, in two ways: by an almost excessive tinkering with the formal working arrangements of discrete institutions (as in 'machinery of government' reform); and, particularly, by taking institutions less seriously, by assuming that informal, fluid processes of elite consensus-seeking and co-optation will provide a satisfactory (albeit obscure) way of accommodating problems and that personal moral virtues of the individuals who take part in institutions are the foundation of good government. Such an analysis suggests that obscurity and flexibility without the institutional solidity of 'state' societies may be the 'efficient' secret of British politics. Institutional theory is less relevant to an understanding of conduct in such a society.

Britain relies on the learning capacity and subtlety of a pluralistic and loose political order in which good people and ideas are expected to float to the surface. The morality of its politics appears to reside in a practice of civility, a universal acknowledgement of the authority of common practices which are seen as the precondition of freedom and of respect for the dignity and individuality of others (Oakeshott, 1975). By contrast, the emphasis of the state tradition on the formal rationality of working arrangements and the institutional embodiment of collective purposes makes them more prone to perceive crises of purpose and coherence, to translate chronic policy failure and indications of civic disobedience into an ideological crisis of institutions, to go back to first principles rather than to live pragmatically. Crisis avoidance may be pursued by compromising politicians addicted to politicking, like Chautemps and Briand in the Third or Queuille and Pleven in the Fourth French Republic. However, ultimately there emerges the leader figure who is preoccupied with the requirements of political order, prone to perceive crisis and disposed to tackle it by direct confrontation. Crisis is used to force through overdue change. The claims to clarity, autonomy and coherence of the institutions that are identified with the idea of the state produce a different kind of vulnerability. A somewhat different style of politics is to be found in Austria and West Germany where a merging of the notion of the state and democracy has helped to reconcile institutional values of autonomy, clarity and coherence with adaptability and complexity. The result is a more high-minded, didactic and moralistic style of political compromise than is to be found in Britain. Political 'deals' are worked out in the context of an appeal to shared fundamentals of purpose and to 'objectivity' and of an anxiety about precipitating the sort of crisis that could bring procedures into question.

epilogue | the end of the idea of the state?

The future of state as a political concept will be partly shaped by the kind of intellectual company it has kept in the past and by evaluations of the political experience with which it has been associated. Since 1945 there has undoubtedly been a new uncertainty in continental Europe about the adequacy and appropriateness of historical and institutional understanding, a sense of past intellectual failures which induced a new intellectual modesty and, until the mid-1960s, a willingness to take a greater interest in American models of politics. While a marked decline of interest in general theories of the state occurred, intellectuals remained reluctant to abandon state as an organizing concept in intellectual life. Its influence was pervasive, even if often subconscious. Nevertheless, grounds existed for anticipating a 'crisis of the state idea' and of the sense of 'stateness' (*Staatsbewusstsein*); namely, that ideological attitudes and cultural dispositions no longer supported it (Quaritsch, 1970; Burdeau, 1949–57, vol. 7). There was a new questioning of the idea of the state as a territorial phenomenon, the unit of international affairs, and of the idea of the state as the institution of political rule at home. Western European political systems appeared to be experiencing a prolonged and complex process of readjustment to fundamental changes and, as a consequence, to be in need of new political forms in order to cope more effectively with these changes. Did the concept of the state continue to be historically and socially relevant?

The idea of the state as a territorial association seemed increasingly irrelevant to the adequate provision of physical security as well as to effective economic and industrial management. A combination of international, economic and technological developments cast doubt on the viability of the state itself as the fundamental unit of politics.

The post-1918 movement from a European 'state system' towards a world-wide 'state system' involved a general drift towards dependency and inter-dependency, one that was vividly underlined by the emergence of the two superpowers, the Soviet Union and the United States, after 1945 (Hintze, 1962b). Continental Europe, which found itself divided into two camps and dependent on one or the other superpower, experienced a new sense that each political unit was embedded more and more intricately within a complex international structure of political, economic and military power and was subject to a speedier and more intense process of diffusion of political ideas and experiences across frontiers. As the state system absorbed the entire world, the individual state appeared to be losing some of its significance. Even those European powers that had played a major role in creating the new worldwide state system lost influence. This common circumstance and an experience of being on the ideological side of West rather than East, and then on the economic side of North rather than South, altered perceptions of frontiers within Western Europe itself. Historical frontiers (*Staatsgrenzen*), with which the idea of the state as a territorial phenomenon had always been intimately associated, began to be seen as hindrances to tackling specific economic, industrial and environmental problems, and there was a willingness to relinquish sovereignty in a pragmatic spirit (Ermacora, 1970). One factor in this changing perception of frontiers was the pressure for a larger scale of operations from within modern capitalism. Economic development seemed to depend on wider markets and the mobility of capital and labour in order to make the harnessing of investment in new, more sophisticated technology possible and worthwhile. This internationalization of capitalism found its most graphic expression in pressures from expanding trans-national corporations on the individual state. The response was a search for new forms of international collaboration to co-ordinate economic and financial policy so as to attain common objectives. However, besides these pragmatic responses to changes in the international balance of power and in modern capitalism, and reinforcing and influencing these responses, there was an element of idealism born of a new attachment to the European idea and of a view of the state as a tragic, even bizarre unit. Historical experience within Western Europe suggests the close connection between, on the one hand, war, threat of war and the search for coalitions against rivals and, on the other, state-building and the formation of national armies that are devoted to warfare (Krippendorf, 1970). A twentieth-century experience of two world wars, initiated in Western Europe, and of their aftermath of profound social and economic dislocation underlined most vividly, and on a vast human scale, the high costs that have always been associated with state-building and were now escalated by technological advances and global politics. The idea of integration into a wider and more flexible political community was, therefore, supported by two types of argument: a utilitarian critique of the adequacy of the individual state as a problem-solving unit, a critique that accompanied a new calculative involvement of elites in forms of supra-national integration like, after 1957, the European Economic Community; and a normative critique of the state as a cultural unit, a critique that seemed to suggest a radical departure in ideas of political rule. Nevertheless, when it came to consideration of the character of this new political community, traditional conceptions proved tenacious. For example, German debate tended to focus on whether Western Europe was witnessing the emergence of a *Staatenbund* (a confederation), which did not exercise an independent *staatliche Gewalt,* or a *Bundesstaat* whose members renounced their sovereignty.

The fundamental doubt about the idea of the state as the institution of political rule involved its ability to provide an adequate principle of or-der for a modern complex society, in which egalitarian and participatory values appeared to be gaining strength, and in which the 'public power' was increasingly judged instrumentally by its effective performance as a problem-solving and want-satisfying enterprise whose boundaries of ac-tion were difficult to observe or define. Affluence and the material security of 'post-industrial' societies brought a decline of interest in the problem of order and the requirements of collective action, in the concerns of, for example, Bodin and Hobbes, and a greater concern for 'authentic' social relationships and for self-realization. The appeal to 'affluent' societies of Marx's model of 'unalienated' man and of Freud's model of 'psychological' man, who was preoccupied with personal self-mastery rather than a public philosophy, reinforced tendencies to take the idealism out of institutions, to see them as strait-jackets on the individual or as crude manipulators of conduct. A 'radical freedom' (Hegel's term) seemed to be further accentu-ated by a preoccupation with extending the participatory and egalitarian characteristics of democracy, a preoccupation that was, at least in part, the political expression of these new social attitudes. Criticism of the elitist quality of democracy in 'state' societies suggested, to some observers more than to others, a deep-seated crisis of authority.

The possibility of a crisis of the idea of the state as the institution of political rule was also intimated by the changing character of the theory and practice of the modern state. A twentieth-century experience of economic crisis, of the economic demands of modern technological warfare and of the immediate social unrest and fear of revolution that followed war underlined the need for the mobilization of men and resources on a new scale. At the same time, paralleling this development, political analysis shifted its attention away from the determination of the formal conditions of political rule, among which had figured prominently the analytical distinction between state and society, to a material analysis that concerned itself with the conditions for the effective and efficient performance of government as an enterprise (Burdeau, 1949–57, vol. 7; Hennis, 1977; Oakeshott, 1975). A 'socialization' (*Vergesellschaftung*) of the state occurred as organized groups, which proliferated in numbers and threatened to overcrowd the public policy process, sought to influence government performance in order to achieve greater satisfaction of their particular wants. Simultaneously, a process of 'statification' (*Verstaatlichung*) of society suggested that public institutions were attempting to shape society by consciously manipulating opinion, for example through corporatist arrangements, so as to be better able to effectuate policy, especially economic strategy (Habermas, 1973; Middlemas, 1979). Both processes blurred the boundaries between state apparatus and society and made it more difficult to entertain the view that the analytical distinction between state and society was any longer relevant to modern politics (Böckenförde, 1976).

Other doubts existed about the adequacy of the idea of the state as the institution of rule and the principle of order. There was a feeling that public institutions were insufficiently adaptive and unwilling to tolerate enough internal complexity (for example, by designing novel machinery and policies) in order to deal with a more rapid rate of social and economic change. One danger that was confronting modern societies appeared to be political stagnation through 'over-institutionalization', the valuing of institutions for their own sake (Huntington, 1968; Schon, 1971). Another problem was the emergence of new centres of power outside the framework of the state apparatus and an increase in the complexity of relationships of dependency which that apparatus had to take into account if it was to be able to realize its purposes. Centrifugal pressures and a subsequent 'neutralization of power by power' seemed to suggest a new 'feudalism' and raised the issue of 'who governs' in an acute form (Ionescu, 1975).

There were doubts about whether it was practical for governments to impose their authority on powerful groups and even about whether 'concertation' could be made to work. According to Crozier (1975): 'The modern European state's basic weakness is its liability to blackmailing tactics'. The more complex the functions and goals of the state itself and the more intimate the relations of the state apparatus to private interests, the more difficult it became to maintain faith in the notion of the unity of action of the state. Finally, the strength of ideas of secularization and individualism seemed to be suggested by the ideological impact both of technical rationality as a model of thought which served to 'demythologize' politics and of an economic model of man as a customer with wants (represented by groups) in place of a political model of the citizen with rights and duties (embodied in the state). Myths were to be exploded rather than recognized as motivators. Satisfaction of individual consumer preferences rather than concern for the character and requirements of political association became the criterion of the good.

These arguments about the threat to the idea of the state as the institution of rule have often involved much simplification and exaggeration as well as a romanticized view of the past. They have, however, reflected a new concern for the values of the state in the midst of rapid economic, social and cultural change and the apparent loosening of the moral constraints once provided by religion, neighbourhood, extended family and class. How long can values of depersonalization, depoliticization, the inherent morality of office and concern for community needs continue to inform elite opinion in this context? How successfully can elites communicate the meaning and purpose of the idea of the state to the public, or is a gap likely to appear between elite attitudes which emphasize state values and mass attitudes of an egoistic, consumer-oriented character? These concerns have produced a variety of theoretical reactions. There are those who welcome the demise of the notion of the state, for they see it as a tragic concept, an expression of inhumanity (Bärsch, 1974). At the other extreme, the conservatives of German *Staatslehre* look backwards with nostalgia to embrace the fear of their Weimar predecessors that there is a 'deficit of state ideology'. Their inspiration is the peculiarly German conception of the *Obrigkeitsstaat*. As a form of political theology or secular religion, their theory of the state is unwilling to accept the openness, uncertainty, imperfection and fragility of democracy. By contrast, Georges Burdeau looks forward, albeit anxiously, to a future of active citizens and a much more fluid polity. Another response has been to return to Hegel's penetrating analysis of modern society, a process encouraged by a resurgence of interest in the Hegelian motifs in Marx. There is a new awareness, which has been prompted by a loss of faith in empirical theory and a new interest in conceptual change, of the need for a wider critical comprehension of existing social and political reality in terms of a historical perspective (Taylor, 1975; Bernstein, 1976). It is this attempt to impose coherence on the complexity of experience and to see politics as a rationally intelligible activity that most promises response to a fundamental question: does the concept of the state need redefinition to take account of social changes, or is a new concept required to deal with the problem of order in contemporary conditions? The second position ought not to be adopted simply because there exist politically authoritarian interpretations of the state, past and present. Western Europe is, however, going through an extended period of political transition, one characterized by uncertainty and experimentation. A sense of direction is only likely to be achieved if philosophy is prepared to marry conceptual analysis to a more comprehensive, historical understanding of social and political experience. Its failure to rise to the challenge will only open the way for crackpot ideas, the tyranny of the fashionable and the degeneration of political ideas into the byproducts of action.

bibliography

Aho, J. A. (1975) *German Realpolitik and American Sociology.* Lewisburg, Pa.: Bucknell University Press.

Albrow, M. (1970) *Bureaucracy.* London: Macmillan.

Allen, J. W. (1928) *A History of Political Thought In the 16th Century.* London: Methuen.

Allum, P. (1973) *Politics and Society in Post-war Naples.* Cambridge, England: Cambridge University Press.

Almond, G. A. and Powell, G. B. (1966) *Comparative Politics: A Developmental Approach.* Boston, Mass.: Little Brown.

Althusius, J. (1948) *Grundbegriffe der Politik, Aus 'Politica methodice digesta' (1603).* Frankfurt: Klostermann.

Altmann, R. (1968) *Späte Nachrichten vom Staat.* Stuttgart: Seewald.

Andersen, P. (1954) *Dansk Statsforfatningsret.* Copenhagen: Gyldendal.

Anderson, P. (1974) *Lineages of the Absolutist State.* London: New Left Books.

Anschütz, G. and Thoma, R. (eds) (1930, 1932) *Handbuch des Deutschen Staatsrechts,* 2 vols. Tübingen: Mohr.

Aris, R. (1929) *Die Staatslehre Adam Müllers.* Tübingen: Mohr.

Aris, R. (1965) *History of Political Thought in Germany from 1789 to 1815.* London: Frank Cass.

Armstrong, J. A. (1973) *The European Administrative Elite.* Princeton, N.J.: Princeton University Press.

Arnold, M. (1869) *Culture and Anarchy.* London: Smith Elder.

Aron, R. (1968) *Main Currents in Sociological Thought.* London: Weidenfeld and Nicolson.

Bähr, O. (1864) *Der Rechtsstaat.* Kassel-Göttingen: G. H. Wigand.

Bakunin, M. (1970) *God and the State.* New York: Dover Publications.

Barker, E. (1915) 'The discredited state', *Political Quarterly,* February, pp: 101–21.

Barker, E. (1930) *Church, State, and Study.* London: Methuen.

Barker, E. (1942) *Reflections on Government.* London: Oxford University Press.

Barker, R. (1978) *Political Ideas in Modern Britain.* London: Methuen.

Barry, B. (1965) *Political Argument.* London: Routledge and Kegan Paul.

Bärsch, C. E. (1974) *Der Staatsbegriff in der Neueren Deutschen Staatslehre und seine Theoretischen Implikationen.* Berlin: Duncker und Humblot.

Barthélemy, J. (1933) *Traité de droit constitutionnel.* Paris: Dalloz.

Bayley, D. (1975) 'The police and political development in Europe', in C. Tilly (ed.) *The Formation of National States in Western Europe*. Princeton, N.J.: Princeton University Press.

Beer, S. (1965) *Modern British Politics*. London: Faber and Faber.

Beetham, D. (1974) *Max Weber and the Theory of Modern Politics*. London: George Allen and Unwin.

Beetham, D. (1977) 'From socialism to fascism: the relation between theory and practice in the work of Robert Michels', *Political Studies*, March, pp: 3–24, and June, pp: 161–81.

Bell, H. E. (1965) *Maitland*. London: Black.

Bentley, A. (1908) *Process of Government*. Chicago: University of Chicago Press.

Berlin, I. (1978) *Concepts and Categories: Philosophical Essays*. London: Hogarth Press.

Bernstein, R. J. (1976) *The Restructuring of Social and Political Theory*. London: Methuen.

Berthélemy, H. (1933) *Traité élémentaire de droit administratif*. Paris: Rousseau.

Beudant, C. (1920) *Le droit individuel et l'État* (3rd edn). Paris: Rousseau.

Birch, A. H. (1968) *The British System of Government* (2nd edn). London: George Allen and Unwin.

Bluntschli, J. K. (1875) *Lehre vom Modernen Staat*, 3 vols. Stuttgart: Cotta.

Böckenförde, E.-W. (1972) *Rechtsfragen der Gegenwart*. Stuttgart: Kohlhammer.

Böckenförde, E.-W. (ed.) (1976) *Staat und Gesellschaft*. Darmstadt: Wissenschaftliche Buchgesellschaft.

Bodin, J. (1962) *The Six Books of a Commonweale*. Cambridge, Mass.: Harvard University Press. (First published in 1576.)

Bonnard, R. (1939) *Le droit et l'État dans la doctrine nationale-socialiste* (2nd edn). Paris: Librairie Générale de Droit et de Jurisprudence.

Bonnecase, J. (1928) *Science du droit et romantisme*. Paris: Sirey.

Bosanquet, B. (1899) *The Philosophical Theory of the State*. London: Macmillan.

Bottomore, T. and Goode, P. (eds) (1978) *Austro-Marxism*. Oxford: Oxford University Press.

Bracher, K.-D. (1968) 'Staatsbegriff und Demokratie in Deutschland', *Politische Vierteljahresschrift*, January, pp: 2–27.

Bruford, W. H. (1975) *The German Tradition of Self-Cultivation*. Cambridge, England: Cambridge University Press.

Brunner, O. (1954) 'Die Freiheitsrechte in der Altständischen Gesellschaft', in *Aus Verfassungs- und Landesgeschichte: Festschrift Theodor Mayer*. Lindau, Thorbecke.

Bulpitt, J. (1978) 'The making of the United Kingdom', *Parliamentary Affairs*, Spring, pp: 174–89.

Burdeau, G. (1949–57) *Traité de science politique*. Paris: Librairie Générale de Droit et de Jurisprudence. Vol. 1, *Le pouvoir politique* (1949); Vol. 2, *L'État* (1949); Vol. 3, *Le statut du pouvoir dans l'État* (1950); Vol. 4, *Les régimes politique* (1952); Vol. 5, *L'État liberal et les techniques de la démocratie gouvernée* (1953); Vol. 6, *La démocratie gouvernante. Son assise sociale et sa philosophie politique* (1956); Vol. 7, *La démocratie gouvernante. Ses structures gouvernmentales* (1957).

Carré de Malberg, R. (1920) *Contribution à la théorie générale de l'État.* Paris: Tenin.

Carrillo, S. (1978) *Euro-communism and the State.* London: Lawrence and Wishart.

Cassesse, S. (1971) *Cultura e Politica del Diritto Administrativo.* Bologna: Il Mulino.

Castberg, F. (1947) *Norges Statsforfatnig,* 2 vols. Oslo: Arbeidernes aktietrykkeri.

Chabod, F. (1958) *Machiavelli and the Renaissance.* Cambridge, Mass.: Harvard University Press.

Chabod, F. (1964) 'Was there a Renaissance state?', in H. Lubasz (ed.) *The Development of the Modern State.* New York: Macmillan.

Chapman, B. (1970) *Police State.* London: Macmillan.

Chardon, H. (1926) *L'Organisation de la république pour la paix.* Paris: Presses Universitaires de France.

Church, W. F. (1969) *Constitutional Thought in 16th-century France.* New York: Octagon Books.

Church, W. F. (1972) *Richelieu and Reason of State* Princeton, N.J.: Princeton University Press.

Clark, G. (1958) *War and Society in the 17th Century.* Cambridge, England: Cambridge University Press.

Clark, T. N. (1973) *Prophets and Patrons.* Cambridge, Mass.: Harvard University Press.

Coleridge, S. T. (1829) *The Constitution of Church and State.* London: Hurst, Chance.

Collini, S. (1976) 'Hobhouse, Bosanquet and the state: philosophical idealism and political argument in England 1880–1918', *Past and Present,* August, pp: 86–111.

Collini, S. (1978) 'Sociology and idealism in Britain', *Archives Européennes de Sociologie,* January, pp: 3–50.

Craig, G. A. (1964) *The Politics of the Prussian Army 1640–1945.* Oxford: Oxford University Press.

Craig, G. A. (1978) *Germany 1866–1945.* Oxford: Clarendon Press.

Croce, B. (1925) *Elementi di Politica.* Bari: Laterza.

Croce, B. (1945) *Etica e Politica.* Bari: Laterza.

Crosland, C. A. R. (1956) *The Future of Socialism.* London: Cape.

Crozier, M. (1964) *The Bureaucratic Phenomenon.* London: Tavistock.

Crozier, M. (1970) *La société bloquée.* Paris: éditions du Seuil.

Crozier, M. (1975) 'Western Europe' in M. Crozier , S.P. Huntington and J. Watanuki. (eds) *The Crisis of Democracy.* New York: New York University Press.

Dabin, J. (1957) *L'État ou le politique, essai de définition.* Paris: Dalloz.

Dahrendorf, R. (1959) *Class and Class Conflict in Industrial Society.* London: Routledge and Kegan Paul.

Dahrendorf, R. (1967) *Society and Democracy in Germany.* London: Weidenfeld and Nicolson.

Deane, H. A. (1955) *The Political Ideas of Harold J. Laski.* New York: Columbia University Press.

Debré, M. (1947) *La mort de l'État républicain.* Paris: Gallimard.

Debré, M. (1963) *Au service de la nation.* Paris: édition Stock.

Demichel, A. (1978) *Le droit administratif.* Paris: Librairie Générale de Droit et de Jurisprudence.

Dicey, A. V. (1895) *Introduction to the Study of the Law of the Constitution.* London: Macmillan.

Donnedieu de Vabres, J. (1954) *L'État.* Paris: Presses Universitaires de France.

Dorwart, R. A. (1972) *The Prussian Welfare State before 1740.* Cambridge, Mass.: Harvard University Press.

Dowdall, H. C. (1923) 'The word state', *Law Quarterly Review,* January, pp: 98–125.

Downs, A. (1957) *An Economic Theory of Democracy.* New York: Harper and Row.

Duguit, L. (1911) *Traité de droit constitutionnel,* 2 vols. Paris: Fontemoing.

Dyson, K. H. F. (1975) 'Left-wing political extremism and the problem of tolerance in Western Germany', *Government and Opposition,* Summer, pp: 306–31.

Dyson, K. H. F. (1977) *Party, State, and Bureaucracy in Western Germany.* Beverly Hills, Calif.: Sage Publications.

Dyson, K. H. F. (1979) 'The ambiguous politics of Western Germany', *European Journal of Political Research,* December, pp: 375–96.

Easton, D. (1965) *A Systems Analysis of Political Life.* New York: Wiley.

Eccleshall, R. (1978) *Order and Reason in Politics.* Oxford: Oxford University Press.

Egbert, D. D. (1970) *Social Radicalism and the Arts.* New York: Knopf.

Ehmke, H. (1962) 'Staat und Gesellschaft als Verfassungstheoretisches Problem', in K. Hesse, S. Reicke and U. Scheuner (eds) *Staatsverfassung und Kirchenordnung, Festgabe für R. Smend.* Tübingen; Mohr.

Eisenmann, C. (1939) *Sur un traité de l'État moderne.* Paris: Archives de Philosophie du Droit.

Elder, N. (1970) *Government in Sweden.* Oxford: Pergamon Press.

Elton, G. R. (1973) *Reform and Renewal: Thomas Cromwell and the Common Weal.* Cambridge, England: Cambridge University Press.

d'Entrèves, A. P. (1967) *The Notion of the State.* Oxford: Clarendon Press.

Ermacora, F. (1970) *Allgemeine Staatslehre: Vom Nationalstaat zum Weltstaat,* 2 vols. Berlin: Duncker and Humblot.

Esmein, A. (1909) *Éléments de droit constitutionnel français et comparé.* Paris: Larose and Tenin.

Femia, J. (1975) 'Hegemony and consciousness in the thought of Antonio Gramsci', *Political Studies,* March, pp: 29–48.

Fiedler, W. (1972) *Sozialer Wandel, Verfassungswandel, Rechtsprechung.* Freiburg: Alber.

Fischer, W. and Lundgreen, P. (1975) 'The recruitment and training of administrative and technical personnel', in C. Tilly (ed.) *The Formation of National States in Western Europe.* Princeton, N.J.: Princeton University Press.

Forsthoff, E. (1964) *Rechtsstaat im Wandel.* Stuttgart: Kohlhammer.

Forsthoff, E. (1966) *Lehrbuch des Verwaltungsrechts* (9th edn). Munich: Beck.

Forsthoff, E. (ed.) (1968) *Rechtsstaatlichkeit und Sozialstaatlichkeit.* Darmstadt: Wissenschaftliche Buchgesellschaft.

Forsthoff, E. (1971) *Der Staat der Industriegesellschaft.* Munich: Beck.

Forsyth, M. (forthcoming) *The Three Dimensions of the State.*

Fraenkel, E. (1941) *The Dual State.* Oxford: Oxford University Press.

Fraenkel, E. and Bracher, K.-D. (eds) (1957) *Staat und Politik.* Frankfurt: Fischer Lexikon.

Freeden, M. (1978) *The New Liberalism.* Oxford: Oxford University Press.

Friedrich, C. J. (1952) *The Age of the Baroque: 1610–1660.* New York: Harper.

Gablentz, O. H. von der (1965) *Einführung in die Politische Wissenschaft.* Opladen: Westdeutscher Verlag.

Gablentz, O. H. von der (1966) 'Der Staat als Mythos und Wirklichkeit', *Politische Vierteljahresschrift,* pp: 138ff.

Gallie, W. B. (1973) 'An ambiguity in the idea of politics and its practical implications', *Political Studies,* December, pp: 442–52.

Gamble, A. (1974) *The Conservative Nation.* London: Routledge and Kegan Paul.

Gehlen, A. (1956) *Urmensch und Spätkultur.* Bonn: Athenäum Verlag.

Gény, F. (1927–30) *Science et technique en droit privé positif,* 4 vols. Paris: Sirey.

Gerber, K. F. von (1865) *Grundzüge des Deutschen Staatsrechts.* Leipzig: Tauchnitz.

Gierke, O. von (1883) 'Lebendes Staatsrecht und die Deutsche Rechtswissenschaft', *Schmollers Jahrbuch,* 1883, pp: 1097ff.

Gierke, O. von (1915) *Die Grundbegriffe des Staatsrechts und die Neuesten Staatsrechtstheorien.* Tübingen: Mohr.

Glucksmann, A. (1977) *Les maîtres penseurs.* Paris: Grasset.

Gneist, R. von (1872) *Der Rechtsstaat.* Berlin: Springer.

Goubert, P. (1969) *L'ancien régime.* Paris: Colin.

Gregor, A. J. (1969) *The Ideology of Fascism.* New York: Free Press.

Guérard, A. (1965) *France in the Classical Age.* New York: Harper and Row.

Gumplowicz, L. (1881) *Rechtsstaat und Sozialismus.* Innsbruck: Wagner.

Gumplowicz, L. (1897) *Allgemeines Staatsrecht.* Innsbruck: Wagner.

Gumplowicz, L. (1902) *Die Soziologische Staatsidee.* Innsbruck: Wagner.

Gurvitch, G. (1932) *L'idée du droit social.* Paris: Sirey.

Häberle, P. (1970) *Offentliches Interesse als Juristisches Problem.* Bad Homburg: Athenäum.

Habermas, J. (1965) *Strukturwandel der Öffentlichkeit* (2nd edn). Neuwied: Luchterhand.

Habermas, J. (1973) *Legitimationsprobleme im Spätkapitalismus.* Frankfurt: Suhrkamp.

Halbecq, M. (1965) *L'État: son autorité, son pouvoir.* Paris: Pichon Durand-Auzias.

Hallis, F. (1930) *Corporate Personality.* London: Oxford University Press.

Hamel, W. (1971 and 1974) *Deutsches Staatsrecht,* 2 vols. Berlin: Duncker and Humblot.

Harris, H. S. (1960) *The Social Philosophy of Giovanni Gentile.* Urbana, Ill.: University of Illinois Press.

Harris, N. (1972) *Competition and the Corporate Society: British Conservatives, the State and Industry 1945–64.* London: Methuen.

Hartung, F. (1961) *Staatsbildende Kräfte der Neuzeit.* Berlin: Duncker and Humblot.

Hartz, L. (1955) *The Liberal Tradition in America.* New York: Harcourt, Brace and World.

Hauriou, M. (1906) *L'institution et le droit statutaire.* Paris.

Hauriou, M. (1923) *Précis de droit constitutionnel.* Paris: Sirey.

Hawthorn, G. (1976) *Enlightenment and Despair.* Cambridge: Cambridge University Press.

Hayward, J. E. S. (1973) *The One and Indivisible French Republic.* London: Weidenfeld and Nicolson.

Hayward, J. E. S. (1975) *Political Inertia.* Hull: University of Hull.

Heclo, H. (1974) *Modern Social Politics in Britain and Sweden.* New Haven: Yale University Press.

Hegel, G. W. F. (1894) *The Philosophy of Mind.* Oxford: Clarendon Press.

Heller, H. (1963) *Staatslehre,* 3rd edn. Leiden: Niemeyer.

Hennis, W. (1968) *Verfassung und Verfassungswirklichkeit.* Tübingen: Mohr.

Hennis, W. (1970) *Demokratisierung: Zur Problematik eines Begriffes.* Cologne: Westdeutscher Verlag.

Hennis, W. (1977) *Organisierter Sozialismus.* Stuttgart: Klett.

Herzog, R. (1971) *Allgemeine Staatslehre.* Frankfurt: Athenäum Verlag.

Hesse, K. (1959) *Die Normative Kraft der Verfassung.* Tübingen: Mohr.

Hesse, K. (1962a) *Der Unitarische Bundesstaat.* Karlsruhe: C. Müller.

Hesse, K. (1962b) 'Der Rechtsstaat im Verfassungssystem des Grundgesetzes', in K. Hesse, S. Reicke and U. Scheuner (eds) *Staatsverfassung und Kirchenordnung, Festgabe für R. Smend.* Tübingen: Mohr.

Hesse, K. (1967) *Grundzüge des Verfassungsrechts der Bundesrepublik Deutschland.* Karlsruhe: C. Müller.

Hexter, J. H. (1973) *The Vision of Politics on the Eve of the Reformation: More, Machiavelli and Seyssel.* London: Allen Lane.

Higley, J., Brofoss, K. and Groholt, K. (1975) 'Top civil servants and the national budget in Norway', in M. Dogan (ed.) *The Mandarins of Western Europe.* Beverly Hills, Calif.: Sage Publications.

Hintze, O. (1962a) 'Der Commissarius und seine Geschichtliche Bedeutung für die Allgemeine Verwaltungsgeschichte', in G. Oestreich (ed.) *Staat und Verfassung.* Göttingen: Vandenhoeck and Ruprecht. (First published in 1910.)

Hintze, O. (1962b) 'Wesen und Wandlung des Modernen Staates', in G. Oestreich (ed.) *Staat und Verfassung.* Göttingen: Vandenhoeck and Ruprecht. (First published in 1931.)

Hintze, O. (1967) *Regierung und Verwaltung.* Göttingen: Vandenhoeck and Ruprecht.

Hoare, Q. and Nowell Smith, G. (eds) (1971) *The Prison Notebooks of Antonio Gramsci.* London: Lawrence and Wishart.

Hobhouse, L. (1918) *The Metaphysical Theory of the State.* London: Allen and Unwin.

Hobson, J. A. (1909) *The Crisis of Liberalism.* London: P. S. King.

Hoffmann, S. (1963) *In Search of France.* Cambridge, Mass.: Harvard University Press.

Hoffmeyer, E. (ed.) (1962) *Velfoerdsteori og Velfoerdsstat.* Copenhagen: Berlingshe.

Hollingdale, R. J. (1973) *Nietzsche.* London: Routledge and Kegan Paul.
Hubatsch, W. (1975) *Frederick the Great: Absolutism and Administration.* London: Thames and Hudson.
Huber, H. (1939) *Demokratie und Staatliche Autorität.* Zurich: Polygraphischer Verlag.
Huber, M. (1915) *Der Schweizerische Staatsgedanke.* Zurich: Rascher.
Hubert, R. (1926) *Le principe d'autorité dans l'organisation démocratique.* Paris: Gamber.
Humboldt, W. von (1947) *Über die Grenzen des Staates.* Düsseldorf: Drei Eulen Verlag. (Written in 1791, first published in 1852.)
Huntington, S. P. (1968) *Political Order in Changing Societies.* New Haven, Conn.: Yale University Press.
Imboden, M. (1945) *Der Schütz vor Staatlicher Willkür.* Zurich: Polygraphischer Verlag.
Innes, H. A. (1950) *Empire and Communications.* Oxford: Clarendon Press.
Ionescu, G. (1975) *Centripetal Politics: Government and the New Centres of Power.* London: MacGibbon.
Jellinek, G. (1900) *Allgemeine Staatslehre.* Berlin: O. Häring.
Jèze, G. (1904) *Principes généraux du droit administratif.* Paris: Berger-Levrault.
Johnson, H. C. (1975) *Frederick the Great and his Officials.* New Haven, Conn.: Yale University Press.
Johnson, N. (1977) *In Search of the Constitution: Reflections on State and Society in Britain.* Oxford: Pergamon Press.
Jouvenel, B. de (1945) *Du pouvoir.* Geneva: Bourquin.
Justi, J. H. G. (1755) *Staatswirtschaft.* Leipzig: Breitkopf.
Kägi, W. (1945) *Die Verfassung als Rechtliche Grundordnung des Staates.* Zurich: Polygraphischer Verlag.
Kant, I. (1797) *Die Metaphysik der Sitten.* Königsberg: F. Nicolovius.
Kauffeldt, C. (1958) *Borger og Stat.* Copenhagen: Busch.
Kaufmann, E. (1921) *Kritisk der Neukantischen Rechtsphilosophie.* Tübingen: Mohr.
Keir, D. L. (1967) *The Constitutional History of Modern Britain since 1485* (8th edn). New York: Norton.
Kelly, G. A. (1969) *Idealism, Politics and History.* Cambridge, England: Cambridge University Press.
Kelsen, H. (1922) *Der Soziologische und Juristische Staatsbegriff.* Tübingen: Mohr.
Kelsen, H. (1925) *Allgemeine Staatslehre.* Berlin: Springer.
Kern, R. W. (1966) *Caciquismo versus Self-government: The Crisis of Liberalism and Local Government in Spain.* Chicago: University of Chicago Press.
Kesselman, M. (1967) *The Ambiguous Consensus.* New York: Knopf.
Keylor, W. R. (1975) *Academy and Community: The Foundation of the French Historical Profession.* Cambridge, Mass.: Harvard University Press.
Kierstead, R. F. (1975) *State and Society in 17th-century France.* New York: New Viewpoints.
Kjellén, R. (1924) *Der Staat als Lebensform* (4th edn). Berlin: K. Vowinckel. Translated from Swedish.
Kogel, R. (1972) *Pierre Charron.* Geneva: Droz.
Krieger, L. (1959) *The German Idea of Freedom.* Boston, Mass.: Beacon Press.

Krippendorf, E. (1970) 'The state as a focus of peace research', *Peace Research Society Papers*, The Rome Conference, XVI, pp: 47–60.

Krockow, C. von (1965) 'Staatsideologie oder Demokratisches Bewusstsein, die Deutsche Alternative', *Politische Vierteljahresschrift*, January, pp: 118ff.

Krüger, H. (1966) *Allgemeine Staatslehre*. Stuttgart: Kohlhammer.

Kuhn, H. (1967) *Der Staat–eine Philosophische Darstellung*. Munich: Kösel.

Laband, P. (1901) *Das Staatsrecht des Deutschen Reiches* (4th edn). Tübingen: Mohr.

La Bigne de Villeneuve, M. de (1929, 1931) *Traité général de l'État*, 2 vols. Paris: Sirey.

Lachmann, L. M. (1970) *The Legacy of Max Weber*. London: Heinemann.

Laski, H. J. (1919) *Authority in the Modern State*. New Haven, Conn.: Yale University Press.

Laski, H. J. (1935) *The State in Theory and Practice*. London: Allen and Unwin.

Laubadère, A. de (1970) *Traité élémentaire de droit administratif*, 3 vols (5th edn). Paris: Librairie Générale de Droit et de Jurisprudence.

Le Fur, L. (1937) *Les grandes problèmes du droit*. Paris: Sirey.

Lehmbruch, G. (1977) 'Liberal corporatism and party government', *Comparative Political Studies*, Vol. 10, pp: 91–126.

Leroy, M. (1918) *Pour gouverner* (3rd edn). Paris: Grasset.

Lichtheim, G. (1971) *From Marx to Hegel*. London: Orbach and Chambers.

Lijphart, A. (1975) *The Politics of Accommodation* (2nd edn). Berkeley: University of California.

Lindsay, A. D. (1914) 'The state in recent political theory', *Political Quarterly*, February, pp: 128–45.

Lindsay, A. D. (1943) *The Modern Democratic State*. Oxford: Oxford University Press.

Linz, J. (1964) 'An authoritarian regime: the case of Spain', in E. Allardt and Y. Littunen (eds) *Cleavages, Ideologies and Party Systems*. Helsinki: Transactions of the Westermarck Society.

List, F. (1841) *Das Nationale System der Politischen Ökonomie*. Stuttgart: J. Cotta.

Lowith, K. (ed.) (1962) *Die Hegelsche Linke*. Stuttgart: Frommann.

Lübbe, H. (ed.) (1962) *Die Hegelsche Rechte*. Stuttgart: Frommann.

Lukes, S. (1973a) *Émile Durkheim*. Harmondsworth: Penguin.

Lukes, S. (1973b) *Individualism*. Oxford: Blackwell.

Macarel, L. A. (1842) *Cours d'administration et de droit administratif professé à la Faculté de Droit de Paris*. Paris: Plon frères.

Machin, H. (1977) *The Prefect in French Public Administration*. London: Croom Helm.

MacIver, R. M. (1926) *The Modern State*. Oxford: The Clarendon Press.

Mager, W. (1968) *Zur Entstehung des Modernen Staatsbegriffes*. Wiesbaden: F. Steiner.

Maier, H. (1966) *Die Ältere Deutsche Staats- und Verwaltungslehre (Polizeiwissenschaft)*. Neuwied-Berlin: Luchterhand.

Maitland, F. W. (1901) 'The crown as corporation', *Law Quarterly Review*, Vol. 17, pp: 131–46.

Mann, G. (1960) 'The German intellectuals', in G. B. de Huszar (ed.) *The Intellectuals: A Controversial Portrait*. Glencoe, Ill.: Free Press.

Mann, T. (1918) *Betrachtungen eines Unpolitischen.* Berlin: S. Fischer.

Marini, F. (ed.) (1971) *Towards a New Public Administration.* Scranton, Pa.: Chandler.

Marshall, G. (1971) *Constitutional Theory.* Oxford: Clarendon Press.

Maspetiol, R. (1957) *La société politique et le droit.* Paris: Domat-Montchrestien.

Maurenbrecher, R. (1837) *Grundsätze des Heutigen Deutschen Staatsrechts.* Frankfurt: Varrentrapp.

Mayer, O. (1895–6) *Deutsches Verwaltungsrecht,* 2 vols. Leipzig: Duncker and Humblot.

McLellan, D. (1974) *Karl Marx: His Life and Thought.* London: Macmillan.

Meinecke, F. (1908) *Weltbürgertum und Nationalstaat.* Munich: R. Oldenbourg.

Meinecke, F. (1957) *Machiavellism.* New Haven, Conn.: Yale University Press.

Meyer, G. (1899) *Lehrbuch des Deutschen Staatsrechtes* (5th edn). Leipzig: Duncker and Humblot.

Middlemas, K. (1979) *The Politics of Industrial Society.* London: Deutsch.

Miliband, R. (1969) *The State in Capitalist Society.* London: Weidenfeld and Nicolson.

Miliband, R. (1977) *Marxism in Politics.* Oxford: Oxford University Press.

Miller, D. (1976) *Social Justice.* Oxford: Clarendon Press.

Miller, R. D. (1970) *Schiller and the Ideal of Freedom.* Oxford: Clarendon Press.

Mitteis, H. (1940) *Der Staat des Hohen Mittelalters.* Weimar: Böhlaus.

Mohl, R. von (1832) *Die Polizei-wissenschaft nach den Grundsätzen des Rechtsstaats,* 3 vols. Tübingen: H. Laupp.

Mohl, R. von (1859) *Encyklopädie der Staatswissenschaften.* Tübingen: H. Laupp.

Mommsen, H. (1966) *Beamtentum im Dritten Reich.* Stuttgart: Deutsche Verlagsanstalt.

Moore, B. (1969) *Social Origins of Dictatorship and Democracy.* Harmondsworth: Penguin.

Mousnier, R. (1970) *La plume, la faucille, et le marteau.* Paris: Presses universitaires de France.

Müller, A. (1922) *Elemente der Staatskunst,* 2 vols. Vienna and Leipzig: Wiener Literarische Anstalt.

Myers, A. R. (1975) *Parliaments and Estates in Europe to 1789.* London: Thames and Hudson.

Nairn, T. (1977) 'The twilight of the British state', *New Left Review,* February, pp: 3–61.

Nettl, J. P. (1968) 'The state as a conceptual variable', *World Politics,* July, pp: 559–92.

Nicholls, D. (1975) *The Pluralist State.* London: Macmillan.

Nisbet, R. A. (1967) *The Sociological Tradition.* London: Heinemann.

Nozick, R. (1975) *Anarchy, State and Utopia.* Oxford: Blackwell.

Oakeshott, M. (1975) *On Human Conduct.* Oxford: Clarendon Press.

Oertzen, P. von (1962) 'Die Bedeutung C. F. von Gerbers für die Deutsche Staatsrechtslehre', in K. Hesse, S. Reicke and U. Scheuner (eds) *Staatsverfassung und Kirchenordnung, Festgabe für R. Smend.* Tübingen: Mohr.

Offe, C. (1972) *Strukturprobleme des Kapitalistischen Staates.* Frankfurt: Suhrkamp.

Oppenheimer, F. (1926) *The State: Its History and Development Viewed Sociologically.* New York: Vanguard Press.

Opzoomer, C. W. (1873) *De Grenzen der Staatsmacht.* Amsterdam: J. H. Gebhard.

Opzoomer, C. W. (1854) *Staatsregtelijk Onderzoek.* Amsterdam: J. H. Gebhard.

Orlando, V. E. (1952) *Principii di Diritto Administrativo* (rev. edn). Florence: G. Barbèra. (First published in 1891.)

Orlow, D. (1973) *The History of the Nazi Party: vol. 2 1933–1945.* Newton Abbot: David and Charles.

Paret, P. (1976) *Clausewitz and the State.* Oxford: Oxford University Press.

Peyrefitte, A. (1976) *Le mal français.* Paris: Plon.

Philip, K. (1947) *Staten og Fattigdommen.* Copenhagen: J. Gjellerup.

Pinson, K. S. (1954) *Modern Germany.* New York: Macmillan.

Plant, R. (1973) *Hegel.* London: Allen and Unwin.

Poggi, G. (1978) *The Development of the Modern State.* London: Hutchinson.

Poulantzas, N. (1969) 'The problem of the capitalist state', *New Left Review,* Winter, pp: 67–78.

Poulantzas, N. (1973) *Political Power and Social Classes.* London: New Left Books.

Poulantzas, N. (1974) *Fascism and Dictatorship.* London: New Left Books.

Prélot, M. (1957) *Institutions politique et droit constitutionnel.* Paris: Dalloz.

Pulzer, P. (1964) *The Rise of Political Antisemitism in Germany and Austria.* New York: Wiley.

Quail, J. (1978) *The Slow Burning Fuse.* London: Paladin.

Quaritsch, H. (1970) *Staat und Souveränität: Band I, Die Grundlagen.* Frankfurt: Athenäum.

Radbruch, G. (1930) 'Die Politischen Parteien im System des Deutschen Verfassungsrechtes', in G. Anschütz and R. Thoma (eds) *Handbuch des Deutschen Staatsrechts,* Vol. I. Tübingen: Mohr.

Radbruch, G. (1950) *Rechtsphilosophie* (4th edn). Stuttgart: Koehler.

Ratzenhofer, G. (1893) *Wesen und Zweck der Politik,* 3 vols. Leipzig: Brockhaus.

Rawls, J. (1972) *A Theory of Justice.* Oxford: Clarendon Press.

Renard, G. (1930) *La théorie de l'institution.* Paris: Sirey.

Renard, G. (1933) *L'institution.* Paris: Flammarion.

Renard, G. (1939) *La philosophie de l'institution.* Paris: Sirey.

Richter, M. (1964) *The Politics of Conscience: T. H. Green and his Age.* London: Weidenfeld and Nicolson.

Ridley, F. F. (1970) *Revolutionary Syndicalism in France.* Cambridge, England: Cambridge University Press.

Rieff, P. (1966) *The Triumph of the Therapeutic.* New York: Harper and Row.

Ringer, F. K. (1969) *The Decline of the German Mandarins.* Cambridge, Mass.: Harvard University Press.

Ritter, G. (ed.) (1973) *Vom Wohlfahrtsauschuss zum Wohlfahrtsstaat. Der Staat in der Modernen Industriegesellschaft.* Cologne: Markus.

Rokkan, S. (1970) *Citizens, Elections, Parties.* New York: McKay.

Rolland, L. (1938) *Précis de droit administratif* (7th edn). Paris: Dalloz.

Romano, S. (1901) *Principii di Diritto Administrativo.* Milan: Società Editrice Libraria.

Romano, S. (1917) *Ordinamento Giuridico.* Pisa: Spoerri.

Römer, P. (1971) 'Die Reine Rechtslehre Hans Kelsens als Ideologie und Ideologiekritik', *Politische Vierteljahresschrift,* pp: 579–98.

Ross, A. (1959) *Statsregtlige Studier.* Copenhagen: Nyt Nordisk Forlag.

Ross, A. (1959–60) *Dansk Statsforfatningsret,* 2 vols. Copenhagen: Nyt Nordisk Forlag.

Saleilles, R. (1922) *De la personnalité juridique* (2nd edn). Paris: Rousseau.

Salmon, J. H. M. (1975) *Society in Crisis: France in the 16th Century.* New York: St Martin's Press.

Schäffle, A. E. F. (1875) *Die Quintessenz des Sozialismus.* Gotha: Perthes.

Schama, S. (1977) *Patriots and Liberators: Revolution in the Netherlands, 1789–1813.* London: Collins.

Scheler, M. (1925) *Die Formen des Wissens und die Bildung.* Bonn: F. Cohen.

Schelsky, H. (1965) *Auf der Suche nach Wirklichkeit.* Düsseldorf–Cologne: E. Diederichs.

Scheuner, U. (1961) 'Die Neuere Entwicklung des Rechtsstaats in Deutschland' in *Hundert Jahre Deutsches Leben, Festschrift zum Hundertjährigen Bestehen des Deutschen Juristentages 1860–1960.* Karlsruhe: C. Müller.

Scheuner, U. (1977) 'Robert von Mohl: Die Begründung einer Verwaltungslehre und einer staatswissenschaftlichen Politik', in *500 Jahre Eberhard-Karls-Universität Tübingen.* Tübingen: Mohr.

Schindler, D. (1932) *Verfassungsrecht und Soziale Struktur.* Zurich: Schulthess.

Schindler, D. (1975) *Schweizerische Eigenheiten in der Staatslehre.* Zurich: Komm. Beer.

Schlözer, A. von (1793) *Allgemeines Statsrecht und Statsverfassungslere.* Göttingen: Vandenhoek and Ruprecht.

Schmitt, C. (1928) *Verfassungslehre.* Munich: Duncker and Humblot. (Reprinted in 1954.)

Schmitt, C. (1932) *Legalität und Legitimität.* Munich: Duncker and Humblot.

Schmitt, C. (1963) *Der Begriff des Politischen.* Berlin: Duncker and Humblot.

Schmitter, P. (1974) 'Still the century of corporatism?', *Review of Politics,* Vol. 36, pp: 85–131.

Schmoller, G. F. von (1900–04) *Grundriss der Allgemeinen Volkswirtschaftslehre,* 2 vols. Leipzig: Duncker and Humblot.

Schnur, R. (1962) *Die Französischen Juristen im Konfessionelen Bürgerkrieg des 16. Jahrhunderts.* Berlin: Duncker and Humblot.

Schoenbaum, D. (1966) *Hitler's Social Revolution.* New York: Doubleday.

Schon, D. (1971) *Beyond the Stable State.* London: Maurice Temple Smith.

Schwab, G. (1970) *The Challenge of the Exception.* Berlin: Duncker and Humblot.

Seydel, M. von (1873) *Grundzüge einer Allgemeinen Staatslehre.* Würzburg: Stuber.

Sharpe, L. J. (1973) 'American democracy reconsidered', *British Journal of Political Science,* Vol. 3, pp: 1–28 and 129–67.

Shennan, J. H. (1974) *The Origins of the Modern European State 1450–1725.* London: Hutchinson.

Shonfield, A. (1965) *Modern Capitalism.* Oxford: Oxford University Press.

Skalweit, S. (1975) *Der Moderne Staat. Ein Historischer Begriff und seine Problematik.* Opladen: Westdeutscher Verlag.

Skinner, Q. (1979) *The Foundation of Modern Political Thought:* Vol. 1, *The Renaissance:* Vol. 2, *The Age of Reformation.* Cambridge, England: Cambridge University Press.

Smend, R. (1928) *Verfassung und Verfassungsrecht.* Munich and Leipzig: Duncker and Humblot.

Smend, R. (1955) *Staatsrechtliche Abhandlungen.* Berlin: Duncker and Humblot.

Smith, G. R. (1978) 'The reintegration of the state in Western Europe', in M. Kolinsky (ed.) *Divided Loyalties.* Manchester: Manchester University Press.

Sontheimer, K. (1962) *Antidemokratisches Denken in der Weimarer Republik.* Munich: Nymphenburger.

Sorel, G. (1950) *Reflections on Violence.* New York: Free Press.

Spann, O. (1921) *Der Wahre Staat.* Leipzig: Quelle and Meyer.

Spencer, H. (1884) *The Man versus the State.* London: Williams and Norgate.

Spengler, O. (1924) *Der Staat.* Munich: C. H. Beck.

Stahl, F. J. (1846) *Die Philosophie des Rechts,* 2 vols. Heidelberg: J. C. B. Mohr.

Stammler, R. (1922) *Lehrbuch der Rechtsphilosophie.* Berlin: W. de Gruyter.

Stankiewicz, W. J. (1969) *In Defence of Sovereignty.* New York: Oxford University Press.

Stassinopoulos, M. (1954) *Traité des actes administratifs.* Athens: Collection de l'Institut Francais d'Athènes.

Stein, L. von (1850) *Die Geschichte der Sozialen Bewegung in Frankreich von 1789 bis auf Unsere Tage,* 3 vols. Leipzig: O. Wigand.

Stein, L. von (1865–8) *Die Verwaltungslehre,* 7 vols. Stuttgart: J. G. Cotta.

Steiner, J. (1974) *Amicable Agreement versus Majority Rule.* University of North Carolina, Chapel Hill.

Steiner, K. (1972) *Politics in Austria.* Boston, Mass.: Little Brown.

Stolleis, M. (ed.) (1977) *Staatsdenker im 17. und 18. Jahrhundert.* Frankfurt: Metzner.

Stone, L. (1965) *The Crisis of the Aristocracy, 1558–1641.* Oxford: Clarendon Press.

Strayer, J. (1970) *On the Medieval Origins of the Modern State.* Princeton, N. J: Princeton University Press.

Strömberg, H. (1962) *Allmän Förvaltningsrätt.* Lund: Gleerup.

Suhr, D. (1975) *Bewusstseinsverfassung und Gesellschaftsverfassung. Über Hegel und Marx zu einer Dialektischen Verfassungstheorie.* Berlin: Duncker and Humblot.

Suleiman, E. (1974) *Politics, Power and Bureaucracy in France.* Princeton, N.J.: Princeton University Press.

Suleiman, E. (1979) *Elites in French Society, the Politics of Survival.* Princeton, N.J.: Princeton University Press.

Sundberg, J. W. F. (1969) 'Civil law, common law and the Scandinavians', *Scandinavian Studies in Law,* Vol. 13, pp: 179–205.

Tannenbaum, E. R. (1973) *Fascism in Italy.* London: Allen Lane.

Tarde, G. (1909) *Les transformations du droit* (6th edn). Paris: Alcan.

Tarrow, S. (1977) *Between Center and Periphery.* New Haven, Conn.: Yale University Press.

Taylor, C. (1975) *Hegel.* Cambridge, England: Cambridge University Press.

Thoma, R. (1923) 'Der Begriff der Modernen Demokratie in seinem Verhält nis zum Staatsbegriff', in M. Palyi (ed.) *Hauptprobleme der Soziologie, Erinnerungsgabe für Max Weber.* Munich-Leipzig: Duncker and Humblot.

Thompson, E. P. (1978) *The Poverty of Theory and Other Essays.* London: Merlin Press.

Tilly, C. (1975) 'Reflections on the history of European state-making', in C. Tilly (ed.) *The Formation of National States in Western Europe.* Princeton, N.J.: Princeton University Press.

Tönnies, F. (1887) *Gemeinschaft und Gesellschaft.* Leipzig: Fues's Verlag.

Treitschke, H. von (1963) *Politics.* New York: Harcourt, Brace and World Inc.

Trevor-Roper, H. R. (1967) *Religion, the Reformation and Social Change.* London: Macmillan.

Triepel, H. (1927) *Staatsrecht und Politik.* Berlin: W. de Gruyter.

Ullmann, W. (1965) *A History of Political Thought: The Middle Ages.* Harmondsworth: Penguin.

Ullmann, W. (1975) *Law and Politics in the Middle Ages.* London: The Sources of History.

Vedel, G. (1949) *Manuel élémentaire de droit constitutionnel.* Paris: Sirey.

Vile, M. J. C. (1967) *Constitutionalism and the Separation of Powers.* Oxford: Clarendon Press.

Vilmar, F. (1973) *Stratagien der Demokratisierung.* 2 vols. Darmstadt: Luchterhand.

Vivien, A. F. A. (1859) *Études administratives* (3rd edn). Paris: Guillaumin.

Waismann, F. (1945) 'Symposium on verifiability', *Proceedings of the Aristotelian Society,* Suppl. XIX, pp: 119–50.

Waline, M. (1957) *Traité élémentaire de droit administratif* (7th edn). Paris: Sirey.

Weber, A. (1925) *Die Krise des Modernen Staatsgedankens in Europa.* Stuttgart: Deutsche Verlagsanstalt.

Weber, M. (1956) *Staatssoziologie* (ed. J. Winkelmann). Berlin: Duncker and Humblot.

Weber, M. (1964) *The Theory of Social and Economic Organization.* New York: Free Press.

Weber, W. (1951) *Spannungen und Kräfte im Westdeutschen Verfassungssystem.* Stuttgart: F. Vorwerk.

Wehler, H.-U. (1973) *Das Deutsche Kaiserreich 1871–1918.* Göttingen: Vandenhoeck and Ruprecht.

Weinacht, P. (1968) *Staat, Studien zur Bedeutungsgeschichte des Wortes von den Anfängen bis ins 19. Jh.* Berlin: Duncker and Humblot.

Weldon, T. D. (1953) *The Vocabulary of Politics.* Harmondsworth: Penguin.

Williams, P. M. (1970) *Wars, Plots and Scandals in Post-War France.* Cambridge, England: Cambridge University Press.

Wilson, W. (1889) *The State.* Boston, Mass.: Heath.

Woolsey, T. D. (1878) *Political Science or the State Theoretically and Practically Considered.* New York: Scribner, Armstrong.

Zachariae, H. A. (1841–5) *Deutsches Staats- und Bundesrecht.* Göttingen: Vandenhoek and Ruprecht.

index of names

The book identifies a complex of individual contributions to what constitutes a rich tapestry of thought about rule. Many of the names to which reference is made in the text will be unfamiliar to an English-speaking audience. Hence, where appropriate, background information is included in this index; its introduction in the body of the book would have proved a clumsy device.

| index of subjects

public interest, 51, 67, 70, 273–7
public power, concept of, x, 19n2, 20–1 n4
public schools, English, 84, 249
public-service state, 85, 90, 121, 147
puissance publique, 20–1 n4, 162
Puritan Revolution, English, 37, 46n9

Radicals' Decree, West German, 10, 264–5
realism, American legal, 112, 133n1, 184n3
  philosophical, 199, 200
  political, 34, 101ff, 133n1, 178
  Scandinavian legal, 12, 184n3
reason of state, 26, 30, 32, 44n2, 82, 102
Rechtsstaat, 11, 17, 21 n5, 35, 54, 87, 108–9,
  116, 120, 122–7, 150, 151, 153, 177,
  221, 223, 227, 257, 265, 267, 268
  sozialer, 127, 149, 178, 251 n4
Reformation, 31, 42
relativism, 142, 268
religion, 75–6, 84, 172–3, 240
Renaissance, 30–1, 42
Renaissance State, 30, 33, 37
representation, 39–40, 137, 208, 209
'République des Professeurs', 246
Roman law, 26, 31, 42–3, 54, 110,
  112–17, 137, 171, 188, 213
Romanticism, German, 103, 130, 140, 144, 151,
  158, 162, 164, 165, 167, 168, 261
Rome, 121, 122, 137, 171
Rule of law, 42, 117
Russia, 31, 223

Sachlichkeit, 65, 211, 227, 270, 276
sale of offices, 33
scholasticism, 82, 167
science administrative, 181–2
secularism, 30–1, 75–6, 286
service public, 218–19
Social Democratic Party, German (SPD),
  86, 99n2, 134n7, 242, 251 n7
social market economy, 95, 96–7
social question, 92, 138, 145
society, as hierarchical order, 139–40
individualistic conception of, 140–3
as community, 143–50
sociology, 89, 90, 92, 93, 94, 192
solidarity, idea of, 147
sovereignty, 19n2, 27, 28, 32, 34, 63, 83,
  113–15, 136, 137, 162–3, 207–8, 229
Sozialstaat, 9, 21 n5, 121, 127, 213, 243,
  247–8, 267
Spain, 29, 68, 156–7, 223
  Franco's (1939), 9, 73–4
  Restoration (1874), 61–2, 75, 77
  Second Republic (1931), 62
Staatsbürger, 177, 184n4, 232
Staatsgebiet, 20n4, 34
Staatsgewalt, 20n4, 34, 162
Staatslehre, allgemeine, 84, 159, 170, 175ff,
  186, 199, 286

Staatspflege, 244
Staatsrechtslehre, 170, 175, 178, 179, 184n4
Staatssouveränität, 115
Staatsvolk, 20n4, 34, 244
'stalemate' society, 263–4
Ständestaat, 26, 53–4, 72, 78n3,
  136, 140, 153, 167
state, the word, 25–8
  idea of, defined, 18–19, 206ff, 256, 270–1, 275
  personality of, 14–15, 218–20
  and society, 21 n8, 189, 228–43,
    250n3 and n4, 265
  as juristic conception, 14–16, 206, 218–20
  as sociological conception, 14–16, 206
'state' societies, x, 6, 8, 18–19, 19n2, 51–2,
  97, 115, 258–9, 272, 277, 280–1, 284
'stateless' societies, x, 19n2, 52, 271–2, 280–1
Statistik, 86–7
Stein-Hardenberg reforms (post-1806), 214
structuralism, 10, 161, 183, 235–6, 238, 239
Stuart dynasty, 62
supra-national organizations, 283–4
surrealism, 261
Sweden, 29, 33, 43–4, 46n10 and n11, 51, 64,
  68, 69, 70, 72–3, 75, 76, 98, 156, 183n1,
  184n3, 223, 232, 233, 245, 259, 275, 279
Switzerland, 10–11, 65, 68, 69, 184n4
syndicalism, 148, 246–7

technical state, 10, 131
technocracy, 131–2, 148, 225, 253, 263
theocracy, 39, 52–3, 114
Thirty Years' War, 28, 82, 114
Toryism, 36, 189–90, 271
towns, rise of, 54
trade unions, 245–7
trust, English legal idea of, 42, 196, 275
Tudors, 37, 45n8

United States, 19–20n2, 38, 105, 112, 186–7, 271
Uppsala school of legal thought,
  47n11, 156, 184n3

Verbändestaat, 8, 242
Verein für Sozialpolitik, 96, 100n6, 159, 186
Vergesellschaftung des Staates, 243, 285
Verstaatlichung der Gesellschaft, 243, 285
Verwaltungslehre, 181–2
Verwaltungsstaat, 256
Volkstaat, 10, 35

warfare, 31–2, 102, 153n1, 283–4, 285
Wars of Religion, French, 136
Willenstheorie, 108, 141, 154n4
Wohlfahrtspolizei, 119
Wohlfahrtsstaat, 21 n5, 118, 120, 134n5
working class, 76, 249–50
world wars, 254, 283

Young Hegelians, 170

www.ingramcontent.com/pod-product-compliance
Lightning Source LLC
Chambersburg PA
CBHW072048020426
42334CB00017B/1425